THE DIAGRAMMATICS OF 'RACE'

The Diagrammatics of ‘Race’

Visualizing Human Relatedness in the History of Physical, Evolutionary, and Genetic Anthropology, ca. 1770–2020

Marianne Sommer

OpenBook Publishers

https://www.openbookpublishers.com

Any digital material and resources associated with this volume will be available at https://doi.org/10.11647/OBP.0396#resources

ISBN Paperback: 978-1-80511-260-0
ISBN Hardback: 978-1-80511-261-7
ISBN Digital (PDF): 978-1-80511-262-4
ISBN Digital eBook (EPUB): 978-1-80511-263-1
ISBN HTML: 978-1-80511-265-5

DOI: 10.11647/OBP.0396

Cover image: Photo by Marc Bloch, 2023, CC-BY
Cover design: Jeevanjot Kaur Nagpal.

Contents

Acknowledgements

My work on the history of (physical, evolutionary, genetic) anthropology has led me to recognize the key role of diagrams in these fields. Tables, graphs, maps, trees, etc. have long been used to establish human categories and produce relations between human groups. Once I turned my full attention to these, I realized I needed to take a much broader look at the scientific and cultural uses of diagrams that establish 'kinship' relations between organisms. This led to the application for a Sinergia Project of the Swiss National Science Foundation on 1 June 2018, with the title "In the Shadow of the Tree: The Diagrammatics of Relatedness as Scientific, Scholarly, and Popular Practice". In the proposal that received five peer-reviews, as well as on the website that we immediately published once the project was approved,[1] we brought together the areas of law, genealogy, natural history, anthropology, ethnology, genetics, and psychology in the periods from the Middle Ages to the present. In the five years of the project's duration, four research groups at five universities discussed *arbores consanguinitates*, bourgeois family trees, ethnographic kinship diagrams, medical and psychiatric pedigrees, genomic admixture diagrams, and much more, looking at the kind of relations they established between organisms and discussing how different diagrams may be connected.

I would like to thank the Swiss National Science Foundation for this grand opportunity and the group leaders Simon Teuscher (University of Zurich), Staffan Müller-Wille (University of Cambridge/University

1 "In the Shadow of the Tree: The Diagrammatics of Relatedness as Scientific, Scholarly, and Popular Practice", University of Lucerne, https://www.unilu.ch/en/faculties/faculty-of-humanities-and-social-sciences/institutes-departements-and-research-centres/department-of-cultural-and-science-studies/chair-of-cultural-studies/research/in-the-shadow-of-the-tree-the-diagrammatics-of-relatedness-as-scientific-scholarly-and-popular-practice-sinergia/

of Lübeck), and Caroline Arni (University of Basel) as well as the postdoctoral and doctoral researchers Eric Hounshell, Lea Pfäffli, Ruth Amstutz, Stéphanie Prieto, Julian Miguez, Niklaas Görsch, Andrea Ceccon, Fiona Vicent, and Amos Kuster for the many stimulating discussions, in which we were often joined by other collaborators and colleagues, including Petter Hellström, Charlotte Bigg, Olivier Doron, Yulia Egorova, Elisabeth Timm, Ted Porter, Helen Gardner, Amir Teicher, Stéphan Jettot, Jean-Paul Zuñiga, Sun Joo Kim, Nick Hopwood, Ariane Dröscher, Hans-Jörg Rheinberger, Cornelius Borck, and Markus Friedrich.

Out of the Sinergia Project came publications discussing diagrams of relatedness within historical and present contexts of anthropological approaches, which serve as a foundation for the analysis in this book. Most important among these are my *British Journal for the History of Science Themes* paper on Charles Darwin and Ernst Haeckel (Sommer 2021), my *History of the Human Sciences* article on early physical anthropology (Sommer 2023a), and my contribution to the volume *Critical Perspectives on Ancient DNA* (Sommer and Amstutz 2024).

In the course of researching this book, I benefitted from access to archival material from the American Philosophical Society Library (particular thanks are due to Valerie-Anne Lutz and Joe Dilullo), Darwin Online, the Ernst Haeckel Haus (online letter edition; particular thanks are due to Thomas Bach), King's College London (particular thanks are due to Oliver Snaith), the American Museum of Natural History (particular thanks are due to Gregory Raml), the Peabody Museum of Archaeology and Ethnology (particular thanks are due to Marie Wasnock and Cynthia Mackey), and the Royal College of Surgeons (particular thanks are due to Saffron Mackay). I am also indebted to my interview partners Nick Patterson and David Morrison, to correspondent Alan Templeton, as well as to the peer reviewers. I am grateful for the kind support I have received from Open Book Publishers, especially Alessandra Tosi and Adèle Kreager. Finally, I would like to thank my academic home, the University of Lucerne (Switzerland), especially student assistant Jennifer De Biasio.

About the Author

Marianne Sommer holds the chair of Kulturwissenschaften at the Department for Cultural and Science Studies at the University of Lucerne, Switzerland. Prior to that, she has held postdoctoral positions at the Max Planck Institute for the History of Science in Berlin, Pennsylvania State University, and the ETH Zurich, followed by a professorship at the University of Zurich. She has been a guest at many institutions, including Stanford University and the University of California, Los Angeles (UCLA). For her research in the history of the earth, life, and human sciences, encompassing processes of narration, visualization, and exhibition, she has received the Swiss National Latsis Prize. Her monograph *History Within* (published with The University of Chicago Press in 2016) engages with the science, politics, and culture related to reconstructions of human evolutionary histories; it traces the generation and circulation of such knowledge from the late nineteenth century to the present, including through venues like the museum, the zoo, literature, or the web. Among her monographs are also *Bones and Ochre: The Curious Afterlife of the Red Lady of Paviland* (published with Harvard University Press in 2007) and *Evolutionäre Anthropologie* (published with Junius in 2015). *Bones and Ochre* tells the scientific and cultural history of paleoanthropology and to a lesser degree archeology through the 'biography' of the most likely first fossil human skeleton discovered in 1823. *Evolutionäre Anthropologi*e is an introduction to the history of evolutionary anthropology for scholars, students, and the interested public.

Introduction

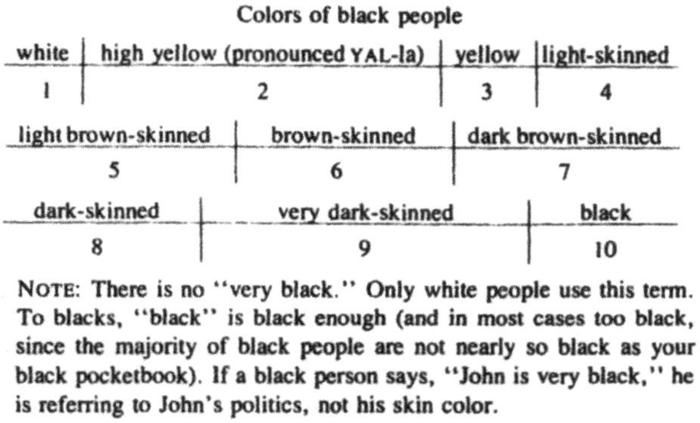

Colors of black people

white	high yellow (pronounced YAL-la)	yellow	light-skinned
1	2	3	4

light brown-skinned	brown-skinned	dark brown-skinned
5	6	7

dark-skinned	very dark-skinned	black
8	9	10

NOTE: There is no "very black." Only white people use this term. To blacks, "black" is black enough (and in most cases too black, since the majority of black people are not nearly so black as your black pocketbook). If a black person says, "John is very black," he is referring to John's politics, not his skin color.

Fig. 0.1 "Colors of [B]lack people". By Fran Ross, from *OREO*, p. 5, © 1974 by Frances D. Ross, all rights reserved. Reprinted by permission of New Directions Publishing Corp.

Fran Ross begins her by now classic novel *Oreo* (1974) with the shock of 'racial mixing'. The shock hits both sides of the family, the African American and the Jewish. Immediately, however, Ross complicates this 'racial mixing' by giving more detailed information on the African American family members' shades of skin color. Continuing the stinging satire, she brings to the aid of the reader a diagram, which should allow to color the book's characters throughout the story (Ross 1974, 5; see Figure 0.1). Oxymoronically titled "Colors of [B]lack people" (ibid.), the numbers 1 to 10 refer to a particular shade from "white" to "black", with attributes like "high yellow", "brown-skinned", and "very dark-skinned" in-between. Throughout the novel, the characters practice grotesque physical anthropology, when they make far-fetched correlations and use hand-made evolutionary classifications. They grapple with 'race' as a fabric made up from the threads of social systems, personal experiences, common sense, and scientific knowledge.

 https://doi.org/10.11647/OBP.0396.00

Ross' diagram of skin colors is part of what I refer to as a *diagrammatics of 'race'* – that is, the construction and representation of 'races' and their relations through diagrams. Figure 0.2 represents a diagram that was actually used in the study of 'racial crosses'. It was designed by the geneticist and anthropologist Reginald Ruggles Gates, one of the figures of interest in this book. Gates explained:

> A colour chart of skin colours, derived entirely from [Black people] X White [people], was published as the frontispiece to *Pedigrees of [Black] Families* (Gates 1949). The skin colours were originally painted on canvas by a portrait painter, and afterwards reproduced on paper, using the spectrophotometer to obtain the correct values in each wave-length of the spectrum. A number of spectrophotometer reflectance curves were also published (Gates 1952) of various [Black persons] and Chinese.[1]

This provides some insight into the practice of diagrammatic anthropology. Gates' diagram was a tool in the establishment of 'races' and their relations to each other, or their classification. In a letter to an anthropologist Gates added: "[T]he frontispiece of the book is a colored plate which reproduces the skin color of nine individuals ranging from pure black to white".[2] As we learn from the original caption of Figure 0.2, number 9, "the skin color of a [W]hite person", was taken from Gates himself. This indicates that such diagrams may provide an identity to the anthropologist in differentiation from various 'others', and that the resulting structure is hierarchical – Gates turned himself into the representative of the highest number, respectively of the lightest shade. That such tools circulated and were discussed between researchers is further demonstrated by the fact that the sheet depicted in Figure 0.2 is taken from the papers of Gates' colleague Earnest Hooton at Harvard University's Peabody Museum archives, among his correspondence with Gates.

1 "Heredity in the Races of Man" 1961, King's College London Archives, Gates, Professor Reginald Ruggles (1882–1962), K/PP65 (hereafter Gates Papers KCL), 4/92/2. The artist Gates was referring to was Ilona E. (Deak-Ebner) Ellinger, who was born in Budapest, Hungary, and gained a PhD from Johns Hopkins University. At the time of the collaboration, she was Professor of Arts at Trinity College, Washington, DC.

2 "To Dr. Juan Comas, Mexico City", 18 November 1949, p. 3, Gates Papers KCL, 4/81/16.

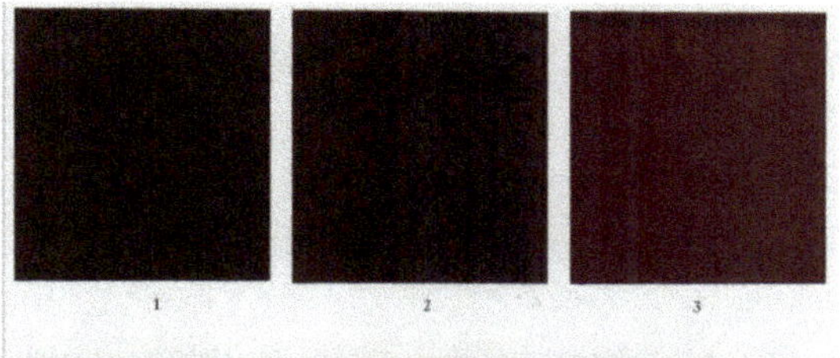
1
2
3
4
5
6
7
8
9
Each rectangle, numbered 1–8, represents the skin color of an individual colored person. No. 9 is the skin color of a white person (the author). For explanation see page 253.

Fig. 0.2 A color chart of skin colors (995-1, Earnest A. Hooton Papers, Peabody Museum of Archaeology and Ethnology Archives, Harvard University, I. Correspondence, G, Correspondence R. Ruggles Gates, Box 10, Folder 4) © Peabody Museum, all rights reserved, reproduced by kind permission.

Such diagrammatic tools and their production of entities like "pure [B]lack" people are satirized by Ross when she captions her diagram of "Colors of [B]lack people" with the note: "There is no 'very black.' Only [W]hite people use this term. To [Black people], black is black enough [...]" (1974, 5). In this book I am interested in diagrams of this kind – in what I refer to as *relating diagrams*. As Figure 0.2 illustrates, *relating* firstly refers to the practice of producing particular (hierarchical) relations between human types; secondly, it entails that these types themselves come into being through this diagrammatic practice; and thirdly, *relating* means 'storytelling'. The last sense reminds us that also diagrams do not stand for themselves. They need to be studied in relation to text, as the indented quote above, with its important information on the production and context of Gates' color chart, suggests. However, we will see that diagrams may also incorporate stories. The third meaning of *relating* further highlights that diagrams themselves may be of a verbal nature. We will encounter this phenomenon throughout the book, for example when I enquire into the role of language in conveying diagrams of relatedness, such as the scale of being and the tree of life.

While Ross suggests that the methods of racial anthropology have come to inform our everyday lives in which we constantly classify, even if unconsciously, the human beings around us, it was far from obvious that the diagrammatic method would be at the core of what was defined as anthropology or ethnology in the decades around 1800. In Part I, I ask how diagrams were integral to a certain approach to the study of human varieties. I focus on the very beginnings of physical anthropology to show how a decidedly diagrammatic tradition was established in competition with the historical-comparative method. I discuss a wide range of diagrammatic imagery that was introduced to produce human 'races' and their relations in the first place, such as geometric renderings of skull outlines, in which the lines for comparative measurement might be shown, skull superimpositions, and tables presenting craniometric results for different 'races'. I also address the violent practices behind such diagrams. Indeed, in the context of imperialism and colonialism and the concomitant atrocities of slavery and genocide, rather than aiming at the creation of kinship, these diagrams were developed to deny close affinities between human groups. Contrary to the long-standing, religious image of the human family that also underlay early anthropology, this new diagrammatic approach could support polygenism and thus work for the justification of 'racial' exploitation and cruelty, even though there was no universal association of either polygenism or monogenism with a specific approach to anthropology (or in fact a specific politics).

The diagram that has become dominant in the presentation of a particular understanding of human evolutionary history and diversity is the tree structure. At the same time, trees did not stand alone, but depended on the continuation of other diagrammatic techniques, such as those discussed in Part I, which were imported from physical anthropology into evolutionary anthropology and paleoanthropology. How the icon of the family tree made it into anthropology, or, better, from which existing visual techniques it was imported, is unclear. Rather than uncovering direct connections to the history of tree diagrams in other cultural realms like religious and secular genealogy or animal breeding, scholars have so far pointed to general discursive and visual formations (Bouquet 1996). The same holds true for the early attempts to bring organismic diversity in general under the order of the tree (e.g., Gontier 2011; Hellström 2012).

The use of trees also to depict intra-human relations entered anthropology independent of an evolutionary understanding. In Part II, I use the first such image that I have found, dating from 1857, to discuss this diagram's links to religious imagery like the *mappa mundi*, the tree of life, and the tree of Jesse, to the hierarchical scale of nature, as well as to other diagrammatic techniques that were used in natural history. The genealogical conception of humanity, which predates the beginnings of anthropology in the eighteenth century, has long been part of Christian cosmology. Also already present in the Christian worldview was the differentiation of humanity and the associated prioritization of certain branches of the tree (Hieke 2003). The human family tree that is so central to our understanding of relatedness within humankind, in medieval and early-modern depictions indicating Noah and the branches emanating from his sons, too, is always both uniting and dividing. The genealogical perspective must be regarded as one inspiration for the transfer of this powerful diagram from the realm of individual descent to panhuman kinship (with the sons of Noah standing for 'nations').

It was this thinking in terms of genealogy that led Charles Darwin to move from human unity to a genealogical conception of the entire living world. Of course, by that time, tree iconography had become most prominent in the practice of representing family genealogies, which increased in importance in the early modern period for royal and princely families, nobility, and urban elites. As I discuss in Part II, Darwin did widely experiment with tree-like shapes, but he did not visually subdivide humans in this way. It was Ernst Haeckel who was prone to excessive and racist phylogenic treeing. To envision the use of the family tree in anthropology as simply the natural continuation of its application in diverse cultural contexts or in natural history and biology is inadequate. Rather, this transfer requires not only explanation but also investigation into its epistemic and political consequences. This transmission shapes human relatedness in three fundamental ways.

First, the tree diagram minimizes variability within taxa. This is why the application of the image that captures kinship between individuals to the relations between species and higher taxa is, in its tendency, typological. In place of individuals, we find entire groups that might be symbolized by species and genera names or even by icons like types of skulls. The same holds true for trees that include inner-human variation. These additionally run the risk of suggesting species status for the human varieties. Tree diagrams therefore maximize the distance between human groups and can even express polygeny. Thirdly, such trees might represent a narrative of local origin and subsequent global distribution. The shape of the tree, sometimes actually projected on a map, therefore communicates that human differentiation was the result of separation through migration and took place without intermixture: human groups split and thereafter evolved in isolation. Thus, the two tendencies of the tree diagram – to minimize variability within, and maximize distance between, human groups – are enhanced through the underlying (or accompanying) narratives. The human family tree can convey the impression of 'pure races' or even separate human species.

There actually existed theories of human classification and evolution in the history of anthropology that corresponded to these underlying notions. Sometimes explicitly drawing on Haeckel's phylogenies that are treated in Part II, I show in Part III how some scientists published polygenist diagrams to convey their understanding of intra-human differences up to the middle of the twentieth century. In these visualization practices, the tree shape was increasingly radicalized or decomposed through prolongation of the lines leading to the modern groups that were thereby constructed in hierarchical order. And this is why there have always been critical voices that opposed this kind of thinking with diagrams. Some of these critics related humans differently, for example through the image of a meandering river, a skein, a trellis, a cable, or a net. It is especially during the interwar period that the racial trees of anthropology began to face criticism for being based on a faulty understanding of genetics and evolution, as well as for being racist – a critique that became louder in the aftermath of World War II. Nonetheless, up until that time, 'human family trees' were disseminated, expressing the belief in very different living human 'races' or even species that had evolved independently of each other, and whose anatomical similarities might be explained by parallel evolution.

While tree-like diagrams can capture important theoretical and methodological elements of the approaches described above, such as typology, evolutionary parallelism, or polygenism and 'racial hierarchies', and can visually distance 'races' from each other and humans from apes, it is harder to account for the diagram's success in human population genetics. These new endeavors worked with very different concepts and theories, such as statistical populations marked by genetic variability, that seem to undermine the tree image. Despite the many possibilities to visualize genetic data on human populations, and despite challenges from diverse fields such as biological and cultural anthropology, linguistics, as well as genetics, from the 1960s onwards, a human population genetics developed that was structured by tree thinking and that represented modern human phylogeny in tree diagrams that, to the layperson, suggest independent development of pure populations (Sommer 2015a).

In Part IV, I begin with tree building and mapping in early blood-group studies, before moving on to the history and present of genetic admixture research and the diagrams pertaining to the so-called 'ancient DNA revolution'. Around 2000, a certain shift in focus took place from the genetic differentiation of populations towards studies of admixture. At the beginning of the third millennium, new theoretical, statistical, and computational approaches could be brought to bear on the organization, analysis, and interpretation of an unprecedented amount of human genomic data. Global genome-wide data was visualized as colored bar plots that showed individual genomes to be mosaics made up of different contributions from several 'ancestral populations'. While I argue that these relating diagrams still carry notions of originally pure populations, with the advent of ancient DNA studies, the phylogenetic trees of human populations have acquired more and more connecting branches. Since these have even come to connect living humans with archaic lines such as the Neanderthals, the human family tree is in jeopardy. Are we entering the post-Linnean and post-Haeckelian age, in which heterarchical understandings of diversity and net-shaped notions of human relatedness take over? And if so, what political connotations does this shift carry?

In the course of this book, I provide spotlights on the history of diagrams in (physical, evolutionary, and genetic) anthropology. While I am interested in 'firsts', that is the possibly first diagrammatics of 'race' or the first application of the family tree to produce intra-human diversity, this kind of inquiry is not in the foreground. Rather, I am concerned with the performativity of diagrams: how was human diversity diagrammatically constructed and reconstructed throughout the history of anthropology? Which kind of practices and inferences underlie diverse relating diagrams, and what are their politics? Did the visual strategies of communication capture the theories of the scientists or did they rather convey contradicting meanings? What kind of controversies, if at all, existed regarding the right kinds of diagrams to capture human kinship and evolution, and were these controversies also about politics? Following these guiding questions leads me from the last decades of the eighteenth century to the present day, with a geographical emphasis on Europe and the United States. I look at eurocentric and Western-centric projects of defining humanity, of subdividing and of ordering it, including the concomitant endeavors to acquire representative samples – bones, blood, or DNA – from all over the world.

Thus, my project is part of what some scholars have referred to as a diagrammatic turn (Bogen and Thürlemann 2003, 3). Diagrammatics has in fact been advanced as an interdisciplinary approach in the humanities and social sciences, with its own introductions, overviews, anthologies, and lexica entries (e.g., Bauer and Ernst 2010; Bender and Marrinan 2010; Ernst 2014; Bigg 2016). Yet, despite there being very thought-provoking theoretical treatises (see, e.g., Schneider, Ernst, and Wöpking 2016), historical reconstruction remains sparse (ibid., 7): Hardly any overviews of the cultural history of diagrams exist (see, however, Bonhoff 1993). At the same time, even though historians of science have only rarely focused their attention on diagrams as such (e.g., Kaiser 2005), diagrams are increasingly seen as an important epistemic tool that needs to be addressed on its own (e.g., Lüthy and Smets 2009; Jardine and Fay 2014; Priest, Findlen, and De Toffoli 2018; Sommer et al. 2018; Arni, Sommer, and Teuscher 2023; Sommer, Arni, and Müller-Wille 2023; Sommer et al. 2024). Diagrams have even been pronounced the secret weapons of the scientific revolution (Franklin 2000). One may speak of diagrams as paper tools with Ursula Klein (2003); as inscriptions, the material, performative, and cultural aspects of which matter (e.g., also Rheinberger, Hagner, and Wahrig-Schmidt 1996); or as technologies in the sense of the arduous work of collecting, selecting, and structuring data, as for example in the case of anthropological research (Sommer et al. 2018, 14–15).

Diagrams seem to suggest themselves as tools for the sciences that aim at classifying human groups, because diagrams are inherently about relations – they represent relations and proportions that characterize a phenomenon. However, they are also constructive – they may bring relations newly into being, and they may be informed by and inform ideological conceptions (Stjernfelt 2000). Despite their omnipresence, the role of diagrams in the history of anthropology has so far largely escaped scholarly attention. There are as yet no comprehensive engagements with visual traditions in anthropology beyond the figurative (there are especially engagements with photographs, (prehistoric) life-scenes, and museum exhibitions, see Sommer 2022a). This, coupled with the realization that understanding the functioning of 'my diagrams' would need a context of academic exchange between different disciplines, led me to initiate the inter-university project "In the Shadow of the Tree: The Diagrammatics of Relatedness as Scientific, Scholarly, and Popular Practice" that the Swiss National Science Foundation has funded from early 2019 to early 2024 (see Acknowledgements). My own goal regarding diagrammatics is to take diagrams seriously in their mediation between image and text as well as thought and action. I ask what went into them, how they were read and used, and how they circulated. I also endeavor to draw connections between diverse diagrammatic traditions, for example between human family trees and religious and natural-historic imagery. Throughout the book, I engage with specific philosophical-theoretical treatises on diagrams, beginning with Charles Sanders Peirce in Part I.

Prior to embarking on these endeavors, a note on terminology is needed. Throughout the book, I have changed the most offensive designations found in my sources. A particularly harmful term and its derivates I have substituted (including in quotes and publication titles) most often with *Black Africans*, as it usually appears alongside other geographical denotations. However, there is variation in terminology within individual sources and among different sources. In other cases,

African Americans as a substitutive term was more appropriate. I have kept *Black* and equivalent terms, but capitalized and adjectivized them when applied to people (without also adding inverted commas). I capitalize *White*, since it does not refer to a real skin color but is a 'racial' grouping, even if mostly meant to be one of superiority. I have replaced disparaging colonial names for smaller populations with current usages where a corresponding self-identification exists. However, throughout the book, I have maintained some of the problematic nomenclature in order to show continuities into present times. This also applies to classifications like 'Caucasian/Caucasoid' and equivalents, which I maintained in quotes or in inverted commas. I have also retained the noun 'race' and the adjective 'racial' (again in inverted commas where distance is not already expressed), because the difference to terms like 'varieties' or 'nations' can be significant. Historical actors like Samuel George Morton, while working with several terms for each of the types they sought to establish, used *Americans* for Indigenous peoples of the Americas, *Australians* for Aboriginal Australians, etc. This is informative, as it highlights just how strongly some of them thought in racial terms. White people in contexts of settler colonialism were, in this racialized outlook, still European. One finds this practice sometimes even in current genetic research. Finally, many of the diagrams I reproduce in this book may be disturbing and contain offending language. They are strictly used as quotes or sources and are to be viewed as if in quotation marks.

PART I. BUILDING A DIAGRAMMATICS OF 'RACE' IN THE EMERGING FIELD OF ANTHROPOLOGY

In the fields of both anthropology and biology, when considering diagrams of relatedness, phylogenetic trees often come to mind. Indeed, as in the case of genealogy, tree diagrams have been identified as "canonical icons" in these realms (Gould 1995; 1997, 30),[1] and they will take center stage in following parts. However, in this part, we will see how other types of diagrams were an integral part of racial anthropology from the start. Various kinds of diagrams were introduced to construct 'racial categories' and to allow the comparison of these categories in the process of establishing the field of physical anthropology out of a more historical-comparative ethnology. The late Stephen Jay Gould has drawn attention to the development of a metric approach in physical anthropology in the nineteenth century that depended on novel instruments, in his now classic *The Mismeasure of Man* (1996 [1981], 62–141). While the constitutive new images were not Gould's focus, Christine Hanke (2007) has shown the connection between metric-statistical procedures and mechanical-objective visualizations, including tables, curves, and drawings, and its role in shaping concepts of race and sex in the context of the journal *Archiv für Anthropologie* during the later period between 1890 and 1915. The diagrammatic repertoire of anthropology more broadly has been the object of a special issue of the journal *History of the Human Sciences* on "Diagrammatic Renderings of Human Evolution and Diversity in Physical, Serological and Molecular Anthropology"; with the exception of the introduction, the issue focuses on the twentieth century (Sommer and Lipphardt 2015).

1 On anthropology, see Sommer, e.g., 2005b and 2015b.

 https://doi.org/10.11647/OBP.0396.01

However, it is the period to which the late George Stocking (1973, xii) has referred to as the dark ages in the history of anthropology, the last decades of the eighteenth to the mid-nineteenth century, that is of particular importance for an understanding of how diagrams came to play such a great role in anthropology. It was a time when practitioners were in the process of defining the field: whose methods would be adopted in the endeavor variously called 'anthropology', 'ethnology', or 'ethnography'? During the transition from environmentalism to physical anthropology, a prominent figure was James Cowles Prichard, who was regarded as the founder of modern anthropology not only by his British contemporaries but also, as will be of particular concern, by Americans. Even though Prichard was not an environmentalist, he stood for the traditional comparative-historical approach to the study of 'man'. At the same time, there were the fledgling beginnings of physical anthropology in the work of such influential authors as Petrus Camper and Johann Friedrich Blumenbach. On all of these drew the so-called father of American physical anthropology: the physician Samuel George Morton. To engage with the transition from a comparative-historical to a comparative-physical approach, I thus focus on a network of researchers whose work has been considered fundamental for the development of anthropology by their contemporaries as well as by historians of science.

Like Camper, Blumenbach, Prichard, and Morton, those who brought change to anthropology in the last decades of the eighteenth to the mid-nineteenth century were in large part trained in anatomy and natural history, and they looked to their fields for inspiration. In the new physical anthropology, skulls became central objects of study. Human skulls were already collected and studied in medicine. However, the new 'science of man' regarded the study of humans as part of natural history and was thus distinct from medical and medico-anatomical inquiry into human beings (Sloan 1995, 113). The comparing and measuring of skulls in anthropology was inspired by the classification efforts in comparative zoology and the nascent field of paleontology (e.g., Stanton 1960, 24–29, 42–43; Roque 2010, 130–31; Armstrong-Fumero 2014, 12–17). As Ann Fabian has put it for Morton: "Morton took up questions that comparative anatomists had asked about the shape and size of skulls of different animals, but instead of looking at various animals, he compared human races" (2010, 30).

However, Morton was also inspired by phrenology, which was entirely focused on the analysis of skull shapes and an important source of diagrammatic and metric methods. Furthermore, Camper especially drew also on diagrammatic techniques from art, another realm in which skulls were collected and studied, and we will see that early physical anthropologists retained some esthetic considerations in their work. Finally, Morton was regularly revered as 'the new Blumenbach' or even 'the new Prichard' already during his lifetime (Stanton 1960, 39), and, in histories of physical anthropology, Camper, Blumenbach, and Morton have long been 'credited' for pioneering the quantitative approach (e.g., Shapiro 1959, 373–76). But the focus on diagrams will reveal that Prichard criticized the metric approach as practiced by Morton and Camper, while beginning to integrate diagrams in his work, and that Blumenbach's method was diagrammatic without necessarily being metric. It was especially the diagrammatic approach, entailing the perception of bodies (and particularly skulls) in terms of proportions and relations, that lay the foundation for the new physical anthropology – a diagrammatic approach that was developed into a diagrammatics of 'race' through the introduction of instruments and measurements, not least in Morton's work.

I will therefore have to ask which qualities of diagrams suited the project of physical anthropologists. This may be approached through the diagrammatology of Charles Sanders Peirce on the basis of some types of diagrams that will be of central importance in this part. For Peirce, the icon is a symbol that is characterized by similarity to the object it represents. Diagrams are one subcategory of icons that are distinguished from the other two subcategories – the image and the metaphor – by representing "the relations [...] of the parts of one thing by analogous relations in their own parts" (Peirce 1998 [1903], 274), such as, in our case, the geometric drawings of the outlines of skulls that served to preserve the proportions of parts for measurement, for which there might be inserted lines. However, these subcategories are not strictly separated. The subcategory of diagrams also contains images, and images can also be read diagrammatically, as when the lithographs of realistic drawings of skulls were studied by observing the relations and proportions of their parts. In doing so, the observer performed a diagrammatic operation, making the image a diagram.

A diagram can also represent a set of objects that stand in rational relation to each other, such as, in our case, the tables containing numbers for the mean cranial capacities of different human groups. Diagrams may thus show relations between the parts of one thing and/or relations between a set of things, as also in a map of 'racial distribution'. Furthermore, there exist relations between diagrams. As rule-based representation of a phenomenon, an actual diagram is less apprehended as the elements and relations of the individual material object than read as a generalized type (as in the attempts to standardize schemata to represent skulls that allowed certain operations and measurements). This already suggests that diagrams are tools for mental experimentation and manipulation, as we will see in practice, for example, when skull types were diagrammatically morphed into each other. For Peirce, this is a great strength of diagrams, but, in operating with a diagram, there also lies the danger of taking the diagram for the thing itself. Characteristics that we associate with objects prior to their analysis – for instance 'primitive' or 'advanced' characters with specific 'races' – may thus enter the experiments carried out with diagrams and lead to the perception of misleading patterns. While diagrams do make knowledge perceptible – diagrams demonstrate something – commonsense, ideological prejudice as well as wishful thinking may enter the production of diagrams and affect how information is presented (Peirce 1998 [1903]; 1906; Stjernfelt 2000; 2007, 23–48).

Another central aspect of diagrams is that, in contrast to objects such as skulls, they can easily travel. The centrality of the processes of accumulation and circulation of objects (of knowledge) for scientific practice through the transformation of things into so-called 'immutable mobiles' has especially been analyzed by Bruno Latour. In *Science in Action* (1987), he investigated the transformations through which events, things, and humans are made into mobile and stable inscriptions that can be combined with each other. In the case under concern here, in cascades of successively higher degrees of abstraction, objects like skulls were transferred onto paper as drawings, transformed into numbers through measurements, and into means in comparative tables that categorized, ordered, and hierarchized. In this process, human remains such as skulls were decontextualized – they no longer carried the traces of their unethical acquisition in contexts of violence and exploitation.

Transformed into diagrams, they could be globally distributed, (re)used, and further processed in the project of sampling, standardizing, and ordering humanity.

In the following, I begin by engaging with Prichard's comparative-historical *Researches into the Physical History of Man* (1813) and ask how he reacted to the physical anthropology, or better craniology, of Camper and Blumenbach, which, as we will see, was esthetic, diagrammatic, and (in the case of Camper) also metric. I then analyze Morton's now decidedly diagrammatic and metric approach to human crania. A close reading of one of his skull atlases, *Crania americana* (1839), in particular, will reveal the intent to instruct in a kind of diagrammatics that had not yet prevailed. Besides making available his huge skull collection through the lithographs in the book's appendix, Morton used diagrams to introduce and explain measuring devices and the carrying out of measurements (on the use of diagrams in connection with instruments, see Gessner 2014 and Higton 2014). He taught the reader how to diagrammatically construct 'racial types'. I shall examine how Prichard was affected in his later editions of *Researches* by the new physical anthropology of Morton, and I will look at Morton's direct legacy through the work *Types of Mankind* (1854), authored by his friends Josiah Clark Nott and George Robin Gliddon: did his fervent supporters also carry through his diagrammatic and metric method?

As already hinted at, there was more at stake than the question of the right methodology or the pre-evolutionary explanation of the causes of human differentiation. Of central concern to the practitioners discussed here was the issue of human origins, of whether humans originated in one pair and in one geographical region, or whether the human varieties had separate origins and at different locations. The terms 'monogenist' and 'polygenist', used to describe the proponents of these views, were actually introduced only in the late 1850s by said Gliddon (Douglas 2008, 53). Connected to this debate was the question of whether humans constituted different varieties that belonged to the same species, or if they could be divided into several species. As we will see, Morton drew on French polygenist writings, and his work was not only foundational for what would be dubbed 'the American school of anthropology' that was associated with polygenism; Morton's crania atlases that instantiated his development of a seemingly rigorously diagrammatic and metric approach triggered follow-up projects internationally and generally were a steppingstone in the development of a polygenist physical anthropology. I will therefore argue that while there was a diagrammatics of relatedness – a way of using diagrams to evidence close human kinship – diagrams were also used to deny genealogical relatedness, to create differences within humankind that amounted to the status of unrelated species. This 'diagrammatics of race', as I call it, was enmeshed in matters of 'racial' politics. Despite aspirations to objectivity, the history of physical anthropology makes it clear that diagrams were not purely epistemological but also political tools in the contexts of imperialism, colonialism, and the 'racial' violence associated with these forms of expansionism (Sommer 2023a, 2–5).

1. Esthetics, Diagrammatics, and Metrics: The Beginnings of Physical Anthropology

Prichard's *Researches into the Physical History of Man*, first published in 1813, was a founding text. He was internationally recognized as the father of modern ethnology or anthropology. As we will see, his encompassing contribution could not be disregarded even by his adversaries (Stocking 1973, ix–xii). Although Prichard called his approach physical history, it rested on classical literature (of historical geographers), later travel writing (by James Cook, Joseph Banks, Johann Forster, Mungo Park, Alexander von Humboldt, etc.), oriental studies, antiquarian and Christian chronological treatises, alongside natural history (Carl von Linné, Georges-Louis Leclerc, Comte de Buffon, George Cuvier, Étienne Geoffroy Saint-Hilaire). Among these influences was William Jones, who had suggested the affinity of the European languages to ancient Sanskrit and their common but lost origin, and who had retraced the history of humanity philologically to a single family in Persia in "A Discourse on the Origin and Families of Nations" (1999 [1807] [1792]). Indeed, the comparative-historical approach to languages was the most important pillar of Prichard's work, followed by studies of religions, political institutions, manners and customs (Stocking 1973, xxxiv–xliii; also Augstein 1997).

However, the beginnings of another anthropology were already taking form, one that aimed at determining human history and kinship on the basis of physical characteristics that were interpreted as durable. The way in which Prichard engaged with this literature is insightful. He at times even seems to have ridiculed what the Dutch physician Camper "fancied" (Prichard 1813, 48). Prichard understood Camper to establish

 https://doi.org/10.11647/OBP.0396.02

a scale of animals and human types according to their beauty and intelligence on the basis of the so-called 'facial angle'. While Prichard in the 558 pages of text in *Researches* could do without illustrations (though he included vocabulary tables and genealogical/chronological lists), Camper's dissertation of 1768, which was posthumously published in 1792 (and translated into German by Samuel Thomas von Soemmerring), was built around diagrams of skulls from his rather modest collection, which, besides crania from his and neighboring countries, contained only eight such from Africa and Asia (Camper 1792, xiv on the collection).

Camper's first two diagrams have since been reproduced frequently, often out of context and adapted in ways so as to enhance their racist appearance (Coghill and Hayes 2024). These showed a row of skulls framed and traversed by lines above a series of corresponding heads (1792, TAB. I and TAB. II [copper plates, n.p.]). They were representations of his method. Camper had aligned a European with his more 'exotic' human skulls and an ape skull for comparison. The inspection of the proportions of the skulls thus arranged made him conclude that the differences between them were captured by a line from the forehead (supraorbital ridge) to the upper lip (incisors). In order to transfer the diagrammatic method into a diagram for measurement and demonstration, Camper invented a construction through which horizontal, vertical, and diagonal strings could be strung. This should allow him to produce geometrical drawings that preserved the skulls' proportions and to arrive at points of comparison and to draw lines (on the technique, see Karliczek and Jank 2010, 71–75). In the drawings, he arranged the skulls along a horizontal line through the base of the nose and the auditory tract, which, together with the first line described above, provided said facial angle. In the resulting first diagram, there is a series of skulls and heads of increasing facial angles from a monkey on the left to a juvenile orangutan and the Angolan child whom he had publicly dissected in Amsterdam in 1758. While the Angolan skull stood in for Black Africans, the fourth skull and head of a "Kalmyk" (Camper 1792, 16) represented all of Asia.[1]

1 The Kalmyk skull was taken to represent all of Asia from Siberia to New Zealand, as well as America; the European stood for Europe, Turkey, Arabia, and Persia; and the Angolan for sub-Saharan Africa. At the same time, Camper recognized that all nations showed a range in facial angle.

The first skull and head on the left of Camper's second diagram referred to a European individual with a facial angle of 80°. Everything above that Camper relegated to the realm of art and everything below 70° he regarded as resembling the apes. Now Camper made explicit use of the experimental nature of diagrams. He changed the European skull's line from forehead to upper lip, step by step, so as to increase the facial angel, or to move from reality into art. When doing so, the head became gradually shorter; in the last figure of the series, in which the facial angle reached its maximum of 100°, the eyes were in the middle of the face. If one were to move above 100°, however, the head would become malformed. Camper explained that the ancient Greeks did go up to the maximum of 100° in their art, as the last figure showed, while the Romans only used 95° as in the second last figure. If one carried out the experiment in the other direction beyond the first diagram, Camper suggested, the Angolan skull would become ape and monkey and then dog and bird. Camper did so in drawing without reproducing the resulting diagram (1792, 16–24). Thus, in playing with the facial angle, Camper made it look as though the Angolan skull would approach the ape, while he at least stated that the similarity disappeared as soon as one considered other regions of the body or the head. At the same time, Camper thought that, due to the correlation of parts, the experimentation with the facial angle enabled one to diagrammatically morph one human type into another. This is demonstrated in Figure I.1 for the transformation of a Black African into a European or vice versa (28–29).

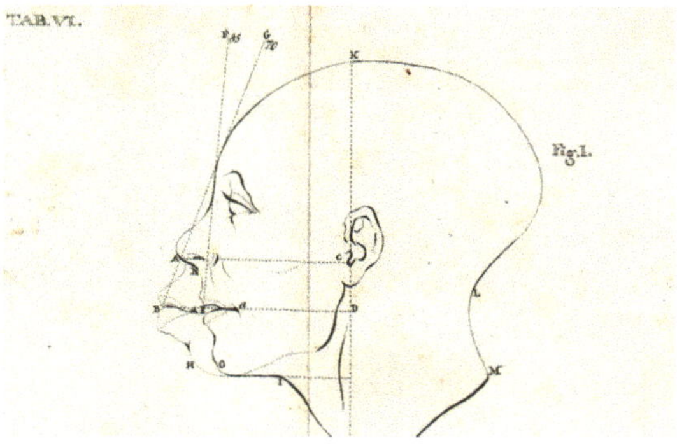

Fig. I.1 The diagrammatic morphing of human varieties. Petrus Camper, *Über den natürlichen Unterschied der Gesichtszüge in Menschen: verschiedener Gegenden und verschiedenen Alters* [...] (Berlin: Voss, 1792), Plate 6, copper plate, appendix. Public domain.

Camper drew, painted, and sculpted human faces as a hobby and noticed that in European art, Black Africans rather looked like Europeans. He was also not satisfied with the existing methods to capture the physically beautiful. In a distinctly diagrammatic way, he wanted to show how beauty resided in relations between parts and that these could be expressed in measures. In doing so, he was drawing on an artistic tradition. In fact, Camper had encountered something similar to his facial angle in Albrecht Dürer's work (Camper 1792, 20). Already Dürer had made extensive use of diagrams to capture different head shapes, their proportions and transformations. Even while it was not his aim to arrive at distinctions between different peoples, he had applied such lines to one Black head as part of the great human variability. Unlike Camper, Dürer had derived his lines from the face, not the skull, and he had not provided measures for the angle between the facial line and the horizontal lines he chose (see Figure I.2; Dürer 1528; Meijer 1999, 102–104).

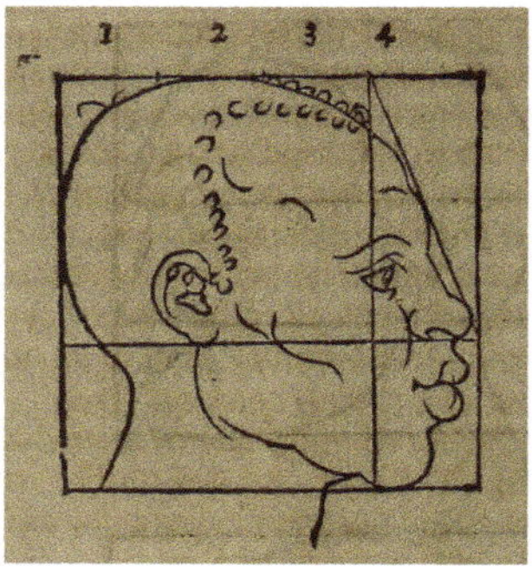

Fig. I.2 Dürer's diagrammatics of the head. Albrecht Dürer, *Hierinn sind begriffen vier Bücher von menschlicher Proportion* [...] (Nuremberg: Hieronymus Andreae Formschneider, 1528), n.p. Public domain.

Beyond art, the correlation of parts would become a central concept in comparative anatomy, and Camper situated his treatise in natural history. He wanted to contribute to the 'natural history of man', and that is how he was understood: the facial angle, the first angular measurement for the comparative analysis of human skulls, became a mainstay of physical anthropology (e.g., Meijer 1999; Visser 1990). Camper, though making esthetic judgments about different human forms, used the power of diagrams to experiment with proportions to demonstrate that the human varieties were exactly that: variations on a single type according to the law of the correlation of parts. This was in support of his belief that all humans were descended from a single pair, Adam and Eve – humans were of one family and bound together by genealogy.

With his scale of perfection through animal and human forms, Camper was part of a longer tradition (even if Camper did not belief in the *scala naturae* as the natural order).[2] However, it was one of his contemporaries who devised another diagrammatic and metric mode of arrangement: the French naturalist Louis Jean-Marie Daubenton, Buffon's assistant, with whom Camper was acquainted. Daubenton (1764) published diagrams of animal and human skulls in which were inserted the lines he used to distinguish between them. In humans, what he defined as the plane of the occipital foramen approached most closely to the horizontal (resulting in the lowest occipital-orbital angle) due to their upright body posture. As in Camper's case, this angle connected the human form with animals in a scale (ape, monkey, dog, and horse). However, Daubenton did not subdivide humans into different 'nations' (Meijer 1999, 110–14). Neither did Johann Gottfried Herder, with regard to the facial angle, but he did partake in the diagrammatic experimentation of molding forms into each other.

In *Ideen zur Philosophie der Geschichte der Menschheit* (1785, 189–218), Herder claimed that his way of comparing human and ape heads resulted from his own study of skulls. Even though he had found the reference to Daubenton's treatise in Blumenbach's writings, he had not read the piece. However, Herder drew on Camper's facial angle and wished that the latter's treatise and diagrams were widely received. Herder thought he had discovered the reason for Camper's findings: if, instead of the ear, one took the last cervical vertebra as the starting point to draw lines to the very back of the skull, to its apex, to the front of the forehead, and the chinbone, it became clear that the form of the head depended on the habitus of the entire organism, on whether it walked

2 The first to have tried to develop *lineae cephalometricae* [cephalometric lines] to distinguish between different animals and humans was Adriaan van den Spiegel in the context of the interest in distinct head forms (*figurae capitis*). One of his lines – the *linea faciei* [facial line] – was drawn from chin to forehead (Spiegel 1632, 21–22; Pierer and Choulant 1816, 520–30; Marinus 1846).

upright. Most importantly, Herder used a diagram in words when mentally transforming one form into the other through the correlation of parts – something Camper had accomplished in drawing: if the center of gravity of the head was changed, the jaws moved forward, the nose flattened, the eyes approached each other, and the front receded as the skull lost its curvature, increasingly resembling that of an ape. If the mental experiment was carried out in the other direction, one transformed an animal form into a human form with its most beautiful and capable head. Within the human form, the angle defined by the degree of protrusion of the lower face and retreat of the forehead marked the difference between mal- and well-formed heads, up to the Greek face that was tilted forward in an esthetically pleasing way. Herder was positive that there would be a science concerned with the correlation of the interior parts that surpasses the superficial approach of physiognomy (1785, 189–218).

By the early nineteenth century, the facial angle had become the stuff of textbooks on natural history. The German comparative anatomist Lorenz Oken used it to support a *scala naturae* as the order of the mammals. In an amalgamation of Camper's and Daubenton's approaches, he proposed also measuring the position of the plane of the occipital hole along with the facial angle (indicating the position of the head on the neck) (1813, 659–60). At the same time, the facial angle had been taken up in Camper's second consideration too, namely, to differentiate between the 'nations' of humankind, while other naturalists had devised further methods for this purpose. The comparative anatomist of the hour, George Cuvier (1800, 3–15), for example, engaged with the facial angle in different 'races' and developed a method for the relative measurement of skull and face – a ratio that, according to him, decreased from Europeans to Asians to Black Africans (and was meant to express relative mental and sensual faculties).[3]

To the contrary, for Prichard (1813, 46–55), it was moot to base the comparison between individuals – which in the case of Camper

3 In his dissertation, Wolter Hendrik Crull (1810) engaged with the existing craniological methods. He treated Camper's, Blumenbach's, and Cuvier's systems, among others, and he also applied Daubenton to the human varieties (for another early overview see Pierer and Choulant 1816, 520–30).

stood for entire human groups – on one measurement.[4] He took issue with other attempts at physical anthropology like Cuvier's and von Soemmerring's, too.[5] But there was one scholar who had pioneered the study of skulls and whom Prichard held in much higher regard – so much so that he dedicated his 1813 *Researches* to him – the Göttingen physician Blumenbach, who was also a friend. Himself referring to Camper (among others), Blumenbach issued his six instalments of *Decas (altera/tertia/quarta/quinta/sexta) collectionis suae carniorum diversarum gentium illustrata* (1790, 1793, 1795, 1800, 1808, 1820), in which a series of ten skulls each was represented on copper plates and described. In his most famous work, *De generis humani varietate nativa* (1775), to the contrary, there were no illustrations of skulls until the third edition of 1795.[6]

Blumenbach (1798, 2) was proud that his skull collection was more extensive and varied than that of his friend Camper, and in this third edition, he distinguished five human varieties on its basis, which he called 'Caucasian', 'Mongolian', 'Ethiopian', 'American' and 'Malayan'. However, the terms 'Caucasian' and 'Mongolian' were not coined by Blumenbach but by Christoph Meiners, the German race theorist and Blumenbach's antagonist at Göttingen due to his polygenist and proslavery advocacy (Quine 2019; Michael 2020a, 90–94). In his own treatise, Blumenbach emphasized that the human varieties showed great variation within themselves and merged into each other through imperceptible gradations; no characteristic had been found that was exclusive to one group. This meant that classification was arbitrary, although Blumenbach did hold that his own was truer to nature than others. He discussed possible causes, including the *Bildungstrieb* [formative drive], climate, way of life, 'bastardization', illnesses and/

4 Prichard did not do justice to the complexity of Camper's analyses. The widespread misinterpretation of Camper's views by anthropologists led to the facial angle being used to establish 'racial hierarchies of intelligence' (Blanckaert 1987).

5 Von Soemmerring had knowledge of Camper's work prior to publication and referred to it in his treatise on the physical differences between 'the African and European races'. He also suggested that Camper's work was mostly only known from an abstract (Soemmerring 1785, 5).

6 I have mainly worked with the German translation of the third edition of 1798, comparing key passages with the Latin (1795) and French (1804) versions of the same edition.

or accidents, of differences in hair color and structure, skin color, face and skull shape, Camper's facial angle, peculiarities in teeth, ears, sexual organs, feet and hands as well as differences in stature. Overall, like Camper and Prichard, Blumenbach wanted to defend the unity of humankind: it constituted one species and was of common origin (Blumenbach 1798, 91–202).

Blumenbach, too, was interested in the relations of parts, especially with respect to the skull, but he accused Camper of not having used his points and lines consistently in his drawings, and he thought that Camper's facial angle did not work as a criterion to distinguish varieties, for more than one reason. There were very different skulls from different 'nations' that may have the same facial angle, while similar skulls may differ in this angle. The profile alone was not very informative. Blumenbach therefore proposed another approach. It seemed nearly impossible to capture all proportions with one line, but this was best achieved with the *Scheitelnorm* [vertex norm], also referred to as *norma verticalis* [vertical norm]. One had to arrange the skulls without lower jaws on their cheekbones (*Jochbein*) along a line on the table and look at them from behind, as illustrated in his diagram that has since become famous and that shows three skulls from different continents from above and behind as well as the line of their orientation (see Figure I.3). This allowed for the simultaneous observation of all important characteristics.

The oval 'Caucasian' skull that Blumenbach put in the middle, which for him possessed most beauty and symmetry, was from a female Georgian (who was captured in the Turkish war by the Russians and died in Moscow, where she was dissected). In comparison, Blumenbach described the 'Ethiopian' skull to its left that was from a female from Guinea (the 'concubine' of a Dutch man who died in Amsterdam, where she was dissected) as having something akin to a beak,[7] and the 'Mongolian' skull to the right, which had belonged to an Evenki person (a 'Reindeer Tungus', who had ostensibly killed himself and was brought home by an army surgeon), looked to him as if it had been flattened and thus protruded on both sides (Blumenbach 1798, 143–61, 203–224, 289–91). The observation that the two 'extreme' varieties seemed to

7 "rostrum" (Blumenbach 1795, 205): 'beak', 'nuzzle', 'snout'.

be 'elongated' and, respectively, 'flattened' versions of the 'Caucasian' skull, combined with the diagram of the skulls adjusted along a visible line, again suggest a diagrammatic approach to skulls in which one variety is molded into the other through correlated changes in parts. Indeed, in this molding, Blumenbach (1798, 204) took the 'Caucasian variety' to be the original: it had developed into the two 'extremes' on both sides, into the 'Ethiopian' and the 'Mongolian'.

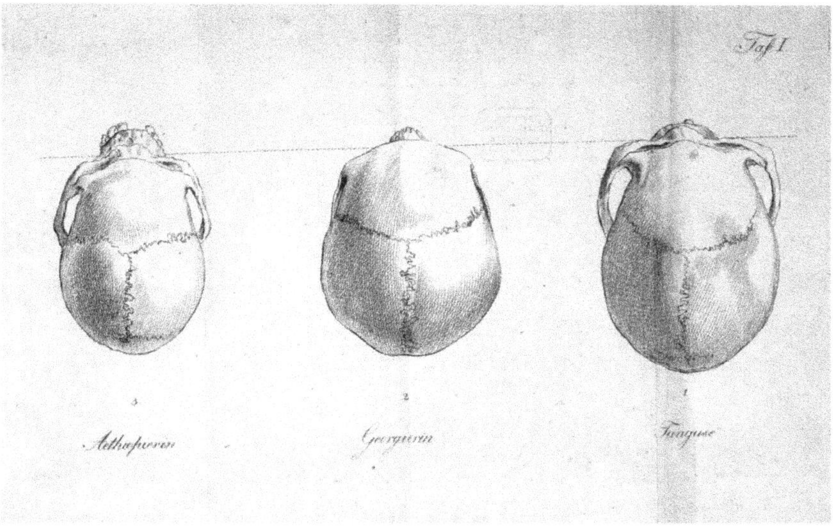

Fig. I.3 Blumenbach's diagrammatic approach. Johann Friedrich Blumenbach, *Über die natürlichen Verschiedenheiten im Menschengeschlechte,* 3rd ed. (Leipzig: Breitkopf und Härtel, 1798), Plate 1, copper plate, appendix. Public domain.

In his second fold-out plate, Blumenbach introduced two new forms on each side of the 'Caucasian', the 'American' (a skull from the Caribbean, acquired by Joseph Banks) on the side of the 'Mongolian' and the 'Malay' (a skull from Tahiti, also acquired by Joseph Banks) on the side of the 'Ethiopian'. But Blumenbach did not think that the 'Caucasian' degenerated, as he called it, first into the 'American' and the 'Malay', and then these forms developed into the 'Mongolian' and the 'Ethiopian' respectively, as this order might suggest. Rather, while he seems to have thought that the 'Malay' had developed from the 'Caucasian', the 'American' was of 'Mongolian' origin (Blumenbach 1798, note to Plate I and II, n.p.). In other words, the arrangement of the skulls does not indicate actual lines of transformation of one form into another; it does not suggest a tree with two shoots branching out from the Caucasian, as has been proposed by Gould (1996 [1981], 401–412, with an image of the 'tree' on 409; see also Junker 2019, who himself proposed another tree structure as underlying Blumenbach's diagram: Fig. 6.4, 109). Blumenbach's visual order is not tree-structured. It is nonhierarchical. It follows anatomical affinity, mostly concerning the breadth of the skull, rather than descent. This is why the 'American' is between the 'Caucasian' and 'Mongolian' instead of to the left of both of them. In other words, for Blumenbach, degeneration was reversible. In adapting to American climates, in diverging from the 'Mongolian', the 'American type' in fact returned somewhat to the 'Caucasian' anatomy.

What a diagrammatic reading of the line of skulls in order of anatomical affinity was meant to convey was not actual genealogy; rather, like Camper's morphing experiments, it was intended to demonstrate that human variation was gradual. It suggested to the eye the possibility of transforming the primordial type into varieties under observation of the relations of parts and, at least to a degree, vice versa. As elaborated in the introduction of this part from the perspective of Peircean diagrammatology, diagrams were not only chosen as the tool of representation because they are inherently about the relation of parts, they were also explored for their potential for experimentation, either by making them dynamic, as in the case of Camper, or by provoking the experiment in the beholder's mind, as in the case of Blumenbach. In the end, like Camper's, Blumenbach's diagrammatics aimed to demonstrate the single origin and unity of humankind, but, unlike Camper's, it was not metric – Blumenbach's approach did not necessarily involve instruments and measurements.[8]

8 Scholars have interpreted Blumenbach's writings on the human varieties rather differently, from being egalitarian and progressive to white supremacist and racist. The latter judgments might well have something to do with the changes the English translations introduced into his texts, as John S. Michael (2017) has aptly argued. Thomas Bendyshe presented Blumenbach's *De generis humani varietate nativa* in his English translation (1865) as constructing five 'races' as distinct, separate, and unequal units. Already in 1787, Blumenbach had concluded in "Observations on the Bodily Conformations and Mental Capacities of [Black Africans]" (English translation 1799) that Black Africans were not inferior to the rest of humanity. He collected books by Black writers, he opposed his colleague Meiners' racism, Friedrich Tiedemann described him as defender of the intellectual power of Black people, and he was drawn on by abolitionists (Michael 2017; also, Douglas 2008; Richards 2018). Additionally, Blumenbach described

Prichard quoted Blumenbach's work in the original Latin and even included a translation of the latter's conclusion with regard to the five skull forms in his *Researches*. At the same time, Prichard observed that the skull bones were strongly shaped in development by the muscular system and that the differences in head shape could not be specific because of the individuality of this system. Prichard declared that none of the peculiarities described were constant and confined to one 'race'. Skull shapes that were considered typical of Black Africans and 'Mongolians' appeared also among Europeans, and even more so the other way around. Though this was acknowledged by Blumenbach, Prichard took issue with what he understood as the other researcher's insistence on the constancy of his descriptions (Prichard 1813, 56–65; for an encompassing treatment of Prichard and his work, see Augstein 1996). In the next chapter I turn to the physical anthropology of the Philadelphia physician Morton, who drew on all of the above: Prichard's ethnological and chronological knowledge, Camper's esthetic and metric as well as Camper's and Blumenbach's diagrammatic approach. However, Morton's work was of different theoretical and political intent and impact. The anthropologists so far treated were monogenists – they believed in a single origin of humankind, a humankind that constituted one species –, and their monogenism was associated with an antislavery position. To the contrary, we will see that Morton's work was taken on by polygenists and advocates for slavery. Morton wanted to have his very own impact on anthropology, ethnology, or ethnography, as he called it (Sommer 2023a, 5–10).

members of all varieties as esthetically pleasing (Michael 2020a, 80–84). However, Blumenbach was not free from the eurocentrism of his time and, in a letter, did compare a Black African skull to that of a monkey (Blumenbach to Camper, 9 September 1784, in Gysel 1983, 138).

2. Samuel George Morton and His (Paper) Skulls

Morton graduated from the University of Pennsylvania with a medical degree, and, after a brief tour of Europe, he returned to Philadelphia, practiced medicine, lectured on anatomy, and wrote on geology, zoology, and paleontology. He wanted to follow Blumenbach and others in the application of the comparative anatomical approach used in these fields to the study of humans. In fact, one of the pioneers of craniometry, the Dutch Jacob Elisa Doornik, persistently tried to persuade Morton to publish his own 'Decas craniorum', i.e., to describe a skull collection of his own. It was also Doornik who advised Morton not to restrict himself fully to the skulls of 'American tribes', "because you deprive your self [sic] exactly of that what you want above all – points of comparison […]".[1] Morton should widen the comparative scope to other 'nations'. However, when working on the different skull forms in the 'five human races' for a lecture held in 1830, Morton had realized that he needed more 'specimens'. Doornik was only one among many who assisted him in remedying the situation. He gave Morton half of his varied skull collection with the drawings for free, offering the other half for sale.[2] On his death in 1851, Morton left behind 867 cleaned and polished skulls

1 Doornik to Morton, 23 June 1835, Samuel George Morton Papers, American Philosophical Society Library, Mss.B.M843: Series I. Correspondence (hereafter Morton Papers APS). Doornik had moved to the United States and between 1828 and 1835 acquired enough of the English language to write to Morton in English rather than French.

2 Ibid., see also Doornik to Morton, 3 July 1835, 11 July 1835, 21 July 1835, Morton Papers APS, in which Doornik provided some information on the history of the skulls. The letters further document how they bickered over the payment and the price of the second half of his collection and drawings.

 https://doi.org/10.11647/OBP.0396.03

from all over the world; nonetheless, remains of Indigenous peoples of the Americas were particularly prominent.

The fact that Morton was of ill health increased the importance of a network of helpers for the so-called American father of physical anthropology. As Ann Fabian (2003; 2010, 9–46) has detailed, it was therefore opportune that Morton was the Corresponding Secretary of the Academy of Natural Sciences in Philadelphia, which meant he oversaw the circulation of information and specimens. He managed to enlist many such helpers for his skull 'collecting', including army men and doctors, missionaries, officials, settlers, explorers, phrenologists, and naturalists. Morton's project was enmeshed with imperialism and colonialism globally and, in particular, with the American frontier violence of the 1830s and 1840s, when eastern nations were forced off their ancestral lands. 'Collectors' would detail their methods of skull acquisition in letters, which, more often than not, involved grave robbing. While there might be rivalries between looters, and while remains might be protected by Native Americans, war and disease were on Morton's side.[3]

The skulls from all over the American continent allowed Morton to approach the question of the identity of the Indigenous peoples of the Americas in his *Crania americana* of 1839. However, Morton's collection was much more encompassing. His gruesome booty encompassed, for example, the heads of 'uncultivated' Anglo-Saxons, "lunatics" and "idiots" (Morton 1849a, n.p.), or more generally of marginalized people such as a Parisian prostitute. He held remains from hospitals and institutions for the poor, of a (most likely Aboriginal) Australian executed for cannibalism, as well as Afghans, Greeks, Black Africans, African Americans, and Chinese. For his second skull atlas – *Crania aegyptiaca* of 1844 – the (former) US consul of Cairo, Gliddon, supplied him with over one hundred Egyptian skulls in a large-scale plundering

3 Morton's correspondence documents this 'collecting mafia' as well as his acquaintance with influential scientists internationally, like William Buckland, Gideon Mantell, Charles Lyell, Alexandre Brongniart, or Edward Hitchcock (Morton Papers APS). It also documents how his interest in mineralogy, geology, and paleontology, as well as in ornithology and zoology more broadly, gave way to a focus on anthropology around the mid-1830s. Rather than shells, minerals, animal specimens, etc., it was now more often skulls that were discussed and transferred in bone or on paper.

project. Morton had to imburse Gliddon for packing, shipping, and other transportation, as well as for services such as grave raiding, bribery in hospitals, and so on, testing Morton's dedication to the project. After all, Morton had limited funds and carried out his ethnology as a pastime. Despite the unethical and uncanny nature of skull 'collecting' and 'collections', Morton made no secret of the origins of his loot in his books and catalogues, and this transparency was maintained by those who followed his lead. Where possible, Morton catalogued the skulls with information on 'race', sex, place of birth, and identity of 'collector'. Where available, stories were given about the persons to whom the remains had belonged and how they had died (Morton 1839, 1844, 1849a).[4] The histories of the human remains were important for the 'science of craniology'; consequently, the skull collections required paper archives, documenting these details (Roque 2010, 118–22).

Morton made his skull series – dubbed the 'American Golgotha' by a 'collector' – available to visitors. He also exchanged skulls with other 'collectors'. Most importantly, however, he circulated his skulls as images and text on paper, so that the series could easily reach the great anthropologists in Europe too. In 1839, Morton did so through his publication *Crania americana; or, A Comparative View of the Skulls of Various Aboriginal Nations of North and South America, to Which Is Prefixed an Essay on the Varieties of the Human Species*. This was not entirely novel; a few years earlier, he had published a groundbreaking work in paleontology dedicated to his colleague and correspondent, the renowned British geologist and paleontologist Gideon Mantell. It was similarly structured, serving as a kind of atlas with a systematic treatment of reptiles, fish, and mollusks of the US Cretaceous, followed by a section containing beautiful plates of specimens (Morton 1834).[5]

Crania americana was nonetheless a novelty in that it introduced a diagrammatic and metric approach to human diversity through a skull atlas. At the same time, this genre, too, had its historical inspirations. Indeed, we may look back as far as the early decades of the seventeenth

4 For more on the 'collecting', see correspondence (with Gliddon), Morton Papers APS; Fabian 2003; Michael 2023.

5 That this kind of lavish illustration was part of a particular genre becomes evident when looking at other works, such as Morton's first American edition of John Mackintosh's authoritative *Principles of Pathology and Practice of Physic*, which contained no images (Mackintosh and Morton 1836).

century, when Adriaan van den Spiegel's *De humani corporis fabrica libri decem* was posthumously published. In his instruction on human anatomy, the Flemish specialist, who might indeed have been the first to carry out craniological measurements, examined the size, shape, and proportions of the head that could be long/short, broad/narrow, high/low, pointed/rounded (Spiegel 1632, 21–22; Marinus 1846). At the end of van den Spiegel's long treatise, there was added a set of woodcuts, including some of skulls in which letters had been inserted to instruct in the anatomy of the parts and their relations to each other (see Figure I.4). As we will see, the transformation of skulls into immutable mobiles (on this term, see Introduction), this diagrammatic way of inspecting the images, and of relating text and image to each other were brought to an apex in Morton's skull atlases.

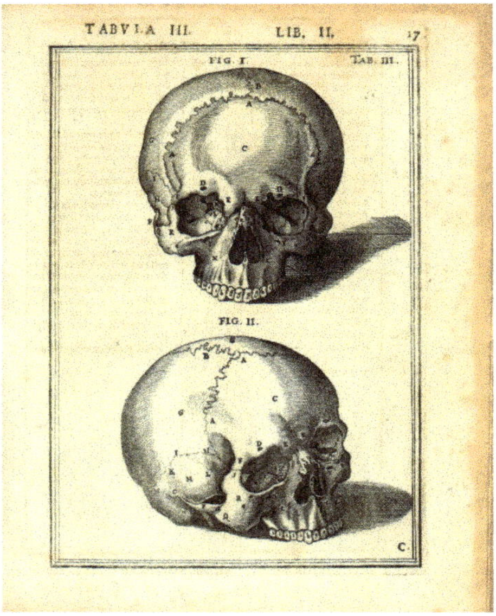

Fig. I.4 Table of skulls. Adriaan van den Spiegel, *De humani corporis fabrica libri decem* (Frankfurt: Impensis & caelo Matthaei Meriani bibliopolae & chalcographi, 1632), Vol. II, Plate 3, appendix. Public domain.

Morton most deeply embedded his work in the tradition of Camper, Blumenbach, and Prichard – the latter representing an approach he partly opposed, the first two representing an approach to which he aspired. Morton's *Crania americana* was more opulent and more extensive than the preceding *Decas* by Blumenbach. Morton had hired the Philadelphia lithographer, John Collins, to draw his skulls onto stone for the substantial appendix of plates. Somewhat surprisingly, the image Morton chose as the frontispiece of *Crania americana* first seems to suggest a traditional ethnological treatise. It is a drawing of a representative of 'another race', such as found in the third edition of Prichard's *Researches* (1836–47; on these images of Prichard, see Augstein 1996, 326–35). It shows a Native American chief who was painted from life by a Philadelphia artist and lithographed by another artist of that city. But its traditional look is misleading. This is not simply a portrait. It is a diagram, or at least Morton wanted the reader to look at the image in that way. As is typical for Morton's play of cross-references between bones and paper, and image and text, he referred the reader to page 292, where he proclaimed the warrior and orator of the Omaha as most characteristic of the Indigenous peoples of the Americas, "as seen in the retreating forehead, the low brow, [...] the large, aquiline nose, the high cheek bones, full mouth and chin, and angular face" (1839, 292).

Before entering the main text, the reader is then presented with the map of the world, reproduced in Figure I.5, "shewing the geographical distribution of the human species" (on map). Morton wrote that the distribution of the 'five races' "in the primitive epochs of the world" (1839, 95) was represented after Blumenbach. However, this map anticipated Morton's main findings that strongly diverged from Blumenbach's views. Morton would not argue but 'demonstrate' that the 'American tribes' constituted their own 'race', with the exception of the ones northern of the 60 degrees latitude, whom Morton considered to have migrated from Asia and to be now a mixture of 'Mongolians' and 'Americans'. But on the map, this intermixture had not yet taken place: the 'great races' were still neatly separated from each other in what Morton largely took to be their original territories. It was only in the course of time, he imagined, that this perfect order would have been disturbed through major migrations and interbreeding. Rather than a relating diagram, this is therefore one that denies a kind of relatedness which, at that time, was still taken more or less for granted: it denied the notion of 'the family of man' in the sense of a humankind that had descended in its entirety from a single pair or stock at a common place of origin, from where, eventually, the earth was populated with humans.

Fig. I.5 "The World – shewing the geographical distribution of the human species". Samuel George Morton, *Crania americana* […] (Philadelphia, PN: J. Dobson, 1839), engraving, after p. v. Public domain.

Morton (1839, 1–95) prefaced *Crania americana* with a ninety-five-page 'essay' on the human 'races' and the twenty-two families he thought they comprised. He provided a list of them with a short general morphological and temperamental description that was followed by longer treatments of each group. Morton estimated that the most intelligent and advanced families belonged to the "Caucasian Race" (5). Typical of his style, his description of the 'Caucasians' reads like a diagram in words with the face, for example, being "small in proportion to the head" and of "well-proportioned features" (ibid.). This already makes clear that while parts of the same skull were set in relation to each other, the judgments ("small", "well-proportioned") depended on the comparison of these proportions to those found in other skulls and 'races'. Morton stated that the 'Caucasians' originated in the area between the Black Sea and the Caspian Sea, from where they migrated and developed into what he considered to be 'the best types'. However, he thought that only the 'more advanced races' in the moderate climates were prone to migrate; generally, everyone "thinks no part of the world so desirable and delightful as his own" (1). Drawing on Blumenbach and reminiscent of Camper's esthetics, Morton described the 'Caucasian' profile as approaching that of the Greek: some 'Caucasians' were as beautiful as classical sculptures. Dissociating himself from Prichard, who had called the 'Caucasian' families 'Indo-European nations', Morton was of the opinion that real affinity was best determined through anatomical study. 'Indo-European' may describe their languages, but anatomy determined the peoples. Morton continued in this vein, with the "Ethiopian Race" (6) – that contained the Black African family and the 'Australian families' among others – taking the lowest rung. Particularly the Khoekhoe or the Khoisan as a whole were described as "the nearest approximation to the lower animals" (90).

However, in *Crania americana*, Morton was most interested in the "American Race" (6), especially in the ancient Peruvians (1839, 96–112). This extinct type was older than the Incas and was only known from remains taken from graves. From the remains that had been robbed from tombs, Morton concluded that, though the ancient Peruvians had lowly features, they had already been civilized. Morton's physical descriptions of the 'American nations' followed the order of the paper skull collection at the end of the book, so that the reader might see the specific characteristics and proportions for himself while contemplating the measurements provided in tables. Plate 4 of the appendix, my Figure I.6, for example, was in the explanatory text described as the type specimen for the ancient Peruvians.

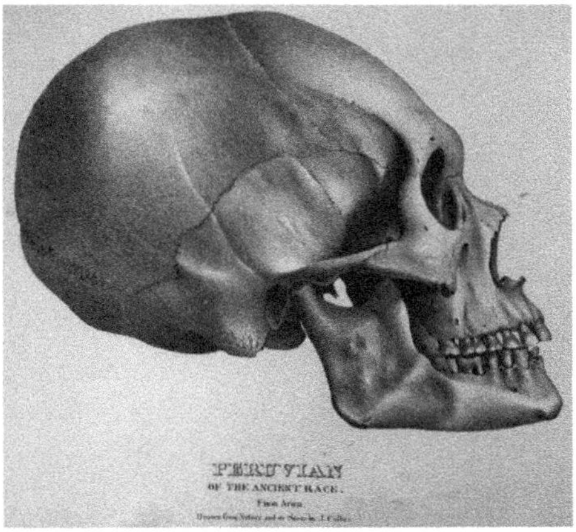

Fig. I.6 "Peruvian of the ancient race". Samuel George Morton, *Crania americana* [...] (Philadelphia, PN: J. Dobson, 1839), Plate 4, lithograph, appendix. Public domain.

In addition, Morton included many outlines of skulls throughout his discussion of the 'American race', and Figure I.7 of 'Mexican skulls' shows that he called these skull drawings 'diagrams'. Figure I.7 makes clear that even if the drawings did not contain lines or numbers, they were set in relation with numbers and looked at with eyes trained in lines, volumes, and the facial angle. The production of these woodcuts had been a challenge. Morton had turned to artists who worked with the camera lucida and the graphic mirror, in vain. In the end, he drew the images himself by means of an instrument adapted for the purpose by John S. Phillips of the American Academy of Sciences. This craniograph, the workings of which were explained in *Crania americana* by means of a diagram, allowed the user to draw the skulls on glass in reduced size while maintaining their proportions. The outlines could then be transferred to paper and wood (Morton 1839, 294).

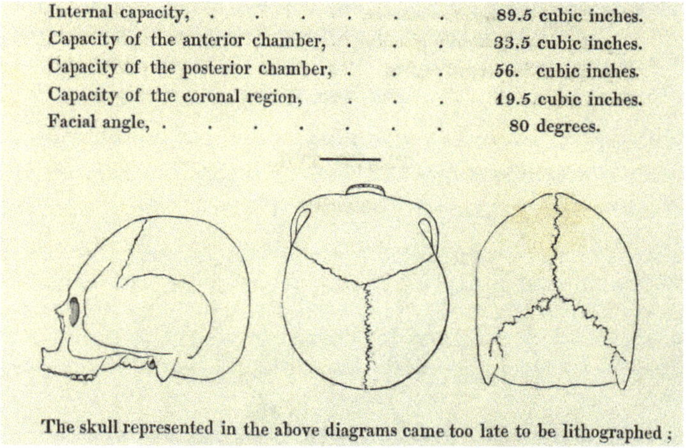
Internal capacity, ... 89.5 cubic inches.
Capacity of the anterior chamber, . . . 33.5 cubic inches.
Capacity of the posterior chamber, . . . 56. cubic inches.
Capacity of the coronal region, . . . 19.5 cubic inches.
Facial angle, ... 80 degrees.
The skull represented in the above diagrams came too late to be lithographed ;

Fig. I.7 Skull woodcuts as diagrams. Samuel George Morton, *Crania americana* [...] (Philadelphia, PN: J. Dobson, 1839), p. 154. Public domain.

The reader was instructed in this kind of diagrammatic analysis to construct self and other in the section on anatomical measurements (Morton 1839, 249–61). Linear measurements could be obtained with craniometer and calipers, but the facial angle after Camper, which elucidated the projection of the face in relation to the head, was of particular importance. Blumenbach's *norma verticalis*, too, was discussed on the basis of the diagram of the three skulls and the line of their orientation (see Figure I.3). In order to render Camper's measure more scientific and accurate, Morton, unlike Camper himself, determined the facial angle directly from the skulls with the original type of facial goniometer (an instrument devised by his friend Dr. Turnpenny). As in the case of the craniograph, this instrument was explained by means of a diagram, as Morton called it (252–53), and it was accompanied by other diagrams (see Figures I.8a–b) showing the lines that gave the facial angle drawn on skulls. *E* gave a facial angle of 66° for the first diagram of a head from the Cowlitz Indian Tribe. In the second, "much better formed head" of a "Peruvian Indian", it amounted to 76° (250), which, however, still compared poorly with a 'Caucasian'.

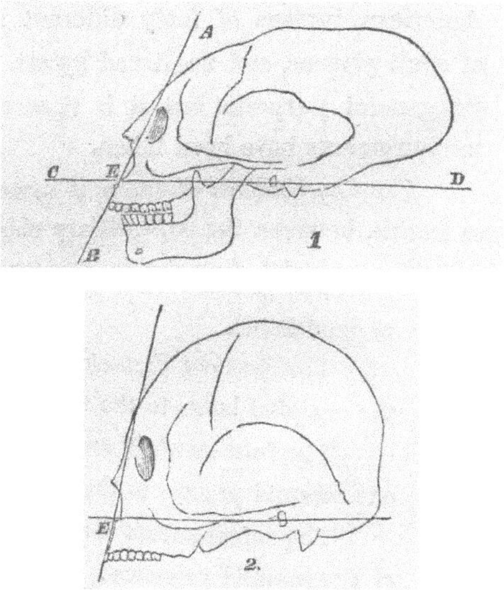

Fig. I.8a and I.8b Camper's facial angle. Samuel George Morton, *Crania americana* [...] (Philadelphia, PN: J. Dobson, 1839), p. 250. Public domain.

Nonetheless, the facial angle was no indication of cranial capacity and thus intelligence in Morton's view (something Camper had never claimed). To determine brain size and intelligence through the measurement of the internal skull capacity, as well as of particular portions of the skull, in cubic inches with white pepper seed, Morton had Phillips design yet another instrument. Morton again included an instructing diagram of that instrument in the book and accompanied it with textual explanations (1839, 253–54). Finally, he provided a table summarizing all the measurements for the 'American' skulls that ran over three pages (257–59). For each skull, the ethnic origin, catalogue and plate number, if present, were given, followed by the measurements. There was no particular order here, and since Morton changed measurements in the table while the book was in print, the table did not always correspond to the text above. It was only by providing the means of the different measurements for the four major divisions he made within the Indigenous peoples of the Americas in another table that the numbers began to gain meaning, but, at the same time, this showed that 'the barbarous nations' had bigger cranial capacities than 'the semi-civilized ones' (Toltecs and ancient Peruvians). Morton could only achieve 'real order' when, after having gone to this length of individually measuring the 'American' skulls, he unified them, namely as a mean in brain size, reintegrating them into Blumenbach's five-part system. Blumenbach's system was thereby transformed into a 'racial hierarchy', based on numbers in a table (Figure I.9).

NOTE.—*On the Internal Capacity of the Cranium in the different Races of Men.*—Having subjected the skulls in my possession, and such also as I could obtain from my friends, to the internal capacity measurement already described, I have obtained the following results. The mean of the American Race, (omitting the fraction) is repeated here merely to complete the Table. The skulls of idiots and persons under age were of course rejected.

RACES.	No. of skulls.	Mean internal capacity in cubic inches.	Largest in the series.	Smallest in the series.
Caucasian.	52	87.	109.	75.
Mongolian.	10	83.	93.	69.
Malay.	18	81.	89.	64.
American.	147	80.	100.	60.
Ethiopian.	29	78.	94.	65.

Fig. I.9 Morton's diagrammatic 'racial hierarchy'. Samuel George Morton, *Crania americana* [...] (Philadelphia, PN: J. Dobson, 1839), p. 260. Public domain.

However, there was an alternative scientific approach present in the book that was as objectifying and judgmental as the ethnological perspective. This was the phrenological system. Morton had studied for an advanced medical degree in Edinburgh (graduating in 1823), then the British center for phrenology, housing the Edinburgh Phrenological Society and its collection of skulls. There, Morton had made the acquaintance of the phrenologists Johann Spurzheim and George Combe. In *Crania americana*, Morton now included a note by Phillips, in which Phillips explained how he had made phrenological measurements of the same skulls with the use of a craniograph, calipers, dividers, a graduated strap and a measuring frame (Phillips in Morton 1839, 262). These measurements related to mental attributes such as self-esteem, firmness, hope, and benevolence, and the results were listed in a table that ran over six pages (263–68). Morton emphasized that he had not carried out the entire work from the phrenological perspective; he called himself a learner and preferred to let the reader judge the two approaches. Nonetheless, he agreed with the phrenological assumption that the brain was the organ of the mind and that different parts performed different functions. Also, the interpretations from phrenology corresponded with his ideas about the "mental character of the Indian" (Morton 1839, n.p.).

These interpretations were those of the famous phrenologist Combe himself, who was on an American tour when he collaborated with Morton, shortly before the appearance of *Crania americana*.[6] Combe, too, was given a voice in the book at the beginning of the appendix (Combe in Morton 1839, 269–91). He had to make his judgments on the 'races' before reading Morton's, so he "solicit[ed] the reader [...] not to condemn phrenology" alone, should the conclusions from ethnology differ from "the phrenological inductions the reader will be enabled to draw by applying the rules now to be laid down" (270). Combe concluded that the 'Caucasians' were the most prone to advance, and within them the "Teutonic race" (271), much more so than the Celtic in France, Scotland, and Ireland. Asians were seen as less likely to reach a high grade of civilization, and Black Africans were not considered predisposed to even make history. Even so, some "African tribes" (ibid.) were more advanced than those "tribes of native Americans" that were still "wandering savages" (272). Combe judged that the "American race" (ibid.) had been and remained barbaric, with no inclination to learn from the Europeans who surrounded them. These 'national differences' were not due to climate, Combe claimed, since 'races' under similar climates differed, nor due to institutions; rather, people developed institutions

6 The American edition of Combe's *Elements in Phrenology* (1826) had sold 1,500 copies within ten months (on Combe's visit to Morton and the work on his collection, see Combe to Morton, 10 October 1838, Morton Papers APS).

according to their inclinations and purposes. For Combe, it was the form (size and proportions) of the brain that corresponded to dispositions and talents of individuals and peoples.

Plate 71 in *Crania americana*, Figure I.10 below, shows a Swiss skull. Combe had included visual aids in the image in the form of lines, so that the reader may be able to observe the extraordinary mental vigor of the Swiss. He led the reader step by step through the diverse measurements with reference to the Swiss skull, adding further diagrams where necessary (Combe in Morton 1839, 280–81). This diagrammatic skull could then "serve as a standard by which to compare the skulls of the other tribes represented in this work": "by comparing the dimensions of this Swiss skull as they appear to the eye in the plate, with those of the other skulls delineated in this work, all being drawn as large as nature, their relative proportions will become apparent" (277–78). Indeed, Combe had already announced to Morton in a letter prior to his work on the skulls that he "would teach the reader of how to judge of them [the 'races'] by the skulls." To that purpose, he wanted his "lines inserted in these drawings" (Combe to Morton, 19 March 1839, Samuel George Morton Papers, American Philosophical Society Library, Mss.B.M843: Series I. Correspondence [hereafter Morton Papers APS]).

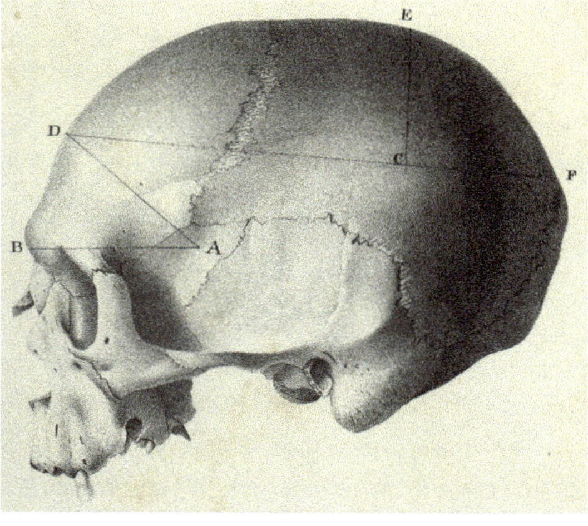

Fig. I.10 "Swiss". Samuel George Morton, *Crania americana* [...] (Philadelphia, PN: J. Dobson, 1839), Plate 71, lithograph, appendix. Public domain.

However, Figure I.10 remained the only lithographed skull to which lines have been added. It is the same kind of image as those of Morton in the appendix (see Figure I.6), only that a diagrammatic approach was indicated in the plate itself for didactic purposes. The reader was thus once again instructed in how to read, as diagrams, the realistic lithographs of skulls in the appendix that did not contain any diagrammatic elements. Nonetheless, even if the phrenologist worked with cranial capacity and facial angle, phrenological readings and measurements were different from ethnological ones. This becomes evident from the phrenological chart following the Swiss skull at the end of *Crania americana* (see Figure I.11). Such phrenological busts, as well as skulls, often with the 'organs' inscribed and numbered, or marked by lines, frequently accompanied phrenological writings, as did diagrams of calipers and craniometers. However, portraits were a more prominent form of illustration, and phrenologists were more concerned with how well-known personalities exemplified certain physical traits and associated faculties, and with the physiognomy and phrenology of the sexes or types such as 'criminals' or the 'mentally ill', than with the differences between 'nations' or 'races' (e.g., Combe 1822, 1826, 1830; Mackenzie 1820). Even where Spurzheim had published on the differences in faces between 'races' in *Phrenology in Connection with the Study of Physiognomy* of 1833, he left the portraits of 'a Malay', 'a Mongol', 'a Jew', and Hannibal without commentary, and illustrated the dispositions of 'European types' on the basis of what he took to be representative personalities (23–29).

At the same time, Spurzheim (1833, 43–46, Plate XIII) did state that heredity was much more important than environment, that physical traits and the characters they stood for were endurable (if the 'nations' did not mingle), and he did present the skulls of an Indigenous person of Brazil, a Native American woman, a Hindoo, and Blumenbach's ancient Greek and described them in terms similar to the ethnology of Morton. There is one further characteristic besides the theoretical emphasis on physical aspects and the head that render phrenological treatises likely inspirations for Morton's crania atlases, and that is the diagrammatic and metric nature of the approach and the visualizations. The phrenological treatises were written as instructions to readers on how to practice 'the science' themselves. Thus, George Mackenzie's *Illustrations of Phrenology* (1820) already contained plates with naturalistic skulls with the phrenological grid inscribed, alongside illustrations of skulls that had not been turned into diagrams but were nonetheless intended to be read as diagrams by the viewer.

In *Crania americana*, both Morton and Combe now went to greater lengths and proceeded much more systematically. The phrenological chart included in the volume should be used by the reader in combination with Combe's corresponding textual explanations to perform a phrenological reading of the 'racial' skulls himself, "to judge of the size of the different parts of the brain in relation to each other" (Combe in Morton 1839, 278). The different regions of the skull were correlated to mental characteristics, measures of which for the skulls in general were given in the six-page-long table after Phillips' note mentioned above. In following Combe's phrenological interpretations of the realistic skull lithographs, the reader should verify that the skull shapes of 'nations' foretold whether they had been or would be subjugated or even exterminated by another, or rather live in civilized freedom (278–83). Colonial histories with all their violence and exploitation were thereby naturalized.

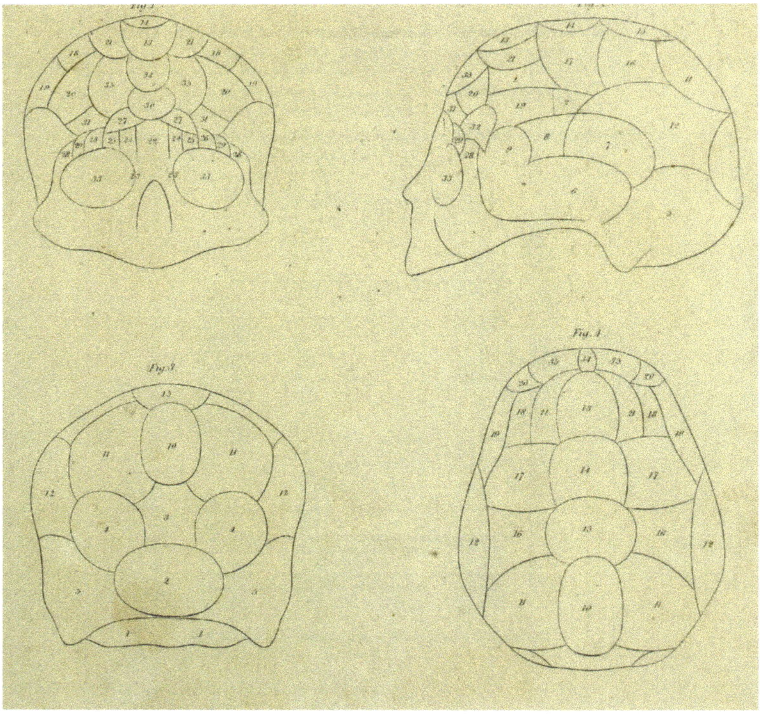

Fig. I.11 "Phrenological Chart". Samuel George Morton, *Crania americana* [...] (Philadelphia, PN: J. Dobson, 1839), Plate 72, appendix. Public domain.

In sum, *Crania americana* was a book that instructed in a new scientific approach, not in the method of comparative philology, history, and culture, but in reading osseous remains to allow the establishment of human 'races' – perceived as (originally) distinct and nearly unchanging entities. This approach was not only diagrammatic, like Blumenbach's, but decidedly metric. While Camper and Blumenbach had used the dynamics of diagrams to show the possibility of the human varieties' development from one original type, Morton, to the contrary, established diagrammatic and metric techniques that effectively froze their anatomies into a hierarchical arrangement. Seemingly no longer part of the same 'genealogical family', they remained juxtaposed to each other like numbers in a table. Morton therefore instructed in the diagrammatic reading of images and made use of the ability of diagrams to set (aspects of) objects in rational relation to each other (see my discussion of Peirce at the beginning of this part) – not in order to demonstrate kinship, but to deny it.

However, *Crania americana* also represents a point at which it was not yet clear whether this new approach would be the one of ethnology or phrenology. This, as Morton and Combe put it, would be decided by the readers and by time. Indeed, scholars allowed themselves to be instructed – some preferred ethnology, some phrenology, and others the combination – and they used Morton's movable images to spread the word and argue for the cause of their chosen camp. Morton himself donated *Crania americana* to European institutions to promote his new science of ethnology. He sent important scholars, such as Alexander von Humboldt, a presentation copy. But, by the late 1830s, these institutions had come into financial difficulties, and the book did not sell well despite Combe's efforts to launch it in the US and Europe (Fabian 2003). At the same time, *Crania americana* was received by institutions from the Asiatic Society of Bengal, the Société Ethnologique in Paris, to the Royal Society of Northern Antiquaries in Copenhagen, which indicates that the volume was understood to contribute to different branches of knowledge (Poskett 2015; 2019, 78–114; Sommer 2023a, 11–21).

3. Kinship Denied and Acknowledged

Into this fray entered Morton's second paper skull atlas, *Crania aegyptiaca* of 1844, which was possible due to the plundering of Egyptian sepulchral grottoes, catacombs, and pyramids largely organized by Gliddon, to whom Morton dedicated the volume. The oldest remains were estimated to be at least 2,500 years old, a timeframe that fell within the date range traditionally attributed to the deluge at 3,154 BC. On this basis, Morton approached the controversial questions of whether the ancient Egyptians were Jews, Arabs, Hindus, Nubians, or Black Africans, and whether civilization had started in Egypt or rather in Ethiopia. To ascertain the position of the ancient Egyptians in the 'hierarchy of races', Morton compared the mummies with the monuments, namely the images and statues of the people, and with the skulls in his collection (1844, 1–3).

Morton concluded that the ancient Egyptians were 'Caucasian'. Most importantly for his overarching argument, he 'showed' that in ancient Egypt the main existing 'races' of his day had already been present, and even exhibited similar relations, including Black Africans as slaves and serfs and some 'Caucasians' as human gods. And with civilizations as old as in Egypt and in the Americas, humankind and the human varieties would have to be referred even further back in time (1844, 65–67). Morton's conclusions from the two skull atlases could therefore be read as arguments in favor of polygenism. However, it seems that it was only in the third edition of his catalogue of 1849 that Morton openly stated the view that the 'main races' were rather groups themselves containing 'races', all of which had originated independently and in the geographical region in which they now lived, and to which they were adapted. In the catalogue, he also gave measures of facial angles and

 https://doi.org/10.11647/OBP.0396.04

cranial capacities to definitively fix the 'hierarchy of races'. Even then, such clear statements were hidden in footnotes (1849a, ix footnote; see also Morton 1849b, 223 footnote).

This seems to fit the observation of Paul Wolff Mitchell and John S. Michael that Morton never took clear sides in the slavery debate, whether in public or in private, and that he had friends and colleagues in both parties, including vocal proslavery race supremacists as well as abolitionists. Even the man who funded the lithographs for *Crania americana* and the lithographer Collins were antislavery activists. Furthermore, while studying in Edinburgh, Morton became friends with the physician Thomas Hodgkin who spoke out for the Native American peoples. At the same time, Morton's close association with polygenist slaveholders and their use of his work for their cause seem to speak for themselves (Mitchell and Michael 2019, 86–87; Sommer 2023a, 21).

Morton drew especially on French polygenist writers in *Crania americana*. One inspiration Morton explicitly mentioned in his preface (1839, iv) was the politically progressive military physician Julien Joseph Virey, who divided the genus *Homo* into two species on the basis of the facial angle (1824, 438). Virey's writing also once again illustrates that the emphasis on the head as the most important source of information was present not only in phrenology, but also in the older approach of physiognomy. Morton cited Virey's *L'Art de perfectionner l'homme* (1808), which concerns the interdependence of environment and the 'soul', morals, 'temperament', and way of life, as well as the physiognomy of peoples. While this environmental approach clearly diverged from Morton's views, the notion that the human body exhibits particular and meaningful proportions and symmetries align with his understanding. Virey claimed that the 'straighter' ("droite") the face, the higher the intellect and civilization, while what he described as the extended "museau" [muzzle] in Black Africans (143) was seen as a decline towards the apes. Playing with the correlation of parts in Cuverian fashion, the elongation of the lower part of the face was said to have the effect of the proportional retreat of the brain, so that while the senses were increased, intelligence decreased (139–59).[1]

1 Indeed, Michael (2021a) has shown that Virey actually manipulated some of Blumenbach's skull illustrations in this way to increase the facial angle of 'the Caucasian' and to decrease that of 'the Ethiopian'.

Another French polygenist was Antoine Desmoulins, who, in his *Histoire naturelle des races humaines* (1826), gave descriptions of head types; although he did not take measurements, he did discuss measurements such as diameters in his work. Desmoulins divided humankind into different *espèces* [species], their '*races*', and their *souches* [families], with references to Camper and Blumenbach among others, and he claimed that each animal and human species was created at a specific place, although this place (the environment) had nothing to do with its form (335). In his treatise, we already encounter the claim that the study of the ancient texts shows that the same human species lived and were recognized at that remote time, and that the parts in which they were then found were where they originated (336; altered human populations, he suggested, were the result of mixtures). Like Morton, Desmoulins held that philology proved nothing when physical characters contradicted it; the affiliation of languages hinted only at political not genealogical affiliation.

Morton also referred to Jean-Baptiste Bory de Saint-Vincent as an important input in the preface of *Crania americana* (1839, iv) and cited him frequently in his treatment of the varieties of the human species. In *L'Homme* (*Homo*) (Bory 1827), the French naturalist, military man, and politician denied that 'the Red and Black races' were consanguineous with 'the White'. Bory claimed that his voyages had given him proof of eleven species and later of fifteen. Of Bory's many human species, "*Homo Japeticus*" (after Japheth) was the most beautiful in proportions, presented the largest facial angle, an oval face, and contained the greatest number of geniuses (Vol. I, 102–162). "*Homo Aethiopicus*", too, was given a close description regarding the form of the skull, its volume (smaller than that of "*Homo Japeticus*", Vol. II, 29–30), the protruding face, etc. (Vol. II, 29–86). It was once again the Khoekhoe or Khoisan, Bory's species number fifteen, who were presented as bridging the gap to the apes (Vol. II, 113–34). In one breath, however, Bory condemned the cruelty inflicted by White people upon Black Africans, including in the context of the slave trade and slavery, while (condescendingly) observing that Haiti's Black population had taken revenge and proven that they could have ideas of freedom. Bory's blatant scientific racism thus exemplifies the complexity of the connections between science and politics, as he strongly opposed slavery and was an antimonarchist, liberal thinker who believed in equality before the law.

In the preface of *Crania americana* (1839, iv), mention was also made of Morton's friend, American race supremacist Charles Caldwell, who might have been the first to explicitly promote polygenism in the English language and who took on Prichard in his *Thoughts on the Original Unity of the Human Race* (1830). Morton (1839, 88) cited Caldwell in support of the old age of both 'the White and Black races' – an age that, according to biblical chronology, did not leave enough time to render the previous transformation of one into the other a possibility.[2] Nonetheless, there were also the voices of monogenists in *Crania americana*, beyond those of Camper and Blumenbach. One of them was the British physician William Lawrence, whose influential *Lectures on Physiology, Zoology, and the Natural History of Man* Morton cited. The lectures had been held by Lawrence as Professor of Anatomy and Surgery at the Royal College of Surgeons and published in 1819, but Lawrence was withheld copyright due to a verdict stating that the book was in parts against the Scripture, and there were accusations of materialism. In spite of this, several editions appeared, and, in 1822, Lawrence was made a member of the American Philosophical Society in Philadelphia (Mudford 1968). Lawrence was clearly a follower of Blumenbach, to whom the book was dedicated and whose ideas structured Lawrence's treatment of

2 Concerning further American sources, Morton for example also highlighted the importance of the monogenists John Collins Warren (e.g., 1822) and Benjamin Hornor Coates (e.g., 1834). Finally, Morton's book was more than a mere comparative anatomy of skulls. To link it to the literature on the distribution, history, language, affiliations, general appearance, customs, religion, commerce, politics, temperament, etc. of diverse peoples, he drew on travelogues and historical and ethnographical studies (beyond Prichard). *Crania americana* was dedicated to Morton's Philadelphia colleague and surgeon of the US Navy, W. S. W. Ruschenberger, who wrote about his voyage around the world and provided Morton with important information especially with respect to Peru (Ruschenberger 1838 – dedicated to Morton in turn). Ruschenberger was among those explicitly listed in the preface of *Crania americana* (Morton 1839, iv). Morton also relied on Ruschenberger's *A Voyage Around the World* (1838) for physical descriptions of peoples, and he referred to the latter's table of "four purely Siamese heads" (Ruschenberger 1838, 299) and their measurements including the facial angle (ibid., 300) (see Morton 1839, 49, also footnote). The same was true for Alexander von Humboldt's (1814) description of the retreating and small forehead of Indigenous peoples of the Americas (Morton 1939, 66) or of features, stature, hair, etc. more generally (ibid., e.g., 69, 71, 143).

the human varieties. The 1822 reprint of *Lectures* also included some of Blumenbach's skull drawings. However, like Prichard before him, Lawrence denied that the climate was the cause of the imperceptible gradations in variation throughout the human species, which must rather spontaneously appear in generation as was the case in domestic animals. At the same time, Lawrence deviated widely from Prichard as well as Blumenbach in his description of Black Africans, inverting the argument against slavery, from the stance that Black Africans were not generally inferior to the stance that their inferiority was a reason against enslavement (1822, 330–36).

With regard to the French-speaking community, *Crania americana* refers to the work of the monogenist Pierre Paul Broc. The Professor of Anatomy and Physiology opened his *Essai sur les races humaines* (1837) with a fold-out of skull lithographs and 'racial portraits'. Broc recognized only one species of 'man' containing different 'races' or varieties. The differences between human groups concerned the form of the skull and face, the proportions of their various parts, as well as the color of skin and hair, but these differences were not essential. It was impossible to reconstruct something like an original state of the 'races', because they had mixed and changed over an immense and unknown period of time. In nature, Broc reasoned, there were in fact no races, only individuals, but the human mind liked to categorize and thus sort humans into groups. So, in a certain sense, those scholars who constructed a great number of races (up to sixty) were closer to the truth. Broc juxtaposed the systems of human classification of Cuvier, the physician Pierre Nicolas Gerdy, Linné, Blumenbach, Virey, Bory, and Desmoulins in a table (1837, 7) and went on to synthesize their racial classifications and descriptions, including the comparative-anatomical traits with a range for the facial angle. Broc also reproduced Prosper Garnot's table of comparative measurements of skulls – a table that indicates that an extensive system was in place before Morton's crania atlases (Broc 1837, 29; see my Figure I.12).

The marine surgeon and naturalist Garnot had been part of an expedition 'around the world' in the first half of the 1820s. They 'collected' skulls and, in the atlas of plates accompanying the published research results, there is one showing the lithographed front, base, and profile of a skull from New Guinea (Duperrey 1826, Plate 1). In the first chapter of the first volume and first part of the research compendium (Lesson and Garnot 1826, 1–116), Garnot carried out a comparison of skulls from Waigeo, New Guinea, New Zealand, Mozambique, and Paris and gave the table reproduced by Broc (Lesson and Garnot 1826, 113–15). In this play of image, measurements, and diagrammatic description of relative proportions and volumes, the impression again emerges that the various human skulls could be arrived at through 'the flattening, squeezing, elongating, etc.' of certain parts, and the correlated changes in others, of the European variety (see also Garnot 1828, in which he mentioned the systems of the scholars treated above; and Garnot 1836, which again contains said table of measurements and a series of plates, with Plate 217 and Plate 221 showing 'portraits of races' and their skulls).

TABLEAU COMPARATIF *des proportions que présentent les diverses parties des crânes de*

	FRANCAIS.	NEGRE MOZAMBIQUE	PAPOU DE WAIGIOU.	ALFOUROUS. NOUVELLE-GUINÉE.	NOUVEAUX ZÉLANDAIS.
	p. l. m.	p. l. m.	p. l. m.	p. l. m.	p. l. m.
Diamètre antéro-postérieur ou occipito frontal.	6 10 0,185	6 4 0,171	6 6 0,176	6 9 0,183	6 8 ,0180
Diamètre transverse ou bipariétal.	4 10 0,131	4 7 0,124	5 4 0,144	4 8 0,126	4 10 0,131
Diamètre perpendiculaire ou sphéno-bregmatique. . . .	5 » 0,135	4 6 0,122	5 3 0,142	5 » 0,135	5 3 0,142
Distance de la protubérance occipitale à la symphyse du menton.	6 10 0,185	7 5 0,201	»	8 » 0,217	7 4 0,198
Distance du sommet de la tête à la symphyse.	8 2 0,221	8 2 0,221	»	8 » 0,217	8 3 0,223
Distance d'une arcade zygomatique à celle opposée. . . .	4 10 0,131	4 6 0,123	» 0,135	5 1 0,138	4 11 0,133
Distance d'un angle de la mâchoire à celui du côté opposé. .	3 10 0.104	3 4 0.090	»	3 6 0,095	3 8 0,099
Distance de l'angle de la mâchoire à l'apophyse condyloïde. .	2 4 0,063	2 3 0,061	»	2 6 0,068	2 5 0,065
Distance d'une apophyse mastoïde à celle du côté opposé. .	3 10 0,104	3 8 0,099	3 8 0,099	3 8 0,099	3 11 0,106
Distance de l'angle orbitaire externe à celui du côté opposé.	3 10 0,104	3 8 0,099	4 » 0,108	4 1 0,111	4 1 0,111
Diamètre transverse de l'orbite.	1 5 0,038	1 6 0,041	1 8 0,045	1 10 0,050	1 7 0,043
Diamètre perpendiculaire.	1 4 0,036	1 4 0,036	1 4 0,036	1 6 0,041	1 5 0,038
Largeur des fosses nasales.	1 11 0,025	1 1 0,029	» 11 0,025	» » 0,027	» 11 0,025
Diamètre antéro-postérieur du trou occipital.	1 3 0,034	1 4 0,036	1 4 0,036	1 3 0,034	2 » 0,054
Diamètre d'une tubérosité molaire de l'os maxillaire supérieur à l'autre.	» 8 0,045	1 8 0,045	1 6 0,041	2 » 0,014	»
Angle formé par une ligne partant de la symphyse du menton à la protubérance occipitale, et par une autre ligne partant de la symphyse à la bosse frontale.	70 degrés.	58 degrés.	» (1)	67 degrés.	67 degrés.

(1) Les têtes qui ont été comparées entre elles n'étant pas parfaitement entières, nous avons été forcés de négliger quelques-unes de leurs dimensions.

Fig. I.12 "Tableau comparatif des proportions que présentent des diverses parties des crânes de" [Comparative table of the proportions presented by the diverse parts of the skulls of]. Pierre Paul Broc, *Essai sur les races humaines* [...] (Brussels: Établissement Encyclographique, 1837), p. 29. Public domain.

Overall, there are competing messages in Broc's 1837 treatise. While he repeated the racist descriptions of other naturalists, he recounted with pride how he had opened up a school in Bogotá with children of all 'races', free and enslaved, motivated by the enormous transformative power of education in all 'races of man', which to him proved the unity of 'mankind'. Broc ended his book with a diagram by a corresponding member of the Royal Academy of Medicine (Antoine Constant Saucerotte) that instantiated a grand synopsis of the then circulating 'knowledge' about the human 'races' and their derivates – their distribution and characteristics (including the range of the facial angle) (Figure I.13).[3]

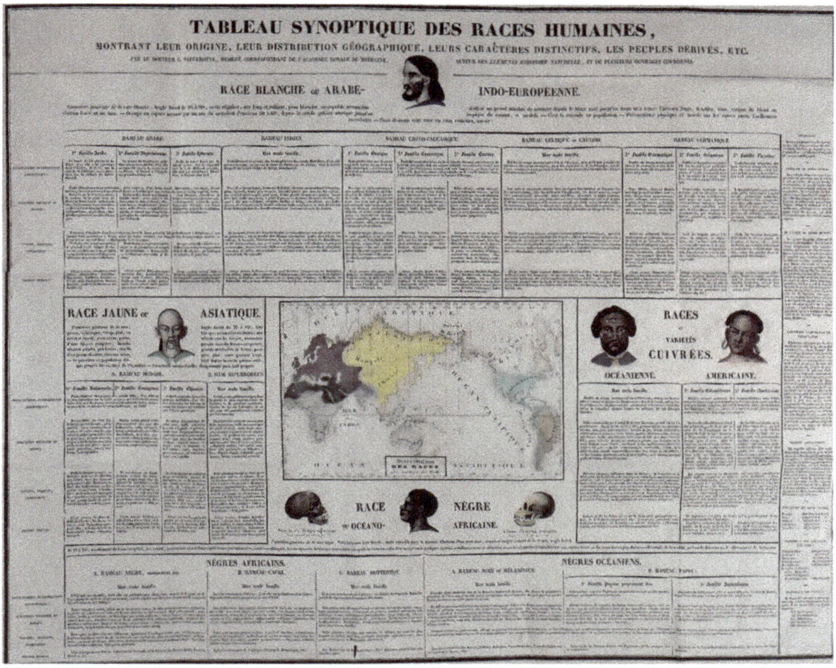

Fig. I.13 "Tableau synoptique des races humaines" [Synoptic table of the human races]. Pierre Paul Broc, *Essai sur les races humaines* [...] (Brussels: Établissement Encyclographique, 1837), appendix. Public domain. A larger version of this image may be viewed at https://hdl.handle.net/20.500.12434/ce1f3d06

All in all, Morton especially relied on French polygenists already in *Crania americana* when establishing a 'racial hierarchy' based on skulls,

3 Saucerotte had published the compendium *Elémens d'histoire naturelle* (1834), which treated botany, zoology, and mineralogy, with each section containing synoptic tables followed by plates. The section on zoology contained a plate with stereotypical drawings of the 'three main human races' (Plate 5) that were described in the synoptic tables under the first order of the "Bimanes" (38), including the facial angle (39, see also 34).

diagrams, and numbers. But he also drew on monogenists, and members of both camps could stand for complex and contradicting politics of knowledge. As we are going to see, it was after Morton's death, and in connection with *Crania aegyptiaca*, that Morton's ethnology was once and for all enlisted for polygenist and racist causes by the Egyptologist Gliddon and the surgeon and Alabama plantation owner Nott.

4. Prichard's Third Edition of *Researches* (1836–47) and Nott's and Gliddon's *Types of Mankind* (1854)

James Poskett (2015) has shown that *Crania americana* instantiated a transatlantic network. Prichard communicated with Morton and displayed Morton's skull lithographs for *Crania americana*, which he received from Morton himself, at a meeting of the British Association for the Advancement of Science (BAAS). Prichard also tried to promote the book. In return, Morton dedicated the 'foreign edition' of *Crania americana* also to Prichard and presented the book as part of the same enquiry (Prichard to Morton, 23 August 1839, 17 February 1840, Morton Papers APS). Through Prichard, Morton was even made an honorary member of the Aborigines' Protection Society. Prichard hoped to secure financial and institutional support for what he, too, had recently come to call 'ethnology'. He wanted a section for it in the BAAS and he received some money for printing and circulating a questionnaire for travelers and others to gather information on the 'races of man' (Combe to Morton, 7 December 1839, Morton Papers APS). In the questionnaire, Prichard referred to the importance of the skull to distinguish 'races'. At the same time, he dismissed phrenology in his review of *Crania americana*, which competed with his ethnology for recognition (Prichard 1841; Poskett 2015; 2019, 78–114).

However, in view of Prichard's third edition of *Researches* that was published in five volumes between 1836 and 1847, these observations are surprising. Prichard may have paid more serious attention to physical

 https://doi.org/10.11647/OBP.0396.05

anthropology, especially craniology, than before, as Poskett (2015, 269) notes. The first volume of the third edition contained nine lithographic plates of skulls and a new chapter on national forms of skulls (Prichard 1836, 275–321). Nonetheless, the entire oeuvre was again one big argument for monogenism that demonstrated the similarities and overlap between the human groups making up the single human species (Prichard 1836–47). Even in the chapter on national skull forms (Chapter 5), Prichard maintained that also the so-called characteristics of the 'Black African race' were found in the other varieties and that it did not approach the ape any closer than other 'races'. Still harboring esthetic concerns, he emphasized that there were many exceedingly beautiful Black African people. Furthermore, he continued to reject the facial angle and the claim that there were constant differences in cranial capacity between 'races' – the very two measurements Morton most relied on.

Rather, Prichard followed Blumenbach in favoring the comparative holistic method; he recommended that the trained eye study different skulls that were aligned from all sides. This approach made him distinguish the symmetrical/oval skull forms mostly found in Europeans and western Asians from the narrow/elongated/prognathous forms mostly found in 'Black nations'. He thereby introduced the description 'prognathous' that would become central, under which he also subsumed the "new" 'Oceanic types' described by Garnot and his colleague René Lesson as discussed at the end of Chapter 3 (Prichard 1836, 298–302, quote on 298; Lesson and Garnot 1826, 113–15). Prichard's skulls looked rather artistic than objectivistic, which might be exemplified by the plate showing his third, pyramidal, broad-, or square-faced skull form, typical among others of the 'Turanian' variety (Prichard's alternative term for the 'Mongolian') given in Figure I.14. The skulls' esthetic appearance that makes them seem somewhat imprecise, or unscientific as judged by Morton's standard, contrasts with the diagrammatic element Prichard introduced into the lithograph. It showed the triangle between the zygomas (cheekbones) and the apex of the forehead: "[...] the lateral projection of the zygomas being so considerable, that if a line drawn from one to the other be taken as a base, this will form with the apex of the forehead a nearly triangular figure" (Prichard 1836, 282).

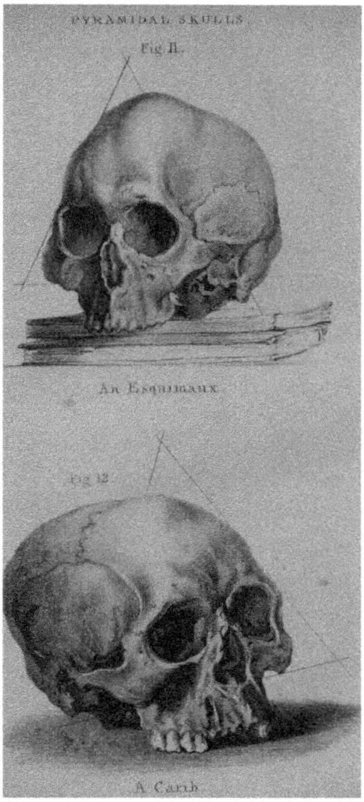

Fig. I.14 "Pyramidal Skulls". James Cowles Prichard, *Researches into the Physical History of Mankind*, 3rd ed. (London: Sherwood, Gilbert, and Piper, 1836), Vol. I, figs. 11 and 12, p. 306. Public domain.

Figure I.14 gives the impression that the triangles had been rather clumsily added to an artistic drawing already in place. It seems that Prichard barely gave in to a diagrammatic anthropology, but certainly not to a metric approach. Rather, he instrumentalized Morton's *Crania americana* to support the notion that the Indigenous peoples of the Americas were of one stock (although Prichard included the Arctic peoples), without discussing Morton's 'polygenism' (Prichard 1847). This understanding is corroborated by Prichard's popular *The Natural History of Man* of 1843, in which he doubted that the physical traits, and, in particular, those of the skull, were the most durable, rather attributing the three main skull shapes to particular ways of life from hunting to nomadism and civilization (105–109). Again deconstructing physical racial anthropology (109–122), he denied that its methods were adequate to establish genealogies, which was better achieved with research into other characteristics such as affinities in language. It was the unity of the human mind, in the end, that furnished clear evidence "that all human races are of one species and one family" (546).

It was after Morton's death that his work was most emphatically embraced, particularly by his friends Nott and Gliddon, in whose hands Morton's polygenism became vocal, and it was Morton's *Crania aegyptiaca* of 1844 that proved most amenable to their polygenist cause. In 1851, Nott and Gliddon gained access to Morton's correspondence and writings, and they used it to produce the expensive volume *Types of Mankind* of 1854, with its 360 woodcuts, which they dedicated to their father of anthropology (ix). At this moment, the politics of the new anthropology became unambiguous. In his introduction, Nott emphasized the importance of the new science's findings for the denunciation of philanthropic arguments against slavery, which was the object of heated controversy at that time (Nott and Gliddon 1854, 49–61). In the US, polygenism was part of the unrest that preceded the Civil War. In 1820, pro- and antislavery factions were fighting in Congress; consequently, the Missouri Compromise was enacted to give them equal power in the Senate. This led to the secessionist agenda of the Confederacy. Between 1836 and 1844, petitions against slavery were prohibited before the House of Representatives, which meant a setback for abolitionists (Keel 2013, 8). Morton's *Crania aegyptiaca* (1844) had sold well, also to proslavery intellectuals; *Types of Mankind* (1854) was highly successful and appealed to some racist southerners (Fabian 2010, 107, 111). In the volume, Nott actually bragged that Morton's crania atlases had even played their role in the issue of slavery as it appeared in the negotiation with Great Britain over the annexation of Texas. The books gave the American Secretary of State ammunition in his support for the institution in denying the perfectibility and equality of all human kinds (Nott and Gliddon 1854, 50–51).

In his contributions to the book, Nott meant to show that progress had only come about through 'Caucasians'. According to his devastating verdict, Black Africans never approached civilization, and the monuments of Peru and Mexico were nothing compared to the achievements of 'Caucasians' from the Egyptians up to the modern Anglo-Americans. Nott claimed that Morton had proven how deficient 'other races', especially Black Africans, were with respect to brain size. Morton's work was also introduced as proof that in the 4,000 years since the Egyptian monuments, Black Africans had remained the same and remained slaves. Progress, Nott declared, had largely been due to the war between 'races', to the 'superior races' who migrated into the territories of the 'stationary ones' and seized their lands. He argued that the replacement of 'lower by higher races' was a law inscribed by the creator. Nott also overtly attacked Prichard and his 'false theory' of monogenism, although he conceded the latter's great achievement in bringing into being ethnology. Since the knowledge from Egypt and Morton's work, however, in Nott's estimate all such views of human unity and equality had become obsolete. To Nott, the 'great human races' were separate creations; they in fact constituted separate species each of which had its own place of origin and comprised original subdivisions (Nott and Gliddon 1854, 49–297, 372–465; further on Nott, see Erickson 1986; Keel 2013).

However, *Types of Mankind* is a confusing and also rather confused volume. Although ostensibly building an edifice to Morton's physical anthropology and containing excerpts from Morton's manuscripts, it does not add much in this respect. If anything, it has more in common with Prichard's approach, for the long Part II and III by Gliddon are an engagement in philology and with different chronological traditions, and are thus part of a more traditional scholarly style (Nott and Gliddon 1854, 466–716). Gliddon tried to figure out to which ethnicities and geographical regions the authors of the Old Testament had referred, and arrived at the conclusion that Genesis 10 only engaged with 'Caucasian' descent. The sons of Noah had all been 'Caucasian'. The authors had known nothing of Ethiopia or sub-Saharan Africa, only about Egypt, and they had been unacquainted with Asia proper and the Americas. Finally, in accordance with the subtitle *Or, Ethnological Researches, Based upon the Ancient Monuments, Paintings, Sculptures, and Crania of Races, and upon Their Natural, Geographical, Philological, and Biblical History* the larger part of the illustrations in the book are reproductions of art.

Nonetheless, there is a section on the comparative anatomy of the 'races' written by Nott that contains skulls and skull series taken from other works like Morton's (Nott and Gliddon 1854, 411–65). However, Nott commented on the drawing of 'the cranial types of mankind' that is given at the end of the section on craniometry (reproduced here as Figure I.15) as follows:

> If, as we have reiterated times and again, those types depicted on the early monuments of Egypt have remained permanent through all subsequent ages – and if no causes are now visibly at work which can transform one type of man into another – they must be received, in Natural History, as primitive and specific. When, therefore, they are placed beside each other (*e.g.* as in Figs. 336–338) such types speak for themselves; and the anatomist has no more need of protracted comparisons to seize their diversities, than the school-boy to distinguish turkeys from peacocks, or pecaries [sic] from Guinea-pigs. (Nott and Gliddon 1854, 456)

Thus, in the end, Nott revealed his intuitive approach to the question of 'human races or species', a deep-rooted knowledge, or what we would call prejudice, about their relative worth and appropriate station in life – no need for elaborate measurements. Yet, while thus seemingly depreciating Morton's grand aim of objectifying racial anthropology with a plethora of instruments and measurements, Nott's series of skulls (reproduced as Figure I.15) worked to the same purpose as Morton's diagrams. Morton had transformed Blumenbach's horizontally overlapping skull characters of the five human varieties into static numbers diagrammatically separated in hierarchical order. Nott's inert series 'from the Caucasian skull down to the Black African skull', too, counteracted Camper's and Blumenbach's dynamic and experimental diagrammatic approach of types that morph into each other: Nott explicitly declared it impossible that anything "can transform one type of man into another". His static and racist diagram is one that denies humans a common genealogy (Sommer 2023a, 21–25).[1]

1 Nott and Gliddon also cooperated on *Indigenous Races of the Earth* (1857), which contained a contribution on "The Cranial Characteristics of the Races of Man" (203–352) by James Aitken Meigs and a tableau-foldout describing the 'knowledge' about the '54 human types' that, among other things, provided facial angles and internal capacities below drawings of skulls mostly from Morton's collection. It stood in the diagrammatic tradition represented by Saucerotte's synopsis reproduced here as Figure I.13.

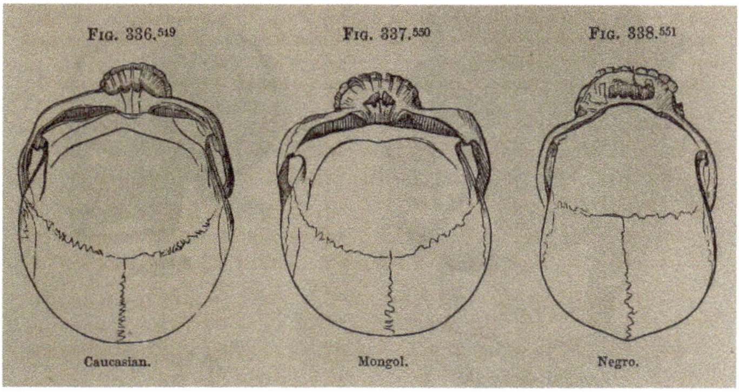

Fig. I.15 Inert skull series. Josiah Clark Nott and George Robin Gliddon, *Types of Mankind* [...] (Philadelphia, PN: J. B. Lippincott, Grambo and Co., 1854), figs. 336–38, p. 457. Public domain.

5. Codifying a Diagrammatics of 'Race'

In the above chapters, I have looked at a time in the history of anthropology when different scholars vied for the power of definition of the new field. While there is a tendency to subsume such 'pioneers' as Camper, Blumenbach, and Morton under the physical anthropological approach, the focus on diagrammatics revealed that not only their conclusions but also their methods differed. Morton wanted to stand on the shoulders of 'the first giants', but he rendered Camper's facial angle 'objective' by measuring it with a precision instrument and he made Blumenbach's general diagrammatic reading of skulls strictly metric. It seems to have been this use of instruments and measurements that began to freeze the dynamics of diagrammatically comparing and morphing proportions in skulls, and thus human varieties, into each other. The practice of ascribing a particular measure, a mean, or even a range to indices, arches, volumes, and angles initiated a process that eventually literally set 'the human races' in stone. In Morton's work, the measures acquired a life of their own, formed the basis of means, and translated human groups into static numbers in hierarchical tables. Through Morton, Camper's transformative facial angle and Blumenbach's morphing comparison of five cranial varieties were turned into instruments in the creation of clearly demarcated and stable 'races' along a vertical axis of increasing intelligence and humanness, qualities that, in the process, were reduced to numbers.

Diagrams were weapons in the battle over the 'real anthropology' and they forged or denied degrees of relatedness between human groups at the times of 'American Indian removal' and of (conflict over) slavery. Morton's work was a crucial step in the direction of establishing a truly racial diagrammatics for a genuinely racial anthropology – a

 https://doi.org/10.11647/OBP.0396.06

diagrammatics that instructed in severing rather than establishing relations. Thus, when Frederick Douglass gave a speech at Western Reserve College in 1854 on the subject of Black African ethnology, he singled out Morton's work for the longest critique, and *Types of Mankind* as the most vicious in its attack on Black Africans. At the same time, he drew on Prichard as an ally. The polygenists' books were used by statesmen to portray the enslavement of Black Africans as natural. The polygenists denied not only 'brotherhood' between Black Africans and Europeans, but also the close relatedness between all African nations, especially regarding the ancient Egyptians. To the contrary, Douglass quoted from Prichard in support of his arguments for the unity of all the people of Africa and their status as "one great branch of the human family" as a whole (Douglass 1999 [1854], 291; for eulogies and other criticism of Morton during his time, see Michael 2020b).

While it would have been possible for Douglass to also draw on the work of Europeans like Camper and Blumenbach in his case for a single human family, Camper and Blumenbach shared aspects of Morton's work more closely than Prichard did. Like Morton, they 'collected' skulls, thus embarking on an activity enmeshed in imperial and colonial projects, wars, as well as marginalizing practices in Europe, Euro-American societies, and the world over. The anthropologists discussed in this part further objectified the 'sampled' people and their communities by studying their remains, by reproducing and distributing these remains, and, not least, through turning them into diagrams – immutable but mobile inscriptions that reduced human beings to readable and measurable angles, proportions, and volumes (Sommer 2023a, 25–26). And their endeavors and Morton's skull atlases did not remain without successor projects, some of which further testify to the fact that the contest between different approaches to the study of 'man' was not yet entirely over.

In the aftermath of *Crania americana* (1839), the French physician Joseph Vimont (1841) produced an atlas of 180 plates from the perspective of comparative phrenology, as he called it, showing skulls of animals and humans and including explanatory diagrams. Carl Gustav Carus (1843), then personal doctor to the king of Saxony, delivered an atlas of 'physiognomic cranioscopy', reproducing the skulls and faces (in original size and proportions) of renowned and noteworthy persons. This still constituted a hodgepodge of specimens – including the skulls of Friedrich Schiller, Immanuel Kant, and Napoleon, as well as skulls that had belonged to 'idiots', persons from Greenland, Scandinavia, Africa, and Malaysia, someone who had committed suicide, and an Egyptian mummy. There were also superimposed outlines of skulls for easy comparison and tables with measures. As the preface indicates, Carus not only knew of the decline of phrenology, he was also aware of the criticism leveled at his own, older approach to the study of mental traits.

In 1857, the French physician Michel-Hyacinthe Deschamps lamented the many racial systems scholars had devised on the basis of different methods (on craniometry, see 94–120); the following year, his countryman, anatomist and polygenist Georges Pouchet (1858), still complained that, despite Camper, Daubenton, Blumenbach, Cuvier, Morton, and others, and despite the dominance of craniometry, the definitive method of anthropology had yet to be established. At the same time, the year before his death, the influential Swedish anatomist and anthropologist, Anders Adolf Retzius (1859 [1860]), who held a skull collection at the Karolinska Institute in Stockholm, left no doubt that he believed to have discovered this method. In the 1840s, Retzius had introduced the cephalic index (ratio of width to length of skull) that determined the anthropological distinction between dolicho- and brachycephalic skulls – a distinction that could be combined with the characteristics of ortho- versus prognathism. Dolichocephalic individuals were of the long-headed types that were considered more advanced than the round-headed types. Degrees of prognathism were meant to refer to the facial angle after Camper, with a more protruding face as a marker of primitiveness. Retzius himself used the criterion of long- versus short-headedness to characterize 'nations', and in his review of the advances in this respect, he provided classificatory lists or keys of human groups for each major global region according to the cephalic index and the degree of pro- versus orthognathism (on the controversy over Retzius' system, see Blanckaert 1989).

Another intricate measuring system for the generation of data was proposed by the Austrians Karl Scherzer and Eduard Schwarz (1858). They provided a table that systematized the measurements they had used on their voyage around the world (15–18, 22–25), including not only the head but also the rest of the body in an extended anthropometry, from which they thought to have arrived at "a natural system of the human races" (18). They clearly meant to be imitated; they even started "a journal to note down the different measurements" (26) to be continued by the reader. In the explanations of the measurements, they used a seemingly idiosyncratic way of demonstrating distances and angles not on a skull, but solely in relations to each other, a procedure which resulted in a diagram of measurements that (re)constructed the head (see Figure I.16). They thereby demonstrated that it worked both ways: not only could realistic renderings of skulls without numbers or lines serve as diagrams, heads could also be constructed purely diagrammatically (Scherzer and Schwarz 1858). Scherzer's and Schwarz's system was received internationally and applauded by figures such as Alexander von Humboldt. They had their treatise translated into other languages and distributed to medical men and men of science in diverse regions of the globe in the hope that these men may expand on their own collection of approximately 12,000 measurements (see Davis 1861, 126–28).

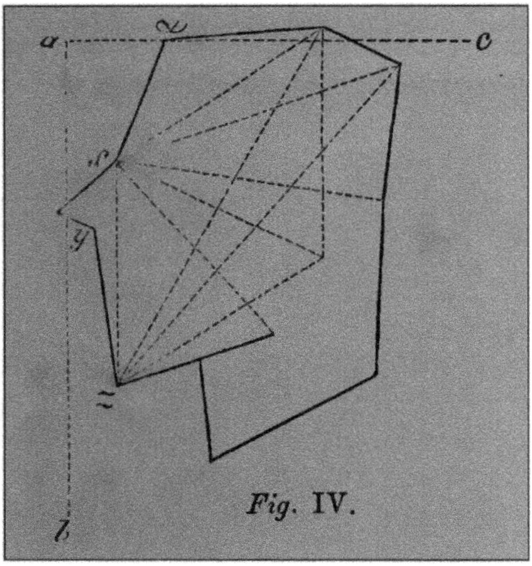

Fig. I.16 A diagrammatic head. Karl Scherzer and Eduard Schwarz, *On Measurements as a Diagnostic Means for Distinguishing the Human Races* [...] (Sydney: Printed for private circulation only, 1858), Fig. 4, p. 12. Public domain.

Another person who set out to remedy the lack of a coherent universal system of craniometry at that time was the physician and natural historian Karl Ernst von Baer. In his *Crania selecta* of 1859, he followed the now established structure. He provided a long list of measurements to be used. He described types of skulls (from Papua, New Guinea, China, from a Kalmyk, etc.) from the St. Petersburg collection with tables containing measures, and, in the accompanying atlas of skulls, he included some superimpositions of skull outlines for easy comparison – a genre of diagram that, too, was becoming standard. Von Baer tried to organize an anthropological congress, again with the aim of standardizing craniometry. As a consequence, in the form of a letter to von Baer, the German physician Johann Christian Gustav Lucae (1861), who had the skull collection of the Senckenberg Museum and Institute of Anatomy in Frankfurt at his disposal (as did von Soemmerring), also presented an atlas of 'racial' skulls with measures (taken after von Baer) in the name of craniometry proper.

Lucae (1861) complained that the number of skulls in collections was small, and that the collections were not accessible to everyone. Craniometric studies tended to be based on small samples, used different methods, and did not allow for remeasurement if there were no images available or if the images were of poor quality. James Aitken Meigs had set the example when he presented an expanded catalogue of the (Morton) Philadelphia collection (that would be followed by other catalogues such as the one by Jan van der Hoeven in 1860). There was also the possibility of providing casts as was done in the case of the Göttinger (Blumenbach's) collection, or photographs. However, Lucae's standard for an exact craniometry was only met by geometric drawings, because they were not only cheap, but also made possible more exact (re)measurements than the objects themselves and they could be superimposed for comparison. The latter diagrammatic practice supposedly demonstrated the 'dramatic racial differences', for example, between a skull from Greenland and a European skull (Lucae 1861, Fig. 9, 49). Lucae mentioned the illustrations of Carus and von Baer as exemplary, while he found fault with the skull reproductions of Blumenbach and Morton. Explaining his drawing instruments through the use of diagrams, Lucae therefore instructed in the production of perfect geometric images such as were appended to his treatise. Such drawings were holistic impression, description, and measurement in one, he claimed. So Lucae agreed with many that a geometric rendering of a skull was a diagram as such that surpassed all other media, even the real thing, in its epistemic value.

Indeed, by that time, there existed a great variety of instruments and measurements, including different methods to arrive at the weight or volume of the brain (Wyman 1868), as well as overviews over these (e.g., Ward 1858 [1838]; Meigs 1861). Within a short time, a number of paper skull collections appeared, such as Giustiniano Nicolucci's *La stirpe ligure in Italia* (1864), Wilhelm His' and Ludwig Rütimeyer's *Crania helvetica* (1864, with geometrical skull drawings after Lucae), and Alexander Ecker's *Crania germaniae* (1865). There were the images of George Busk's *Crania typica*,[1] a *Crania gallica* was announced, and Joseph Barnard Davis and John Thurnam (1865) added their *Crania britannica* (originally published in six 'Decades' between 1856 and 1865 [according to Harlan 2018, 66]). *Crania britannica* was built on the model of Morton's *Crania americana* and dedicated to him and Blumenbach, opening with an emblem joining the two men's busts in profile. Though Prichard's voice remained an important presence, Morton's influence indeed once again showed itself in the very structure of the book. It gave an explanation of tools and measurements and provided tables of measures, skull lithographs (that were produced by drawing the outline of skulls directly on stone in the original size), as well as small outlines of skulls of ¼ in diameter of the original size in facial, vertical, and posterior views at the head of every "descriptive picture of every skull lithographed as we are able to delineate in words" (Davis and Thurnam 1865, 12).

Davis was a polygenist, claiming that the ancient Britons and inhabitants of other countries were autochthonous to their lands. He also opened the illustrated catalogue of his enormous collection of 1,474 skulls, for which he made more than 25,000 measurements, with a rejection of "the unity of man's origin" (Davis 1867, see the preface, v–xvii, quote on v, which also contains an overview of existing collections and catalogues as well as the specification of his measurements). In the catalogue, Davis emphasized that he not only surpassed Morton

1 Busk seems to have been working on a substantial treatise, *Crania typica*, giving descriptions and lithographs of skulls, that was never published; but the plates were deposited in the library of the Anthropological Institute (W. H. F. 1887). In 1861, Busk presented his craniometric system that drew on von Baer's – including instruments, measurements, and drawing techniques – as a way of announcing the *Crania typica* (Busk 1861).

in terms of his collection, but also in the number of measurements presented. Indeed, Davis (1867, 345–62) even compared the results of his measurements to those provided by Morton in words and tables. It is further noteworthy that Davis, although dealing with the ancient Britons in his works, was cautious vis-à-vis the novel concept of human antiquity as it presented itself with the discovery of prehistoric cultures and human fossil remains. This is why in the supplement to his catalogue, Davis (1875, vii) depreciated the achievements of the widely lauded *Crania ethnica* (Quatrefages and Hamy 1882), installments of which circulated before the book's publication. *Crania ethnica* was a hallmark of the new prehistoric studies and added to the system of recent human 'races' those no longer in existence.

Crania ethnica, as well as its precedent *Reliquiae aquitanicae* (Lartet and Christy 1875 [1865–75]), documented the slow and heterogeneous uptake of evolutionary perspectives in anthropology as well as of the notion of human antiquity (Sommer 2007, Part I). They followed in the wake of such lavishly illustrated books as John Lubbock's *Pre-historic Times as Represented by Ancient Remains and the Manners and Customs of Modern Savages* (1865). The banker, politician, and natural historian discussed the Darwinian theory and synthesized knowledge from archeology, ethnology, geology, anthropology, and to a lesser extent history and philology into a new prehistoric archeology. Lubbock refined the Scandinavian tripartite division of prehistory into Stone, Bronze, and Iron Age by differentiating the Paleolithic (the Old Stone Age of chipped or flaked stone tools) from the Neolithic (the New Stone Age marked by polished stone tools).

Reliquiae aquitanicae presented the work of the French paleontologist Édouard Lartet, who had introduced a chronological system for the different prehistoric cultures, and the gentleman scientist Henry Christy. It described and integrated the archeological industries and fossil bones from the south of France, but it did not yet constitute a unitary evolutionary framework. As indicated by its title and subtitle, *Crania ethnica: Les crânes des races humaines* stood in the tradition of Morton's *Crania americana* and *Crania aegyptiaca*, but it was a compendium and classification of not only the living but also 'the fossil human races', including the Canstadt (Neanderthals) and the Cro-Magnon 'race'. Its appendix contained 100 plates with lithographs, and close to 500 illustrations accompanied the texts. The authors Jean Louis Armand de

Quatrefages and Jules Ernest Théodore Hamy compiled the material at the Muséum d'Histoire Naturelle, where de Quatrefages held the Chair of Anthropology and Hamy was his assistant. De Quatrefages was not a proponent of human evolution from simian origins, but he defended human antiquity and monogenism. This was his motivation for carrying out the comprehensive study of the collections at his museum, of the anthropological society in Paris, and other major collections at home and abroad (Sommer 2007, 123–30).

The anatomist and anthropologist Paul Broca, too, was among the French authorities contributing to *Reliquiae aquitanicae*. He defined the Cro-Magnon 'race' as an amalgam of superior characteristics and inferior traits. The description, including features such as a large brain size, a highly developed frontal region, a dolichocephalic and orthognathic upper face, alongside broad-faced features and alveolar prognathism, indicates that these newly discovered humans were measured diagrammatically within the existing 'hierarchical system of races': Broca concluded that the 'Paleolithic troglodytes' had, in some respects, approached the living 'inferior human races' and even the anthropoids. At the same time, they surpassed the 'most civilized' of existing humans in cranial capacity. Broca also invoked the prehistoric typological diversity in Europe as evidence of polygenism. He emphasized that the Quaternary human remains from Les Eyzies (Cro-Magnons) belonged to a different 'race' than those from the Belgium caves (Neanderthals) (Broca 1875 [1865–75], 120–22; see also Broca 1868; Sommer 2007, 126, 130).

Broca's influence on anthropology was decisive. Between 1860 and 1880, drawing on his knowledge of physics and mathematics, he invented many prototypes of anthropometric instruments for comparative measurement (for details, see Hoyme 1953, 418), defined a good part of the standard methodology, and accumulated a great amount of craniological data, flanked by such figures as Retzius in Sweden, James Hunt in England, and Rudolf Virchow in Germany. Although in Paris the first regular courses in anthropology were held by the monogenist de Quatrefages at the Muséum National d'Histoire Naturelle, Broca's polygenist race concept gained broad acceptance through the institutions he co-founded: the Société d'Anthropologie de Paris (1859) and its *Bulletins* as well as the Laboratoire d'Anthropologie (1868) and the *Revue d'Anthropologie* (1872, together with Paul Topinard). The gaining of ground of physical anthropology – often with a polygenist slant – vis-à-vis the philological, geographical, and historical approaches manifested itself in the foundation of similar institutions internationally, such as the Anthropological Society under Hunt in London (Sommer 2015b, 46–58).

The year *Reliquiae aquitanicae* was finished, Broca (1875) codified his field with craniological and craniometric instructions in the name of a commission of the Société d'Anthropologie and in the society's *Mémoires*. In these instructions, Broca covered the collection of skulls, their documentation, reparation and conservation, cranial anatomy, craniometric instruments, measurements, and the handling of numbers as in the formation of means. With regard to instruments, Broca, for example, commended Morton's goniometer for measuring the facial angle while presenting his own lighter and cheaper design by means of a diagram (82–83). Broca not only discussed Camper's facial angle and its derivates, but also the one introduced by Daubenton, explaining the instrument for its determination on the basis of a diagram – as was the case for all lines, diameters, arches, and angles. This instrument, however, was demonstrated in action on a longitudinal section of a skull (even though it was to be applied on the skull in its entirety) (see Figure I.17).

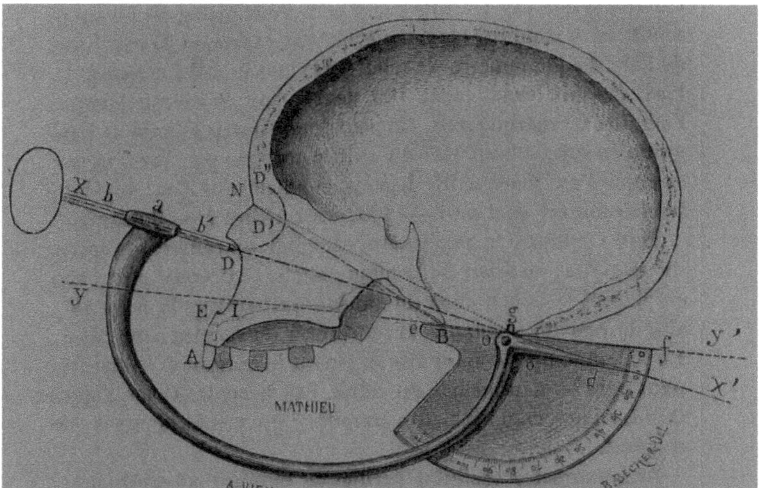

Fig. I.17 "Le goniomètre à arc appliqué sur un crâne [africain]" [The ganiometer with the arc applied to the skull of a Black African]. Paul Broca, "Instructions craniologiques et craniométriques" (*Mémoires de la Société d'Anthropologie de Paris* 2.2 [1875]: 1–203), Fig. 8, p. 91. Public domain.

In the same craniometric instructions, Broca spent quite some space on the diverse ways of measuring the capacity of entire and damaged skulls, but, in the end, it was the relation of parts (as expressed in indices) that was most informative. Reminiscent of Scherzer's and Schwarz's diagrammatic construction of a head out of measures alone, Broca mused that these indices allow the form of the skull to appear before one's eyes ("[...] qui font, en quelque sorte, apparaître cette forme devant les yeux" [1875, 171]). Skulls could be looked at as diagrams and could be constructed purely diagrammatically. Accordingly, Broca introduced the reader to craniography – the art of transferring skulls on paper for exact measurement. Such geometric drawings (that in contrast to photography could replace the skull itself for the physical anthropologist) had to be provided from diverse aspects, certainly including Blumenbach's *norma verticalis*. Different solutions had been proposed for the alignment of skulls for drawing by Blumenbach, Camper, van Baer, and Hamy. There existed also different instruments for obtaining the drawings, including Lucae's instruments, or the craniograph, stereograph, and diagraph (114–25).

Broca now was also careful to have the practitioner differentiate skulls according to age, sex, and deformation when preparing series. Once a series of skulls of the same provenance was established, each cranium had to be directly inscribed with a number on the forehead to put it in relation to the other skulls as well as to the inscriptions produced on its basis, including diagrams. Furthermore, the name of the series had to be written on the left parietal of each cranium. Even a person's sex, age, and name should be inscribed on his or her skull, if, and only if, these were of absolute certainty (1875, 158–59). Broca provided directions on how to describe the skulls in words and a table as an example of how to identify each skull and register the individual measurements and means. He suggested measuring each skull in a series at once for the same measure and making in a row all the measures that needed the same instrument.

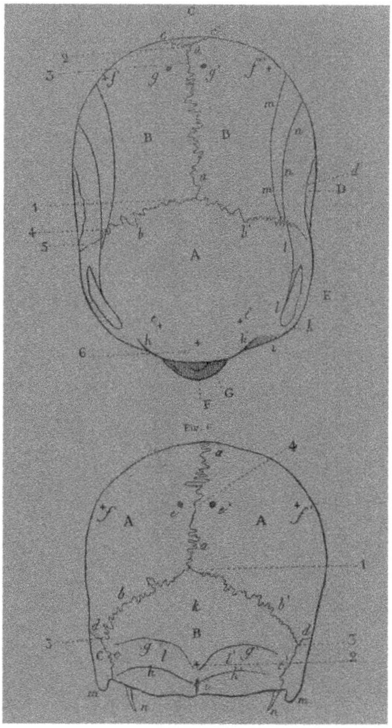

Fig. I.18 Plate with skull diagrams. Paul Broca, "Instructions craniologiques et craniométriques" (*Mémoires de la Société d'Anthropologie de Paris* 2.2 [1875]: 1–203), Plate 3, appendix. Public domain.

Finally, Broca included an appendix with skulls from all sides (in the case of the upper skull in Figure I.18 in the *norma verticalis*), in which the anatomical parts as well as craniometric reference points and lines were indicated. And he gave the name and address of a man in Paris who, for twenty-five francs, could provide the reader with an exercise skull, a skull on which craniometric points of reference and lines in agreement with the instructions had been drawn. He also gave the address of an instrument maker, with a list of instruments and prices, and pointed the reader to the editors of the Société d'Anthropologie, from whom (some 144 pages of) model registers for the compilation of measurements and means could be obtained for free. All in all, reading Broca's lessons conjures up the working anthropologist, immersed in the practice of establishing a system of reference of increasing abstraction, an interplay between bones, texts, diagrams, and numbers. In the process, individual skulls are grouped into series, and from these series the numeric means are calculated for a hypothetical "*crâne moyen*" (1875, 175), a 'racial type' that could be set in relation to other such 'racial types'. Broca's "Instructions" are once again just that, instructions with the purpose to standardize physical anthropology and to spread its techniques even beyond the men of science.

Broca's work was a cornerstone in the grand project of establishing a diagrammatics and metrics of 'race' that constructed human groups as fixed entities in hierarchical relation and, especially in its polygenist expression, this project was entangled with colonial and racial politics not only in the US. The Anthropological Society of London, for example, provided the Empire with legitimation – even the massacre under Governor John Eyre in Jamaica in 1865 – and supported the Confederation in the American Civil War (e.g., Livingstone 2008, Chs. 3 and 7). At that time, however, a particular diagram of a different nature and with its own success story had already been introduced to express human relatedness: the tree shape. As we will see in Part II, rather than entering anthropology on the tide of evolutionary theory, it first appeared as a means of classification. And while the tree diagram is, from its origin, connected to a genealogical understanding of human unity (that need not be evolutionary), it could also be transformed so as to deny human kinship and give expression to new versions of polygenism, even within an evolutionary understanding of human history. What the work of those who followed in the footsteps of Camper, Blumenbach, Morton, and others shows is that Darwin embarked on the application of his theory of evolution to humans at a time when polygenism was far from uprooted – to the contrary, and as is of concern in Part II, *The Descent of Man* (1871ab) can be seen as a reaction to it.

PART II. MAPS, SCALES, AND TREES AS (INTERTWINED) DIAGRAMS OF HUMAN GENEALOGY AND EVOLUTION

> Genealogy became the great problem of zoology and botany, of palaeontology, and of all allied studies. The mighty maze of organic life was no longer without plan [...] Philology was remodelled; ethnology took a new face; sociology, as a complete science, first really began to be. Even such studies as law and history felt the remote effects of the great Darwinian wave. (Allen 1882, 307)

The man who wrote the above lines emphasized the revolution the genealogical approach meant for different scientific and scholarly endeavors – a revolution brought about by Charles Darwin. At the same time, the author of this obituary left no doubt about the fact that Darwin's work and writings were part and parcel of his time and of a certain tradition. After all, we have seen in Part I that the genealogical approach was central to pre-evolutionary scholars like Johann Friedrich Blumenbach and James Cowles Prichard, if only with regard to humankind or organisms that pertained to the same species. Accordingly, Darwin's *The Descent of Man, and Selection in Relation to Sex* (Darwin 1871ab) evidences ties to, as well as a break away from, the pre-evolutionary anthropology that was under concern in Part I. In *The Descent of Man*, Darwin treated some of Blumenbach's views (even if mostly through other authors), referred indirectly to Petrus Camper, and drew on Prichard (the third and fourth editions of *Researches*).

Scholars have described Prichard as a precursor to Darwin, in terms of the analogy with artificial selection in breeding and the concepts of natural selection and heredity, as well as in the application of evolution and progress to man's physical and mental characteristics, and/or

 https://doi.org/10.11647/OBP.0396.07

his understanding of geographical distribution and variation (see Stocking 1973). At the other end of the spectrum, some argue that the idea of Prichard as a precursor to Darwin is a myth born in secondary literature, and that Darwin was not much concerned with Prichard's writings. According to this perspective, considering his opposition to transformationism, Prichard can hardly be seen as a forerunner of Darwin (Augstein 1996, 20, 528–29). Nonetheless, Darwin wrote into his copy of the first volume of the fourth edition of Prichard's *Researches* (1851), "How like my Book this will be" (see *Catalogue of the Library of Charles Darwin*, Rutherford 1908, xi), and his references to Prichard also in the second volume of *Descent* (1871b) suggest that with regard to sexual selection, too, Darwin found inspiration in Prichard's writing.[1]

Samuel George Morton made only one appearance in *Descent*, when Darwin observed that even though 'man' was the best researched animal, the most renowned scientists disagreed vastly on the question of race, and that there existed estimates from one to sixty-three races, with Morton proposing twenty-two (Darwin 1871a, 226). Morton's *Crania americana* was on Darwin's list of books to be read, but seems to have remained there (Darwin 1838–51 – it still appears on that list of 1852–60). Darwin was acquainted with some of Morton's papers on species, 'races', and hybridization, as well as paleontology; and he did possess a copy of *Types of Mankind* (Nott and Gliddon 1854) (see *Catalogue of the Library of Charles Darwin*, Rutherford 1908, 31). However far Darwin might have been influenced by Prichard, he distrusted Morton's research and warned Charles Lyell: "I do not think Dr. Morton a safe man to quote from" (Darwin to Lyell, 2 June 1847, in Mitchell and Michael 2019, 77; CUL-DAR146.166 in Wyhe 2002).

The above must be seen in view of the fact that *The Descent of Man* was, in some measure, a reaction to the polygenist anthropology discussed in Part I. Adrian Desmond and James Moore show in their *Darwin's Sacred Cause* (2009) how Darwin moved in circles of abolitionists, with his mother's side of the family active for the cause. The authors meticulously reconstruct how the knowledge Darwin gained about genocide and

1 The last observation is true also with regard to William Lawrence's *Lectures on Physiology*. Note that already the Scottish naturalist Arthur J. Thomson (1909), following the British evolutionary biologist Edward Poulton, discussed Prichard as a predecessor of Darwin.

slavery, including the gruesome outcomes of its abolition, on the five-year voyage of the *Beagle* around the world (1831–36), radicalized him to a certain extent. Darwin was also aware of the involvement of science in 'racial' exploitation and violence, especially with the support that polygenist theories gave such social institutions in the American south. These doctrines were strongly contradicted by his observations in South America, especially in Brazil, where Europeans, Black Africans, and Indigenous peoples had intermixed and graded into each other.

However, in the course of time the constant wars between groups, evidenced by the Xhosa Wars, for example, would make more of an impression on Darwin than peoples' ability to find a way of coexisting. And a Darwin who was losing his religious faith rated ethnicities on the basis of his understanding of morality and civilization. He compared Europeans to domesticated animals, while the 'savages' had remained wild. Such 'savages' helped him to imagine 'his' progenitors, and ancestral ties between groups might be uncovered through relations between languages or comparisons of parasites. Such a paternalistic stance towards the 'primitives' was also taken by anthropologists like John Lubbock and Edward Tylor, with whom Darwin clearly felt more aligned than with the craniologists and polygenists. Furthermore, Darwin certainly applied to 'the human family' his understanding of the British class and gender systems, in which he perceived 'natural hierarchies', notwithstanding the concession that a lower-class member could become more refined and even women might improve themselves through education (Darwin 1871a, 232–34; Desmond and Moore 2009, especially Chs. 4–6, 13).

Taken together, the above observations amount to a complex mixture for developing a coherent theory and diagrammatic image of human descent. And the fledgling attempts at applying transformationism to humankind that were in place might not have been to Darwin's liking. According to transformationist theories like those of Jean-Baptiste Lamarck and Robert Grant, with which Darwin was acquainted, evolution did not amount to diversification from a common origin, but consisted in a series of parallel developments through the same pedigree. In this view, rather than humans and apes having branched from a common progenitor, humans had passed through the apes' phase on their own line. Some even envisioned such independent phylogenies for the human 'races', meaning that the living 'races' did not share a common ancestor. Rather, White people constituted the oldest and highest form on the separate but parallel ladders of progress, a rung 'other races' had not yet achieved (Desmond and Moore 2009, 111).

Darwin's conception of descent stood in stark contrast to such views: "Common ancestry had been his innovation: a chartable pedigree for the whole of life, and not just for the human aristocrats" (Desmond and Moore 2009, 141). Desmond and Moore suggest that Darwin preferred 'descent' over 'evolution', because "[h]uman genealogy was more than a metaphor for Darwin's common-descent evolution. It was the prototype explanation" (375). And in accordance with this prototype explanation, Darwin worked with the image of the tree. Family genealogy suggested that some branches of the tree of life would flourish while others withered or perished, just like families rose to influential dynasties or died out; similarly, common 'racial' descent and 'racial' extinction reinforced the notion of a tree of life, with many branches having been wiped out. Indeed, Desmond and Moore propose that it is from Darwin's conception of the relationship between the human 'races' that he ventured into the entire animal kingdom and arrived at the notion of "the genealogy of all living beings" (Darwin to Joseph Hooker, July 13, 1858, in L. Huxley 1918, 499). In sum, "racial unity was his starting point for explaining the common descent of all life using a pedigree approach" (Desmond and Moore 2009, 126).

All of this suggests the tree as the perfect diagram to capture the descent of 'man' and contradict the polygenists. Indeed, Darwin did experiment with tree-like drawings of phylogenies. At the same time, we will see that his ideas and use of language evoke the great chain of being (Sommer 2021, 45–47). As the initial remarks regarding Darwin's hybrid stance towards human varieties imply, the two diagrams were not mutually exclusive, and both have a longer history within natural history and without. Before engaging with Darwin's own struggle to develop a diagrammatics to capture his new way of conceptualizing human relatedness, I therefore examine the ways in which genealogy and eventually evolution, the chain, and the tree were interlinked. Finally, another image was associated with the tree in the context of humanity, that of the map, and this trinity of map, chain, and tree is remarkably obvious in the first image I have discovered that included the human 'races' in a tree-shaped system of classification. A close engagement with its visual references will lead us to the issues Darwin was tackling.

This means that the experimentality inherent in diagrams that I discussed for Charles Sanders Peirce in Part I will retain center stage in this part. It also means that diagrammatic metaphors will be a major concern. Peirce distinguished three subcategories of the icon – the image, the metaphor, and the diagram. While the image-icon shares simple qualities (such as color) with its object, the diagram is a skeleton-like sketch of its relations, and the metaphor represents an object by finding similarity in something else. As we have seen, the subcategories of this triad are not exclusive, however. Rather, an image can be read diagrammatically, and metaphors include both images and diagrams. The diagrammatic analysis of an object indeed seems to be a prerequisite for forming a typical metaphor, because through it one recognizes the fundamental structure of an object that in the metaphor is used to understand another phenomenon. The metaphor of the family tree requires that the basic scheme of the tree is applied to that of the family and, in my case, to 'the family of man' (Stjernfelt 2000, 358–60).

6. The First Tree of the Human 'Races': *Mappa Mundi*, Chain of Being, and Tree of Life

Fig. II.1 The wall chart "A General View of the Animal Kingdom" by Anna Maria Redfield (1857). With great thanks to the Yale University Peabody Museum and Senior Collection Manager Susan H. Butts for the photograph. Public domain. A larger version of this image may be viewed at https://hdl.handle.net/20.500.12434/a91688e4

https://doi.org/10.11647/OBP.0396.08

In 1857, a most astonishing image appeared that was to educate students and laypeople in the art of zoological classification: "A General View of the Animal Kingdom" by the Canadian-born Anna Maria Redfield, shown in Figure II.1. The wall chart, carried out with the assistance of a friend, a Reverend E. D. Maltbie of Syracuse (New York), measures 1560 to 1560 mm in size, a lithograph consisting of thirty-two sections that were laid down on linen. Redfield was from a wealthy family; she collected shells, minerals, and plants as well as studying scientific literature. She attained the equivalent of a Master's Degree from Ingham University, the first such institution for women in the United States. The American writer and historian Elizabeth Ellet wrote of her in 1867 as a lady in Syracuse "whose social influence has been salutary and widely acknowledged" (Ellet 1867, 309–310, quote on 309). A large part of this was due to Redfield's popular book *Zoölogical Science* (1858); this was the elaboration of the wall chart in text form, although, as I will discuss later, it contained its own tree of the animal kingdom. The Swiss-born Louis Agassiz, an internationally renowned Professor of Zoology and Geology at Harvard University, praised the book highly (Sommer 2022b, 273).

Redfield's wall chart is primarily spectacular and of great importance in my context because it is the first use of the tree for zoological classification that I have so far found that includes not only humans as a species, but the human varieties (Sommer 2022b, 273).[1] Beyond this unique characteristic, Redfield's wall chart presents the perfect opportunity to move from the topics of Part I to those of Part II, because she drew on the anthropologists of the first hour whom I discussed in Part I, and, at the same time, she leads us to the issues of the phylogenetic tree and the evolutionary view of life. The latter is the case even though Redfield worked within a religious framework, thus demonstrating that the uptake of the tree image in biology and anthropology could be independent of evolutionary theory. Before paying attention to these issues, however, it is well worth taking a closer look at Figure II.1 itself, for it in fact incorporates not one but three long-standing traditions of thinking and visualizing diversity: it evokes the *mappa mundi*, the chain of being, and the tree of life. I therefore set out with a consideration of the cultural history of these three iconographies in this chapter.

1 J. David Archibald includes the image in his concise history of visualizing the natural order, but without noticing this unique feature, the inclusion of the human varieties (Archibald 2014, 74–76).

To begin with, as part of a chain of being that surrounds the tree in Figure II.1, in the four corners of the wall chart, we find hunting scenes (see close-ups in Figure II.2a–d). These scenes are set in Europe (II.2a), Asia (II.2b), America (II.2c), and Africa (II.2d). In each of these, placed in a typical landscape, men (and, in one case, a woman) are using weapons and domesticated animals. In all four images, the figures' prowess and dignity as hunters is expressed. We are presented with the hunt of a stag with horses and dogs; of a tiger with elephants, rifle, and spears; of a buffalo with horses, spears, and bow and arrow; and of a zebra with horse and spear. The people wear European hats, suits, and a dress; turbans; feather headdresses; and a kind of cape. Adorning the corners of what is therefore also a map, the scenes stand for four continents, the 'corners of the world'. If we read in a clockwise manner, humankind thus unfolds from the White variety – a motif to which I will return.

Figs. II.2a–d Close-up of Europe (top left), Asia (top right), America (bottom right), and Africa (bottom left) in the four corners of the wall chart by Anna Maria Redfield (1857). With great thanks to the Yale University Peabody Museum and Senior Collection Manager Susan H. Butts for the photograph. Public domain.

The most prominent early depiction of what David N. Livingstone has called "racial cartography" is the *mappa mundi* tradition, which stems from the encyclopedist and historian Isidore of Seville, from the sixth and early seventh century (Livingstone 2010, quote on 206; see Figure II.3). These diagrams show the three known continents Asia, Africa, and Europe in a T within an O arrangement, so that the T, or the cross, cuts the space within the O, or the orb, into three parts. The three continents in turn became associated, possibly in the ninth century, with Noah's sons Shem, Ham, and Japheth, who were posited as the fathers of the main human lines: 'the Asian, the African, and the European'. Already at that time, their face and skin color, their size and temperament, became linked to the different climates they inhabited (Livingstone 2010, 206–207; also 2008, 5–6).

Fig. II.3 "T and O style *mappa mundi* (map of the known world) from the first printed version of Isidorus' *Etymologiae* (Kraus 13). The book was written in 623 and first printed in 1472 at *Augsburg* by one *Günther Zainer* (*Guntherus Ziner*), Isidor's sketch thus becoming the oldest printed map of the occident." "This T and O map, from the first printed version of Isidore's Etymologiae, identifies the three known continents as populated by descendants of Sem (Shem), Iafeth (Japheth) and Cham (Ham)". Wikimedia, public domain, https://commons.wikimedia.org/wiki/File:T_and_O_map_Guntherus_Ziner_1472.jpg

However, the historian Benjamin Braude has cautioned that the division of the world into three or more continents did not exist before the seventeenth century. Although the terms 'Asia', 'Africa' (or 'Libya'), and 'Europe' were used centuries earlier, they did not carry their current meaning. They referred to regions of one world rather than separate continents. They were little more than continental exposures to the Mediterranean Sea. The only tradition in which the tripartite system was constant was indeed that of the Isidorean or T and O maps, which were not maps in the modern sense. They did not represent geographical space, and should thus rather be called Cross and Orb icons. They were not even the work of Isidore of Seville himself, only appearing in copies of his work after his death. The first such icon is of the eleventh century and it only gives the names of Noah's sons, not the 'continents'. Neat and clear-cut continental divisions among the three sons were not only absent from the biblical text, they would also have been incomprehensible to the ancient and medieval world. Braude argues that it was only with print capitalism, coincident with the 'invention of Africa and America', that the story of the sons of Noah that was more polyphonic in ancient and medieval times began to consolidate. The slaving expeditions to Africa during the fifteenth century aided the association of Ham with black skin and with a curse interpreted as one of serfdom (Braude 1997).

What is important in my context is that Noah's sons did eventually become associated with the different continents and with their inhabitants – establishing a genealogical geography of the main human types and the human family at large, which has been at stake in Part I of this book, but that, as we will see, reverberates throughout anthropological histories up until today. And this genealogical geography was increasingly hierarchical. With it was established a Christian visual cosmology that already contained the tension between unity and diversity – a diversity with which differential value judgments could be associated. Indeed, since the Middle Ages biblical history could be represented in tree-like forms in which Noah constituted the root, while his three sons were the founding fathers of the branches. Joachim of Flora, in a twelfth-century diagram, had the branches of Japheth (Christians) and Sem (Jews) intertwine, while the branch of Ham was only of short life. In the course of the early modern period, more clearly arboreal shapes came to represent the descent of nations from Noah. And once again, such a tree could be linked also visually (not only conceptually) to the map, as in the case of a Swedish scholar who planted Noah's tree in the old world, which was drawn on a kind of globe (Hellström 2019, 165–72).

Redfield gave classical renderings of the four continents and their peoples at a time when there were well-established 'racial hierarchies'. Interestingly, in the wall charts' chain of being, the European and Asian scenes contain also an ape that is partly separated from the hunting scene, while the American scene features a monkey; the African scene is devoid of this 'missing link'. Furthermore, her continental scenes in the four corners of the wall chart also resonate with the tradition of allegorical renderings of the four continents, their peoples, animals, and plants on textiles, as ceramics, or on metal, glass, stone, and earth ware (Cooper Union Museum for the Arts of Decoration 1961; Le Corbeiller 1961).

Fig. II.4 'America' in the octagon of the Galleria Vittorio Emanuele II, around 1880. Photograph by © Benjamin Hemer, all rights reserved, reproduced by kind permission of the artist, https://imaginoso.de/italien/mailand/viktor-emanuel-ii-galerie-luenette-amerika-oktagons

A 'racial geography' that like in Redfield's scheme depicts the continents with their peoples in one image and arranges them in space is most common in drawing or painting, such as in Andrea Pozzo's spectacular ceiling fresco *Triumph of St. Ignatius of Loyola,* completed in 1685 for the Church of Sant-Ignazio in Rome (Müller-Wille 2021) or in Giovanni Battista Tiepolo's ceiling fresco in the Residenz in Würzburg (1753). A later classical rendering can be found in the Galleria Vittorio Emanuele II in Milan. The shopping arcade opened in 1867 and is decorated with four mosaics (originally frescos) of the continents on opposite walls of an octagonal hall leading into different corridors. It seems that, befitting colonial times and a mall celebrating the wealth of things one could acquire in Italy, in each painting, local people are offering goods to a female. Indeed, in 'America', the female figure is sided by a Native American man but to her right are enslaved people from Africa (see Figure II.4). The White female in each of the four pictures could either represent the four continents ('Africa' in fact was given Egyptian attributes), or they could all be personifications of Europe, who (maybe with the exception of 'Africa') is only slightly adjusted to the different continents through her headdress.[2]

Fig. II.5 Close-up of aspects of the chain of being in the wall chart by Anna Maria Redfield (1857). With great thanks to the Yale University Peabody Museum and Senior Collection Manager Susan H. Butts for the photograph. Public domain.

The four corners of the earth are embedded in a chain of being in Redfield's wall chart. This chain of being communicates with the tree that it frames through its botanical rendering. It is itself made-up of two wooden stems, intertwined to form a chain, that sprout little branches with leaves. Within the chains, animals of different kinds are nested, without any apparent order. Some chains contain diverse animals such as an insect and a squirrel, or a tiger with its prey (see Figure II.5).

2 In the few sources on the paintings/mosaics that I have found, the females are taken to represent the different continents, without discussing the issue that they exhibit what was taken to be a European appearance (e.g., Bandmann 1966, 81).

The chain of being as the underlying order of all things expressing the will, power, and goodness of God was also part of medieval Christian cosmology. The historian Arthur O. Lovejoy (1964) has paid particular attention to the concepts of plenitude, continuity, and gradation the chain embodies, which are themselves historically versatile elements (Wilson 1987). From these concepts developed by Plato and Aristotle, scholars conceived a linear scale of perfection in which all natural entities would have to be arranged (metaphors of chains, cords, ladders, and stairways for the natural order go very far back in Middle Eastern and European intellectual and religious thought). However, in Redfield's wall chart, the chain of being is morphed into a highly vivid botanical and zoological visual metaphor, framing the tree of life and connecting the different peoples of the earth. It is a closed chain, thus appearing nonhierarchical, rather emphasizing the unity and completeness of creation.

The simultaneity of horizontal and hierarchical imagery rather seems to be due to the tree of life that figures most prominently in Redfield's wall chart. In fact, the tree of life could also present a hierarchical scale of nature (Gontier 2011, 523). While Redfield did not use the expression 'tree of life' in her accompanying *Zoölogical Science* (simply referring to the wall-chart image as a 'tree'), historians have attributed an important role to the tree-of-life iconography. This symbolic and mythic tree is one of the oldest and most universal images, related to notions of cosmic origin and unity, growth, fertility, and regeneration or rebirth. Visualizations go back to ancient times, and in the Christian Middle Ages it could recount the history of Christ or of humankind on its way to salvation (Philpot 1897; James 1966; Cook 1988; Demandt 2005; 2014). In Genesis, the tree of life, together with the tree of knowledge of good and evil, appears at the center of the Garden of Eden. It figured regularly in medieval illustrations of the Fall as a symbol of the way to salvation as expressed by Christ. This liminal quality was emphasized in early Christian art by positioning the tree of life on portals, sarcophagi, and tombs. The botanical iconography varied because of diverse biblical references but also due to the fact that, in the Middle Ages, there was as yet no categorical distinction between a tree, a shrub, or a vine. Artists portrayed the tree of life in various forms, sometimes as botanically unidentifiable, and other times as a vine, acanthus, fig, olive, date palm, or a combination of these plants. Thus, as in the mosaic pavement on the floor of the Cathedral of St. Maria Annunziata in Otranto, Italy

(1163–65), the tree of life often does not look very tree-like to the modern beholder. In this image of the history of the world, men climb and fall from the tree's branches in their struggle to get away from the Fall and move towards the altar, or heaven. There is therefore a clear direction to 'history' that is associated with progress in the sense of salvation (Salonius 2020).

Further according to Pippa Salonius, not only the tree of life (*lignum vitae*) but also the tree of Christ (tree of Jesse) could offer an optimistic image of a growth towards heaven and map a path towards God:

> Vertical growth was fundamental to the diagrammatic structures of the *Tree of Jesse*, the *Lignum vitae* and the *ordensstammbäume*, which were all meant to be read proceeding heavenward through the founding ancestor [...] to culminate in a visual reference to God. The upward progression of the arboreal schemata should be read as a transition from earth towards the heavens, from the human towards the divine, an ascent towards spiritual perfection. (Salonius 2020, 321)

In the Old Testament's Book of Isaiah, Christ is a flower growing from the root of Jesse, which gave rise to the successful iconography of the tree of Jesse beginning in the eleventh century. Such trees could be a summary of salvation and lead the contemplating on his or her own way to salvation along the axis of the son of God's earthly ancestry. In this sense, the tree of Jesse could also be a tree of life. Furthermore, although Salonius adds that genealogies of Christ and trees of life differed from dynastic stemma that were read from top to bottom or from the *arbores consanguinitates* that did not have tree imagery until the thirteenth century, the *arbores*, too, could help in the conceptualization of time and history. Their main role was to determine degrees of family relatedness that were under the incest prohibitions (see Figure II.20 below). However, in a few cases in the twelfth century, they were regarded as supplementary to biblical genealogy, connecting human history to individual family history. Complementing the stemmata of Christ's genealogy, they, too, were identified with the *lignum vitae*. These special cases of *arbores consanguinitates* looked particularly tree-like. In historical treatises, an *arbor consanguinitatis* could work as a reflection on the human dimension of time, and it could also appear in the context of genealogies of earthly dynasties (Worm 2014).

These elements of the tree of life in its diverse forms, the Christian image of unity and diversity, of genealogical continuity in humankind, of history and progression, as well as the atypical iconography for our current understanding, are remarkably present in Redfield's tree. Her wall chart shown in Figure II.1 looks more like a fern than a tree, and is, in fact, reminiscent of some of the tree-of-life imagery, such as Figure II.6 with its bending branches, its fruits, leaves, and multiple parallel roots.

Fig. II.6 Tympanum, Altneushul, Prague, circa 1260. Photograph by Paul Asman and Jill Lenoble (2015), https://www.flickr.com/photos/pauljill/25752643044/, CC BY 2.0

Of course, by Redfield's time, tree iconography had become most prominent in family genealogy. In the early modern period, royal and princely families, nobility, and urban elites legitimated their authority and guaranteed the transfer of power and wealth through the demonstration of great antiquity and noble bloodlines in the form of family trees (especially in Germany, but also in Great Britain, France, and Italy) (Heck 2000; 2002). While between the sixteenth and seventeenth century, genealogy was 'scientized' and based on family and state archives (Kellner 2004; Klapisch-Zuber 2004; Gierl 2012, 102–112), up to about 1800, family trees could still be *généalogies fabuleuses* [fantastical genealogies] and reach back to national chieftains of the

Migration Period and even to Trojans or Adam (Bizzocchi 2010). The family tree was instrumental in the transfer from religious to secular legitimation of noble and mostly male sovereignty. Therefore, while related to technologies of antiquity, tree building is seen as a sign of scholarly modernity, also as a tool in the service of clarity and reduction of complexity at a time when the amount of knowledge appeared increasingly unmanageable (Blair 2010). By the nineteenth century, genealogical tree building had become a popular practice, and was, for example, taught in English schools (Castañeda 2002, 59; Sommer et al. 2018, 6; Sommer et al. 2024). Figure II.7 is a particularly striking example, as it connects the members of the imperial family through bodily material.

Fig. II.7 "Maison Bonaparte devenue Impériale de France", a family tree made out of hair by Elisa Montazzi, second half of the nineteenth century, Musée de la Maison Bonaparte. Photograph by Sailko (2019). Wikimedia, CC BY 3.0, https://commons.wikimedia.org/wiki/File:Albero_genealogico_della_famiglia_bonaparte,_1850_ca.jpg

While I can only speculate how far the above religious and secular traditions influenced Redfield's choice of visual metaphors, several developments took place that show the family resemblance between the three diagrammatic traditions intertwined by Redfield – map, scale, and tree – also in the history of natural history.

7. Map, Scale, and Tree in Natural History

It was in the eighteenth century that the image of the chain or scale of nature was most influential. It was seen as representing the order in God's creation, including the conception that every individual and social class had a designated place in the order of society and every group of humans had a position in the hierarchy of civilizations, which were to be accepted and filled to the best of everyone's ability (Diekmann 1992, 53–81). There are, in fact, artistic images that express orders of social rank (see, e.g., Archibald 2014, 6–7). I have not come across a similar visualization of the human ethnic varieties, although one can of course regard the instrumentalizations of Camper's series of skulls/heads for the purpose of the hierarchization of the human 'races', such as carried out (visually), for example, by the English anatomist and polygenist Charles White in *An Account of the Regular Gradation of Nature in Man* (1799), as such scales of the human varieties (Bowler 2021, 71–72). Certainly, in natural history more generally, the linear scale was seen as the underlying order arranging all natural entities according to rungs of perfection.

 https://doi.org/10.11647/OBP.0396.09

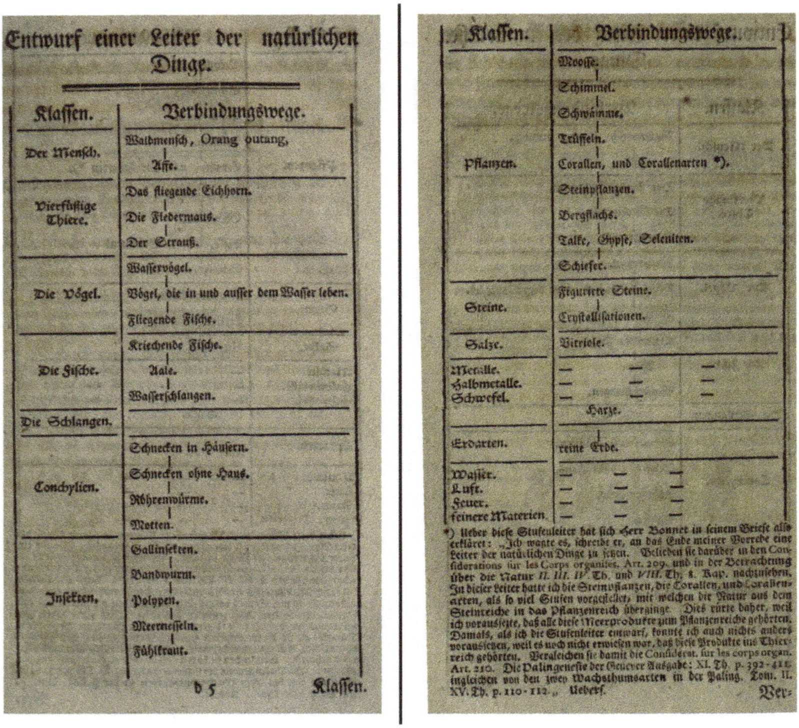

Entwurf einer Leiter der natürlichen Dinge.

Klassen.	Verbindungswege.
Der Mensch.	Waldmensch, Orang outang, | Affe.
Vierfüßige Thiere.	Das fliegende Eichhorn. | Die Fledermaus. | Der Strauß.
Die Vögel.	Wasservögel. | Vögel, die in und ausser dem Wasser leben. | Fliegende Fische.
Die Fische.	Kriechende Fische. | Aale. | Wasserschlangen.
Die Schlangen.	
Conchylien.	Schnecken in Häusern. | Schnecken ohne Haus. | Röhrenwürme. | Motten.
Insekten.	Gallinsekten. | Bandwurm. | Polypen. | Meernesseln. | Fühlkraut.

d 5 Klassen.

Klassen.	Verbindungswege.
Pflanzen.	Moosse. | Schimmel. | Schwämme. | Trüffeln. | Corallen, und Corallenarten *). | Steinpflanzen. | Bergflachs. | Talke, Gypse, Seleniten. | Schiefer.
Steine.	Figurirte Steine. | Crystallisationen.
Salze.	Vitriole.
Metalle. Halbmetalle. Schwefel.	— — — — — — — — — Harze.
Erdarten.	| reine Erde.
Wasser. Luft. Feuer. feinere Materien	— — — — — — — — — — — —

*) Ueber diese Stufenleiter hat sich Herr Bonnet in seinem Briefe also erkläret: „Ich wagte es, schreibt er, an das Ende meiner Vorrede eine Leiter der natürlichen Dinge zu setzen. Belieben sie darüber in den Considerations sur les Corps organises. Art. 209. und in der Betrachtung über die Natur *II. III. IV.* Th. und *VIII.* Th. 8. Kap. nachzusehen. Zu dieser Leiter hatte ich die Steinpflanzen, die Corallen, und Corallenarten, als so viel Stufen vorgestellet, mit welchen die Natur aus dem Steinreiche in das Pflanzenreich übergienge. Dies rührte daher, weil ich voraussetzte, daß alle diese Meerprodukte zum Pflanzenreiche gehörten. Damals, als ich die Stufenleiter entwarf, konnte ich auch nichts anders voraussetzen, weil es noch nicht erwiesen war, daß diese Produkte ins Thierreich gehörten. Vergleichen sie damit die Considerat. sur les corps organ. Art. 210. Die Palingenesie der Genever Ausgabe: XI. Th. p. 392-411. ingleichen von den zwey Wachsthumsarten in der Paling. Tom. II. XV. Th. p. 110-112." Uebers.

Ver-

Fig. II.8 "Entwurf einer Leiter der natürlichen Dinge" [Draft of a ladder of the natural things]. J. A. E. Goeze, in Charles Bonnet, *Herrn Karl Bonnets Abhandlungen aus der Insektologie* (Halle: Bey J. J. Gebauers Wittwe und Joh. Jac. Gebauer, 1773), Vol. I, pp. 57–58. Public domain.

Figure II.8 shows a scale of perfection of the natural world. It appeared in the German translation of a treatise on insects by the famous Swiss naturalist Charles Bonnet. Bonnet, too, had a diagram of the scale of nature (*scala naturae*) in his original (1745, after preface), but the translator complexified it by adding a second column to emphasize the role of intermediaries. Thus, humans were linked to the four-footed animals via half-humans, orangutans, and monkeys. The categories in the right column connected each class of animals, plants, stones, salts, metals, and earths of the left column to the class above and below. While the scale of nature, especially in the way rendered by this translator, therefore nicely captured gradation and perfection, the idea of fullness was even more strongly expressed in the chain of being. For a chain to work, it needs all its links – hence the associated search for 'missing links', also expressed in Figure II.8: the right column is headed "Verbindungswege", approximately 'connecting links', that is, links that are not missing. These connecting links not only joined classes of animals as well as animals and plants, but also the organic and inorganic world, and even integrated the different natural elements.

While in antiquity and the Middle Ages, there was held a primarily static view of nature frequently expressed in the image of the *scala naturae*, the idea of nature as well as the scale of nature could acquire a dynamic aspect in the early modern period (Thienemann 1910). Lovejoy saw the chain of being as taking on a dynamic form with the German polymath Gottfried Wilhelm Leibniz, who could conceive of the possibility that perfection had not once and for all been given, but gradually approached in a process of development. It is unclear how much branching the linear progress in this scheme of the chain did allow for, but it seems that Leibniz, and later the German philosopher Immanuel Kant, worked with notions of diversification as well as continuous development. With thinkers like Georges-Louis Leclerc, Comte de Buffon, too, the eighteenth century witnessed speculations about the transformation of species, even if in a limited sense and mainly still within the rather rigid pattern of the scale of nature (Lovejoy 1964, 242–87, with 256–59 on Leibniz, 265–68 on Kant; Rheinberger 1990; Sloan 2006).

The linear scale was certainly put to the test by the vast expansion in knowledge of animals and plants from many parts of the world during the seventeenth and eighteenth century; it caused an "Erfahrungsdruck" [pressure of experience] (Lepenies 1976, 63) that forced natural historians to experiment with diagrams to capture the bountiful diversity of life. In one sense, the ladder literally exploded, so that Bonnet talked of a nearly infinite number of scales of perfection (1745, xxx), and he speculated whether the scale of nature, which he had so influentially visualized diagrammatically, actually had branches (Bonnet 1764; see, e.g., Thienemann 1910, 250). The Berlin zoologist Peter Simon Pallas described a tree in 1766 that illustrated an original separation in animals and plants, and in which, within the animal kingdom, the branches of insects and birds diverged from the ideal scale of increasing complexity from fish to amphibians to quadrupeds (see, e.g., Thienemann 1910, 251). The concept of the scale of nature remained clearly dominant in the image of the Baltic German geologist Karl Eduard von Eichwald in the early nineteenth century. Even though he called it a tree, or more precisely a tree of life ("*Arbor vitae animalis*", Eichwald 1829, 41), one rather recognizes several parallel scales of being (see Figure II.9) (Ragan 2009, n.p.; Archibald 2014, 57–59).

Fig. II.9 "*Arbor vitae animalis*" [Tree of life of the animals]. Karl Eduard von Eichwald, *Zoologia* [...] (Vilnae: J. Zawadzki, 1829), Vol. I, between p. 40 and p. 41. Public domain.

As the historian of science Petter Hellström (2019, 57–135) has shown, the French naturalist Augustin Augier, too, failed to arrange all plants in one continuous series, which made him consider the genealogical tree as the natural botanical order, albeit a family tree that was made up of several ladders. It was presumably the first published classificatory tree, and its iconography interrelated elements of natural trees with elements of heraldry (Augier 1801, foldout after preface). Drawing on the genealogical social fabric of Old Regime France, Augier employed terms such as 'kingdom', 'tribe', 'class', 'order', and 'family' instead of the prominent 'genus', 'species', and 'variety', again demonstrating the interrelatedness of the social and natural order. However, the tree had by no means become the main model. When at the end of the seventeenth century debates emerged in natural history about whether diagrams were able to reflect the natural affinities among organisms, other forms were suggested (Sloan 1972; Lefèvre 2001; Scharf 2009; Müller-Wille 2014). Carl von Linné introduced the metaphor of the map of life, and up until Darwin's influence, in botany and zoology, relatedness was predominantly represented by keys, map-like and reticulate diagrams. This diagrammatic imagery had crisscrossing lines to interconnect organisms in all directions; or it used blobs, circles, or polygons to represent nested groups of affiliated organisms (Rheinberger 1986; Barsanti 1988; 1992; O'Hara 1991; Larson 1994; Ragan 2009; Rieppel 2010; Archibald 2014; Sommer et al. 2018, 6–8).

Maps of variously adjoining territories could better capture the still widely held notion of a nature that does not take jumps, but that, once entirely known, would fill each and every niche with kinds of organisms. As August Thienemann (1910, 247–57) has already discussed, for some eighteenth-century naturalists, this could also be achieved by the chain of being. Naturalists multiplied it, and provided the chains with links to interrelate to the degree of forming nets, or threads interwoven to tissue. The ways in which affinities were conceptualized therefore seem to have suggested three-dimensional constructs, with groups of organisms touching on others in their diverse characteristics all around – as in the case of the Italian natural historian Vitaliano Donati, who in the mid-eighteenth century connected the chains through links into a net, and of Lorenz Oken, in whose mind the ladder became a 'stereotic' net, i.e., a ladder, the basis of which was a net.[1] Chains could

1 "Der Standpunkt und die Verwandschaften der Thiere zu einander und zu den übrigen Producten der Natur möge im folgenden Schema übersehen werden, damit es sich sogleich zeige, dass die Natur, weder nach einer blossen Leiter, noch nach einem flachen Neze die Thiere geordnet habe, sondern nach einem stereotischen Neze, nach einer Leiter, deren Basis ein Nez ist" [The position and relations of the animals to each other and to the other products of nature may be looked over in the following diagram, so that it may be shown at once that nature has not arranged the animals according to a mere ladder, nor according to a flat

thus not only form 'trees', as in Eichwald's case, but also anastomose to form other three-dimensional bodies like networks or maps (also Giessmann 2007).

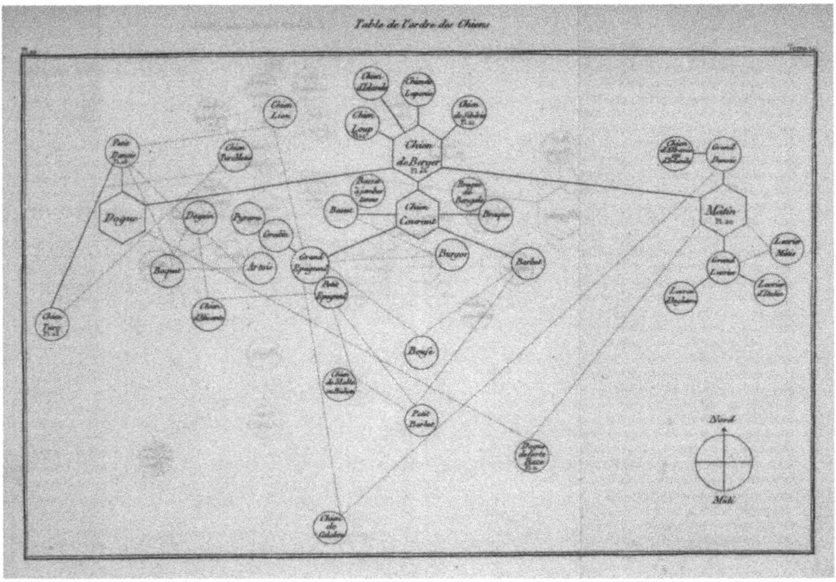

Fig. II.10 "Table de l'ordre des chiens" [Table of the order of the dogs]. Georges-Louis Leclerc, Comte de Buffon, *Histoire naturelle* [...] (Paris: l'Imprimerie royale, 1755), Vol. V, between p. 228 and p. 229. Public domain.

These complex diagrams were mainly not created with the ambition to introduce a temporal dimension or speculate about common descent, and this was true even for the few diagrams that did resemble trees like Augier's *Arbre botanique* [botanical tree] discussed above (Hellström, André, and Philippe 2017). The only exception seems to have been diagrams that illustrated relations of hybridization and geographic variation among races *within* one species. The French botanist Antoine Nicolas Duchèsne drew the descent of cultivated kinds of strawberries as a genealogical 'tree' ("Généalogie des fraisiers" by Duchèsne 1766, opposite 228; e.g., in Toepfer 2011, 40), thereby suggesting connections between the tree diagrams in human family genealogy and in plant

net, but according to a stereotic net, according to a ladder whose base is a net] (Oken 1805, 203).

and animal breeding – connections that Augier made explicit for his botanical tree of 1801 (Ratcliff 2007). Similarly, Buffon's "Table de l'ordre des chiens" [table of the order of dogs] connected breeds or races of dogs in a net-like diagram (1755, between 228 and 229; see Figure II.10 above). Also Buffon conceived of his diagram as a genealogical tree, but one that was oriented like a geographical map. He thought about the genealogy of dogs in analogy to human family genealogy on the microlevel, and to the genealogy of humankind's descent from Adam on the macrolevel (Hellström 2019, 84–91). Thus, Buffon introduced what we will encounter throughout this history of relating diagrams: a tree-map structure that integrates temporal and spatial elements.[2] The diagram relates to a story of common origin and subsequent differentiation through distribution in space (into different climates).

According to the historian of science Olivier Doron (2012), it was Buffon who introduced a decidedly genealogical understanding of races and species into natural history, an understanding that influenced successors like Blumenbach and Prichard. Prior to the mid-eighteenth century, natural history followed the model of botany in a classificatory approach according to differences and affinities. For example, the family did not express kinship but logical relationships. Before the eighteenth century, 'race' was used in nobiliary discourse for different royal dynasties and nobility; 'race' could also refer to the transmission of sin and spiritual status, as in the human race whose members all inherited the original sin through descent from Adam. The third area where 'race' was prominent prior to the eighteenth century was breeding, and natural historians from Buffon to Prichard used it as an analogy for the new way of conceptualizing humankind: "Through Buffon's analysis, it is the whole vocabulary of kinship, the entirety of genealogical knowledge from nobiliary, juridical or breeding practices which enters natural history" (Doron 2012, 101). 'Race' thus pertains to the genealogical style of reasoning. Reproduction was made the basis for classification and the understanding of species and races as natural categories. However, when Buffon went so far as to carry this line of reasoning 'within family genealogy' to its 'logical' end in the conception of the living world as

2 With 'tree-map' I refer to diagrams that combine a tree structure with a cartographic arrangement. It therefore differs from what designer Manuel Lima (2014, 144–47) calls 'treemap'.

descended from a single species, he rejected such a notion as contrary to the authority of the Bible (Doron 2012; 2016).

This is not to say that the Enlightenment did not also bring forward notions of 'true' evolution, such as most forcibly expressed by Lamarck's *Philosophie zoologique* (1809) in the new century. Nonetheless, although Lamarck was clearly working with the transformation of species and did use the branching structure to visually communicate that idea (with more 'trees' in his *Histoire naturelle* of 1815),[3] even within his framework, the ideal order underlying the diversity of life was still the linear series, and Lamarck relied on ongoing spontaneous creation. Again, the 'branches of his trees' stood rather for deviation from the ideal chain (in his case due to adaptation) than for the crucial element of his theory of transformation. Thus, the phylogenetic tree to represent the branching transformationist view of biodiversity appeared later in the nineteenth century (Tassy 2011; also 1991; Pietsch 2012, 7–9). Even in the early decades of the nineteenth century, naturalists still used diverse geometric figures, often including circles, to suggest affinities and/or analogies between organisms (Illies 1983; Ragan 2009; Toepfer 2011, 34–36; Sommer et al. 2018, 6–8; Bowler 2021, 27–41, 177–78).

That for some naturalists the tree diagram to convey natural orders presented serious problems might be elucidated with an example from Agassiz. Agassiz was strongly opposed to transformationist ideas, but nonetheless combined the structure of the zoological map with that of the genealogical tree in his influential *Recherches sur les poissons fossils* (1833–43) (see Figure II.11). Once again, this was done due to the inadequacy of the model of a single series, but by this time, also to bestow a historical dimension on affinities between groups: fish would show such affinities among themselves at each moment in time, and also with those forms that existed before and those that came to exist after. In his description of Figure II.11, Agassiz already made it clear that he was well aware of the support the shape of a true tree would lend to an evolutionary interpretation. In contrast, his tree-map had a historical dimension without implying the transformation of species; it stood for repeated divine creative intervention. This was visualized by groups of fish appearing and disappearing through geological time. Indeed,

3 Archibald (2009, 565) is among those who refer to Lamarck's branching diagram in *Philosophie zoologique* (1809, 463) as the first evolutionary tree of life.

one would hardly think of the image as a tree, because it shows the orders of fish in parallel to each other. Agassiz expressly noted that he did not connect even the families within each order to 'the main stem', because he did not believe in genealogical relations between them, all the same referring to the diagram as a genealogy of the fish class. Finally, Agassiz also indicated the prevalence of a species by the breadth of the 'branches', as he called them (Agassiz 1833, Vol. I, 169–71 and accompanying diagram; Archibald 2014, 69–70; Hellström 2019, 123).

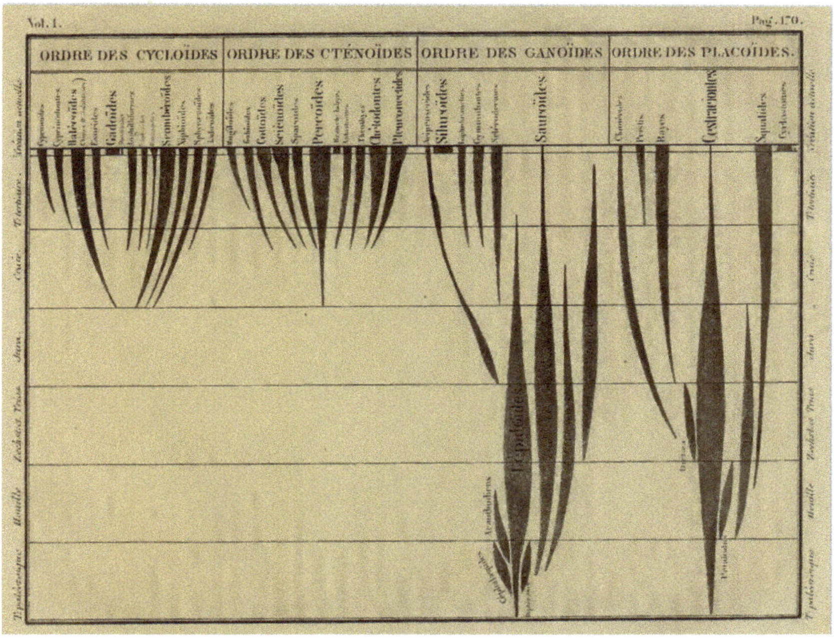

Fig. II.11 "Généalogie de la classe des poissons" [Genealogy of the class of fish]. Louis Agassiz, *Recherches sur les poissons fossiles* (Neuchâtel: Petitpierre, 1833), Vol. I, opposite p. 170. Public domain.

Agassiz's colleague, the German geologist and paleontologist Heinrich Georg Bronn, included similar images in his highly diagrammatic *Untersuchungen über die Entwicklungs-Gesetze der organischen Welt während der Bildungs-Zeit unserer Erd-Oberfläche* (1858). These diagrams visualized the appearance, existence, and disappearance as well as prevalence of taxa throughout geological time. According to Bronn, they demonstrated that the groups of organisms appeared when and where the circumstances were suitable to them, the less 'perfect' groups generally appearing earlier. Being initially similar, the groups increasingly differentiated over time, as did their surroundings. However, this progress towards the present was not brought about by transformation, but by novel creations (Bronn 1858, 484: "fortdauernde Schöpfung neuer Arten"). Most astonishingly, Bronn used a veritable tree in his book (see Figure II.12). He explained that the tree shape was the only one that could express the above findings: higher types could be placed higher up in the tree, even though they might belong to a branch that appeared earlier than that of less progressive forms that were lower down the tree. Thus, in Figure II.12, *f* on branch *A* is more advanced than *d*, but its branch *A* appeared before *B*, and *f* on branch *A* is on the same level as *f* on branch *E*, although branch *E* is younger and thus started off in a more progressed form than *A*. *A* to *G* might refer to groups of invertebrates, to fish, reptiles, birds, and mammals, with the top of the tree signifying the human line. Bronn did not differentiate humankind further – neither in his tree nor in his text (Bronn 1858, 481–82; Archibald 2014, 76–78). Thus, Bronn demonstrated the ability of the tree diagram to code for scales of progression.

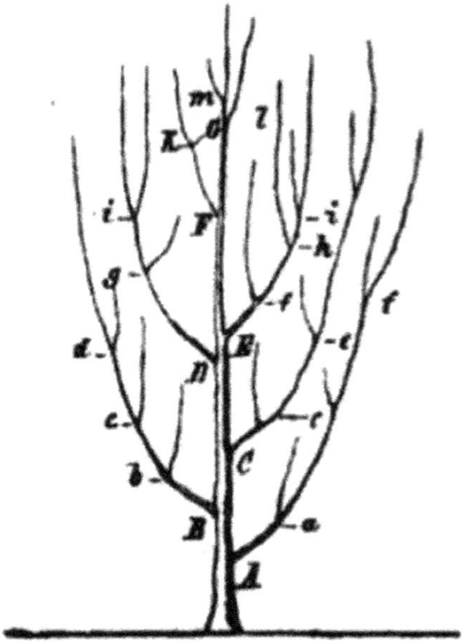

Fig. II.12 "Baum-förmige[s] Bilde des Systemes" [Tree-shaped image of the system]. Heinrich Georg Bronn, *Untersuchungen über die Entwicklungs-Gesetze der organischen Welt* [...] (Stuttgart: E. Schweizerbart, 1858), p. 481. Public domain.

While Bronn's tree once again illustrates that the tree diagram was not necessarily associated with an evolutionary understanding of the organismic world, Agassiz placed the tree squarely in the transformationist approach. Agassiz's hybrid figure was a way to work around the tree, and it once again renders clear that naturalists experimented with and integrated elements from diverse visual traditions to arrive at diagrams that seemed to capture best their understanding of the natural order. Agassiz's diagram makes visible a tendency generally manifest in relating diagrams, including, as we will see, diagrams of the human varieties: newly introduced diagrams may retain older conceptions of the order of nature, while extant diagrammatic traditions can be adjusted to incorporate new ideas. It also seems that there was no clear line of development, from, say, a linear chain or scale to a tree, and eventually to a network or map (a linear development that has sometimes been suggested, e.g., Kull 2003). The network appeared early as a diagram of relatedness, and elements of the three kinds were often combined. Diverse fields might have influenced the ways in which organismic relatedness was visually conceived, from Christian cosmology and iconography, religious and secular genealogy, plant and animal pedigrees, to imagery specifically developed in natural history.

The above observations can also be made for Redfield's trees, which were produced around the same time as Bronn's but which also subdivide humankind. I speak of 'trees' in the plural, because there was a second tree that prefaced her *Zoölogical Science* (1858) (see Figure II.13). While the rendering of the tree in the artistic wall chart exhibits inspiration from the iconography of the corners of the world, the chain of being, and probably the tree of life in its various religious expressions (see Figure II.1), her book and its frontispiece more clearly evidence her acquaintance with natural history and its images, certainly with Agassiz's diagram. Redfield's trees and book were intended to illustrate the natural relations between animals in order to acquaint school children with zoological classification. Like Agassiz and Bronn, Redfield did not believe in the transformation of species and would not begin to do so after the publications of Darwin and others – her textbook *Zoölogical Science* of 1858 was re-issued until 1874. This did not prevent her from drawing on Darwin's natural history, and she also included fossil animals in her wall chart. What Redfield's trees show are the four branches of the animal kingdom after George Cuvier: *Radiata, Mollusca, Articulata,* and *Vertebrata* (Archibald 2014, 74–76). The branching structure of this order is implied in Cuvier's term *embranchements.* With his classification of the living forms in four branches standing beside each other, Cuvier (1817, xx–xxi, 57–61), himself not working within a phylogenetic framework, opposed the concept of the *scala naturae,* the linear series of organisms.

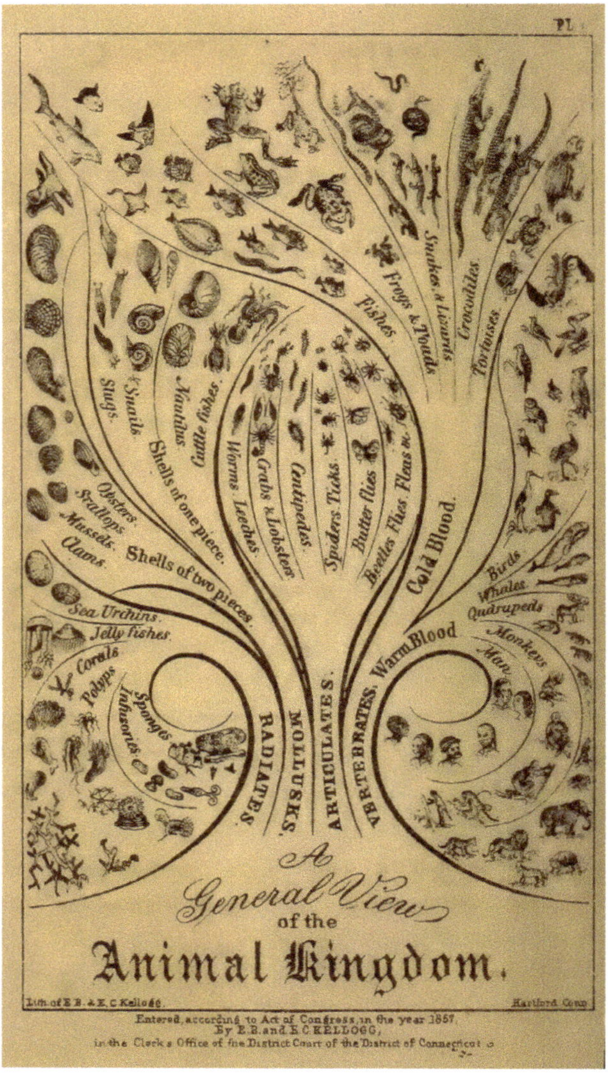

Fig. II.13 "A General View of the Animal Kingdom". Anna Maria Redfield, *Zoölogical Science* [...] (New York: E. B. and E. C. Kellogg, 1858), Plate 1, frontispiece. Public domain.

Interestingly enough, in Redfield's trees, humans are not at the top, as in Bronn's tree, and as the chain of being would suggest. However, a closer look indicates that also in Redfield's wall chart and frontispiece, the 'natural order' is still in place. If we read the trees from left to right instead of from bottom to top, we do climb along the branches of the animal kingdom in the direction of increasing organismal complexity. This is supported by the fact that, in her book, Redfield (1858, 20 and 279) drew on the American geologist Edward Hitchcock who visualized 'man' literally as a crown – the crown of creation – in his "Paleontological Chart" of the influential *Elementary Geology* (1840) that was published in over thirty editions (see Figure II.14). Behind Hitchcock's "two trees" (99) for the plant and animal kingdom stood a non-evolutionary, or rather antievolutionary, rationale in the shape of a ladder towards increasing perfection. Like Redfield after him, Hitchcock structured the animal kingdom on the basis of Cuvier's four *embranchements*, arranging them in a way that made them appear to run in parallel. Like Agassiz, Hitchcock already used the iconography of the geological layers to indicate the progression of life through the ages, to which I will return in the context of evolutionary trees in Part III. Seemingly unaware of Agassiz's visual 'genealogy', Hitchcock (1840, 100) thought that he was the first to have come up with such a kind of image, encountering a similar diagram by Bronn (1837, Plate I) only when his own was already in press. The time was obviously ripe for this geo-paleontological visual language, but not for an evolutionary one. In fact, J. David Archibald has argued that once the tree was clearly attached to an evolutionary meaning some twenty years later, Hitchcock no longer included the chart in the editions of *Elementary Geology* (Archibald 2009, with figure on 578; also 2014, 70–74).

In Redfield's wall chart, the human varieties not only appear last in the twirl from left to right through the *embranchements* and their sub-branches as well as within their own branch of the mammals (and thus quasi 'at the top of the tree'), they also form a 'hierarchy of races' with the "White" at the apex and the "Olive", "Brown", "[R]ed", and "Black" varieties approaching the apes and monkeys (see Figure II.15).

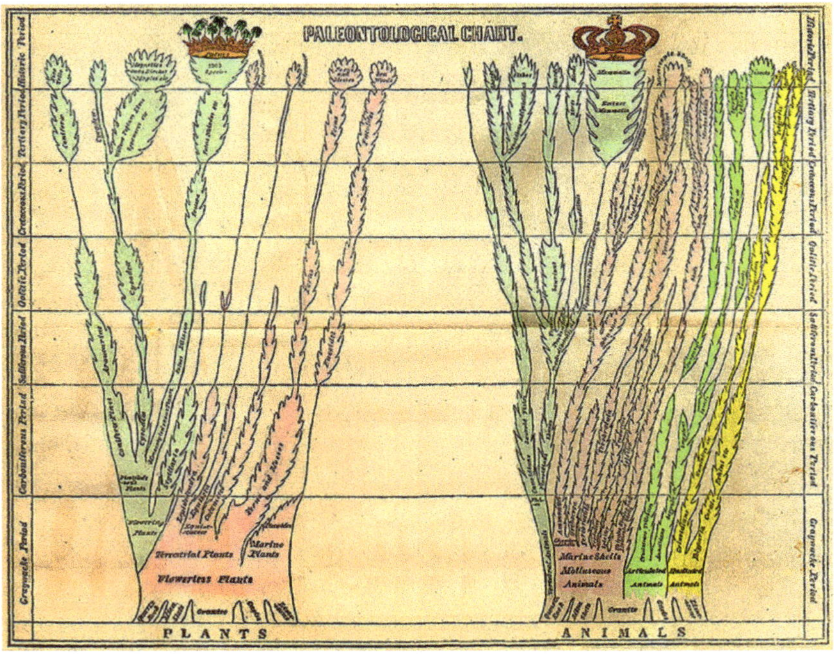

Fig. II.14 "Paleontological Chart". Edward Hitchcock, *Elementary Geology* (Amherst: J. S. and C. Adams, 1840), foldout vis-à-vis title page. Wikimedia, public domain, https://commons.wikimedia.org/wiki/File:Edward_Hitchcock_Paleontological_Chart.jpg

At the same time, the frontispiece of *Zoölogical Science* (1858) rather suggests that the "White race" is the original variety, as the human branch seems to unfold from them (see Figure II.13). Redfield probably had the system of Blumenbach in mind, according to which, as we have seen, the "Mongolian", "Malays", "Americans", and "Ethiopian" diverged from an original "Caucasian" form. Indeed, in the wall chart, we also find his designations, with the addition of Prichard's alternative for the "Mongolian" ("Turanian of Dr. Pritchard"). Could it be that this is why, in the wall chart as well as the frontispiece, only the 'Caucasian' variety is represented by a couple (see Figure II.13 and Figure II.15)?

Despite the fact that Redfield's diagrams rather relied on Cuvier's 'branches' and Blumenbach's 'racial geography' than on the 'racial hierarchy' of the scale of nature, the 'tree' in the wall chart is framed by a chain of being, and her 'trees' do have a hierarchal structure. Accordingly, within the book *Zoölogical Science* (1858), Cuvier's *embranchements* were reworked into a scale of nature in image and text. The kind of visual technique of having life scenes from different geological epochs follow each other in a column that Redfield employed in Figure II.16 had its own tradition – a tradition that was closely entwined with the use of geological layers as exhibited by Agassiz, Bronn, and Hitchcock in the diagrams discussed above. In congruence with the visual *scala naturae* of Figure II.16, in the text of *Zoölogical Science*, Redfield led the reader down through the animal kingdom from the *Bimana* or humans (of the vertebrates) down to the protozoa (of the radiates). The *Bimana* were presented as the link between the animals and the spiritual beings. And in the text, she also applied the scale to produce clear hierarchies within the climatically and culturally based human varieties, from the Khoekhoe to the "Caucasians": "In respect both to mental power, and attainments in art and science, the Caucasians have ever stood in the foremost rank" (Redfield 1858, 29; see Sommer 2022b, 273–76).

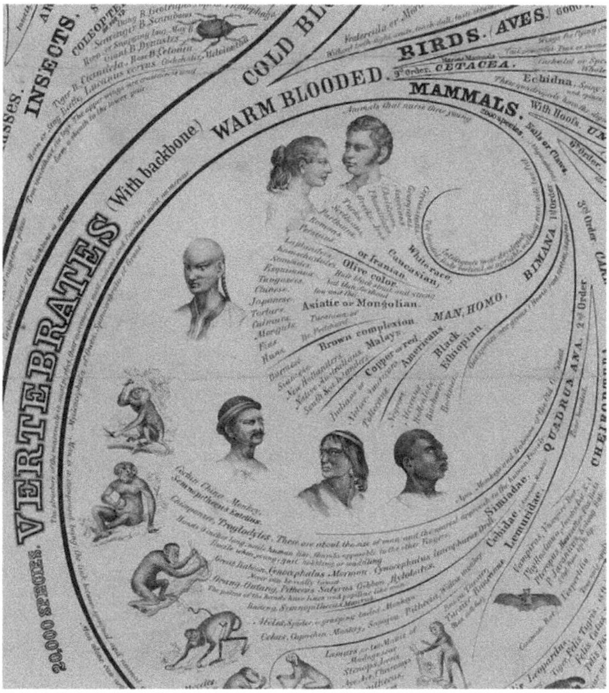

Fig. II.15 Close-up of the human 'races' in the wall chart by Anna Maria Redfield (1857). With great thanks to the Yale University Peabody Museum and Senior Collection Manager Susan H. Butts for the photograph. Public domain.

Fig. II.16 Cuvier's *embranchements* as a scale of nature. Anna Maria Redfield, *Zoölogical Science* [...] (New York: E. B. and E. C. Kellogg, 1858), Plate 2, p. 16. Public domain.

Already the champion of the *scala naturae*, Bonnet, had applied the diagram's linear hierarchy to intra-human differentiation in physical appearance, behavior, morals, intelligence, art, technology, etc. (Thienemann 1910, 239). Redfield, at her point in time, besides characteristics such as skin and hair color, made use of further criteria identified by the physical anthropologists we met in Part I to substantiate the ladder, such as the shape of the skull and face as among other things captured by the facial angle. Redfield (1858, 30) also quoted Morton as the reference regarding the different brain sizes. At the same time as expressing a racism that was seemingly scientifically based, with Blumenbach and Prichard, she emphasized human unity (29).

Thus, through the wall chart together with the frontispiece and explanations in the book, pupils should learn to differentiate the human 'races' physically and mentally. They should then be able to answer the questions in this regard provided in the book (Redfield 1858, 30–31), but, in a mix rather reminiscent of the later Prichard, the teacher may also want to combine this with exercises in geographical and historical knowledge about the customs, religions, degrees of civilization, etc. of the different peoples of the world. In sum, Redfield inscribed herself into the tradition of naturalists who regarded natural history as a way to enhance the love of God and his creation, including the 'brotherhood of men', exactly because everything had been adjusted to its place by the creator in perfect gradations (693–94). In the end, despite her reliance on the scale of nature, however, it was the tree shape that could express her vision best also with regard to humankind: the unity and at the same time the diversity, the linear gradation and hierarchy but also the differentiation (Sommer 2022b, 273–76).

As I discuss next, the coexistence of different diagrammatic elements also characterized Darwin's verbal and visual imagery, even though it was with the works of Alfred Russel Wallace and Darwin that tree metaphors and diagrams came to be used to convey a branching as well as evolutionary understanding of organismic relatedness, a phylogeny of diversification from one or a small number of original forms. In this chapter we have seen that the tree that included human diversity appeared early, if not for the first time, in educational and popular science. This hints at the diagram's ability to transfer content across scientific disciplines and between science and diverse publics. In fact, Hellström (2019) has discussed the first tree-like structures in natural history, philology, and harmony and found that each of their makers was concerned with pedagogy. This ability of the tree diagram to build bridges that we will notice for exchanges between biology and linguistics may be linked to the ubiquity of tree images in different cultural traditions, but what appears to be so straightforward carries a plethora of suppositions that already concerned Darwin. Darwin was inspired by family genealogy in the application of the genealogical view to humanity at large and, from there, to the entire living world. One might therefore think that the use of tree imagery suggested itself. However, he was skeptical of detailed phylogenies and most likely of the tree diagram in particular in its application to intra-human diversity. He left the excessive phylogenetics to Ernst Haeckel.

8. Map, Scale, and Tree in Darwin, Haeckel and Co.: The Genealogy of the Human Species

Desmond and Moore have shown that "[h]uman genealogy was more than a metaphor for Darwin's common-descent evolution. It was the prototype explanation" (2009, 375), that "racial unity was his starting point for explaining the common descent of all life using a pedigree approach" (126). Thus, like Buffon and others before him, Darwin worked with the concept of genealogy; for him, the application of family genealogy and the family tree to human history and kinship and beyond was more than metaphoric.[1] However, in spite of Darwin's strong reliance on genealogy, I argue that he was less interested in "a chartable pedigree of the whole of life" (Desmond and Moore 2009, 141) than in the mechanisms that shaped that pedigree. Furthermore, where the diagrammatics of relatedness are concerned, Darwin's use of language suggests that he was still strongly influenced by the great chain of being. In fact, Darwin does not use the word 'tree' in the sense of a genealogical tree in *The Descent of Man* (1871ab), and he very rarely draws on tree-related metaphors such as 'branch' or 'stem'. These are mostly contained to his discussion of primate phylogeny. Interestingly enough, Darwin drew a phylogenetic tree of the primates in the context of his work on *Descent*, but he did not include it in the book (Voss 2010, 243).

That Darwin did not omit his tree of the primates due to a general disregard for the value of images in the generation and communication

1 Arthur J. Thomson has noted that already Kant "speaks of 'the great Family of creatures, for as a Family we must conceive it, if the above-mentioned continuous and connected relationship has a real foundation'" (1909, 6).

 https://doi.org/10.11647/OBP.0396.10

of knowledge becomes clear from their importance to his work. Scholars like Julia Voss (2010) have shown the enormous epistemic power the production and use of images had for Darwin. They have also brought to light the relations to the arts and the wider context of Darwin's visual culture (e.g., Donald and Munro 2009; Smith 2009). Against this backdrop, it comes as a surprise that there are no images of humans in *Descent* (1871ab), except of a human embryo and ear, even despite the book's main title. The imagery that is mostly taken from publications of other authors – such as Alfred Brehm's *Tierleben* – largely concerns Darwin's reasonings on sexual selection in animals. Regarding *Descent*, Voss (2010, Ch. 3) thus mainly focuses on the famous pictures of (the ornaments on) the Argus pheasant's feathers. More specifically regarding my interest, scholars have studied Darwin's diagramming in the context of his scientific practice, in the context of thinking about phylogenies (Priest 2018). So why not publish the phylogeny of the primates that he drew when working on *Descent*?

The omission of the tree diagram from the publication seems all the more significant considering Heather Brink-Roby's argument with regard to Darwin's famous foldout 'tree-like' diagram in *On the Origin of Species* (1859) that the seriality of written language made naturalists like Darwin recognize the necessity for diagrams to convey their novel understanding of natural relations as non-linear (Brink-Roby 2009). At the same time, it has become clear that naturalists devised diagrams other than tree structures for nonlinear conceptions, that branching structures did not have to stand for evolutionary relations, and that these could still represent mostly linear and progressive models. Furthermore, as Redfield's earliest trees that include the human 'races' indicate, tree thinking and iconography may produce 'racial hierarchies'. As we will see, the tree structure can even be seen as reifying what Darwin is said to have combated: polygenism. So how exactly did Darwin capture the descent of 'man'?

In the first chapter of *Descent*, Darwin elaborated from comparative anatomy, comparative embryology, and rudimentary organs that 'man' descended from the animal kingdom. In the process of reconstructing man's genealogy – or "pedigree" (Darwin 1871a, 213), as he also called it – he employed words from the semantic field of the *scala naturae*. He tried to establish hierarchies of infinite gradations, specifically with regard to mental powers, throughout the animal kingdom and within humankind:

> We must also admit that there is a much wider interval in mental power between one of the lowest fishes, as a lamprey or lancelet, and one of the higher apes, than between an ape and man; yet this immense interval is filled up by numberless gradations. Nor is the difference slight in moral disposition [...] and in intellect, between a savage who does not use any abstract terms, and a Newton or Shakspeare [sic]. Differences of this kind between the highest men of the highest races and the lowest savages, are connected by the finest gradations. Therefore it is possible that they might pass and be developed into each other. (Darwin 1871a, 35)

As we have seen, the *scala-naturae* concept and image stem from a time before Darwin and predate an evolutionary conception of the living world (Lovejoy 1964), but the associated notions of a complete chain, a series without gaps, and a hierarchy of infinite gradations have a strong presence in Darwin's wordings, as is further exemplified in these phrases: "the animals which come next to him ['man'] in the series"; "[i]n the vertebrate series"; "some animals extremely low in the scale"; "the ascending organic scale" (1871a, 36, 46, 106). From a reasoning in terms of a scale in matters of instincts and mental faculties, Darwin consequently conveyed the evolution of cultural traits such as 'religion' along similar lines: "The same high mental faculties which first led man to believe in unseen spiritual agencies, then in fetishism, polytheism, and ultimately in monotheism, would infallibly lead him, as long as his reasoning powers remained poorly developed, to various strange superstitions and customs" (68).

One of the basis of evidence for Darwin's gradual scale of physical, mental, and cultural development was the use of ontogeny as an analogy for phylogeny:

> In a future chapter I shall make some few remarks on the probable steps and means by which the several mental and moral faculties of man have been gradually evolved. That this at least is possible ought not to be denied, when we daily see their development in every infant; and when we may trace a perfect gradation from the mind of an utter idiot, lower than that of the lowest animal, to the mind of a Newton. (Darwin 1871a, 106)

Even though Darwin turned what appeared to him to be contemporary developmental and 'racial' scales into progressive evolutionary lines of descent, the way in which the parallel between ontogeny and phylogeny was conceptualized had undergone a change. Karl Ernst von Baer's

(1828–37) description of ontogeny as a process of differentiation and individuation had been analogized to the view of evolution as a system of divergent development. Thereby, the ideal (*Naturphilosophie*) and/or non-evolutionary (Cuvier, Richard Owen, von Baer) notion of archetypes of taxonomic groups such as fish, reptiles, birds, and mammals had been turned into real common progenitors, even if their fossil bones had not yet been found.[2] As we have seen, Cuvier worked with a system of *embranchements* to arrange the animal kingdom, and his writing that Darwin had taken onto the *Beagle* was one site where the latter met with the idea of "the various branches of the great family of mankind" (Cuvier 1827, 155). Now Darwin integrated von Baerian embryology and a view of evolution as a process of divergence in a recapitulationist framework. Already in the notebooks of the late 1830s, he had embraced recapitulation theory; in *On the Origin of Species* (1859), he argued:

> As the embryonic state of each species and group of species partially shows us the structure of their less modified ancient progenitors, we can clearly see why ancient and extinct forms of life should resemble the embryos of their descendants, – our existing species [...] Embryology rises greatly in interest, when we thus look at the embryo as a picture, more or less obscured, of the common parent-form of each great class of animals. (449–50)

The von Baerian principle of differentiation suggested not a linear scale as the natural system but a tree structure. In his scandalous, because transformationist, *Vestiges of the Natural History of Creation* (1844), Robert Chambers had actually deduced an evolutionary tree-like diagram from embryological reasoning (see Figure II.17; Archibald 2014, 68–69). According to this diagram, the fetus of all the classes advances up to point A, then the embryological path of the fish diverges, the same is true for the reptiles and birds at later stages in the advance to the mature mammals. Chambers prompted his readers to continue the diagram in their heads, adding more and more ramifications as they included the orders, tribes, families, genera, and so on in the diagram "of the affinities of genealogy" (Chambers 1844, 212–13; quote from Chambers 1845, 73; see also Bowler 2021, 55).

2 On recapitulation theory see Russell 1916; Ospovat 1976; Gould 1977; Sommer 2005a, 238.

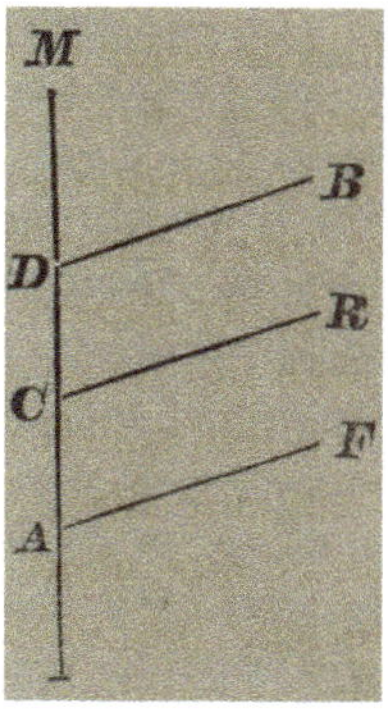

Fig. II.17 "Diagram". Robert Chambers, *Vestiges of the Natural History of Creation* (London: John Churchill, 1844), p. 212. Public domain.

The tree structure could also solve another problem that appeared when adding a time-dimension to the animate world: some living animal groups seemed not to have been modified as much as others. As Darwin wrote in *Descent*: "Some old forms appear to have survived from inhabiting protected sites, where they have not been exposed to very severe competition." Only within the structure of a tree can such 'old' contemporary forms not only be explained, but also provide insights into phylogeny, for "these often aid us in constructing our genealogies, by giving us a fair idea of former and lost populations" (1871a, 212). There appeared to be a simultaneity of the non-simultaneous visible in the current organismic diversity, a phenomenon that complicated kinship and could only be accommodated by the tree model. In the conclusion to the sixth chapter of *Descent*, Darwin once more expressed the importance of von Baerian embryology for this kind of genealogy of the living world:

> The best definition of advancement or progress in the organic scale ever given, is that by Von Baer [sic]; and this rests on the amount of differentiation and specialisation of the several parts of the same being, when arrived, as I should be inclined to add, at maturity. Now as organisms have become slowly adapted by means of natural selection for diversified lines of life, their parts will have become, from the advantage gained by the division of physiological labour, more and more differentiated and specialised for various functions [...] But each organism will still retain the general type of structure of the progenitor from which it was aboriginally derived. In accordance with this view it seems, if we turn to geological evidence, that organisation on the whole

> has advanced throughout the world by slow and interrupted steps. (Darwin 1871a, 211)[3]

Thus, the model of differentiation from the homogeneous to the heterogeneous, from the simple to the complex, though taking the form of a tree, still allowed for progress in the "organic scale". Correspondingly, Darwin's sixth chapter is about the "Position of man in the animal series" and at the same time about the proof that "The natural system [is] genealogical" (Darwin 1871a, 185). In fact, despite the renewed reference to the series, this chapter relates to the tree of primates that Darwin drew on 21 April 1868, but did not publish in *Descent* (see Figure II.18). J. David Archibald (2014, 106–112) provides a close reading of the diagram and reconstructs the steps through which it possibly went. In the following, I focus on how far it corresponds with the passages in *Descent*, and it seems that said Chapter 6 is the verbal consequence of the drawing experiment with ink on paper.

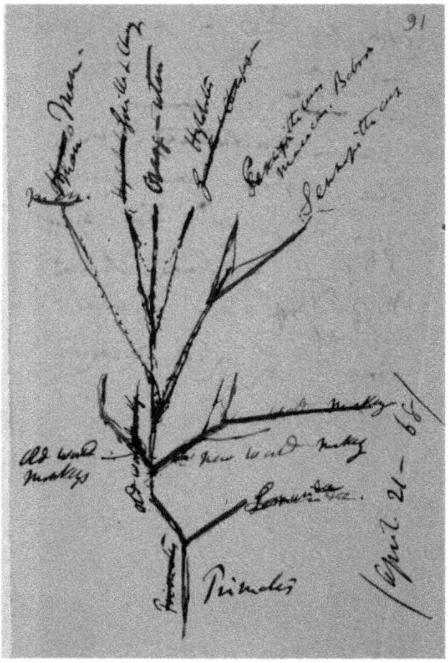

Fig. II.18 Tree of primates by Charles Darwin (Cambridge University Library MS DAR 80; B91r, https://cudl.lib.cam.ac.uk/view/MS-DAR-00080/227, all rights reserved). Reproduced by kind permission of the Syndics of Cambridge University Library.

3 Note that one of Darwin's unpublished pages from the 1850s actually shows his experimenting with combining comparative embryology and phylogeny in the construction of genealogical trees (Priest 2018, 162–64).

Darwin agreed with Linné and Thomas Henry Huxley that humans did not constitute a separate order from the primates. He suggested that it was a question of how to weigh which characteristics. Darwin had worked with the "simile of tree and classification" for some time (Darwin to Hooker, 23 December 1859, in F. Darwin 1887, Vol. II, 247), and following the metaphor of the tree, he could now speculate about some branches growing faster than others in the tree of the primates:

> If we imagine three lines of descent proceeding from a common source, it is quite conceivable that two of them might after the lapse of ages be so slightly changed as still to remain as species of the same genus; whilst the third line might become so greatly modified as to deserve to rank as a distinct Sub-family, Family, or even Order. But in this case it is almost certain that the third line would still retain through inheritance numerous small points of resemblance with the other two lines. (Darwin 1871a, 195)

Although attaching most importance to the great modifications, and thus providing 'man' with a special place would be "the safest", the many little similarities seemed to suggest that integrating 'man' within the primates was "the most correct as giving a truly natural classification" (Darwin 1871a, 195).

As visualized in Figure II.18, Darwin went further than Huxley (1869, 99) and concluded that "under a genealogical point of view it appears that this rank [of a Sub-order] is too high, and that man ought to form merely a Family, or possibly even only a Sub-family" (Darwin 1871a, 195). Also in agreement with his drawing of the tree, he suggested that a group resembling the progenitors of the *Lemuridae* "branched off into two great stems" (213), old world monkeys and new world monkeys. And via the progenitors of the *Lemuridae*, one could connect the primates to "forms standing very low in the mammalian series" (202). Again "under a genealogical point of view", 'man' was "an offshoot from the Old World Simian stem" (196). Humans belonged to the branch of the anthropoid apes (in the image labelled "Gorilla&Chimp", "Orang-utan", "Holybates") that was separate from the branch of *Semnopithecus* on the one hand and that of *Macacus* ("Cercopithecus", "Macacas", "Baboons" on the tree) on the other. "[S]ome ancient member of the anthropomorphous sub-group gave birth to man" (197), and because – as evident in the tree – the gorilla and chimpanzee were closest to 'man', one could speculate on an African origin of the human stem (199).

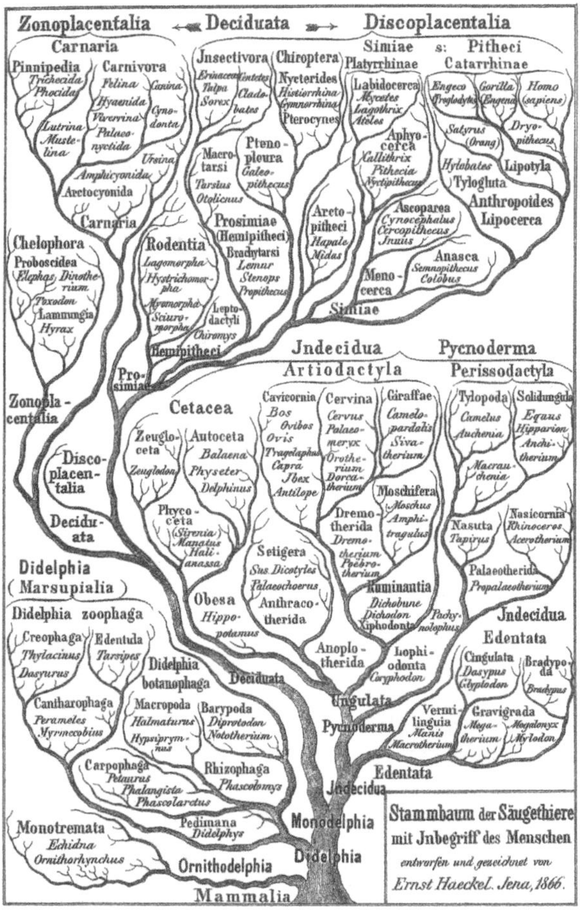

Fig. II.19 "Stammbaum der Säugethiere mit Inbegriff des Menschen" [Family tree of the mammals including humans]. Ernst Haeckel, *Generelle Morphologie der Organismen* (Berlin: Walter de Gruyter, 1866), Vol. II, Plate 8, appendix. Wikimedia, public domain, https://commons.wikimedia.org/wiki/File:Ernst_Haeckel_-_Stammbaum_der_S%C3%A4ugethiere_mit_Inbegriff_des_Menschen_(1866).tif

However, although Darwin verbally drew his tree of the primates, using language such as 'stock', 'common source', 'stem', 'diverge', 'branch (off)', 'lines (of descent)', 'offshoot', etc., he simultaneously relied on the metaphor of the chain of being, as when he wrote about "[t]he great break in the organic chain between man and his nearest allies, which cannot be bridged over by any extinct or living species [...]" (1871a, 200).

This again shows how the thinking along the lines of scales and chains that form linear hierarchies was carried over to a certain extent into the novel understanding of evolution as divergent also by Darwin. As we have already seen, he certainly used vocabulary denoting progress: "In accordance with this view it seems, if we turn to geological evidence, that organisation on the whole has advanced throughout the world by slow and interrupted steps. In the great kingdom of the Vertebrata it has culminated in man" (211–12).[4]

As discussed in the preceding chapter, when Darwin wrote *Descent*, tree-like images to capture classifications of fossil and extent forms, even such that included humans, were no longer a novelty. In fact, there already existed trees to represent understandings of phylogeny. Prior to the drawn tree of primate evolution, Darwin himself had experimented with tree-like structures on more than a dozen sheets of paper, among them an earlier and more rudimentary version of a primate phylogeny – none of which he published, however, with the exception of the one diagram that entered *On the Origin of Species* (1859) (Archibald 2012; 2014, 80–112). Francesca Bigoni and Giulio Barsanti (2011) have also drawn attention to the evolutionary primate trees of 1865 and 1867 by the British zoologist St. George Mivart that included *Homo* and predated Darwin's tree in question here, and on which Darwin drew with regard to his "genealogy of man" (1871a, 185, 196–97, quote from title of Ch. 6).

However, those who preceded Darwin with the application of antiquity and evolution to humankind, and to publications of whom Darwin referred in the introduction of *Descent* (1871a, 4), did not include human phylogenies therein: Huxley (1863), Lyell (1863), Carl Vogt (1863ab), Wallace (1864), John Lubbock (1865), Friedrich Rolle (1866), Ludwig Büchner (1868), and others.[5] The exception was Haeckel,

---

4 On the ambiguities in Darwin's thinking that found expression in the metaphor of the tree that could encompass teleology and hierarchical judgment as well as accommodate social inequality, see also Hellström 2012.

5 In their influential books, Huxley, and to a lesser extent Lyell, made use of the kinds of diagrams that we have found introduced into anthropology in Part I in order to establish hierarchical ('racial') series (for example superimpositions of skulls), including the 'fossil races', but they did not provide phylogenies. Huxley had published an article in which he included a diagram to show his classification of the human stocks on the basis of hair structure, skull shape, and skin and hair color (1865, 269). He did not discuss this in terms of phylogeny, however. Darwin

whom Darwin (1871a, 4) singled out from among his precursors with regard to human evolution. Haeckel had published eight phylogenies in the form of trees in *Generelle Morphologie der Organismen*, among them a "Stammbaum der Säugetiere" [family or genealogical tree of the mammals] that contained *Homo* at the upper right hand of the image, in 1866 (see Figure II.19 above), the year Emma Darwin wrote into her diary "Prof. Haeckel came".[6] Darwin reported to Haeckel that Agassiz "was very savage at [Haeckel's] genealogical tables", which is in line with the above observation that Agassiz was aware of the support the tree diagram could lend to evolutionary theories (theories that Agassiz opposed).[7] Unimpressed by critics, Haeckel followed up with tree-like genealogies in *Natürliche Schöpfungsgeschichte* (1868), and, with *Anthropogenie* (1874), there would soon be the famous "Stammbaum des Menschen" [family tree of man] in the form of an oak with humans as the crown (Haeckel 1874, Table 12).[8]

Darwin informed Haeckel that he had shortened in his manuscript of *Descent* some of the subjects that Haeckel had treated, instead referring his readers to Haeckel. And indeed, Darwin did refer to both *Morphologie* and *Schöpfungsgeschichte* in the chapter on human genealogy in *Descent* (1871a, 199, 203; Darwin to Haeckel, 23 June 1870, in *Ernst Haeckel Online Briefedition*, Ernst Haeckel Haus Jena, https://haeckel-briefwechsel-projekt.uni-jena.de/de [hereafter EHA Jena], A 9877). So why not follow Haeckel also with regard to publishing the primate phylogeny? Why did Darwin use words to draw his primate tree but did not publish the diagram? In fact, Darwin considered Haeckel's trees too speculative, and when Haeckel had sent him a "genealogical tree" by letter, he expressed disagreement with aspects of it (Darwin to Haeckel, 30 March 1868, EHA Jena, A 9870). Later that year, Darwin had written the following to Haeckel, after struggling with *Morphologie* and while

(1871a, 229) drew on this paper in *Descent* to connect his evolutionary to the monogenist perspective.

6 21 October 1866, Emma Darwin's Diary 1824–82, entry for 1866, CUL-DAR242[.30] (in Wyhe 2002). It appears to have been their first personal encounter (Darwin to Haeckel, 20 October 1866, in *Ernst Haeckel Online Briefedition*, Ernst Haeckel Haus Jena, https://haeckel-briefwechsel-projekt.uni-jena.de/de [hereafter EHA Jena], A 9864).

7 Darwin to Haeckel, 4 July 1867, EHA Jena, A 9868.

8 For reproductions of Haeckel's trees, also from other than first editions, see Pietsch 2012, 98–122.

"reading a good deal" in *Schöpfungsgeschichte*, the style of which was "beautifully clear and easy" (Darwin to Haeckel, 19 November 1868, in F. Darwin 1887, Vol. 3, 104; see also EHA Jena, A 9873):[9]

> Your boldness, however, sometimes makes me tremble, but as Huxley remarked some one must be bold enough to make a beginning in drawing up tables of descent. Although you fully admit the imperfection of the geological record, yet Huxley agreed with me in thinking that you are sometimes rather rash in venturing to say at what periods the several groups first appeared. (Darwin to Haeckel, 19 November 1868, in F. Darwin 1887, Vol. 3, 105)

Similarly, in the fifth edition of *On the Origin of Species* (1869 [1859], 515) of around that time, Darwin adopted Haeckel's term 'phylogeny', but considered Haeckel's actual drawings of the lines of descent "bold[]" and "in the future" of classification. It is also noteworthy that in the letter to his "dear Haeckel" quoted above, Darwin used the word 'tables' instead of 'trees', again referring to an older tradition of visualizing natural affinities. As stated at the beginning of this chapter, the word 'tree', in the sense of phylogenetic tree, is absent from *Descent*, and on the reverse side of the paper on which Darwin drew the never-published primate family tree, he wrote: "Arrangement as far as I can make out by comparing the ~~work~~ views of ~~Huxley~~ various naturalists as

9 However, Darwin later wrote to Haeckel, after having received the fourth edition of *Schöpfungsgeschichte* of 1873, that he had never been able "to read it thoroughly in German" (Darwin to Haeckel, 25 September 1873, in F. Darwin 1887, Vol. 3, 180). *Morphologie* was never translated and *Schöpfungsgeschichte* only appeared in English in 1876. Of course, Darwin would have had no problems studying the images. The answer to the question of how well Darwin was acquainted with the text of *Schöpfungsgeschichte* is further complicated by what Darwin wrote about it in the introduction of *Descent*: "If this work had appeared before my essay had been written, I should probably never have completed it. Almost all the conclusions at which I have arrived I find confirmed by this naturalist, whose knowledge on many points is much fuller than mine. Wherever I have added any fact or view from Prof. Häckel's [sic] writings, I give his authority in the text, other statements I leave as they originally stood in my manuscript, occasionally giving in the foot-notes references to his works, as a confirmation of the more doubtful or interesting points" (1871a, 4). While Darwin had obviously been first with his evolutionary theory and very much welcomed Haeckel's great support in campaigning for it, Haeckel had applied an evolutionary perspective to humans prior to Darwin, and even though Darwin paid tribute to this in his introduction to *Descent*, Haeckel felt he could have referenced his work more.

in whose judgment much reliance can be placed – For myself I have no clues whatever to form an opinion" (Cambridge University Library MS DAR 80; B91v, cited in Archibald 2014, 112).

In short, although for Darwin tree drawing obviously constituted an important technique of mental experimentation on evolutionary mechanisms as well as organismic relations, he was cautious with regard to fleshed-out phylogenies, and indeed hardly ever entered the names of taxa into his nearly twenty unpublished tree-like sketches (for a discussion and reproductions of the drawings, see Archibald 2014, 80–112). In the context of his paraphrasing the tree of primate phylogeny in *Descent*, Darwin hinted at his reservations about attempts at reconstruction beyond the mammals:

> In attempting to trace the genealogy of the Mammalia, and therefore of man, lower down in the series, we become involved in greater and greater obscurity. He who wishes to see what ingenuity and knowledge can effect, may consult Prof. Häckel's [sic] works. I will content myself with a few general remarks. (1871a, 203)

With reference to Haeckel's genealogical diagrams in *Generelle Morphologie* (1866) and, with regard to 'man', in *Natürliche Schöpfungsgeschichte* (1868), Darwin in this passage of *Descent* once more brought to the fore the force of the tree as an icon that can combine a dendritic pedigree with serial or linear progress. The imagery in the quote appears geological, with the strata lower in the series being less illuminated. This coalesces nicely with the notion that Darwin himself would dare only a few remarks on a subject largely in the dark, so that Haeckel's so-called "ingenuity" seems to denote 'inventiveness'. As already alluded to, specific phylogenies by Haeckel were contested by others,[10] and Darwin was not alone in criticizing Haeckel's bold speculations – Rudolf Virchow, for one, even called him a "fanatic" with regard to his construction of overall concrete

10 E.g., Wilhelm Olbers Focke to Haeckel, 1 July 1867, EHA Jena, A 1840; Wilhelm Heinrich Immanuel Bleek to Haeckel, 25 May 1869, EHA Jena, A 7050; Wilhelm Breitenbach to Haeckel, 20 September 1895, EHA Jena, A 5951; Wilhelm Breitenbach to Haeckel, 18 March 1908, EHA Jena, A 6043.

systems of descent in the form of family trees (my translation from Virchow to Haeckel, 25 January 1868, EHA Jena, A 43743).[11]

Haeckel was obsessed with family genealogy as well as evolutionary phylogeny, which were often more or less humorously linked in his correspondence (see, e.g., his correspondence with Max Fürbringer, EHA Jena; Ernst Haeckel to Charlotte Haeckel, 8 February 1868, EHA Jena, A 38707). But could it be that Darwin also thought of Haeckel's trees as too progressive and even teleological, as too hierarchical, and, in some cases, as too focused on humans? After all, Haeckel put Darwin's theory on a par with Lamarck's and Johann Wolfgang von Goethe's, thus emphasizing the inheritance of acquired characteristics and particularly his biogenetic law, the very strong expression of the notion that ontogeny recapitulates phylogeny. In Haeckel's work, the merging of the *scala naturae* with the branching structure is obvious in his derivation of the tree from the line: the ontogeny and evolution of one species are progressive and linear processes; the tree form that mirrors the natural classification system only results from comparative embryology and paleontology. Haeckel referred to this phenomenon as the three-fold parallelism, a parallelism in tree structure. It allowed humans to remain the apex of evolutionary history (Haeckel 1868, 227–58; on Haeckel's tree building, see Dayrat 2003; Sommer 2015b, 40–45).

For Darwin, to the contrary, if 'man' was the apex of the living world, as many passages in *Descent* suggest, then this was the result of contingence and could only be seen in retrospect, by this very being who had acquired a high degree of intelligence and who tended to form the world in its own shape:

> Thus we have given to man a pedigree of prodigious length, but not, it may be said, of noble quality. The world, it has often been remarked, appears as if it had long been preparing for the advent

11 Darwin had generally cautioned Haeckel against expressing his views too loudly and attacking other opinions too forcefully. It seemed to him "doubtful policy to speak too positively on any complex subject however much a man may feel convinced of the truth of his own conclusions" – in contrast to such an approach, Darwin saw the merit of his own work in "the large accumulation of facts by which certain positions are I think established" (Darwin to Haeckel, 12 April 1867, EHA Jena, A 9866). Again, it seems that statements like "I [...] admired the boldness of your expressions" might have been polite talk (Darwin to Haeckel, 19 July 1864, EHA Jena, A 9857).

> of man; and this, in one sense is strictly true, for he owes his birth to a long line of progenitors. If any single link in this chain had never existed, man would not have been exactly what he now is. Unless we wilfully close our eyes, we may, with our present knowledge, approximately recognise our parentage; nor need we feel ashamed of it. The most humble organism is something much higher than the inorganic dust under our feet; and no one with an unbiassed mind can study any living creature, however humble, without being struck with enthusiasm at its marvellous structure and properties. (1871a, 213)

While the analogy to family genealogy (of the Victorian aristocracy) seems particularly strong in this passage, we find a cacophony of images and messages: 'an ignoble pedigree' versus 'the ascending links in the chain of being'; 'there is always one lower down this chain' versus 'every organism needs to be valued on its own terms'. But one thing seemed clear: the world had only been prepared for 'man' in 'man's eyes'. Maybe this 'illusion' was one of the pitfalls of tree building. Phylogenetic trees focused on the outcome rather than the process or even the history of evolution. They tended to obscure the false starts, stutters, reversals, and the crisscrossing. Voss (2010, Ch. 2) has situated Darwin's diagrams that culminated in the one in *On the Origin of Species* in the attempts to capture the natural order in drawing during this time, and she emphasizes the importance Darwin put on a visual language for the unpredictability and irregularity of the process that brought about 'that order'. Obviously, Darwin had not freed himself entirely of the notion of progress that was associated with the scale of nature. At the same time, the phylogenetic trees in circulation might have occurred to him as still too strongly associated with this concept, even if they also expressed the idea of divergence. So, while Desmond and Moore (2009) are certainly right in that Darwin strongly relied on notions of genealogy, pedigree, and descent, it seems that he considered phylogenetic trees with caveats – and such caveats are most expedient when the tree icon is used to convey intra-human phylogeny (Sommer 2021, 48–54).

9. Map, Scale, and Tree in Darwin, Haeckel and Co.: The Genealogy of the Human 'Races'

That the tree-like structures that came to be proposed as representations of phylogenies could still encompass the notion of a linear sequence seems to have been particularly true for anthropology, where the acceptance of human antiquity and the turn towards evolutionism added the parameters of time and development to a 'racial hierarchy' already in place. Incorporating the new insights from comparative ethnology and prehistoric archeology, an inevitable series of ever higher cultural and anatomical stages came to be seen as mandatory passages for all human 'races' and civilizations.[1] The 'savage races' came to be understood as simultaneously offshoots of the line leading to the 'modern civilized races' and stages through which the latter had passed in their evolution. They were projected back in time, so that a *scala-naturae* structure was essentially maintained within the diagram of the tree (Sommer, e.g., 2015b, Part 1).

That Darwin shared this conceptualization of a series of steps in a general advancement finds expression in *Descent*:

> The evidence that all civilised nations are the descendants of barbarians, consists, on the one side, of clear traces of their former low condition in still-existing customs, beliefs, language, &c.; and on the other side, of proofs that savages are independently able to

1 The literature on these issues is expansive, if not focused on diagrams of relatedness. Among the classics are certainly George Stocking's works, for example, *Race, Culture, and Evolution: Essays in the History of Anthropology* (1968).

 https://doi.org/10.11647/OBP.0396.11

> raise themselves a few steps in the scale of civilisation, and have actually thus risen. (1871a, 181)

This progression from 'savage to civilized', or 'primitive to modern', was again analogized to individual embryonic development, which drew attention to so-called 'atavisms'. A recapitulationist model of evolution suggested that stagnation or reversion in embryonic development resulted in an individual that in certain aspects represented more primitive phylogenetic stages:

> *Arrests of Development.*– [...] It will suffice for our purpose to refer to the arrested brain-development of **microcephalous idiots** [...] Their skulls are smaller, and the convolutions of the brain are less complex than in normal men. The frontal sinus, or the projection over the eye-brows, is largely developed, and the jaws are prognathous to an '*effrayant*' degree; so that these idiots somewhat resemble **the lower types of mankind**. Their intelligence and most of their mental faculties are extremely feeble [...] They often ascend stairs **on all-fours**; and are curiously fond of **climbing up furniture or trees**. We are thus reminded of the delight shewn by almost all **boys** in climbing trees [...]. (Darwin 1871a, 121–22, my emphases in bold)[2]

In this discussion of the phenomenon of arrest of development, supposedly phylogenetically and ontogenetically earlier and lower stages, such as "the lower types of mankind", children, and apes (and quadrupeds), are brought in to characterize the arrested or reverted state of "microcephalous idiots". It seems as though the 'atavistic' trait of a microcephalous brain rendered the affected individuals 'atavistic' in morphology and behavior more generally. They showed anatomical characters that we have seen established as markers of primitiveness in Part I: small skulls, protruding brow ridges, and prognathism. Thus, von Baerian embryology, when translated into evolutionary embryology (and the notion of atavism this suggested), functioned as an integrative element between the 'older' linear conceptions of the order of beings and the concept of organismic divergence, since there seemed to be

2 Darwin based his speculations on the microcephalous condition on Vogt, who argued that fossil hominids, supposedly 'lower extant races', and 'microcephalous idiots' represent missing links between the living 'White races' and the recent great apes (Vogt 1863b, 277–79).

evidence that organisms, including humans, could fall from their branches of the family tree, as it were, and land on a lower branch, or rather, at a fork in the tree. In the atavism and throwback survived the notion of the missing link that, as we have seen, was etymologically as well as conceptually connected to the image of the great chain of being (Sommer 2005a, 239–40).

While there was a 'racial hierarchy' in the human family tree from the beginning, which I have noted for Redfield's trees, some anthropologists still considered the tree diagram suitable to express the monogenist understanding of human diversity. In *Descent*, Darwin made frequent reference to Jean Louis Armand de Quatrefages' *Unité de l'espèce humaine* (1861a). As we have seen in Chapter 5, de Quatrefages was a monogenist but not an evolutionist. Together with his colleague Isidore Geoffroy Saint-Hilaire, he emphasized the utility of the tree, the branches of which all lead back to the same stem, as the form to capture the relations of the races of a species (Quatrefages 1861b, 436 and note 437; also 1861a, 70–72). De Quatrefages positioned this diagram of human relatedness against the erroneous doctrines of 'the heads of the American school of anthropology' (namely Morton, Josiah Clark Nott, and George Robin Gliddon) as well as against Paul Broca in his own country. Although for de Quatrefages intra-human diversity was of a gradual nature, and although he emphasized the process of "croisement" [crossing] (already in the title of his work), he considered the tree, when thought of as spread on the globe, a good diagram to represent the monogenist history of humanity.

In communicating his own monogenist view, Darwin like de Quatrefages relied on the tradition of monogenism discussed in Part I that promoted a narrative of human history in accordance with the religious perception of a common origin with subsequent dispersal across the earth. In the *Beagle* library had been Lyell's indispensable *Principles of Geology*, in which Darwin read about the "the great human family" that extended "over the habitable globe" (1832, 62):

> We may refer the reader to the writings of Blumenbach, Prichard, Lawrence, and others, for convincing proofs that the varieties of form, colour, and organization of different races of men, are perfectly consistent with the generally received opinion, that all the individuals of the species have originated from a single

> pair; and while they exhibit in man as many diversities of a physiological nature, as appear in any other species, they confirm also the opinion of the slight deviation from a common standard of which a species is capable. (Lyell 1832, 62)

It was also Lyell who, viewing the earth through geological time, so influentially came to accept the newly known 'fossil races of man' as part of this human family. Regarding the Neanderthals, he wrote in *The Geological Evidences of the Antiquity of Man* of 1863 to which Darwin referred in the introduction of *Descent* (1871a, 4): "The human skeletons of the Belgian caverns of times coeval with the mammoth and other extinct mammalia do not betray any signs of a marked departure in their structure, whether of skull or limb, from the modern standard of certain living races of the human family" (Lyell 1863, 375). As discussed in the introduction to this part, Darwin had knowledge of the ideas of scholars like Blumenbach, Prichard, and William Lawrence, discussed in Part I, not only through Lyell. For example, the abstract of a talk Prichard had given at the meeting of the British Association for the Advancement of Science in 1832 had been on board the *Beagle*, in which Prichard brought together the evidence from philology and natural history to argue for monogenism and against polygenism: the proofs these fields constituted for the connectedness of "the branches of the human family" (Prichard 1833, 530). It had, among others, been Chambers who made this genealogical view of "the branches of the human family" (1844, 314) part of an evolutionary interpretation of the living world as a whole that gave new vigor to the search for the geographic origin and ways of dispersal of humankind. I have reproduced Chambers' embryonic tree of vertebrate development in the preceding chapter (Figure II.17), and also in this respect, he progressed diagrammatically:

> Assuming that the human race is *one*, we are next called upon to inquire in what part of the earth it may most probably be supposed to have originated. One obvious mode of approximating to a solution of this question is to trace backward the lines in which the principal tribes appear to have migrated, and to see if these converge nearly to a point. It is very remarkable that the lines do converge, and are concentrated about the region of Hindostan. (Chambers 1844, 294–95)

When drawing lines back along the migration routes of the various peoples, branches of the human family tree would successively merge until they converged in a single trunk (even though Chambers' racism made him have some doubts with regard to the Black African line [see 1844, 296]). The tree structure of human kinship was thus, on the one hand, established through the migratory understanding of human history and genealogy (already instantiated in Christian narratives and images of Noah's progeny), and, on the other hand, as on the species and higher levels of evolution, through the understanding of comparative embryonic development, according to which individuals belonging to the "Caucasian type" passed through stages similar to the embryos of 'lower races' (Chambers 1844, 306–307): "*The leading characters, in short, of the various races of mankind, are simply representations of particular stages in the development of the highest or Caucasian type*" (307).

Furthermore, it was from the genealogical understanding of the family of humankind that Darwin conceptualized the pedigree of all living organisms, and underlying the genealogical conception of 'man' was the family unit relating all individuals in degrees as in an *arbor consanguinitatis* (see Figure II.20). In Notebook C from 1838, Darwin wrote: "I cannot help thinking good analogy might be traced between relationship of all men now living & the classification of animals. — talking of men as related in the third & fourth degree. —" (38).[3] The 'father' of kinship studies, the American ethnologist Lewis Henry Morgan, who was among Darwin's acquaintances, and on whose work Darwin drew in *Descent*, actually made use of the *arbor consanguinitatis* in his seminal *Systems of Consanguinity and Affinity of the Human Family* (1871). The diagram shown as Figure II.20 and modifications thereof were published in the appendix to Morgan's book. Through them, Morgan made visible his main argument: while the Roman system of kin terms was nearly perfectly descriptive (reflecting actual blood relations within societies that are strictly structured by monogamous marriage), and the British constituted a variation thereof, other societies had much

3 Darwin , C. R. 1859 [1964]. 1838.02–1838.07. *Notebook* C: [Transmutation of species]. CUL-DAR122 (in Wyhe 2002). Of course, already *On the Origin of Species* (not only *Descent*) was understood as reconstructing "the genealogy of man", in which "the monkey is his brother" and "the horse his cousin" (e.g. Bowen 1860, 475). Especially in more popular accounts, one encounters human kin terms applied to the animal kingdom, as for example in Dennis Hird's *An Easy Outline of Evolution*: "By the whole theory of Evolution, the highest ape can only be a far distant cousin of the human family, and cousins far removed do not look for any connecting link except ancestry, and this link we have already abundantly furnished" (1903, 212).

less differentiated systems (which Morgan called 'classificatory'). This meant that for a Seneca man (a member of an Iroquoian-speaking Native American people), for example, not only his own children, but also those of his brothers and male cousins were 'sons' and 'daughters'.

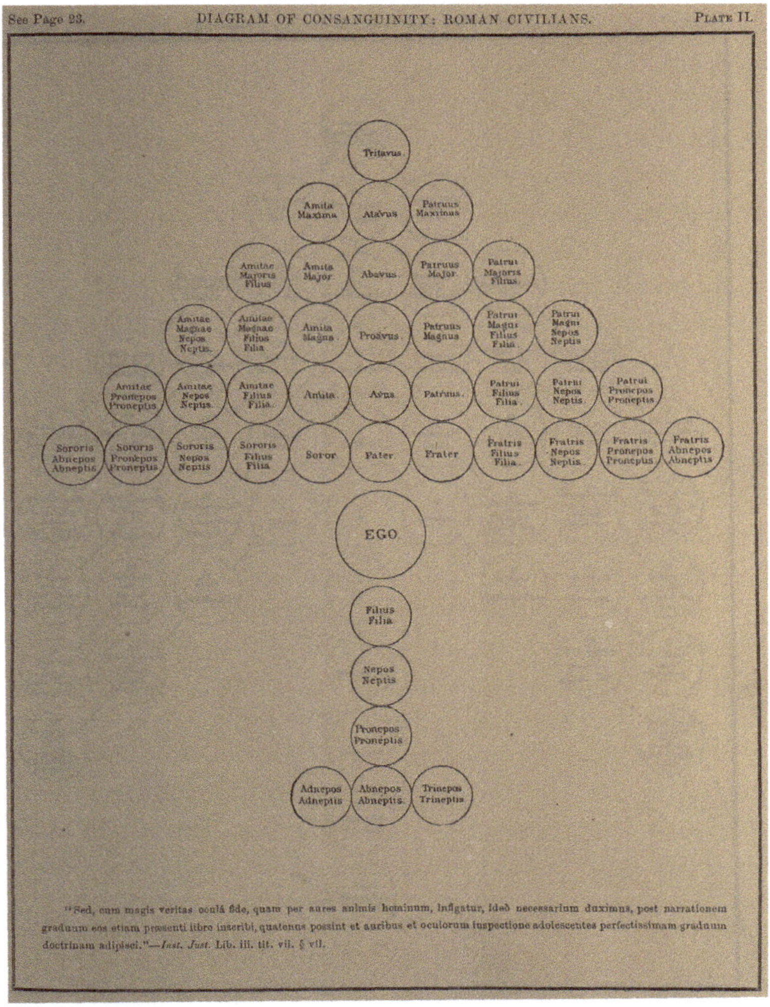

Fig. II.20 "Diagram of Consanguinity: Roman Civilians". Lewis Henry Morgan, *Systems of Consanguinity and Affinity of the Human Family* (Washington, DC: Smithsonian Institution, 1871), Plate 2, appendix. Public domain.

Morgan reasoned that such older and 'more primitive' systems of kin terms like the one of the Seneca Nation could still have been true to nature at a time when peoples were more promiscuous. On the basis of such comparisons and hierarchizations of systems of kin terms worldwide, Morgan eventually arrived at "successive stages of advancement", "successive links of a common chain" (1871, vii), "a great progressive series" (487). At the same time, situating his research in philology (which sometimes confounded languages and 'nations'), Morgan thought in terms of branches of "the entire human family" (5), thus again merging the scale with the tree. Humankind must have differentiated at a very early period into independent 'nations', and from then up until now, they have advanced to different degrees. Like Darwin, Morgan, who often referred to Prichard's writings, wanted to prove monogenism and extended from the genealogy of the family (in the sense of an *arbor consanguinitatis*) to "the human family" of his book title:

> If we ascend from ancestor to ancestor in the lineal line, and again descend through the several collateral lines until the widening circle of kindred circumscribes millions of the living and the dead, all of these individuals, in virtue of their descent from common ancestors, are bound to the '*Ego*' by the chain of consanguinity. (Morgan 1871, 11)

We have already seen that the research on the history of languages was another important element in the turn towards tree thinking, drawing as it was on the image of the Tower of Babel and the confusion of tongues as well as on the biblical stories of Adam and Eve and of Noah's descendants. Hellström (2019, 137–52) has actually discussed an early nineteenth-century tree of languages that not only looked like a family genealogy but that was also a world map, once again uniting temporal narrative, tree, and map (Fig. 3.1., 139). In *On the Origin of Species*, Darwin equated the pedigree of human 'races' with the genealogy of languages, and in *Descent* he wrote: "Languages, like organic beings, can be classed in groups under groups; and they can be classed either naturally according to descent, or artificially by other characters" (1871a, 60).

Simone Roggenbuck (2005a, 303–304) has discussed how, in the nineteenth century, scholars drew on the methods of botany and anatomy to conceptualize the practices of collection and classification in the comparative study of languages as a way to unravel their genealogy and history. Like the boom in biological classification, these linguistic practices related to the blossoming of colonial and missionary activities.

The introduction of the genealogical tree into linguistics was at first a parallel phenomenon to the emerging field of evolutionary biology. The German philologist August Schleicher published his first language tree in 1853. Subsequently, however, tree building in the separate fields took place under reciprocal influence (see Figure II.21). Schleicher's impact was especially great on Haeckel, for whom the only natural system consisted in the genealogical or family tree, in 'the true phylogeny'. Through Haeckel, Schleicher read Darwin, and Darwin was made aware of Schleicher's notion of the evolution of languages.[4]

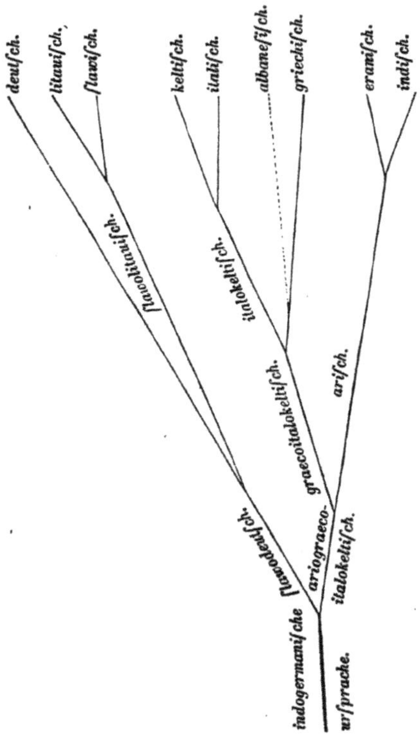

Fig. II.21 Indo-European language tree. August Schleicher, *Compendium der vergleichenden Grammatik der indogermanischen Sprachen* (Weimar: Böhlau, 1861), p. 7. Wikimedia, public domain, https://commons.wikimedia.org/wiki/File:Schleicher_Tree.jpg

4 The literature on the exchanges between comparative philology and evolutionary biology is extensive, e.g., Alter 1999, Ch. 4 on *The Descent of Man*; Richards 2002a; 2002c, Ch. 8; for the role of arborescence in the interdisciplinary history of linguistics, see Roggenbuck 2005b. Darwin felt that Schleicher "well supported the views" he and Haeckel shared (Darwin to Haeckel, 20 December 1868, EHA Jena, A 9874; also 19 July 1864, EHA Jena, A 9857).

In view of the ubiquity of the tree diagram as metaphor, and its presence as image, in the diverse scholarly fields engaging with humankind on which Darwin drew, we may ask why, as far as we know, Darwin never even experimented on drawing a phylogenetic tree that included intra-human differentiation. The answer may be that by the time *Descent* appeared, the diagram that philologists, ethnologists, anthropologists, natural historians, etc. had applied to the relations between human varieties in a monogenist sense had already been driven beyond its initial purpose. We have seen in the last chapter that Darwin considered Haeckel's general phylogenetic trees too speculative and possibly too teleological. To this must be added that Haeckel's views on the human 'races' had already found expression in racist imagery in the form of a series of heads in profile, from monkeys, to apes, and 'primitive and higher races', up to the Greek form on the frontispiece of *Natürliche Schöpfungsgeschichte* (1868). This was meant to suggest that the 'lower human types' were much closer to the apes than to the 'higher human forms' (555). Even more to the point, in the same book Haeckel published a 'primate family tree including man', in which the *Lissotriches* ['plain-haired' humans] and *Ulotriches* ['woolly-haired' humans] arose as separate branches directly from the first speaking hominids and their invented ancestor *Pithecanthropus* ['ape-man'] or *Alalus* ['speechless man'] (Haeckel 1868, 493) (see Figure II.22).

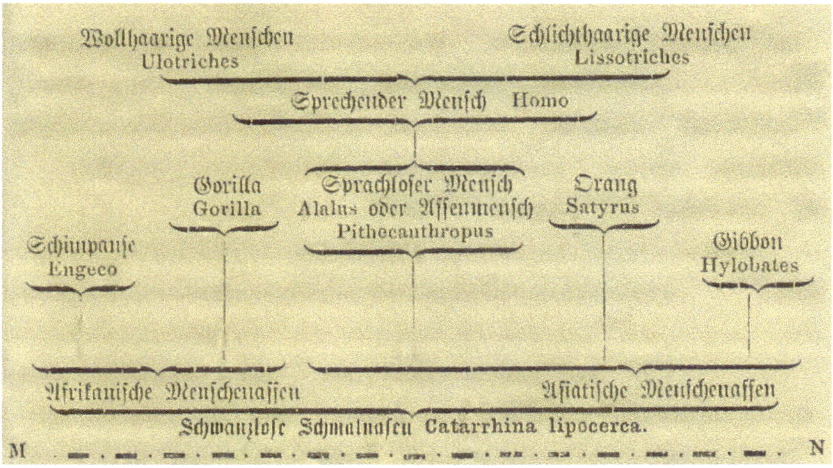

Fig. II.22 Excerpt of "Stammbaum der Affen mit Inbegriff des Menschen" [Primate family tree including man]. Ernst Haeckel, *Natürliche Schöpfungs-Geschichte* [...] (Berlin: Georg Reimer, 1868), p. 493. Public domain.

For Haeckel (1868, 512), a tree with branches separating the human groups was actually an adequate rendition, because he considered them to have the status of different species. He referred to his table of the ten human species (see Figure II.23) as indicating "Stammesverwandtschaft" [phylogenetic kinship] (512). The diagram is actually an alternative representation of a phylogenetic tree showing the human species and their 'races'. Even though Haeckel himself admitted that his genealogies were hypotheses, the table that presents his view of human descent ending with "Homo caucasicus" (species no. X) and its 'Germanic subspecies no. 40' has nothing tentative about it. The table again originally separates the *Lissotriches* and *Ulotriches* that root independently in different branches of 'primordial man' (species no. I: "Homo primigenius").

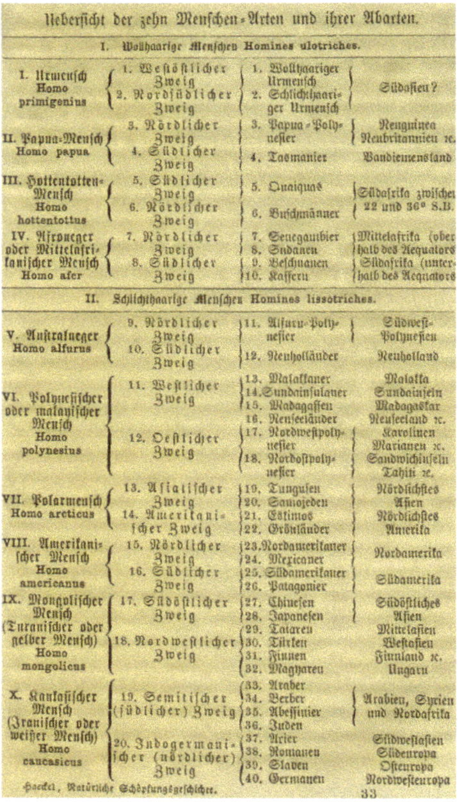
Uebersicht der zehn Menschen-Arten und ihrer Abarten.

I. Wollhaarige Menschen Homines ulotriches.			
I. Urmensch Homo primigenius	1. Westöstlicher Zweig	1. Wollhaariger Urmensch	Südasien?
	2. Nordsüdlicher Zweig	2. Schlichthaariger Urmensch	
II. Papua-Mensch Homo papua	3. Nördlicher Zweig	3. Papua-Polynesier	Neuguinea Neubritannien &c.
	4. Südlicher Zweig	4. Tasmanier	Vandiemensland
III. Hottentotten-Mensch Homo hottentottus	5. Südlicher Zweig	5. Quaiquas	Südafrika zwischen 22 und 36° S.B.
	6. Nördlicher Zweig	6. Buschmänner	
IV. Afroneger oder Mittelafrikanischer Mensch Homo afer	7. Nördlicher Zweig	7. Senegambier	Mittelafrika (oberhalb des Aequators
		8. Sudanen	
	8. Südlicher Zweig	9. Beschuanen	Südafrika (unterhalb des Aequators
		10. Kaffern	
II. Schlichthaarige Menschen Homines lissotriches.			
V. Australneger Homo alfurus	9. Nördlicher Zweig	11. Alfuru-Polynesier	Südwest-Polynesien
	10. Südlicher Zweig	12. Neuholländer	Neuholland
VI. Polynesischer oder malayischer Mensch Homo polynesius	11. Westlicher Zweig	13. Malakkaner	Malakka
		14. Sundainsulaner	Sundainseln
		15. Madagassen	Madagaskar
	12. Oestlicher Zweig	16. Neuseeländer	Neuseeland &c.
		17. Nordwestpolynesier	Karolinen Marianen &c.
		18. Nordostpolynesier	Sandwichinseln Tahiti &c.
VII. Polarmensch Homo arcticus	13. Asiatischer Zweig	19. Tungusen	Nördlichstes Asien
		20. Samojeden	
	14. Amerikanischer Zweig	21. Eskimos	Nördlichstes Amerika
		22. Grönländer	
VIII. Amerikanischer Mensch Homo americanus	15. Nördlicher Zweig	23. Nordamerikaner	Nordamerika
		24. Mexicaner	
	16. Südlicher Zweig	25. Südamerikaner	Südamerika
		26. Patagonier	
IX. Mongolischer Mensch (Turanischer oder gelber Mensch) Homo mongolicus	17. Südöstlicher Zweig	27. Chinesen	Südöstliches Asien
		28. Japanesen	
	18. Nordwestlicher Zweig	29. Tataren	Mittelasien
		30. Türken	Westasien
		31. Finnen	Finnland &c.
		32. Magyaren	Ungarn
X. Kaukasischer Mensch (Iranischer oder weißer Mensch) Homo caucasicus	19. Semitischer (südlicher) Zweig	33. Araber	Arabien, Syrien und Nordafrika
		34. Berber	
		35. Abessinier	
		36. Juden	
	20. Indogermanischer (nördlicher) Zweig	37. Arier	Südwestasien
		38. Romanen	Südeuropa
		39. Slaven	Osteuropa
		40. Germanen	Nordwesteuropa

Haeckel, Natürliche Schöpfungsgeschichte. 33

Fig. II.23 "Übersicht der zehn Menschen-Arten und ihrer Abarten" [Overview of the ten human species and subspecies]. Ernst Haeckel, *Natürliche Schöpfungs-Geschichte* [...] (Berlin: Georg Reimer, 1868), p. 513. Public domain.

Haeckel's work therefore illustrates that trees may convey polygenism. Assuming a plural or polyphyletic origin of human language in reference to Schleicher, he in analogy conjectured that the several human species had originated independently from different species of *Pithecanthropi* and had acquired the human hallmarks (including language) neither at the same time nor to the same degree (1868, 510). This conviction culminated in a phylogenetic tree of the now 'twelve species of man' differentiating from primeval forms all the way up to the 'highest species', the 'Mid-landers', and their subspecies the 'Indo-Germans', that he included in *Natürliche Schöpfungsgeschichte* from the second edition of 1870 onwards (605). The twelve human species constituted the two original stems of *Lisso-* and *Ulotriches*, although the second does not take up much space in the image but seems to be held down in the left bottom corner by the towering 'plain-haired' group. From the eighth edition of 1889 onwards, these two main stems originate in *Protanthropi* that are very close to the ape-men or *Alali* (see Figure II.24) (Sommer 2015b, 43–45; 2022b, 276–80).

It thus appears plausible that, to Darwin, a tree of intra-human kinship must have appeared even more risky than one of inter-species relatedness, because it could have contradicted his arguments against polygenism, which, as Desmond and Moore (2009) have worked out in detail, were central to *Descent* as a whole. In his seventh chapter, "On the Races of Man" (1871a, 214), Darwin worked through the arguments for and against the conception of humans as forming a single species, and he took issue with polygenist views such as those put forward by Nott and Gliddon (Darwin 1871a, 217–18). He found that the most salient argument for their status as 'races', apart from interbreeding, was that they graded into each other; that is, they did not form clearly demarcated groups: "But the most weighty of all the arguments against treating the races of man as distinct species, is that they graduate into each other, independently in many cases, as far as we can judge, of their having intercrossed" (226). This was what made it so hard to come up with a sound intra-human classification. There was no character distinctive of any 'race'. In fact, Darwin observed that even though 'man' was the best-researched animal, authors such as Julien Joseph Virey, Kant, Blumenbach, Buffon, Jean-Baptiste Bory de Saint-Vincent, Antoine Desmoulins, Morton, etc. (the subjects of Part I) disagreed on the question, with estimates for the number of 'human races or species' ranging from one to sixty-three (ibid.).

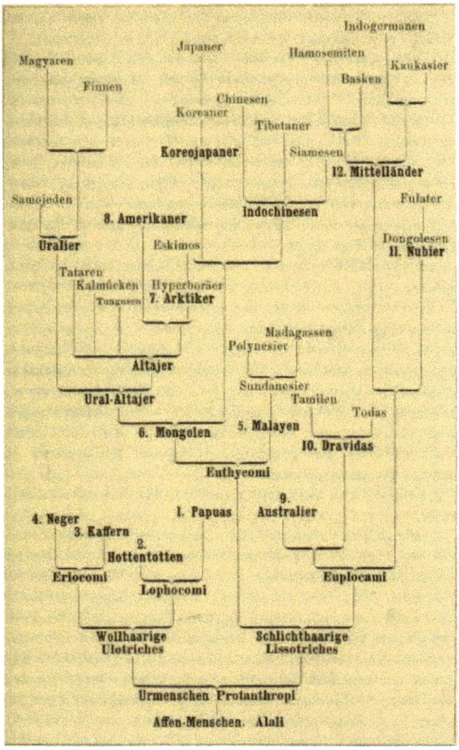

Fig. II.24 "Stammbaum der zwölf Menschen-Arten" [Genealogy of the twelve human species]. Ernst Haeckel, *Natürliche Schöpfungs-Geschichte* [...], 8th ed. (Berlin: Georg Reimer, 1889), p. 727. Public domain. (In somewhat different form, but also with two originally separated stems of *Ulo-* and *Lissotriches*, already in Haeckel's second edition, published in 1870, p. 605.)

If the living human groups do not form clearly demarcated units to begin with, then the tree that inevitably creates them as discrete, seemingly pure, and distant entities – or even as species – is the wrong tool for visualizing current human kinship. Given the tree structure would not have captured Darwin's understanding of intra-human classification adequately, would it have conformed to his view of the history of human diversification? As we have seen, trees can correspond to narratives of migration and distribution from a center across the globe, suggesting a process of differentiation without simultaneous integration. In fact, Haeckel might have been the first to make this visually obvious when, from the second edition of *Natürliche Schöpfungsgeschichte* of 1870, in which he first published the tree of the twelve human species, he projected that tree on a map of the world (Table 15). The resulting diagram indicates that humans originated on the hypothetical landmass of Lemuria, from where they began to wander and branch out, successively splitting and migrating into different regions of the globe, thereby forming the 'twelve species and their races'. Figure II.25 shows the same image from the eighth edition of *Natürliche Schöpfungsgeschichte*, thus constituting a transformation of the tree of Figure II.24 into a map of migrations. By this time, Lemuria had been replaced by South Asia as the point of origin. While Haeckel called the image a "hypothetical sketch of the monophyletic origin and the distribution of the 12 human species from South Asia across the earth" (my translation), also on the map, the "U" and "L" at the very origin of the 'tree' suggest initially separate stems of *Ulo-* and *Lissotriches*.

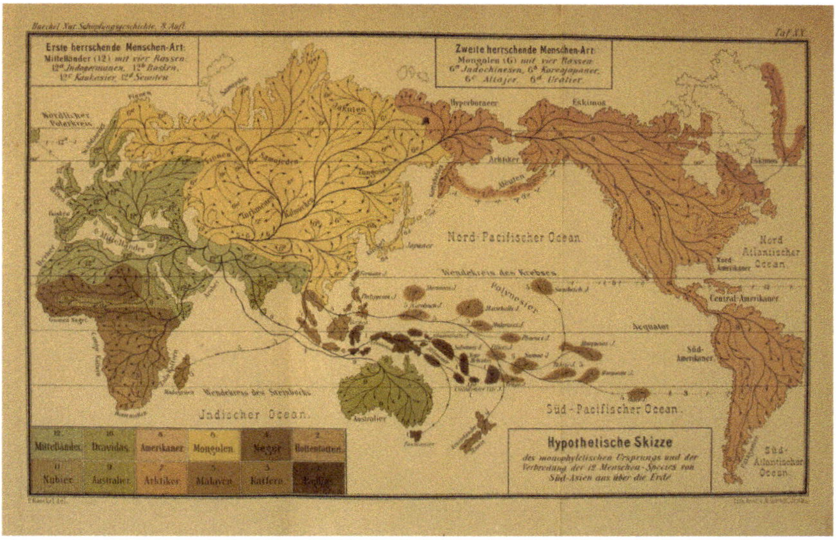

Fig. II.25 "Hypothetische Skizze des monophyletischen Ursprungs und der Verbreitung der 12 Menschen-Species von Süd-Asien aus über die Erde" [Hypothetical sketch of the monophyletic origin and the distribution of the twelve human species from South Asia across the earth]. Ernst Haeckel, *Natürliche Schöpfungs-Geschichte* [...], 8th ed. (Berlin: Georg Reimer, 1889), Plate 20, end of book. Public domain. (In a somewhat different form already in Haeckel's second edition of 1870.)

In contrast to such a tree-map diagram, in *Descent*, isolation in space through migration plays a relatively small part. Darwin did think that the differentiation of the human 'races' would have succeeded their distribution across large parts of the globe (1871a, 234). However, their characteristic differences did not correspond with climate and could not satisfactorily be explained by the direct influence of the conditions of life. Nor could they be explained by the use or disuse of parts or the principle of correlation. Most significantly, natural selection failed as an explanation for the physical differences between the 'races', because they were of no advantage (240–49). The latter was not true for the intellectual capacities and moral or social instincts, though. To account for these, Darwin referred to a kind of natural selection that we today call group selection. He argued that in the course of evolution, human groups with a higher degree of cooperation and organization had an advantage in competition with groups whose members acted more selfishly and possessed less sense of community, a process that favored the development of sociality and morality. The same mechanism of group selection could explain the evolution of other traits, such as general intelligence, inventiveness, and courage (Darwin 1871a, Ch. 5; see also Richards 2002b, 549–52; Sommer 2015b, 26–27).

Aggressive group selection constituted *the* mechanism of 'racial' extinction in past and present:

> Extinction follows chiefly from the competition of tribe with tribe, and race with race [...] If from any cause any one of these checks [natural and social factors like famine, illness, or conflict] is lessened, even in a slight degree, the tribe thus favoured will tend to increase; and when one of two adjoining tribes becomes more numerous and powerful than the other, the contest is soon settled by war, slaughter, cannibalism, slavery, and absorption. Even when a weaker tribe is not thus abruptly swept away, if it once begins to decrease, it generally goes on decreasing until it is extinct. (Darwin 1871a, 238)

The history of European expansion had made clear that "[w]hen civilised nations come into contact with barbarians the struggle is short, except where a deadly climate gives its aid to the native race" (Darwin 1871a, 238). Indeed, "[t]he grade of civilisation seems a most important element in the success of nations which come in competition" (239). So whether group selection spurred the increase of positive traits or the advance of civilization as such, or whether it eradicated the less fortunate, it interacted with environmental factors. Most importantly for my context, it presupposed group contact. And group selection, though relying on differences between "tribes", "nations", or "races" in the intellects of community members and social integration or grade of civilization, was treated rather as a means of general perfection by Darwin – a means of diffusing these qualities throughout the world – than as a means of differentiation. 'Racial' extinction, too, while widening the gap to the nearest nonhuman taxa, tended to make the human species more homogeneous (160 and 163).

Darwin's main mechanism to explain the physical differences between the 'races' was sexual selection. Because he regarded most of these characteristics, such as skin shade, hair quality and color, and skull shape, as of no adaptive value, he could not explain them satisfactorily by group or natural selection alone. In *Descent*, he therefore spent most of the space on sexual selection, deriving the mechanism from the animal kingdom: "For my own part I conclude that of all the causes which have led to the differences in external appearance between the races of man, and to a certain extent between man and the lower animals, sexual selection has been by far the most efficient" (1871b, 384). Males or, in the 'more primitive' populations to a lesser extent, females, would choose their partners according to the esthetic standards of their group, thereby driving external 'racial' differentiation.

Sexual selection was about more than superficial differences, however.[5] In the struggle over females as well as in the safeguarding of and providing for females and young, males would have acquired both physical and mental prowess. But because these were reproductively advantageous, it was hard to clearly distinguish the influence of natural selection from that of this kind of sexual selection: "But these latter as well as the former faculties will have been developed in man, partly through sexual selection, – that is, through the contest of rival males, and partly through natural selection, – that is, from success in the general struggle for life" (Darwin 1871b, 328). And from the above observations we may add: and partly through group selection. Again, though this kind of sexual selection acted more strongly in certain periods of time and in certain communities, it had nonetheless acted on all men in a similar way. It therefore seems that like group selection, it worked towards a general increase in mental and behavioral capacities that, if at all, led to a differentiation of the human 'races' along a grade of perfection.

5 It has been observed by other scholars that, with the mechanism of sexual selection, Darwin naturalized what he perceived to be the bodily and intellectual superiority of men over women (e.g., Milam 2010, 16–17).

In sum, for 'racial' diversification to occur along the lines of a tree, the women of the different 'races' had to be chosen according to idiosyncratic esthetic standards over long periods of time. Therefore, this kind of selection seems to be the mechanism most in need of isolation through migration. Darwin wrote:

> Let us suppose the members of a tribe, in which some form of marriage was practised, to spread over an unoccupied continent; they would soon split up into distinct hordes, which would be separated from each other by various barriers, and still more effectually by the incessant wars between all barbarous nations [...] [E]ach isolated tribe would form for itself a slightly different standard of beauty; and then un-conscious selection would come into action through the more powerful and leading savages preferring certain women to others. Thus the differences between the tribes, at first very slight, would gradually and inevitably be increased to a greater and greater degree. (1871b, 370–71)

However, if this passage conjures up the image of branching paths of migration on a continental map, the image is flawed. The quote suggests that even in passages that at least approach a picture of human evolution along the lines of the tree structure in foregrounding diversification through diffusion and isolation, Darwin imagined human populations in interaction. There were "the incessant wars between all barbarous nations" (Darwin 1871b, 370), which though strengthening intra-group unity and inter-group isolation, could also result in the "absorption" of the women of the subjected "tribe" by the victorious one (see quote above from Darwin 1871a, 238). In fact, stealing women from rival groups constituted a common practice according to Darwin (on sexual selection in humans in general, see his Chs. 19 and 20).

We may therefore conclude that Darwin first demonstrated – against the prevalent polygenist thinking – that humans were divided into 'races' or subspecies only. They did not form clearly demarcated entities. He further supported this with the assumption of the prevalence of group encounter and intermixture throughout human evolution. One concession Darwin did make to the polygenists, however, is that the selection of females had been a much greater factor towards human differentiation in the early stages, when men had been less licentious, and there had as yet been no infanticide, female slavery, or child marriage:

> Hence we may infer that the races of men were differentiated, as far as sexual selection is concerned, in chief part during a very remote epoch; and this conclusion throws light on the remarkable fact that at the most ancient period, of which we have as yet obtained any record, the races of man had already come to differ nearly or quite as much as they do at the present day. (1871b, 383)

Unfortunately, for once, there is no footnote, so that we cannot know how ancient the epoch is to which Darwin referred the different "races" back. Taking into consideration his other statements, it would have been subsequent to humankind's substantial migrations to far apart regions of the world (Sommer 2021, 54–59).[6]

6 On Darwin's problems with the concept of sexual selection and his assumption of the great antiquity of human differentiation, see also Seth 2016. On Darwin's theory in *Descent* in the context of theories of human evolution in general see, e.g., Bowler 1986; Ruse 1996; Sommer 2015b.

10. About Treeing...

Darwin's explanations in *Descent* allow some inferences with regard to the issues related to the tree diagram, of which we find metonyms in *Descent* but no visualization. These explanations and Darwin's work at large suggest that he considered that a rightly drawn branching structure might capture in important ways the natural order down to the species level (as far as the fossil record allowed for it). This interpretation is supported by the many tree-like drawings he has left behind. Darwin's tree sketches are lines of thinking and experimenting rather than fleshed-out phylogenies, however, and the diversification of life takes place in all directions and not at a constant speed or with regular intensity. The diagram in *On the Origin of Species* is a diagram in essence in that it represents the understanding and tentative visual capturing of extinction and speciation on the basis of natural selection working on the variation within populations. In fact, Brink-Roby (2009, 256) has noted that even his only published diagram, which in its foldout materiality could transcend the page of the text, appeared too simple and orderly to Darwin. When verbally drawing the tree of life in *On the Origin of Species* (1859, 129–30), he made the reader see a tree in constant motion to allow the simultaneity of the non-simultaneous to appear in a dynamic fashion.

It is therefore not surprising that Darwin, though at times embracing the tree structure to capture natural relations, also felt its limitations and tried to transcend those by coming up with something like a coral or a seaweed.[1] In the end, Darwin needed language to act together with the drawn diagrams to create the intended meaning. A new way of understanding the natural world – its historicity and its present order

1 Horst Bredekamp (2019) has argued most pronouncedly for the centrality of the model of the coral for Darwin's evolutionary thinking.

 https://doi.org/10.11647/OBP.0396.12

– required novel ways of communicating. This, as we have seen, was even more of a challenge as both language and iconography carried traces of older conceptualizations such as the scale of nature. The tree diagram is an image of wide scope in Howard E. Gruber's sense: It is "capable of assimilating to itself a wide range of perceptions, actions, ideas" (2005, 254). The incredibly manifold and changeful interrelations of organisms – the tangled bank – was the spectacle of present complexity that the tree of life, in historicizing, should not reduce to pure symmetry, regularity, simplicity, or cleanliness.

The limitations of tree iconography were more severe in the case of 'racial' evolution, as the tree diagram could support the polygenist cause. In strong opposition to Darwin's insights, it presented human groups as clearly demarcated categories, and though with a common origin (possibly somewhere far down the tree), as having evolved independently from each other – it could suggest species status. Where Darwin played into the polygenists' hands, however, was in referring 'racial' differentiation through sexual selection far back in time. Furthermore, Darwin was not free from religious and social preconceptions with respect to hierarchical scales, chains, or series, the apex of which was the 'White civilized man'. With regard to both 'racial' and gender relations, his ideas were shaped by current prejudices and inequalities. They entered his view of modern human evolution, which though a reticulate process, produced clear gradations. As he wrote in his last paragraph of *Descent*:

> Man may be excused for feeling some pride at having risen, though not through his own exertions, to the very summit of the organic scale; and the fact of his having thus risen, instead of having been aboriginally placed there, may give him hopes for a still higher destiny in the distant future. But we are not here concerned with hopes or fears, only with the truth as far as our reason allows us to discover it. I have given the evidence to the best of my ability; and we must acknowledge, as it seems to me, that man with all his noble qualities, with sympathy which feels for the most debased, with benevolence which extends not only to other men but to the humblest living creature, with his god-like intellect which has penetrated into the movements and constitution of the solar system – with all these exalted powers – Man still bears in his bodily frame the indelible stamp of his lowly origin. (1871b, 405)

The appearance of man in evolution was thus not an inevitable outcome, but a result of some bodily and mental qualities he was given on his way by contingent evolution, which propelled him to "the very summit of the organic scale" and enabled him to conquer the world and beyond. And here, as in many instances in *Descent*, 'man' really means White human male. It has proven impossible to separate the question of race from the question of sex. As in the scale of nature, they are implicated in the family tree. While Darwin, in the footsteps of Blumenbach and Prichard, intended to fight polygenism with a genealogical understanding of humankind, his theories were adapted to all kinds of politics, including sexisms and racisms, and despite his prudence in this regard, his name became forever linked to the tree of life and the 'family tree of man' (Sommer 2021, 60–61).[2]

With Haeckel, phylogenetic tree building became not only standard in biology and anthropology, but the tree also entered the public sphere as the icon to support and spread the ideas of evolution and phylogeny. As Haeckel's correspondence illustrates, the phylogenetic tree was widely used in publications for wider readerships and lantern slides of tree diagrams accompanied public lectures. Additionally, as we have already seen for Redfield's trees of the animal kingdom, the phylogenetic tree was used as pedagogic tool to teach the new view of the living world to school children. With regard to human phylogenies, fossil kin – 'Heidelberg, Neanderthal, and Cro-Magnon Man' – was added beyond *Pithecanthropus*, the cipher that came to be filled with bones from Java right when the century was ending.[3] Haeckel celebrated that his 'family tree of man' had even reached the "Mongolian race",[4] the famous popular writer Wilhelm Bölsche boasted that his Kosmos booklet on the phylogenetic tree of the insects had sold 86,000 times, while the one on the phylogenetic tree of the animals had reached a sale of 47,000,[5] and

2 Pertinent to the politics and politicization of 'Darwinism' are, among many others, Diane Paul's texts, e.g., "Darwin, Social Darwinism and Eugenics" (2006); see for example also the special issue on *The Descent of Man* of the *British Journal for the History of Science Themes* (Milam and Seth 2021).

3 E.g., Wilhelm Breitenbach to Haeckel, 7 October 1880, EHA Jena, A 5921; Breitenbach to Haeckel, 7 December 1909, EHA Jena, A 6075; Fritz Bartels to Haeckel, 27 May 1912, EHA Jena, A 8112.

4 "mongolische[] Rasse" (my translation from Ernst Haeckel to Charlotte Haeckel [mother], 30 June 1871, EHA Jena, A 38615).

5 Bölsche to Haeckel, 7 June 1919, EHA Jena, A 9752.

the biologist Wilhelm Breitenbach bragged about the approximately one hundred people who had attended his lecture on human phylogeny (Breitenbach to Haeckel, 18 March 1908, EHA Jena, A 6043).

Finally, we have seen in this part how Haeckel was the one who not only introduced the tree in anthropology but also already triggered the development towards its disintegration. His polygenism made him imagine human 'racial' evolution rather as parallel lines than as diverging branches (his diagrams of hominid evolution really look rather like classification keys than natural trees). Living human groups were regarded as separate species that had developed at unequal tempi and to different degrees. It is the apex of evolutionary polygenism à la Haeckel that will take center stage in Part III. In the next part, the radicalization of the human family tree will also be tied to the diagram's ideological meanings. In fact, already in Haeckel's case the tree structure stood for a narrative of violence. In an idiosyncratic interpretation of Darwin's selection between prehistoric tribes, Haeckel justified contemporary imperialism and genocide as natural processes that had been driving human evolution since its beginning. In this scenario, progress in human anatomy and culture depended on the displacement of 'lower' by 'higher human species'. Haeckel claimed that 'the woolly-haired human species' were not capable of developing higher civilizations. It was therefore the fate of the 'midland species', and especially the 'Indo-Germanic race', to expand their rule across the earth by virtue of their intelligence and culture. Haeckel prophesied that the species of the temperate zones would extinguish the 'lower human types', except maybe in the tropic and polar zones. It was a process that he believed to be underway with regard to the Native Americans and Aboriginal Australians, the Khoekhoe, 'Papuans', and other Indigenous peoples (1898 [1868], 729–65).[6]

6 Haeckel's work also contains eugenic propaganda and antisemitism (e.g., Hoßfeld 2005).

PART III. RADICALIZING VERSUS DECONSTRUCTING THE FAMILY TREE OF THE HUMAN 'RACES'

In the wake of Ernst Haeckel's phylogenies, 'the racial family tree' reached its heyday in the twentieth century, and it came to carry strange blossoms. Paleoanthropology came of age with the discovery of fossil remains of *Pithecanthropus erectus*, named after Haeckel's invented taxon (today *Homo erectus*), in Java at the end of the nineteenth century (1891–92), in addition to the increasing knowledge about Neanderthals and Cro-Magnons. The German anatomist Gustav Schwalbe incorporated the newly found missing link into a linear line of descent that went from *Pithecanthropus erectus* via the Neanderthals to modern humans. In doing so, Schwalbe (e.g., 1904) defined the Neanderthals as a separate species (*Homo primigenius*), rather than as a 'fossil human race' as done by Thomas Henry Huxley, thereby enlisting them unambiguously for an evolutionary understanding.

Schwalbe followed Charles Darwin in his monogenism and Haeckel in his conception of evolution as progressive. As a physical anthropologist, he adopted the tools of the trade from the study and classification of the recent human 'races' (see Part I) to the description and incorporation of the fossil forms. He also partook in methodological development. In fact, his extended study of the *Pithecanthropus* remains appeared in the first issue of his newly founded *Zeitschrift* für *Morphologie und Anthropologie* – a journal that was to be dedicated solely to the morphology and phylogeny of humankind, taking good account of paleontology. Its goal was to elaborate the natural hominid order in the shape of a "Stammbaum" [family tree] (Schwalbe 1899a, quote on 6). The treatise on *Pithecanthropus* that followed Schwalbe's programmatic introduction was a more than 230-page-long exercise in comparative measurement, precision, and statistical analysis, ripe with tables, diagrammatic skull

 https://doi.org/10.11647/OBP.0396.13

outlines, skull superimpositions, and with the obligatory skull plates at the end (Schwalbe 1899b). Its aim was to craniometrically establish the position of *Pithecanthropus* in relation to monkeys and apes, on the one hand, and to the Neanderthals and recent human forms, on the other: *Homo primigenius* linked living humans to *Pithecanthropus*, while the latter continued the series in the direction of the apes.

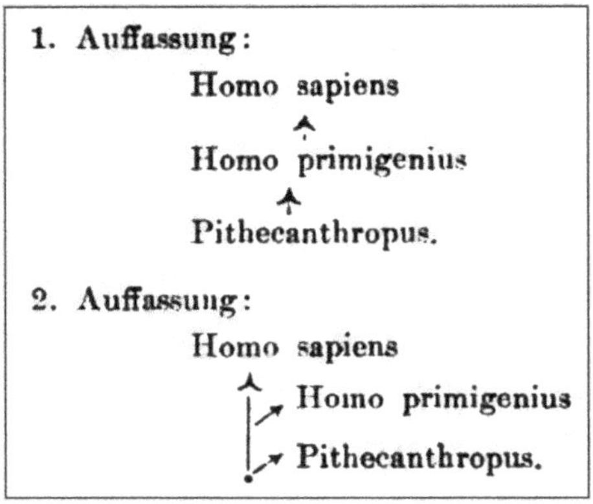

Fig. III.1 A tree could still be a scale. Gustav Schwalbe, *Studien zur Vorgeschichte des Menschen* (Stuttgart: E. Schweizerbartsche, 1906), p. 14. Public domain.

Although this outlook was popular in international anthropological circles, the unilinear model was soon challenged. In the aftermath of these publications by Schwalbe, uncertainty with regard to the dating of known fossils led to the rejection of a unilinear conception of human evolution in favor of a branching model. This process began with the Neanderthals being relegated to a side branch of the human ascent. It was the French doyen of anthropology, Marcellin Boule (e.g., 1908), who initiated this shift, also by emphasizing the species' simian traits (in this process, too, visualizations played a key role, see Sommer 2006). French anthropology, not least due to the richness of fossil human remains and archeological sites in France, was internationally very influential. However, the differences between a unilinear and a branching phylogeny must not be considerable, as Schwalbe (1906, 13–15) himself pointed out. With Figure III.1, Schwalbe indicated that even if the fossil skull cap of *Pithecanthropus* were from a time when *Homo* had already existed, the genus could still be ancestral to the Neanderthal species and modern humans: it could have appeared earlier than *Homo* but survived relatively unmodified into *Homo*'s times. *Pithecanthropus* could be projected back along its branch to where it met the trunk, reinstituting the linear genealogy (see dot on trunk in Figure III.1). So could the Neanderthals.

Such trees in which some branches could stand for the stagnation of hominid types in regions considered unfavorable to progressive evolution were quite common, just like some living human varieties were often seen as 'old types', as already evidenced by Haeckel. However, though conceptually similar to direct descent, such trees still distanced known taxa from each other in time – and the use of tree structures did more than that. While the use of tree diagrams to symbolize evolutionary descent in anthropology might seem straightforward, given the longstanding traditions of conveying religious and secular genealogies and plant and animal pedigrees in similar ways, it supports certain conceptions. To begin with, the transfer of a structure that connects individuals to one that connects groups of organisms may introduce a typological element. Entire genera, with all their natural variety, can be condensed into an individual specimen or type. As we have seen in Part II, an additional consequence of also applying the tree structure to current human diversity is that human populations appear to be as different from each other as species or higher taxa; in the case of Haeckel, this consequence was intended. Showing the living human varieties to have independent lines of descent disregards hybridization between them, which constituted a central process in Darwin's explanation of human variation. The branching structure for intra-human phylogeny per se underestimates kinship between the living human varieties.

Therefore, while genealogical trees are devices to connect people, to show how the individuals of a family are related through blood (even if they at the same time exclude certain individuals), anthropological family trees can be tools for distancing. In fact, although Boule, as was common, strongly worked with the visualized anatomical series of bones to denote overall evolutionary progress, he could imagine *Pithecanthropus* to be on a branch of the anthropoid rather than hominid line, and he prophesied: "As science progresses, we see that these various branches, while retaining their autonomy, extend downward, and their welds to the main branches, or to the main trunk, are more and more distant, too often beyond the points reached so far by our research" (1921, 109–110, my translation).[1] Indeed, Boule's stance set in motion a trend that led to an underestimation of kinship between fossil and living human forms, between different fossil hominids, between apes and humans, as well as between the recent varieties. The trend was also due to a 'fossil' that turned out to be fake: 'Piltdown Man' or *Eoanthropus*. It was a forgery from Great Britain comprised of an ape jaw and a human skull that haunted the anthropological communities from the early 1910s onward. This big-brained 'hominid', as well as other modern-looking bones and supposedly human-made tools that were postulated to be of considerable antiquity, supported the notion that modern human anatomy was of great age, which disqualified 'other' hominid fossils as direct ancestors of living humans, because they were too young or too primitive. They tended to be relegated to dead-ending branches of the human family tree. The ancestors of modern humans were thus again unknown (also called the pre-*sapiens* theory).

The modern human 'types or races', too, came to be conceptualized as having great antiquity and therefore as being the outcome of parallel evolution. This interpretation, in the contexts of nationalism and racial supremacism, could serve to provide an anthropologist's nation with a long and noble genealogy independent of 'the other races', or for "putting the Nordic Race at the apex of the main stem" of the phylogenetic tree (Smith [1924, 11] in Sommer 2007, 190). Even if for those anthropologists, like the just quoted Australian-born Grafton Elliot Smith, human differentiation took place after the *Homo sapiens* stage had been reached, human evolution and history were linked, and in the human family tree, some fossil human forms (like the Cro-Magnon or Grimaldi 'races') could bud later from the stem than some of the living 'races', again turning these populations into relics belonging to the evolutionary past of supposedly advanced populations. Especially the Aboriginal Australians often functioned as a template for imagining the most recent common ancestor of the *Homo-sapiens* forms (see Smith's family tree, 1929, Fig. 16, 54).

1 "A mesure que la science progresse, nous voyons ces diverses branches s'allonger vers le bas, tout en gardant leur autonomie, et leurs soudures aux branches maitresses, ou au tronc principal, se faire de plus en plus loin, trop souvent au delà des points atteints jusqu'ici par nos recherches." For Schwalbe's reception of Boule's Neanderthal study, see Schwalbe 1914.

Smith opposed Nordic superiority claims as expressed in the so-called 'Aryan theory', and he condemned slavery and war as outgrowths of modern societies. All the same, the 'racial hierarchy' established by his trees was justified not only by differences in pigmentation but also by brain evolution. Although Smith did not equate 'race' with culture, this led him to put forth racist opinions regarding the differential potential to advance culturally. Diagrammatic distancing of human 'races' from each other, especially through extended parallel lines of descent in family trees, could be part of imperialistic theories à la Haeckel, in which the geographic expansion of 'higher types' and thereby the replacement of 'lower types' was seen as a mechanism of progressive evolution. In Smith's case, his racial-succession and cultural-diffusion paradigm led him to work with maps, some of which are similar to the one discussed for Haeckel in Part II in that Smith (1929, Fig. 13, 49) showed the migration of the *Homo-sapiens* types from a center in Asia across the globe. From the experiences of World War I, some anthropologists also theorized about war as an expression of 'racial' antagonism or a 'race-forming' process in human evolution (Sommer 2007, Part II).

This is where my Part III takes up the story. We will see how tree-like diagrams and diagrams that were called 'trees' in evolutionary anthropology even came to deny relatedness by pushing the above tendencies to their extremes. In the diagrams of some authors of anthropological treatises, the tree or cactus structure of human phylogeny was in effect decomposed, as if the branches had been moved deeper and deeper downward along the trunk until the tree structure collapsed. The recent human groups could thus be seen as having independent origins, as having sprung from different ancestors, and even as separate species. At the same time, the tree came to be contested in other quarters for exactly these tendencies. Into these processes – the radicalization as well as the contestation of the tree – I enter with a radical example: the diagram of human phylogeny by Reginald Ruggles Gates that will guide me through this part. With Gates, I choose a figure who rather occupied the margins of anthropology, but who was networked with those at its very center and who proved more than capable of irritating some of the big names not in accord with him. Starting from and repeatedly returning to him allows me to look at the controversies between those who radicalized the tree structure because, for them, it overemphasized intra-human similarity and relatedness, and those who deconstructed it because they thought the tree underrepresented human similarity and relatedness. I start from Gates' extreme – in the sense of non-relating – diagram to show that some of the world's most prominent scientists contributing to anthropological knowledge not only paved the way but also held similar views. Gates' diagram serves as a platform from which to investigate its relations to other diagrams and to the social world.

While we have seen that the diagrammatology in the tradition of Charles Sanders Peirce goes beyond an analytical toolbox for studying 'purely epistemic' aspects of diagrams, it is in some of the work of Michel Foucault and Gilles Deleuze that the diagram figures as an abstraction and as the instantiation of a certain 'physics' of power. In their understanding, the diagram consists of practices that structure society as much as reasoning and thought. In *Discipline and Punish* (1977 [1975]), Foucault described a new kind of power characteristic of modernity that renders visible, registers, compares, and differentiates bodies in order to define ways to intervene. The panopticon turns out to be a diagram that not only represents "a pure architectural and optical system" but "is in fact a figure of political technology that may and must be detached from any specific use" (205). The diagram as a materialized political technology, whether in stone or on paper, constitutes a modern type of discipline that ensures the ordering of human diversity. Deleuze expanded on this notion of diagrams to the degree that they appear to be co-extensive with (the history of) the social world. Diagrams are embedded in, and implement, realities of difference and power. But as an intra- and intersocial machine, a diagram "never functions in order to represent a persisting world but produces a new kind of reality, a new model of truth [...] It makes history by unmaking preceding realities and significations [...]" (Deleuze 1988 [1986], 35). With Foucault and Deleuze, new forms of relating diagrams might be viewed as bringing an order of things into place in relation to struggles over the exercise of power and the ordering of bodies in space (Sommer et al. 2018, 13).

11. Denying Even the Tree-Structured Human Kinship

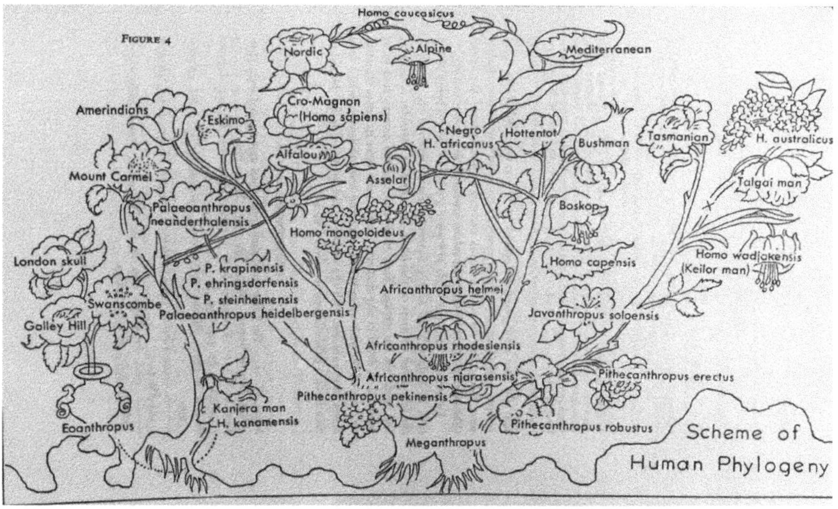

Fig. III.2 "Scheme of Human Phylogeny". Reginald Ruggles Gates, *Human Ancestry from a Genetical Point of View* (Cambridge: Harvard University Press, 1948), Fig. 4, p. 161 © 1948 By the President and Fellows of Harvard College, all rights reserved.

Figure III.2 is a diagram of human phylogeny by the Canadian-born geneticist Reginald Ruggles Gates of 1948 (Fig. 4, 161). Although Gates published important genetic work in botany, he also profusely contributed to human heredity and anthropology. Gates moved between Canada, the United Kingdom, and the United States. He had been at King's College London, among other institutions, before relocating to the US during World War II, from which point he was mainly associated with

 https://doi.org/10.11647/OBP.0396.14

Harvard University as a Research Fellow in Botany and Anthropology.[1] He and his diagram, reproduced here as Figure III.2, will serve as a red thread through this part. To begin with, with the names of species and genera placed in flowers growing on stalks, the diagram is reminiscent of the iconography of genealogies of Christ and secular family trees in which individuals were sometimes depicted in blossoms. As we have seen, the tree of Jesse was probably the original use of 'the family tree' for genealogical representation (known from since the eleventh century). There are many examples in medieval psalters, in stained glass windows, as stone carvings around the portals of medieval cathedrals and as paintings on walls and ceilings. The tree of Jesse also appeared in smaller art forms such as embroideries and ivories. Figure III.3 shows an early-modern painting in the dome of Limburg (Germany, sixteenth century), in which the male kin of Jesus as well as him and Mary are placed in flowers (for further examples see Klapisch-Zuber 2004; also, Watson 1934; Siegel 2009, 62–64).

However, while the similarity of Gates' diagram of human phylogeny to the traditional motif suggests a quasi-religious understanding of human unity based on genealogical relatedness, a closer look at Figure III.2 proves otherwise. Directly out of the fossil ape *Meganthropus* grow different stalks towards the species "Homo mongoloideus", "H. africanus", "Homo capensis", and "H. australicus". In fact, the 'Caucasian stalk' is separated even more severely from the other hominids and towers over them. Without any connection to the other human stems, *Homo sapiens* (Cro-Magnons) and finally "Homo caucasicus" develop from *Eoanthropus* (Piltdown) – a 'missing link' with a big brain from Great Britain that was later shown to be a forgery made up of an ape jaw and a human skull. Only the "Nordic" type that ascends from this line is the true *Homo sapiens*, since the diagram clearly suggests that 'the Alpines' are already in the process of descending. Furthermore, only this

1 Gates was appointed to the Readership in Botany at King's College London in 1919 and was made Chair in 1921. Previously, Gates had been Demonstrator in Botany at McGill University (Canada), Senior Fellow and Assistant in Botany at the University of Chicago (US), Lecturer in Biology at St. Thomas' Hospital Medical School (UK), and acting Associate Professor of Zoology at the University of California (US) among other institutions (*Nature*, 6 February 1919, and 2 June 1921, Press Cuttings, Vol. 1, 1915–31, Gates Papers KCL, 9/1). Between 1942, when he resigned his Chair at King's College London, and 1957, he was in the US; then, five years before his death, he again moved to England.

flower roots in a pot (at the left lower corner, called *Eoanthropus*), as if it had been clear from the beginning that this is the cultivated plant. Thus, even though the image may appear rhizomatic at first glance, Gates rather disaggregated the 'tree' to deny as "Nordic" all relatedness to 'the others': this scheme of human phylogeny is no longer a genealogical tree but a bed of disconnected flowers.

Fig. III.3 Genealogy of Christ in the dome of Limburg. Photograph by SteveK, crop by Bennylin (2011). Wikimedia, CC BY-SA 3.0, https://commons.wikimedia.org/wiki/File:Ahnenreihe_Jesu_im_Limburger_Dom-crop.jpg

The diagram appeared in *Human Ancestry from a Genetical Point of View* (1948, Fig. 4, 161), in which Gates postulated different places of origin, different ancestral genera, and independent evolution of the 'racial types', which for him had species status. He tried to apply genetics to human phylogeny and classification while maintaining the notion of human types. He suggested that parallel mutations had directed the 'racial' lines towards their present state:

> We recognize different species, and even genera, of man coexisting in Pleistocene times and giving rise to such different types as the Australian, the Bushman, and the Caucasian from *independent* lines of descent, yet as a convention arising from man's self-conceit we try to crowd them together into one species, implying simple divergence from one ancestry. The evidence is clear, however, that the primary so-called races of living man have arisen *independently from different ancestral species in different continents at different times.* They have shown some *parallel developments* [...] Yet there is no evidence for convergence [...] Consistency therefore necessitates the recognition of *Homo australicus, H. capensis, H. africanus* ([Black Africans]), *H. mongoloideus* (including the Amerinds as a geographic subspecies), and *H. caucasicus*, as species, each having its own geographical expression despite the migrations and intercrossing which have taken place *especially within historical time.* (Gates 1948, 366–67, my emphases)[2]

Orthogenesis – the theory according to which organisms had inborn tendencies to evolve in certain directions – had been dominantly expressed, among others, by the director of the American Museum of Natural History in New York, Henry Fairfield Osborn, to whom Gates mainly referred his theory of parallelism. Osborn had developed his brand of orthogenesis by maintaining elements from the 'Lamarckian' and recapitulationist approaches as well as through borrowing from the new genetics and Darwinism. At a time of controversy over heredity and evolution, Osborn worked out a theory to account for the trends he recognized in the fossil record of some mammals. In this view,

2 It appears that the phylogenetic diagram does not coincide with the text in every respect. In the text, in which, as typical for Gates' writings, he mostly gave the interpretations of others without a strong author's voice, Gates noted that Franz Weidenreich's suggestion that hominids evolved from *Meganthropus* was unlikely (Gates 1948, 85–86; on Gates, see Sommer 2015b, 128–29).

environment and habit over long periods of time impacted ontological development, thus triggering the hereditary potential in the germplasm and provoking gradual evolution along determinate lines. Natural selection thus worked among the end products of evolutionary trends rather than being a mechanism in their formation.

Applied to human phylogeny, Osborn's orthogenetic theory provided a 'tree' with different hominid genera, species, and 'races' on parallel branches. Such a 'tree' showed no connections between the 'racial' lines, since Osborn thought of 'miscegenation' as a relatively recent phenomenon. Due to the 'race'-specific germplasms and the different living conditions and habitual behaviors exhibited in their evolutionary histories, the current human 'races' were intellectually, temperamentally, and spiritually, as well as anatomically, diverse. Over time, these 'racial' distinctions became more pronounced in Osborn's mind. While in *Men of the Old Stone Age* (1915) hominids and *Homo sapiens* were still presented as being relatively young, in *Man Rises to Parnassus* (1927), which stood for the so-called 'dawn man' theory of the 1920s and 30s, modern humans appeared to have evolved in parallel with the ape family since the Oligocene, when they had sprung from a neutral common stock (Sommer 2016a, 39–40, Part I in general).

In diagrams as the one reproduced from Osborn as Figure III.4, the hominids are represented by outlines of skulls. This is interesting for at least two reasons. First, because it is reminiscent of the portraits of people in genealogical family trees, and, second, because the practice refers to the central importance of the shape and size of the skull in (paleo)anthropology. The observer of Osborn's "Ascent or Phylogeny of Man" would immediately have grasped that the hominid skulls in the left half of the diagram are 'more advanced' than the simian crania on the right, and that there was a hierarchy constructed for the recent time on the top of the left image side that was made to correspond to a progressive improvement of the brain from the "Australian" at the bottom via Black Africans and the "Chinese" up to the "White". This hierarchy is even more conspicuous in the list in the lower left corner of the diagram, where eleven steps including the fossil hominids (and Piltdown) are given.

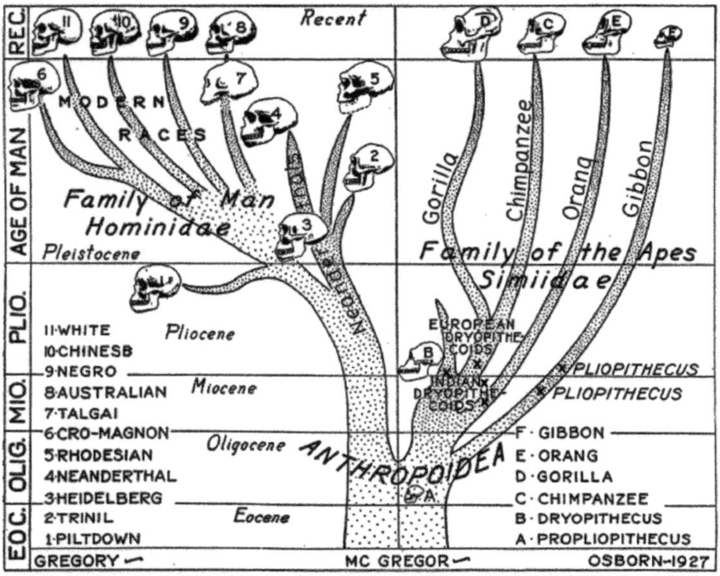

FIGURE 2. RECENT EVIDENCE AS TO THE ASCENT OR PHYLOGENY OF MAN

(LEFT) FAMILY OF MAN, *Hominidæ*, DIVIDING INTO THE NEANDERTHALOID (RIGHT) AND MODERN RACIAL (LEFT) STOCKS. PRESENT GEOLOGIC LOCATION OF THE PILTDOWN, HEIDELBERG, TRINIL, NEANDERTHAL AND RHODESIAN FOSSIL RACES (LEFT). (RIGHT) FAMILY OF THE APES, *Simiidæ*, INCLUDING THE PLIOCENE AND MIOCENE DRYOPITHECOIDS NEAREST THE ANCESTRAL STOCK OF THE *Anthropoidea;* ALSO THE LINES LEADING TO THE GORILLA, ORANG, CHIMPANZEE AND GIBBON. *Anthropoidea*—THE COMMON OLIGOCENE ANCESTORS OF THE *Hominidæ* (LEFT) AND OF THE *Simiidæ* (RIGHT).

Fig. III.4 "The Ascent or Phylogeny of Man". Henry Fairfield Osborn, "Recent Discoveries Relating to the Origin and Antiquity of Man" (*Science* 65.1690 [1927]: 481–88), Fig. 2, p. 486. Public domain.

This once again indicates that the branching diagrams to convey human relatedness in anthropology could still incorporate the notion of scales – the linear hierarchical series that were used to order the cosmos since antiquity. Further to the serial arrangement, the tree structure, with its numbers, letters, and skull-outlines, is contained in a rectangle, the sections of which stand for layers of the earth and therefore for geological epochs, from the Eocene to recent times. This iconicity was taken over from the widely used imagery of stratigraphic series in geology. It gives a third meaning to the skulls: they appear to be the fossil remains resting in the geological epochs during which the hominids lived, respectively in the stratigraphic layers in which they were found. Osborn's reference to "recent evidence as to the ascent or phylogeny of man" in the caption underlines this indexical character of the skulls in the image. In a sense then, this is a variant of the tree-on-a-map diagram, only that the space mapped belongs to the interior of the earth. As we have seen in Part II, already Darwin used this image as a metaphor, even if he could not see as far down the layers as Osborn thought he could. In shaping his tree with the mechanism of orthogenesis, Osborn could convey evolutionary relationships, while at the same time denying close kinship not only between the so-called 'races', but also of 'man' to other hominid taxa, and between the "Family of Man" and the "Family of the Apes". Visually divided from each other by a vertical line, hominids and anthropoids constitute separate families, barely touching each other in the Oligocene at least sixteen million years ago, where they merge in a very distant and diffuse Anthropoidea stock (marked by *Propliopithecus*) (Sommer 2023b).[3]

Osborn, who staged international eugenics congresses and exhibitions at the museum, wanted a noble genealogy for the "White". No fossil form so far found – not even the beautiful and artistic Cro-Magnons – was good enough to be put on their direct evolutionary line, to be their direct ancestor; and the tree provided the living 'races' with long, independent lines of descent. Just as the phylogenetic gap between apes and humans was considerably enlarged, Osborn argued that the living human 'races' in fact constituted different zoological species or even genera, with for example *Homo europaeus* ('Caucasians') comprising the species *nordicus*, *alpinus*, and *mediterraneus* (Osborn 1927, 169). However, Osborn felt that in his reality the 'perfect order' depicted in the tree, with the human 'races' keeping to themselves at very safe distances, was in jeopardy. He considered it vital to prevent 'excessive' immigration of 'southern European and Asian types' to America, to preserve 'his racial stock' and 'the order of the races'. In the course of his life, he was engaged in the Immigration Restriction League, the Galton Society, the American Eugenics Society, and the Aryan Society. The same Nordic supremacism lay beneath Osborn's genealogical self-identification as being of Scandinavian and pure English stock; he was a member of the Fairfield Historical Society and the New England

3 There were several attempts to distance the human from the anthropoid line. Also drawing on parallelism, the British anthropologist Frederic Wood Jones (e.g., 1919; 1929) for example postulated that 'man' and the anthropoid apes had arisen and evolved independently from a basal primate stock.

Historical Genealogical Society (Sommer 2016a, 23–26, Part I in general; also Regal 2002, Ch. 5).

There were also alternative models of human relatedness in the US of the 1920s, which, too, were connected to politics and conceptions of society. Osborn and the American biologist Edwin Grant Conklin sided in the fight against the attempts to ban evolutionary theory from schools and universities (e.g., Osborn and Conklin 1922). The religiously motivated antievolutionary campaigns were one other motif for Osborn to distance 'man' from the apes in his evolutionary trees. However, Osborn's and Conklin's diagrams of human relatedness differed. Conklin as well was concerned with the question of progress, but he linked individuals of a family and all humankind not in a tree but in "a net in which every individual is represented by a knot formed by the union of two lines which may be traced backward and forward to an ever-increasing number of knots and lines until all are united in this vast genealogical net of humanity" (1921, 134). The genealogical threads woven throughout humanity amounted to the "universal brotherhood of man" (139): "Each individual or family is not a separate and independent entity, but merely a minor unit in the great organism of mankind" (138). Conklin not only argued with Mendelian genetics against a model of human relatedness as tree-shaped, but he also criticized the biological determinism inherent in much of the eugenic literature. Instead, he emphasized the role of environment, and he declared that class, 'race', and national antagonism were no biological necessities but cultural and political phenomena (Sommer 2016a, 281–85).[4]

In fact, the hyper-diversity view of human phylogeny came to be challenged from several angles. Regarding paleoanthropological evidence, it was the australopithecine discoveries beginning in 1924 that contested not only Asia as the cradle of humankind, a view promoted

4 For Conklin's anti-eugenics writings from the 1910s onward, especially his emphasis of the role of environment and education in the shaping of the human individual, see Cooke 2002. Conklin's ideas on heredity and eugenics were not always consistent and changed over time. In an analysis of some of his correspondence Miriam G. Reumann and Anne Fausto-Sterling (2001) have shown how contradictory his statements – pro and contra eugenic measures – could be. Even after World War II, the continuation of the "better human types" remained a concern to him. Nonetheless, Conklin was part of the group of American geneticists who publicly criticized eugenics from the 1920s (Cravens 1978, 158–90; Kevles 1995 [1985], 122).

by Osborn and others, but also evolutionary parallelism. The African fossils opened the possibility of a (re)inclusion of *Pithecanthropus erectus* into the line leading to modern humans and made the Piltdown 'specimen' look odder than ever; it was definitively exposed as a forgery in the 1950s. Piltdown or *Eoanthropus*, especially, comprising a modern human brain case considered to be of great antiquity, made real fossil remains look like primitive survivals of earlier evolutionary stages. However, it was not until the 1930s that the significance of the australopithecine remains began to be more widely recognized (e.g., Gundling 2005; Sommer 2015b, 111–23). One step in this direction was taken by Osborn's employee and co-paleontologist at the American Museum of Natural History, William King Gregory. Although Gregory had begun to disagree with Osborn earlier (Gregory 1927), he used *Australopithecus*, with its progressive anthropoid brain and primitive human dentition, to issue "A Critique of Professor Osborn's Theory of Human Origins" (1930). This paper was particularly triggered by an article of Osborn's in which he reproduced the family tree shown in Figure III.4 (Osborn 1930, 3). With the australopithecine's morphology, Gregory argued against Osborn's claim that the hominid branch had left the common hominid-anthropoid stock already in the Oligocene; after all, the australopithecine find was no older than late Tertiary. Overall, the australopithecines added weight to the theory of a close relationship between the African apes and humans.

In this context it is interesting to look at the relating diagram that Gregory included in his *Man's Place among the Anthropoids* of 1934. This "Family Tree of the Primates" was exhibited in the paleontological halls of the museum that were visited by millions of people (see Figure III.5). It depicts the human 'races' like persons in a genealogical tree and thus pushes the typological in this kind of imagery to its apex. Correspondingly, the "White", "Yellow", "Red", and "African Race" are represented by figures rendered in a classical style, with a Greek 'Adonis' standing in for the "White". Even though, at this time, Gregory had come to criticize Osborn's extreme parallelism, in this tree, none of the fossil hominids are connected in direct descent to living humans, and the living 'races' have emerged in longstanding isolation. Anatomical similarities between current forms – in particular between the "Australian Race", who are placed further down and who branch off first, and the rest of present-day humans – would partly have to be explained by means of parallel evolution rather than close kinship. Parallelism and a progressive understanding of evolution seem further implied in that it is the main stem that leads to modern humans, which can be traced all the way back to the root, while all other primates split off as branches, beginning with the Lemuroids and Tarsioids. The image thus seems to contradict Gregory's theory. In fact, Osborn was positively surprised about the inclusion of a diagram in Gregory's treatise that could be read as supporting his own orthogenesis, rather than Gregory's markedly different views (Sommer 2016a, 125; Sommer 2022b, 281–84, 286–87).

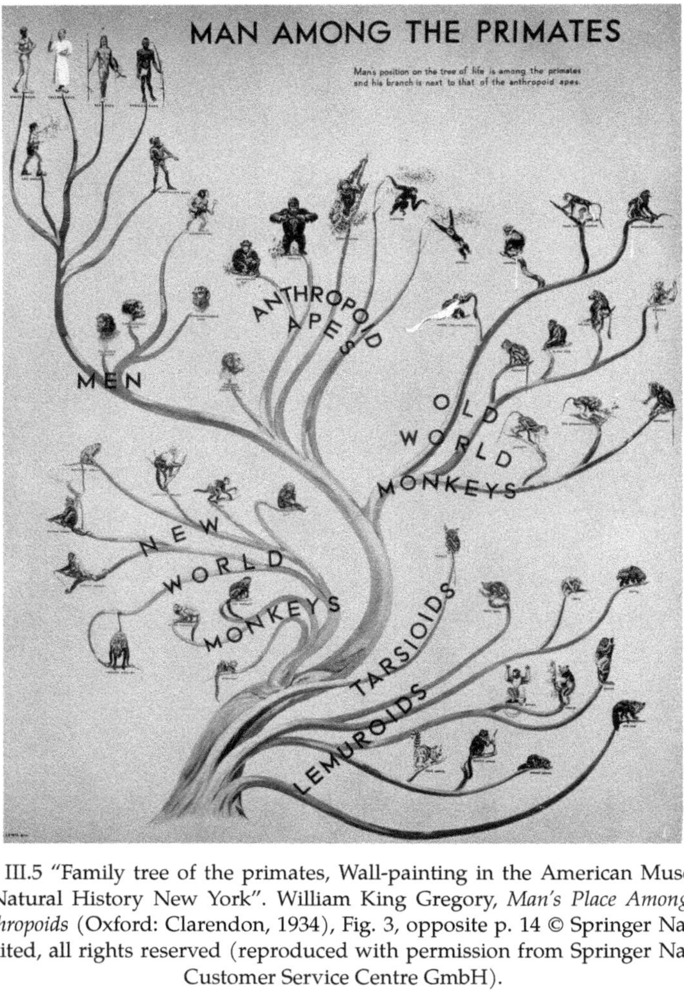

Fig. III.5 "Family tree of the primates, Wall-painting in the American Museum of Natural History New York". William King Gregory, *Man's Place Among the Anthropoids* (Oxford: Clarendon, 1934), Fig. 3, opposite p. 14 © Springer Nature Limited, all rights reserved (reproduced with permission from Springer Nature Customer Service Centre GmbH).

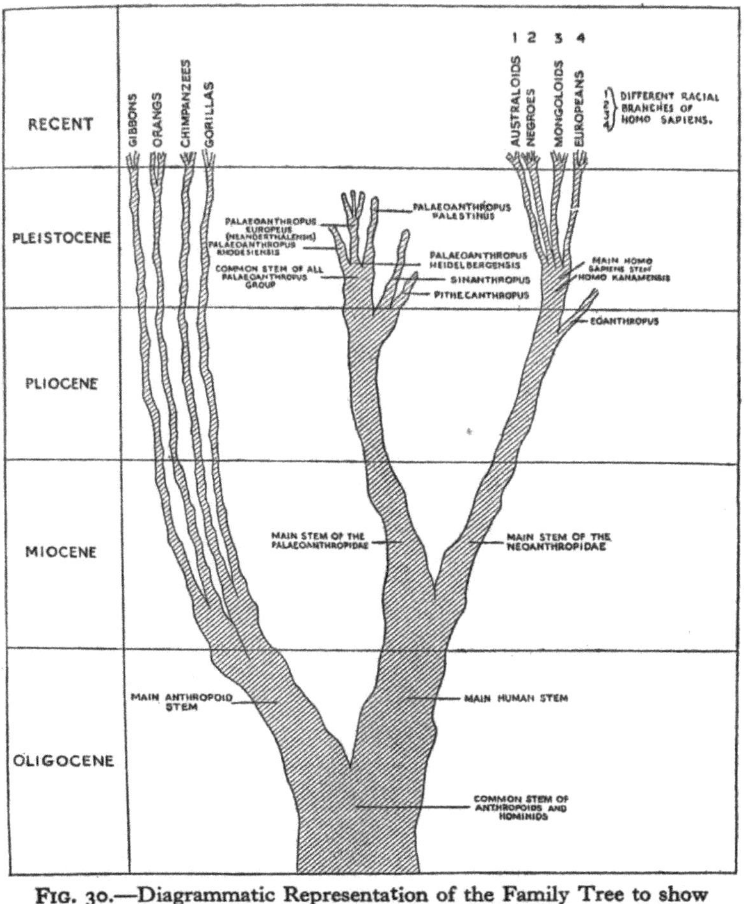

Fig. 30.—Diagrammatic Representation of the Family Tree to show the supposed Relationship of the Different Types of Men and Anthropoid Ape discussed in this book.

Fig. III.6 "Diagrammatic Representation of the Family Tree". From: *Adam's Ancestors* [...], by Louis Leakey (London: Methuen, 1934), Fig. 30, p. 227,

While Gregory's tree did figure the australopithecine as 'the missing link' between "Men" and "Anthropoid Apes", further support for parallelism and orthogenesis came the same year from Wilfrid Le Gros Clark (1934), who, like Osborn, also applied the concepts to primate and mammalian evolution in general. The British primate phylogeny expert of the University of Oxford followed Osborn in his assumption of evolutionary trends programmed into the germplasm that would lead the evolution of related forms into similar directions. He subsumed the australopithecine under the fossil remains of African anthropoid apes. Yet another book of 1934, Louis Leakey's *Adam's Ancestors*, disregarded the fossil and gave support to the concept of a great antiquity of modern human anatomy. Leakey had been born in Africa as the son of English missionaries and, after graduating in anthropology from the University of Cambridge, he returned to Kenya, then a British colony officially named British East Africa, to apply the newly developed archeological techniques of Europe to this 'un-ploughed territory'. Leakey was convinced that Africa was the cradle of humankind, and found this conviction substantiated. With *Adam's Ancestors* of 1934 that went through three editions in that year, Leakey intended to bring the insights from anthropology and prehistoric archeology to the attention of a wider public. In seductively simple language, he presented such complex and unresolved problems as the definitive distinction between human-made and naturally created flints, or the attribution of a skull to a certain 'racial type', as entirely straightforward and uncontroversial.

As visualized in Figure III.6, Leakey split the hominid line in the Miocene into Palaeoanthropidae and Neoanthropidae. At the beginning of the Pleistocene, the first, 'primitive' line of these two hominid subfamilies gave rise to three genera, one of them being *Pithecanthropus* and another containing the Neanderthal species. The second, new or modified line that was very clearly distanced from the first yielded the genus *Eoanthropus* as a side branch and contained *Homo kanamensis* as the only fossil type or ancestor of humans all the way down to the common stock of anthropoids and hominids in the Oligocene. This main branch of the genus *Homo* differentiated into the "Australoids", "[Black Africans]", "Mongoloids", and Europeans in the Pleistocene (again depicted in a hierarchical series, this time from left to right and from one to four). The reason why Leakey did not position (the forged) Piltdown as direct ancestor of modern humans but as a close cousin was its supposed approximate contemporaneity with 'Kanam Man'. Being his own discovery, 'Kanam Man' ended up as the sole direct human ancestor – an ancestor from Africa (Sommer 2015b, 119–20).[5] It therefore

5 Leakey's work and theory were not welcomed by all. Earnest Hooton for one remarked: "Leakey has not the necessary knowledge to speak on the thing ['Kanam Man']: It is such a jaw as should go with H. Rhodesiensis [...] Leakey is only an amateur in a hurry" (Hooton to Keith, 21 November 1935, Peabody

does not come as a surprise that his "Diagrammatic Representation of the Family Tree", like Osborn's "Phylogeny of Man", hardly looks like a tree – there is no natural branching. It rather appears to be a petrified plant, foreign to the current world, but such strange creatures were increasingly contested.

Museum of Archaeology and Ethnology Archives, Earnest A. Hooton Papers, 995-1, I. Correspondence [hereafter Hooton Papers PMA], K, Correspondence Sir Arthur Keith, Box 15). For another unrelenting appraisal of Leakey's character and work, see, for example, Johanson and Edey 1981, 86–88.

12. Meandering Rivers and Synthetic Networks against Polygenism

One development that was going to render Leakey's phylogeny fossil also in an epistemic sense, and Gates' bed of flowers untenable, was the evolutionary synthesis emerging from Mendelian genetics and the Darwinian theory of evolution that began to take hold on paleoanthropology in the following decades. For this development, the shift from a typological to a populational and adaptational approach to the interpretation of physical-anthropological and paleoanthropological material was central. The geneticist Theodosius Dobzhansky, the systematist Ernst Mayr, as well as the paleontologist George Gaylord Simpson undertook a rewriting of human paleontology based on a biological concept of species, interpreting the hominid fossil record within the framework of variation within populations and possible reproductive isolation between groups (polymorphic species as reproductive, ecological, and genetic units). The existence of the taxonomic entities established through this new systematics could be explained by the mechanisms of natural selection, adaptation, and genetic drift. Still lingering conceptions like 'Lamarckism', recapitulation theory, parallelism and orthogenesis, species status of human populations, and typology were undermined.[1] The latter may, too, be indicated by a diagram. Simpson, who also worked at the American Museum of

1 On the old versus new systematics see, e.g., Mayr 1942, 6–8. The American paleontologist Clark Howell's work is often seen as indicative of this shift; he attempted to explain European Upper Pleistocene variation in populational and adaptive terms. He, for example, considered Neanderthal variability as a possible result of climate and genetic isolation (e.g., Trinkaus 1982, 267).

 https://doi.org/10.11647/OBP.0396.15

Natural History and was one of the most influential paleontologists of the twentieth century, insisted that there were no archetypes, but species made up of individual diversity: "A species is not a model to which individuals are referred as more or less perfect reproductions, but a defined field of varying individuals" (Simpson 1941, 14; Sommer 2016a, 128–31). As the diagram reproduced as Figure III.7 shows, in practice species were therefore statistical entities.

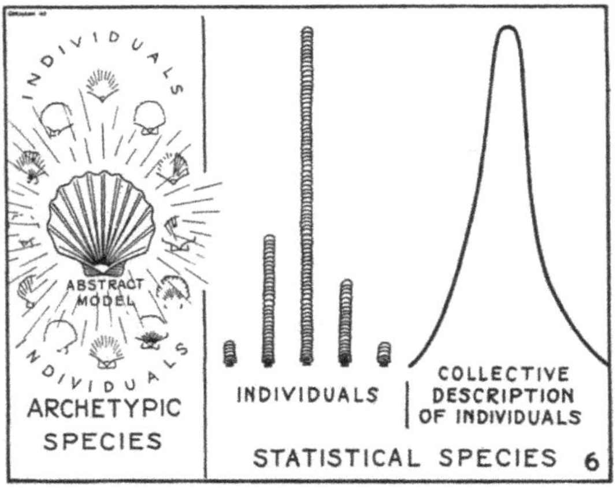

Fig. III.7 Archetypic versus statistical species. George Gaylord Simpson, "The Role of the Individual in Evolution" (*Journal of the Washington Academy of Sciences* 31.1 [1941], 1–20), p. 11.

The British biologist and synthesist Julian Huxley (1938a), too, emphasized that species were natural groups that were reproductively isolated from other such groups. In the influential volume *The New Systematics* that did not deal with humans, Huxley considered it necessary to insist that human evolution had not been mainly a process of differentiation but of convergence through intermixture. Not only could there have been no speciation event; there were no subspecies comparable to those in the rest of the animal kingdom, because humankind "exhibits a peculiar form of reticulate descent consequent upon extreme migration" (1940, 21). Huxley's role in such issues went further back. In the interwar years, he and some of his friends had brought the new understandings of heredity and evolution to bear on anthropology and human genetics, following in Conklin's footsteps when turning them into a political weapon in science and society against 'classical eugenics' and racism.

Key was the book *We Europeans* that Huxley co-authored with the anthropologist Alfred Haddon, in which they already marked humans as an exception in the animal kingdom: "In other animals, the term *sub-species* has been substituted for 'race.' In man, migration and crossing have produced such a fluid state of affairs that no such clear-cut term, as applied to existing conditions, is permissible" (1935, 107–108). There existed no human groups in the sense of geographical isolates. The categorization as subspecies would demand the presence of constant traits sufficient to define a distinct 'race' that were genetically transmitted through common descent – i.e., an isolated branch in a tree. But human groups were of mixed ancestries, they had constantly interbred with each other. Tree diagrams therefore appeared to be part of a racial anthropology, the science of which was outdated and the politics of which were to be challenged. Tree diagrams were doubly wrong when applied to modern human phylogeny: "[i]n man, the branches constantly meet and unite and produce new types of shoots"; "[t]he conventional ancestral tree may have some advantages for representing the descent of animal types; it is wholly unsuitable and misleading for man" (266). In fact, *We Europeans* was essentially a history of human migration and intermixture co-extensive with the history of the genus *Homo*. When a fraction of these processes was mapped onto Europe, the result was not a neat tree but a confusing network that nonetheless came short of representing the true complexity. The evolution and relatedness of modern human populations had to be conceptualized as a net, or one might think of endlessly merging and diverging streams.

In *We Europeans* (1935), Huxley deconstructed the typological race concept that fits the tree structure so well. Anthropology lagged behind biology. It had not yet sufficiently incorporated the novel understanding of species and subspecies, the new genetics and the methods of the biometrician, in the approach to its large amount of data on non-European and European ethnicities. Evidently, the anthropologist had no access to the genetic composition of populations. Nonetheless, Huxley and Haddon suggested taking traits that might have little adaptive value as substitutes for genes; samples should be large and random and analyzed statistically. There should be an emphasis on variation-ranges rather than mean values for traits. In this way, in the case of humans, neither scientific concepts of race (or subspecies), nor popular misconceptions thereof, could be substantiated through anthropometric or blood group data. Such glib, but meaningless expressions as 'racial traits' or 'national characters' were exposed as referring to complicated amalgams of genetic and environmental factors, impossible to disentangle (Sommer 2014; more generally, Sommer 2016a, Part II).

The methods suggested by Huxley and Haddon were particularly difficult to apply in paleoanthropology. An early and rigorous attempt to replace the descriptive-comparative method with statistical analysis was undertaken by Geoffrey McKay Morant in his biometrical studies on prehistoric and ancient crania. Morant worked in Karl Pearson's Biometric Laboratory at University College London; Pearson, along with Francis Galton, had been one of the pioneers of this approach. Morant actually attempted to arrive at a 'racial typology' through the production and analysis of a huge amount of data. Alas, the more data he integrated, the more complicated the picture became. Being aware of the complexity of human relatedness in space and time, he wrote "[i]f a three-dimensional model representing it can be imagined it would resemble a web of irregular pattern rather than a ramifying tree, since the crossing between different branches must have occurred frequently" (1934, 100).

In 1939, in the footsteps of *We Europeans* that constituted a popular critique of Nazism and racism in general, Morant published *The Races of Central Europe* as an argument against Nazi racial theory and the nearly universal notion that languages define 'biological races'. He showed that contrary to the political uses of 'race', cultural characteristics, especially language, did not correlate with biological groupings. His statistics suggested that the distribution of biological markers like skin, hair, and eye color, cranial indices, or blood groups in central Europe was not discrete but showed continuous gradations that must not correlate between traits (Sommer 2015b, 89–91; Clever 2023, 28–36). As in *We Europeans*, maps were the favored images used to communicate the knowledge obtained. Morant positioned his maps in contrast to "the language map" with its longstanding tradition, which, when "accepted as a racial map" (1939, 142) raised the differences between populations to "a fictious maximum" (143). However, Morant still worked with character means (against Huxley's warning), which is why his maps, too, fell short of conveying the fact that "the differences between the group averages are much smaller than those found between the individuals belonging to any particular one of the groups [...]" (142).

Neither *The Races of Central Europe* nor *We Europeans* were much concerned with pre-*Homo* evolution, however. Huxley and Haddon (1935, 33) explicitly stated that since the pre-*Homo* forms like *Pithecanthropus* had died out, they need not dwell on them. It seems that it was the German anatomist Franz Weidenreich who, for the first time, applied the populational understanding to the whole "Pedigree of the Hominidae" (Figure III.8). Weidenreich had held a Professorship in Anatomy at the University of Strasbourg, where he had been assistant to Schwalbe, and subsequently held a post in the Medical Faculty at the University of Heidelberg. Since the end of World War I, Weidenreich encountered obstacles in his career due to antisemitism. However, in 1928 he was made head of the Institute for Physical Anthropology and Racial Science that was financed by the Central Society of Jewish Germans and was meant to bring forth objective knowledge in opposition to racial and antisemitic myths (Hartkopf 2012). Indeed, Weidenreich criticized politically motivated writings on 'race' in *Rasse und Körperbau* [race and anatomy] of 1927, and at the University of Frankfurt, where he held positions from 1929, he partook in a lecture series against racial anthropology that started in 1930.

In his Frankfurt lecture, Weidenreich (1932) emphasized that humans had always migrated, that their subdivision into 'races' was purely conventional, and that characteristics varied along gradients, were not restricted to one group, and were often influenced by factors other than 'race' (such as sex, age, and environment). Indeed, the racial schemas were "fictions" (11) to the criteria of which hardly any real human being fit. Weidenreich accused physical anthropologists of treating individuals and groups that do not fit one of their fictions as hybrids between 'pure races' in order to address this problem. However, in reality, there were only intermediaries in a continuum of variation. It seemed particularly important to deconstruct the correlations of brain characteristics such as size with intelligence or temperament and the associated hierarchization of human groups: one could not read the state of a culture or the intelligence of a person from the scale of cubic centimeters on a measuring cylinder (21). Using the diagrammatic tools of the trade, Weidenreich (1932) presented measurement tables (giving the means of skull volumes) as well as maps (indicating the distribution of head forms) to undermine the claims of racial anthropology and, in particular, the notion of Nordic superiority. In his writings addressed to both science and the public, Weidenreich (e.g., 1931) argued for the beneficial effect of 'racial crossing' and contradicted the views on 'the nature of the Jew' of such illustrious personalities as the race-hygienist Eugen Fischer, who directed the Kaiser Wilhelm Institute for Anthropology, Human Heredity, and Eugenics.

Weidenreich eventually lost his position in Frankfurt because of national socialism. In 1934, he went to the University of Chicago as a Visiting Professor. The following year, he was able to secure the Professorship in Anatomy at the Peking Union Medical College, but then had to leave China due to Japanese occupation and moved to New York, taking up employment at the American Museum of Natural History in 1941. At the end of his career and life, still in American exile (even if as an American citizen), Weidenreich published his monograph on human evolution, *Apes, Giants, and Man* (1946a). Right at the outset, he positioned himself against polygenism (1–3). He once more deconstructed the typological race concept, propagating a populational understanding of anthropological 'races':

> As the matter stands now, the only thing that can be done about the definition of races is [...] to trace these features through the whole of mankind without regard to any previous racial definition or classification. Then the frequency of each combination and its geographical distribution should be noted and a framework built of the final subgrouping of the populations of the earth. This method is in agreement with the views of leading geneticists, like Dobzhansky [...]. (Weidenreich 1946a, 90, see also Ch. 4)

Rather than being comprised of different species, Weidenreich described humankind as a single species of continuous variations. He even argued that not only the living but also the known fossil hominids had to be included in the same species, while he maintained the prevalent nomenclature. Weidenreich held that Australian, 'Mongolian', African, and Eurasian populations had all evolved through the sequence of Archanthropinae (including *Meganthropus*/*Pithecanthropus*/*Sinanthropus*)[2] – Paleoanthropinae (Neanderthaloids) – Neanthropinae (anatomically modern humans), without speciation taking place.[3]

2 The name *Meganthropus* referred to what was thought to be the remains of a large hominid found in Java in 1941; *Sinanthropus pekinensis* (today *Homo erectus*) is similar to *Pithecanthropus* and was found near Beijing in China (1927–29).

3 Weidenreich rejected the Piltdown 'remains' and considered the australopithecines as between the hominid and anthropoid lines. There were other

The geographically distributed groups would have shown local specializations as indicated by the fossil record of a particular region while preserving a certain uniformity through continuous interchange of genes (Weidenreich 1946a, Chs. 1–4). Diagrammatically visualized, this understanding resulted in a network (see Figure III.8), in which the vertical lines stand for descent, the horizontal for distribution and specialization, and the diagonal for gene transfer (Sommer 2015b, 123–25; 2022b, 284–85; on Weidenreich's life and work, see Wolpoff and Caspari 1997, Ch. 7).

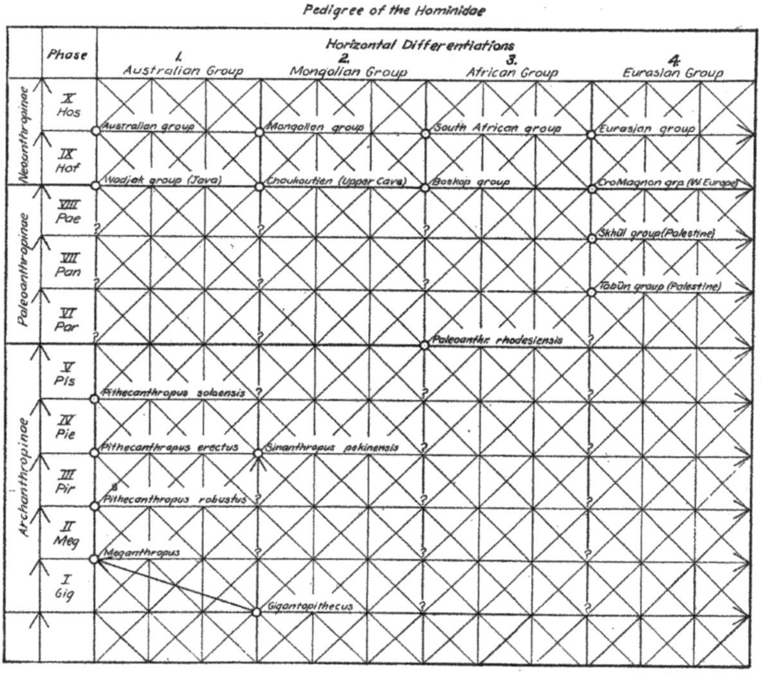

Fig. III.8 "Pedigree of the Hominidae". From *Apes, Giants, and Man* by Franz Weidenreich, Fig. 30, p. 30.

proponents of a Neanderthal-ancestry or -admixture, such as Aleš Hrdlička and Arthur Keith but also Hans Weinert, who in accordance with his rejection of the pre-*sapiens* view was skeptical of the unity and meaningfulness of the Piltdown fragments (Hrdlička 1927; Weinert 1932, 261–70; Keith 1948). While both Hrdlička and Weinert seem to have favored a unilinear view of evolution in the tradition of Weidenreich's intellectual father, Schwalbe (Weinert 1932, 264, explicitly criticized the tendency of relegating the known hominid fossils to side branches) – although their exact views on which Neanderthals gave rise to *Homo sapiens*, and where, differed –, Keith presented a multilinear model (see below). For an earlier expression of Weidenreich's theory, see, e.g., Weidenreich 1940.

For Dobzhansky (1944, 257–65), who like Huxley and others became an outspoken critic of current understandings of race and biological determinism (e.g., Beatty 1994; Sommer 2010a), the concept that hominid evolution had taken place on the 'racial' level, with no more than one hominid species at any time horizon, allowed a synthesis between the classic model of evolution at a center with successive radiation and replacement and Weidenreich's multiregional but unilinear evolution. According to this synthesis, Weidenreich might have been right in that several local fossil varieties were ancestral to living humankind, but not each local type had been transformed into a different human 'race'. The classic view might therefore have been correct in that some of the past 'races' had contributed more than others to the genetic makeup of present humanity. Local adaptations might have spread through the whole species, replacing and absorbing others on their way. Dobzhansky rejected the tree model in which the known fossils represented extinct branches and were thus not part of the trunk leading to modern humans, which split into different branches of modern 'races'.[4] The systematist Mayr, too, was part of the initiative of merging taxa based on the single-species hypothesis. Mayr (1950) included also the australopithecines within the range of variation of *Homo* and regarded all yet known hominids as representing a single line of descent (*Homo transvalensis* [*Australopithecus*] – *Homo erectus* – *Homo sapiens*) (Sommer 2015b, 125–26).

Against this backdrop, it is not astonishing that when Gates' *Human Ancestry* appeared in 1948, it caused controversy. We have so far seen that Gates' understanding of human evolution and kinship did not appear out of nowhere. To the contrary, the overemphasis of parallelism, and the refusal of close kinship among living humans to the degree of classifying them as different species, had been integral to the work of other, well-established scientists. Gates took such notions to their extreme, thus himself rejecting the phylogenetic tree to capture the nature of human kinship, even if for reasons opposite to those of the synthesists:

4 Dobzhansky's claim that only one human or prehuman species existed in any one territory at any one time in evolutionary history was challenged by the diversity of the genus *Australopithecus*, two species of which seemed to have been contemporaneous in South Africa. Dobzhansky accepted two genera, *Australopithecus* and *Homo*, the latter with two species, *erectus* and *sapiens* (Dobzhansky 1962, Ch. 7; see also 1942; 1950, for his ideas on evolution intelligible to the general reading public).

> A real difficulty in the construction of phylogenetic 'trees' is that the diverging branches and twigs of a tree inadequately represent what takes place in the evolution of any group or phylum of organisms. They represent the divergent variations, but take no account of the equally numerous parallel mutations. (Gates 1948, 18)

However, we have also seen that, already in the 1930s, the tide began to turn for evidential, theoretical, and political reasons. Gates resisted these trends. In a review of *We Europeans*, the book that set the new tone regarding race science, he rejected the idea that humankind formed but one species, instead postulating several species, the similarities between which were due to parallel evolution (Gates 1936a). By the time Gates' *Human Ancestry* (1948) appeared, the anthropologist Wilton Marion Krogman of Pennsylvania University warned that "[t]he reader is led, even though perhaps unconsciously, into a racist patterning of thought, both culturally and biologically" (1949, 21). However, the press mainly took on Gates' somewhat cryptic passage on the self-elimination of the 'Caucasian race' and the rise to dominance of people of color. The reports stayed astonishingly calm about the concept of several human species of independent origins. But, as the *Book of the Month* humorously predicted, it caused controversy or even war within science (see Figure III.9).

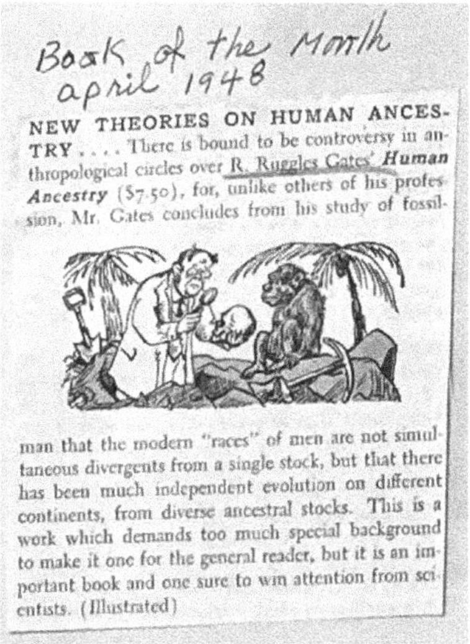
Book of the Month april 1948

NEW THEORIES ON HUMAN ANCESTRY .... There is bound to be controversy in anthropological circles over R. Ruggles Gates' ***Human Ancestry*** ($7.50), for, unlike others of his profession, Mr. Gates concludes from his study of fossil-man that the modern "races" of men are not simultaneous divergents from a single stock, but that there has been much independent evolution on different continents, from diverse ancestral stocks. This is a work which demands too much special background to make it one for the general reader, but it is an important book and one sure to win attention from scientists. (Illustrated)

Fig. III.9 "There is bound to be controversy in anthropological circles" (*Book of the Month*, April 1948, Press Cuttings, Vol. 3, 1936–54, King's College London Archives, Gates, Professor Reginald Ruggles [1882–1962], K/PP65, 9/3), all rights reserved, with kind permission from King's College London Archives.

The British zoologist Solly Zuckerman (1949), among other things an expert on primates, labelled the contents of *Human Ancestry* "Genealogical Guesses" and, in addition to pointing to shortcomings in passages on anatomy, accused Gates of ignorance concerning Zuckerman's own pet methods: biometry and statistics. The American geneticist and editor of *The Journal of Heredity*, Robert C. Cook, tore the book apart, mocking "the paradoxical conclusion that the 'so-called races' are not even cousins" and "the thinness of the speculative ice on which the author skates".[5] Cook also directly tackled the phylogenetic diagrams. With a pun on Gates' botanical roots, he called them "a strange amalgam of botany and anthropology, the branches giving rise in weird disorder to columbines, peas, lilies, and forget-me-nots!" The affront was that "some so-called races are depicted as remote relatives who sprang from a very different line of Pithecanthropus and are hardly to be included in the human family at all."[6] The influential German-born, but US-based, primatologist Adolph Hans Schultz denied anthropological expertise to the geneticist Gates. Among many things, Schultz took issue with Gates' primate tree, which to him looked as confusing as Gates' scheme of human phylogeny: "These chapters include a large, summarizing family-tree in full bloom, entitled 'Scheme of Higher Primate Evolution,' which in some respects is so new or naive as to be startling to primatologists" (1948, 146).

Similarly, with another hint at Gates' background in botany, Simpson considered "[t]he strange, pseudo-botanical phylogenies" confusing and contradictory. The first of these suggested to him relations between different human and anthropoid stems, even though he may "be following the wrong tendrils on this plant" (Simpson to Gates, 7 February 1950, King's College London Archives, Gates, Professor Reginald Ruggles [1882–1962], K/PP65 [hereafter Gates Papers KCL], 7/19/3). As further commentaries indicate, Simpson was not alone with this reading (draft letters to newspapers, Gates Papers KCL, 4/81/13).[7] In

5 "The Heirs of Pithecanthropus", *New York Times Book Review*, 6 June 1948, Press Cuttings, Vol. 3, 1936–54, Gates Papers KCL, 9/3.

6 Ibid.

7 Indeed, the scheme of higher primate evolution already contains a scheme of human phylogeny (Gates 1948, 56) that blatantly contradicts Figure III.2. In the scheme of higher primate evolution, rather than having "*H. caucasicus*" as the most isolated stalk (that nonetheless in the more recent time meets with "*H. africanus*"

Simpson's opinion, the thesis that Gates' phylogenetic trees distributed – "that living men represent several distinct species that have evolved separately and in a polyphyletic manner" – was not only unscientific but "socially a dangerous doctrine"; he cautioned Gates that scientists were "responsible for the social and ethical consequences of [their] work and publications" (Simpson to Gates, 7 February 1950, Gates Papers KCL, 7/19/3). In contrast, Simpson emphasized his belief in "the brotherhood of all men" (Simpson to Gates, 21 February 1950, Gates Papers KCL, 7/19/3; and the quarrel went on: Simpson to Gates, 2 and 14 March 1950, Gates Papers KCL, 7/19/3). Gates' book seems to have been considered important enough even by Simpson to also attack its "revival of old ideas of independent, parallel evolution of modern man as several distinct species" in his *The Meaning of Evolution* (1949, 92, note 5, continued on 93, see also 96).

Dobzhansky, too, had strongly objected to Gates' and others' "excesses of splitting" humans into different species in his correspondence with Gates (Dobzhansky to Gates, 2 March 1945, Gates Papers KCL, 7/16/1). It was difficult for Dobzhansky "to understand how a geneticist can possibly adhere to such a view" (Dobzhansky to Gates, 5 March 1945, Gates Papers KCL, 7/16/1). Gates, on his part, criticized Dobzhansky's 'lumping' view of human evolution in *Human Ancestry* (1948, 404–405). The book ignited the heated debate to the degree that Dobzhansky called Gates a 'mutant' and his book 'excrement' in correspondence with Ashley Montagu (Marks 2010, 197), who discussed it for the *Saturday Review* (Yudell 2014, 131).[8] Gates was also aware of a review

via the Mediterraneans), this species groups with "*H. africanus*", while it is "*H. mongoloideus*", "*americanus*", and "*australicus*" that are unrelated to other humans. It seems that the discrepancy between the two diagrams has to do with the fact that Gates recognized orangoid, gorilloid, and australophitecoid lines based on the absence and presence of bow ridges, respectively a middle position. He classified both "*H. caucasicus*" and "*africanus*" with the first, but "*H. australicus*" with the second (and "*mongoloideus*" with the third). However, he thought of these 'lines' as purely morphological not genealogical. The text of Chapter 3, "Evolution of the Mammals" (44–77), does not explain or clearly support the scheme of higher primate evolution. Rather, Gates in the text treats the different studies and views of others, often without taking a clear stance, which is typical for his writings.

8 Ashley Montagu, "Inequality of Man", *N. Y. Saturday Literary Review*, 28 February 1848, 23, Press Cuttings, Vol. 3, 1936–54, Gates Papers KCL, 9/3. For Gates' reply to Montagu's criticism of *Human Ancestry*, see draft letter to a newspaper, 4 March 1948, Gates Papers KCL, 4/81/13/6, and Gates, "Human Ancestry", *N. Y. Saturday*

by the serologist William C. Boyd in the *American Journal of Physical Anthropology*, in which Boyd accused him of being a racist of the mold of the German Nazis (Gates to Hooton, 26 October 1948, Peabody Museum of Archaeology and Ethnology Archives, Earnest A. Hooton Papers, 995-1, I. Correspondence [hereafter Hooton Papers PMA], G, Correspondence R. Ruggles Gates [International Eugenics Congress], Box 10, Folder 4).[9]

Gates was mainly defended by other scientists and scholars whose views had become marginalized, like the psychologist and segregationist Henry E. Garrett from the Department of Psychology at Columbia University, with whom he would found *Mankind Quarterly* (see below). Garrett fought against Krogman on the pages of *Science*: "On the contrary, its [*Human Ancestry*'s] emphasis upon biology provides a much needed and refreshing antidote to the wishful thinking of the apostles of the 'new anthropology.' It should be read by every psychologist, and should be required reading for all sociologists" (Garrett and Krogman 1950).[10] With "new anthropology", Garrett was referring to yet another trend: neither the discovery of important fossils like the australopithecines, nor the new synthetic approach, but to cultural anthropology. Its gaining ground was also irritating to some physical anthropologists. To this I turn in the next chapter with the example of Earnest Hooton as a starting point for witnessing the reaffirmation of the polygenist tree. Hooton was the leading physical anthropologist in America in the interwar years. He conferred with his countryman and colleague Carlton Coon, one of his protégés, on the latter's recommendation of *Human Ancestry* for publication to Harvard University Press and wrote the foreword to Gates' book.[11]

Review of Literature, 3 April 1948, Press Cuttings, Vol. 3, 1936–54, Gates Papers KCL, 9/3.

9 Interestingly, Simpson's and Mayr's writings were treated rather positively in Gates' *Human Ancestry* while Gates attacked Dobzhansky (Gates 1948, Ch. 12).

10 There were also rather neutral discussions of the book (e.g., "Review of '*Human Ancestry' from a Genetical Point of View*, by R. Ruggles Gates" 1948; Lubran 1951; also Aiyappan 1949; Dodson 1949).

11 Hooton to Gates, 24 October 1946, Gates Papers KCL, 7/16/1; Coon to Hooton, 3 December 1946, Hooton Papers PMA, C, Correspondence Carleton S. Coon, Box 6, Folder 3; Gates 1948, see xv–xvi for Hooton's foreword.

13. The Reaffirmation of the Polygenist 'Tree'

Even before the publication of Morant's book (1939) on the biometrical approach treated in the last chapter, Hooton discussed the notion of race and explained that there was no consensus on the term's definition or meaning and meaningfulness for human beings in his *Up from the Ape* (1931). He classified the anthropologists as divided into the environmentalists (Boasians), who denied any cultural or psychological correlates of 'race', the racists (ethnomaniacs), who saw a close affinity between 'racial type', culture, and psychology without scientific proof, and the biometricians, who were somewhere in between in that they carried out measurements but no 'racial' classification. Hooton seems to have positioned himself as moderate, but, all the same, tried to come up with the missing proof for the reality of human 'races' by the methods of biometry; this was true even for the correlation of mental traits with physical characteristics that supposedly determined 'races'. 'Race' to him was a useful category to classify humanity and, after a discussion of morphological and physiological traits that may serve to do so, he proposed the division into Black Africans, Asians, Europeans, and 'Composites', and then went on to subdivide these further (Hooton 1931, 394–605; on Hooton, see, e.g., Barkan 1992, 101–108; Sommer 2015b, 93–99).

The ambiguous stance towards the race question became even more evident in a paper in *Science* of 1935, where Hooton observed that, until the turn of the twentieth century, 'races' had been based on language, geography, or nationality, while they had now come to be defined by common descent and common hereditary characteristics. We have seen in Part I and Part II that the genealogical understanding of the

 https://doi.org/10.11647/OBP.0396.16

human varieties/'races' goes back to eighteenth-century natural history and the measuring approach also had its fledgling beginnings in that century. But Hooton felt that with the introduction of genetics, the physical anthropologist had to measure minutely for small differences between types that could refer to hereditary units. The insights from experimental geneticists required great carefulness in the definition of what might be hereditary. At the 'extreme' end of the spectrum of opinions on the scientific concept of race, Hooton again identified the countermovement of Franz Boas' powerful school of environmentalists, who were particularly against the Nordic propaganda. Like Morant, Hooton himself was of the opinion that with Pearson's biometry, his sampling methods and statistical tools, much had been added to the reliability of physical anthropology, and technological revolutions such as the electric calculator had worked wonders in handling data of large series of individuals. He was therefore optimistic that if an adequate amount of data from each 'racial' group were subjected to these new approaches with the help of these new technologies, a 'definitive racial classification' could be established. Until that would be the case, he conceded, assertions of 'racial inferiority or superiority' had to be regarded as unscientific (Hooton 1935).

At the same time, Hooton defended Gates "against the wrath of the egalitarians" as late as the 1950s when the latter applied for a research grant to the Permanent Science Fund of the American Academy of Arts and Sciences.[1] To the American Philosophical Society, Hooton wrote:

> Professor Ruggles Gates is a somewhat controversial figure amongst geneticists and physical anthropologists because he holds decided views on the diversity of human species and upon racial differences. Partly for this reason he has been under violent attack by certain anthropologists who desire to minimize racial differences. Some of these attacks have been most unfair, in my opinion. The work in genetics has been subjected to similar criticism. While I cannot state that Professor Gates seems to me to be an absolutely topflight anthropological investigator, I do feel

1 Hooton to the Permanent Science Fund of the American Academy of Arts and Sciences, 12 February 1952 (see also 21 January 1954), Hooton Papers PMA, G, Correspondence R. Ruggles Gates (International Eugenics Congress), Box 10, Folder 4.

> that he is likely to produce something worthwhile if this modest request for aid is granted.[2]

It is also interesting to consider Hooton in relation to Gates regarding visualizations of human phylogeny. In the first edition of *Up from the Ape* of 1931, Hooton stated that "[t]he constructing of family trees of man and the primates is the perennial sport of the student of human origins" (390). He called his primate family tree of 1931 "a good orthodox tree, built upon the general consensus of anthropological opinion [...]" (393). His second diagram of modern human kinship (Fig. 58, 582) stood for the notion that the 'racial stocks' began to differentiate millions of years ago through mutations. Eventually, these 'primary races' gave rise to 'secondary races' through 'miscegenation events' and the stabilization and further change of hybrids. The relating diagram Hooton produced to capture this vision of modern human history was less orthodox and "not a family tree, but a sort of arterial trunk with offshoots and connecting vessels" (583). Hooton's "good orthodox tree" of the primates from 1931 was still part of the phase when anthropologists tended to grow branches for fossil hominids apart from those leading to modern humans, as exemplified by Osborn's and Leakey's trees in Figure III.4 and Figure III.6. By the time of the second edition of *Up from the Ape* of 1946, Hooton's "Family tree of man" had taken a step in the direction that Gates – on whom Hooton drew in the section on human genetics – radicalized: Hooton provided the branches leading to the modern human 'races' with different fossil ancestors (1946 [1931], Fig. 61, 413). The lines of the "Basic White" and "Australoids" contain such different 'fossil' forms as *Eoanthropus* (Piltdown) and *Pithecanthropus* respectively, and they are far apart in the image space. It is images like Figure III.10 that stand for the apex of diagrammatic 'racial' distancing.

2 Hooton to the American Philosophical Society, 1953, Hooton Papers PMA, G, Correspondence R. Ruggles Gates (International Eugenics Congress), Box 10, Folder 4; further on Hooton's support in finding funding for Gates, see Hooton to Gates, 27 February 1946, Gates Papers KCL, 7/16/1; Hooton to Gates, 12 April 1949, Gates Papers KCL, 7/18/2; Hooton to Gates, 7 December 1950, Gates Papers KCL, 7/19/2. On Hooton's science and politics, see Barkan 1992, 101–108, 312–18.

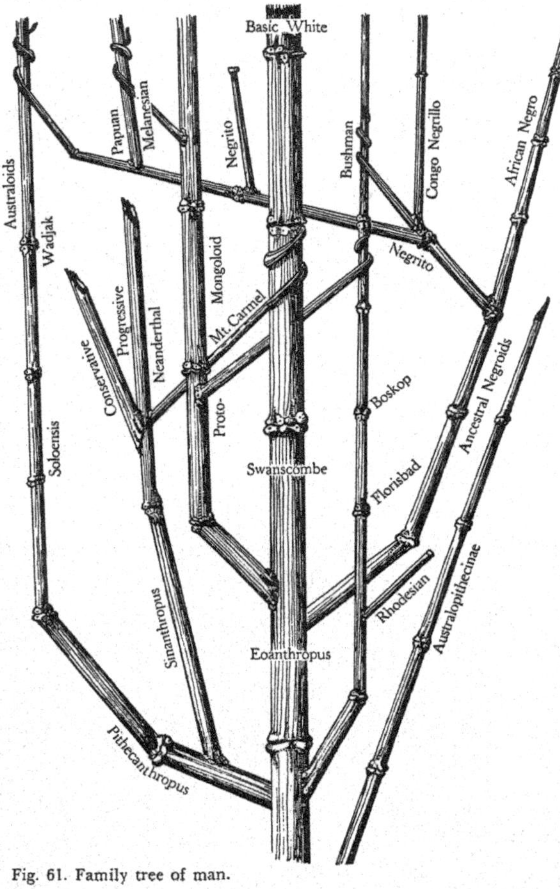

Fig. 61. Family tree of man.

Fig. III.10 "Family tree of man". Earnest Albert Hooton, *Up from the Ape*, 2nd ed. (New York: Macmillan, 1946), Fig. 61, p. 413. Public domain.

Simpson for one called the revised *Up from the Ape* "[a] flippant and personal interpretation" of human origin and affinities (Simpson 1949, 93, note 5). Hooton seems to have been inspired by Weidenreich (Hooton 1946 [1931], 410–21), but the matrix of genetic exchange throughout hominid evolution of Weidenreich's phylogenetic network in Figure III.8 has degenerated to a few branches that "parasitically entwine themselves with other branches and grow into them" (Hooton 1946 [1931], 414). The "Basic White" are only thus affected by a certain group of Neanderthals, and the tree otherwise conveys independent and parallel 'racial' evolution. In fact, rather than a tree with branches (much less a network), the image is reminiscent of bamboo stalks that grow besides each other in similar directions – in Hooton's case, they appear to follow the strongest central stalk of the "Basic White" with more or less success.

This leads on to Hooton's idol Arthur Keith.[3] The influential British anthropologist had initially conceptualized hominid phylogeny as unilinear similar to Schwalbe. However, he soon changed to the shape of a tree, not least to provide the British with a long and noble ancestry. He, like his friend and correspondent Osborn, had been among those who removed all the known (pre-*sapiens*) hominids from the lines leading to modern humans (Sommer 2007, 197–212).[4] Eventually, however, he propagated a model similar to Gates'. Keith saw their "interpretations of things come closer" and felt they were "both indebted to friend Hooton" (Keith to Gates, 14 August 1945, Gates Papers KCL, 7/16/2). After Keith had read *Human Ancestry*, which Gates presented to him with an inscription, he pointed out that there was "a large measure of agreement"[5] between them, and that his forthcoming *A New Theory of Human Evolution* (1948) "corresponds to your 'Human Ancestry'" (Keith to Gates, 30 March 1948, Gates Papers KCL, 7/16/2).

This agreement or correspondence is corroborated by Keith's new diagram of human phylogeny: he referred the branches leading to the modern human 'races' back millions of years in time and stocked them with different (postulated) fossil genera, without the assumption of gene transfer between the lines. These very long, independent lines of ascent were already differentiated at the stage of ground-dwelling anthropoids and Dartians (australopithecines). Out of these forms supposedly evolved in parallel through *Pithecanthropus* and several fossil stages the "Australian"; through 'Kanam Man' and *Homo rhodesiensis* (fossil cranium found 1921 in Zambia) the "African"; through *Sinanthropus* the "Sinasian"; respectively through Neanderthals from northern Israel and Cro-Magnons the "Caucasian" (Keith 1948, diagram on 158–59; see also

3 See particularly Hooton Papers PMA, K, Correspondence Sir Arthur Keith, Box 15. Hooton agreed with Keith's Piltdown reconstruction and emphasized how inspired he was by the elder's work in whose footsteps he wanted to follow.

4 Osborn welcomed Keith's new phylogeny in the 'updated' version of *The Antiquity of Man* (1925 [1915]) (Osborn to Keith, May 11, 1931, correspondence with Arthur Keith, Henry Fairfield Osborn Papers, American Museum of Natural History Museum Archives, Mss. O835 [hereafter Osborn Papers AMNH], Box 12, Folder 2).

5 Keith to Gates, 19 May 1948, Gates Papers KCL, 7/18/3.

Ch. 6; 1950, 599).[6] Keith's diagram shown in Figure III.11 again remotely resembles a dead tree, and, like Gates' phylogeny, it is reminiscent of the early multilinear, or polygenist, theories advanced by Haeckel and even of the polyphyletic view of Hermann Klaatsch.

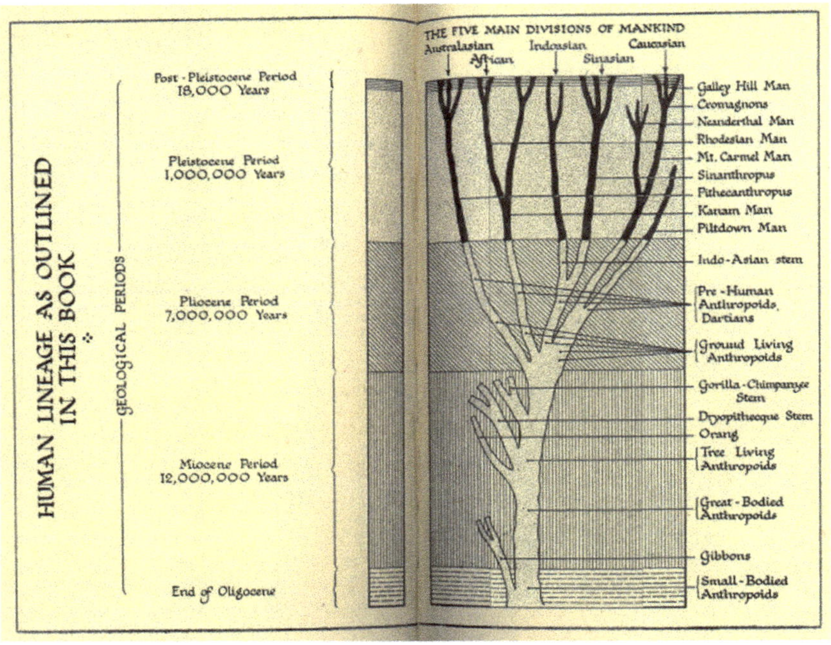

Fig. III.11 "Human Lineage". Arthur Keith, *A New Theory of Human Evolution* (London: Watts, 1948), pp. 158–59.

6 Keith's view on the Neanderthals' place in the hominid family differed from Weidenreich's, Weinert's, and Hrdlička's (whose views also differed from each other), in that he only regarded early non-European Neanderthals as ancestral ('pre-Neanderthal stage of man'), and as ancestral only to the 'Caucasian' line (on the so-called 'Neanderthal-phase' and 'pre-Neanderthal-stage-of-man' theories see Bowler 1986, 105–111). It is interesting to observe that Hooton, who as we have seen generally agreed with Keith's theory of the great antiquity of modern human anatomy, seems to have been slightly disappointed by Keith's reintegration of the Neanderthals into the human line. Even more so, since Hooton like others regarded the discovery of 'Swanscombe Man' (a modern-looking brain case from Swanscombe, East Kent, from Lower Paleolithic/Acheulean, discovered 1935/36 by Alvan T. Marston) and 'Fontéchevade Man' (modern-looking cranial remains from the Charente, France, discovered by Germaine Henri-Martin in 1947) as confirming the correctness of the older view (Hooton Papers PMA, K, Correspondence Sir Arthur Keith, Box 15; for a discussion of whether these 'fossils' could support the Neanderthal-phase, pre-Neanderthal-stage, or pre-*sapiens* hypothesis, see Vallois 1954).

While it was Keith who positioned himself in the tradition of Haeckel, the similarity of Gates' phylogeny to that of Klaatsch had not escaped the attention of contemporaries like Zuckerman or Cook, who pointed it out in their reviews of *Human Ancestry*.[7] With *Der Werdegang der Menschheit und die Entstehung der Kultur* (1920), the German anthropologist Klaatsch had been an early proponent of a kind of parallel evolution that even aligned different recent 'races' with different ape genera. The fact that the Neanderthals were associated with an African fauna, while the Cro-Magnons seemed to belong to Asian animals, made Klaatsch speculate on human migrations. His subsequent comparative studies of the anthropoid apes of the respective continents led him to infer a particularly close relationship between the Neanderthals and gorillas on the one hand, and the Cro-Magnons and orangutans on the other. Generally speaking, he believed in an early separation of the hominid-anthropoid group into a western and an eastern branch from which had evolved the anthropoids and human 'races' still found in these regions. Klaatsch considered the common hominid-anthropoid ancestors to have been more humanoid than anthropoid; the apes had degenerated from that original state. Klaatsch even speculated that the Aboriginal Australians represented an isolated survival of this original stock of which *Pithecanthropus erectus* gave testimony (see Figure III.12). Similar to Haeckel, Klaatsch conjectured that the common origin of both groups might have been a now submerged continent in the Indian Ocean (Klaatsch 1920, e.g., 89–92, 255–386).[8]

---

7 Zuckerman 1949, 742; Cook, "The Heirs of Pithecanthropus", *New York Times Book Review*, 6 June 1948, Press Cuttings, Vol. 3, 1936–54, Gates Papers KCL, 9/3. Gates attempted to defend himself against his alignment with Klaatsch by Cook (letter [to the editor of the *New York Times Book Review*] by R. Ruggles Gates, 26 July and 30 August 1948, Press Cuttings, Vol. 3, 1936–54, Gates Papers KCL, 9/3). As indicated above, Gates recognized orangoid, gorilloid, and australopithecoid lines based on the absence and presence of brow ridges, respectively a middle position. '*Homo caucasicus*' and '*africanus*' he attributed to the first, '*Homo australicus*' to the second (and '*mongoloideus*' to the third). However, he understood these 'lines' as purely morphological not genealogical (Gates 1948, 44–77).

8 *Der Werdegang der Menschheit* was published posthumously, as Klaatsch had died in 1916. There existed several polyphyletic theories of this extreme form that linked different human groups to different apes or even monkeys. Human groups were, in this case, seen as more closely related to some nonhuman primates than to the remainder of humankind and usually correspondingly as constituting different species or genera. Criteria for grouping particular humans with particular nonhuman primates were, for example, head shape (dolicho- versus brachycephaly)

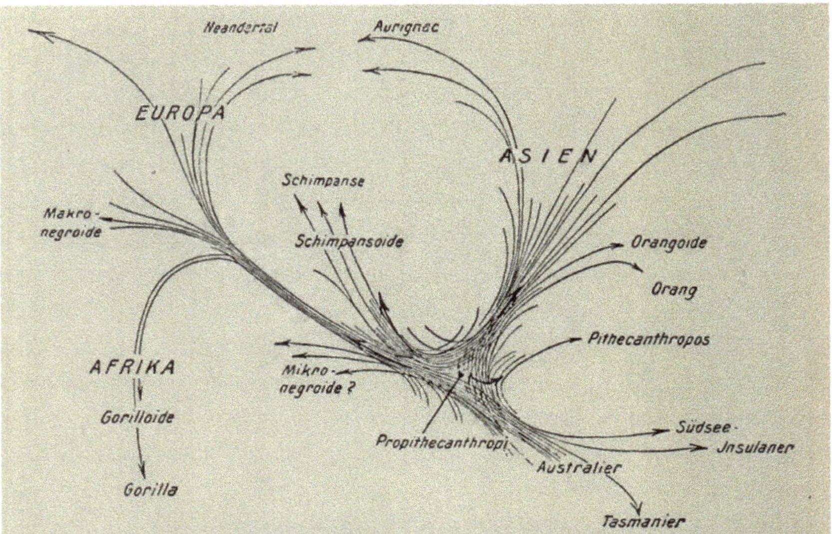

Abb. 273. Versuch eines Schemas zur Erläuterung der Verbreitung der Menschenrassen und Menschenaffen. Nach Klaatsch.
Gibbon und Mongolen sind nicht berücksichtigt worden.

Fig. III.12 "Verbreitung der Menschenrassen und Menschenaffen" [Distribution of the human races and the anthropoid apes]. Hermann Klaatsch, *Der Werdegang der Menschheit und die Entstehung der Kultur* (Berlin: Bong, 1920), Fig. 273, p. 330. Public domain.

Keith was one of the more prolific tree builders and, as mentioned above, he regarded himself as in the footsteps of Haeckel, this "pioneer and prince of pedigree-makers" (Keith 1934, 2) who "immediately saw life as a great tree rooted deeply in the geological past with trunk and branches dead, buried and fossilized [...]" (2–3). It seems therefore that a "pedigree or family tree" (8), "human genealogies", or "evolutionary

or facial characteristics (e.g., Vogt 1863ab; Sergi 1908, see particularly figures on 82 and 530; Sera 1917). Maurus Horst (1913), to give a particularly radical example, separated the human 'races' into phyla that originated as far down in the primate order as the lemurs. The French anthropologist Henri V. Vallois has referred to these kind of theories as "polyphyletic theories (*sensu stricto*)" or as "external polyphyletism", while theories such as those of Gates (1948) and Keith (1948) that have parallel 'racial' lines throughout the *Hominidae* would constitute "internal polyphyletism" (Vallois 1952, 70). Even though one can debate this, given Keith's differentiated ground-living anthropoids as points of origin for the human lines, Vallois (1952, 69) thus noticed that they are clearly a form of polygenism, which some proponents were not shy of stating themselves, as can be judged from the Italian anthropologist Giuseppe Sergi's title "L'apologia del mio poligenismo" ('the apology for my polygenism', 1909).

pedigrees" (10) really were supposed to look like dead, fossil plants. Beyond Haeckel, we have seen that Keith realized the similarity of his theory to those of Hooton and Gates, and, oddly enough, in the same breath, he also included Weidenreich in the club of like-minded (Keith 1948, 256 footnote; see also 1947). In fact, Gates drew very strongly, at times nearly exclusively, on Weidenreich's research in his treatment of human evolution in *Human Ancestry*, and Keith even claimed priority with regard to Weidenreich's interpretation, since his own presentation of the multilinear human phylogeny in *A New Theory of Human Evolution* had been preceded by a presidential address to the British Speleological Association as early as 1936: "This was, so far as I know, the first time the conception had been put forward that modern races of mankind are the direct descendants of early Pleistocene forms of humanity" (Keith 1948, 256 footnote).

Reminiscent of the orthogenesis of Keith's by then deceased friend Osborn, in this address, Keith had suggested parallel development due to genetic predispositions, or "independent evolution of the races of mankind during the whole length of the pleistocene [sic] period [...]" when "separated branches of the human family appear to have been unfolding a programme of latent qualities" (1937, 6) – that is for some half-million years. Keith (1937) explicitly rejected a relatively recent common ancestor and a common geographical origin and center of dispersion for the modern human 'races' by referring to this model as the biblical story. He supplanted it with independent geographical origins, thus making reference to the pre-evolutionary polygenist theories. The very year Keith's radicalization or decomposition of the human family tree was published, Gates (1937), too, discussed the independent origin and parallel evolution of the human 'races' that in fact had species status.

Disregarding the deep-rooted differences between his polygenism and Weidenreich's single-species hypothesis, Keith suggested that Weidenreich had independently come up with a similar model five years later. This enlistment of Weidenreich was not neutral, because Keith's 'tree' stood for his Haeckelian understanding that violence between groups, as exemplified in recent times in imperialism and wars, had been going on between hominid genera, species, and 'races' throughout their evolution, and had been and was a motor of progress (Sommer 2007,

207–209).[9] Indeed, Keith's correspondence with Gates demonstrates their growing antisemitism (including antisemitic conspiracy theories) as well as racism. Keith echoed Gates' sentiments with laments about "the chosen race" and its emphasis, even embracement, of 'racial intermixture' to the extent of confessing "I now understand Hitler's attitude".[10] Despite his appropriation of Weidenreich in publications, Keith grew weary of Weidenreich when the latter began to attack Gates. Weidenreich contested Gates' polygenism, as well as Gates' scientific expertise, in 1946, which unleashed a battle between the two concerning the taxonomic status of human (fossil and recent) varieties.[11] After all, Weidenreich was "one of the chosen race", and Keith now found him "lack[ing] in understanding and power of thinking" (Keith to Gates, 9 June 1948, Gates Papers KCL, 7/18/3).[12]

Weidenreich's theory and worldview indeed stood in stark contrast to those of Keith and Gates. He emphasized that all humans are "fundamentally the same" (1946a, 2): while there had been different local lines of descent, these varieties had remained within the species boundary through genetic exchange. Furthermore, Keith's claim of priority was not only misguided conceptually but also chronologically. Weidenreich had introduced the notion of a humanity that was marked by a considerable degree of variation as well as interbreeding early on in his phylogenetic work. Nonetheless, this notion, too, was structured around the conception of a "Stufenleiter der Entwicklung" [ladder of development], on which not all 'races' had advanced to the same degree with regard to certain anatomical characteristics (1928, 57; see also 1947b, 202). Still: Weidenreich's model of human evolution was unilinear. Haeckel's, Klaatsch's, Hooton's, Keith's, and Gates', to the

9 Osborn had disagreed on the question of the 'eugenic' role of war, particularly World War I, however. This was not due to the fact that he abhorred war in general, but rather because he considered it 'dysgenic' to have representatives of the 'Nordic race' on both sides and the 'fittest' of the nations at the front (correspondence with Arthur Keith, Osborn Papers AMNH, Box 12, Folder 2).

10 Keith to Gates, 20 November 1950, Gates Papers KCL, 7/19/2; also Keith to Gates, 23 February 1950, Gates Papers KCL, 7/19/2; Gates to Hooton, 27 January 1949, Hooton Papers PMA, G, Correspondence R. Ruggles Gates (International Eugenics Congress), Box 10, Folder 4.

11 Weidenreich 1946b; 1947a; Gates 1947; Gates, "Species and Genera of Mankind", 1947, Gates Papers KCL, 4/66/1, 4/75/17, 4/75/18.

12 See also Royal College of Surgeons of England Archives, Papers of Arthur Keith, General Correspondence G: Gates, Reginald Ruggles, MS0018/1/6/4.

contrary, were multilinear and in certain ways polygenist. Weidenreich himself was clear about this fact. In the context of his "Family tree of the hominid-anthropoid stock" (1946a, Fig. 26, 24), he observed that the "diagram presented in Figure 26 departs from the usual form of those pedigrees. An attempt has been made to indicate, also by graphic means (crosslines), the obvious tendency of the listed forms to exchange specific acquired features" (25) (see Figure III.13).

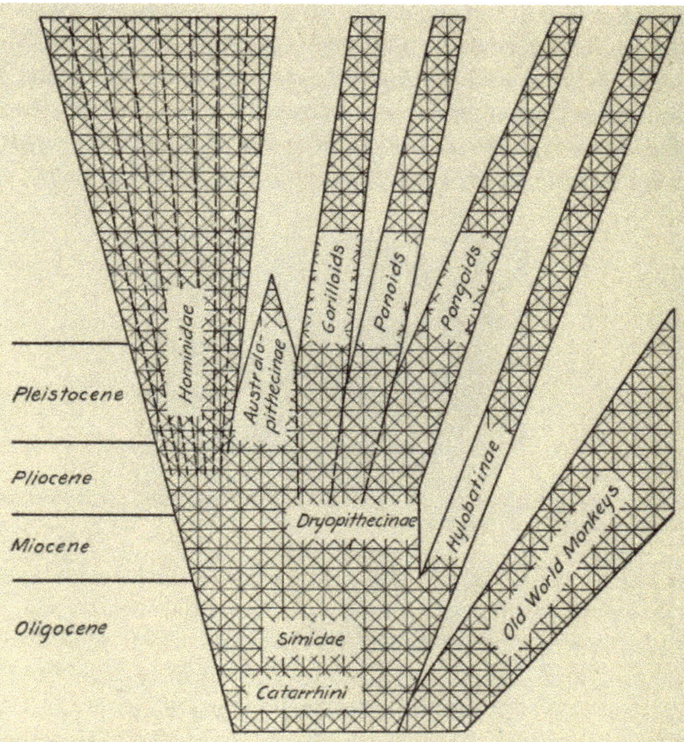

FIG. 26.—Family tree of the hominid-anthropoid stock of the primate order. (For details see text.)

Fig. III.13 "Family tree of the hominid-anthropoid stock". From *Apes, Giants, and Man* by Franz Weidenreich, Fig. 26, p. 24. © 1946 by The University of Chicago. All rights reserved. Reprinted by permission of The University of Chicago Press.

Hooton's, Gates', and in particular Keith's drawing on, or rather distortion of, Weidenreich's ideas and imagery may explain why Weidenreich's diagrammatics were so often misunderstood. In fact, in his review of *Apes, Giants, and Man*, Krogman (1947) paid close attention to Weidenreich's main tenets, including the notion of a human evolution without speciation. At the same time, he came up with his own diagram for Weidenreich's evolutionary phases that suggested parallel and independent evolution (see Figure III.14). In 1952, the French anthropologist Henri V. Vallois (1952, 75–76) classified Weidenreich's diagram among the polygenist and polyphyletic ones. And in 1959, the American physical anthropologist William Howells (1959, 236) categorized different phylogenetic interpretations and described Weidenreich's model as typical of "the Polyphyletic or Candelabra School" that he diagrammatically represented by parallel and independent lines of descent from an unspecified source up to the "Australians", "Mongoloids", "Africans", and "Eurasians", even though, in the text (235), Howells granted that Weidenreich had included gene flow and worked with the single-species concept.[13]

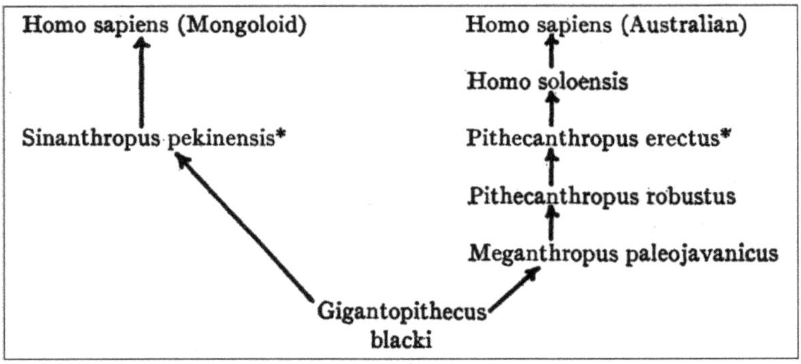

Fig. III.14 A diagrammatic re-rendering of Weidenreich. Wilton Marion Krogman, "Review of *Apes, Giants and Man*, by Franz Weidenreich" . Reproduced by permission of the American Anthropological Association from *American Anthropologist*, 49.I [1947], p. 116. Not for sale or further reproduction.

13 See also Howells' review of *Giants, Apes, and Man* for the same mistake and the repetition of Keith's misunderstanding that Weidenreich had his theory from him (Howells 1947; see also Wolpoff and Caspari 1997, 174–77). As under concern in Part IV, it was and is not uncommon to summarize (the history of) phylogenetic interpretations by grouping them according to several diagrammatic schemes. Boule, for example, had done so regarding the relative positioning of *Pithecanthropus* (1921, 107) and the hominid branch (448) within "'arbres généalogiques' des Primates" [primate family trees] (447). In fact, I have come up with such schemes myself in the appendix of *Bones and Ochre* (2007) to give readers some guidance through the text (see also Sommer 2015b, 111–34; Bowler 1986, 61–146).

Finally, the American anthropologist Carlton Coon, who had read the manuscript of *Human Ancestry* for Gates, also developed a human phylogeny that departed from Weidenreich's in important ways, although he credited Weidenreich as his source of inspiration and dedicated *The Origin of Races* (1962) to him. Coon had studied under Hooton, and after a professorship at Harvard moved to a professorship in anthropology at the University of Pennsylvania in 1948. In his theory of human evolution, Coon spoke of the concept of grades, which referred to adaptive stages of culture through which hominid evolution had passed, such as gathering, hunting, and agriculture. Such grades corresponded with morphological stages "in our family tree" (334), of which Coon identified a series of three: dryopithecine, australopithecine, and hominine. In Coon's scenario, a polytypic species of *Australopithecus* had developed into *Homo* in the old-world tropics. The evolution of polytypic *Homo* went through the stages of local *Homo erectus*, in certain cases Neanderthaloids, and *Homo sapiens* in the five lines giving rise to the "Australoid", "Mongoloid, "Caucasoid", "Capoid", and "Congoid" subspecies respectively. The five human subspecies lines had evolved through these stages in parallel, and at different paces, in the respective geographical regions of the world (Sommer 2015b, 129–30; also Wolpoff and Caspari 1997, 137–65, 209–212).

In line with this scenario, Coon's relating diagram was rather a table with separate, parallel columns than a tree (see Figure III.15). Coon held that the columns or lines of descent in which full humanization had occurred first, namely the "Caucasoid" and "Mongoloid", contained the most advanced forms in the present. However, even though Coon's diagram lacks the connecting diagonal lines signifying gene transfer in Weidenreich's phylogenetic networks (Figure III.8 and Figure III.13), in contrast to Gates and Keith, Coon reasoned that, during their evolution, the different lines had been kept within the species boundary by gene flow (Coon 1962, see particularly 305–309, 332–37).

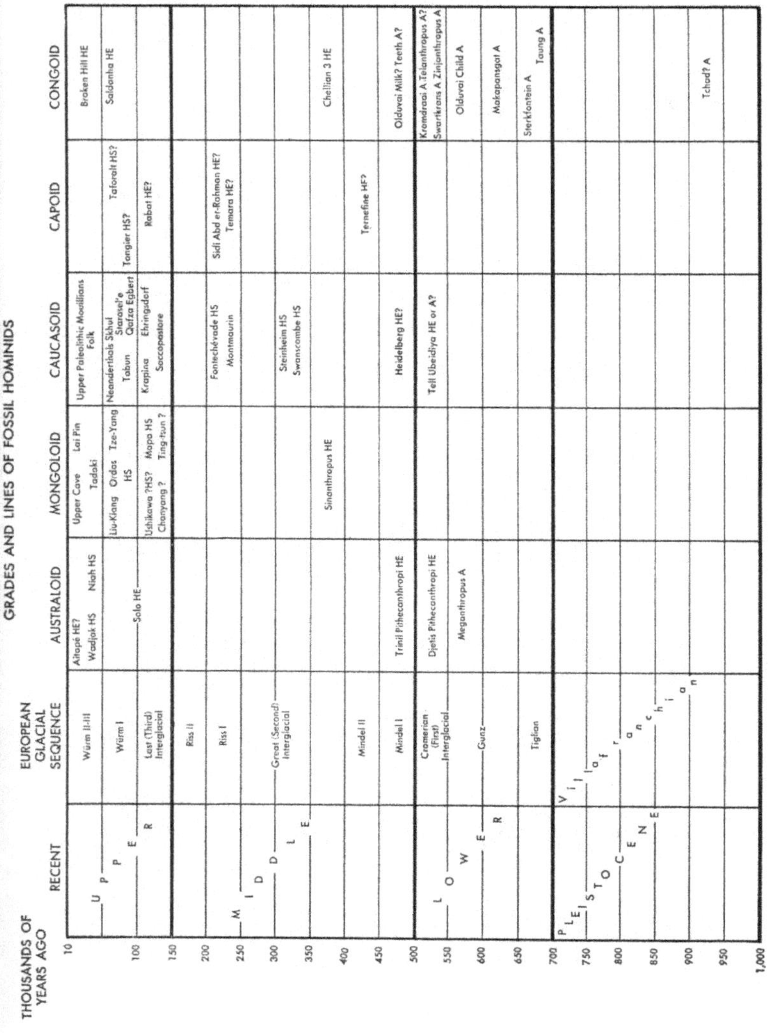
GRADES AND LINES OF FOSSIL HOMINIDS
THOUSANDS OF YEARS AGO
RECENT
EUROPEAN GLACIAL SEQUENCE
AUSTRALOID
MONGOLOID
CAUCASOID
CAPOID
CONGOID
Würm III-III
Würm I
Last (Third) Interglacial
Riss II
Riss I
Great (Second) Interglacial
Mindel II
Mindel I
Cromerian (First) Interglacial
Gunz
Tiglian
Villafranchian
U P P E R
M I D D L E
L O W E R
P L E I S T O C E N E
Aitapé HE?
Wadjak HS
Niah HS
Solo HE
Trinil Pithecanthropi HE
Djetis Pithecanthropi HE
Meganthropus A
Upper Cave
Tadaki
Lai Pin
Liu-Kiang
Ordos HS
Tze-Yang
Ushikawa ?HS?
Mapa HS
Chanyang ?
Ting-tsun ?
Sinanthropus HE
Upper Paleolithic Mousllians Folk
Neanderthals Skhul
Starosel'e
Tabun
Qafza Egbert
Krapina
Ehringsdorf
Saccopastore
Fontechévade HS
Montmaurin
Steinheim HS
Swanscombe HS
Heidelberg HE?
Tell Ubeidiya HE or A?
Tangier HS?
Taforalt HS?
Rabat HE?
Sidi Abd er-Rahman HE?
Temara HE?
Ternefine HE?
Broken Hill HE
Saldanha HE
Chellian 3 HE
Olduvai Milk? Teeth A?
Kromdraai A Telanthropus A?
Swartkrans A Zinjanthropus A
Olduvai Child A
Makapansgat A
Sterkfontein A
Taung A
Tchad? A
HS = Homo sapiens
HE = Homo erectus
A = Australopithecine
FIG. 44

Fig. III.15 "Grades and Lines of Fossil Hominids". Carleton Stevens Coon, *The Origin of Races* (New York: Alfred A. Knopf, 1962), Fig. 44, p. 335.

14. Cable or Tangled Skein?

Despite the fact that contrary to Gates and Keith, Coon thought of the different 'racial' lines as part of a single evolutionary development connected through gene flow, even if with different temporalities, Coon's *The Origin of Races* (1962) incited some of those who stood for the newer cultural approach in anthropology or the synthetic approach even more than Gates' *Human Ancestry* of fourteen years ago. And politically, Coon's treatise once again entered the armory of segregationists in the south and beyond, now in the fight against the civil rights movement's demands (Jackson 2001). In a line leading from the 'physical anthropologist of the first hour', Morton, up to the 'last polygenists', the diagrammatics of 'race' as it was developed in anthropology found its way onto the streets. However, within academia, Coon's book was understood differently by diverse readers. From within academia, it was especially the co-drafters of the UNESCO Statement on Race, Montagu and Dobzhansky, who attacked Coon, as they had previously attacked Gates for his *Human Ancestry*.

The fact that there were different understandings of Coon's meaning, even among allies like Mayr, Dobzhansky, and Simpson, is evidenced in the volume *Classification and Human Evolution* (1963) that was edited by the American physical anthropologist, pioneer primatologist, and synthesist Sherwood Washburn. In the volume, Mayr, Simpson, and Dobzhansky restated their synthetic views of hominid classification and evolution, and they made reference to Coon's *The Origin of Races* (1962). Mayr called Coon the authority regarding the solution to the problem of one polytypic species evolving into another by considering that 'races' may have exhibited different rates of evolution and could have coexisted at different evolutionary stages: it was possible that the *sapiens* grade was first reached by 'Heidelberg Man' (a Neanderthal-like fossil found near Heidelberg in 1907) as *Homo sapiens heidelbergensis* in Europe, while

 https://doi.org/10.11647/OBP.0396.17

the other 'racial' lines lagged behind at the stage of *Homo erectus* (Mayr 1963, 337). Dobzhansky (1963b) was the only one of the three to engage critically with Coon's *The Origin of Races* in the volume. Coon's book appeared after Dobzhansky had sent his contribution to *Classification and Human Evolution* to the publisher. He therefore included an addendum to say that he agreed with Coon that a polytypic *Homo sapiens* arose in the mid-Pleistocene from a polytypic *Homo erectus*. However, he objected to Coon's notion that this transition had happened five times in different places and at different points in time, which for Dobzhansky would only make sense (and, even then, seemed very improbable) if no gene flow between the 'racial' lines was assumed (which Coon however did). This made Coon's work "attractive to racist pamphleteers" (Dobzhansky 1963b, 361).

To the contrary, Mayr observed that in a typological framework, within which one type is the ancestor of another, the coexistence of lower and higher types must indicate that they cannot be linked by direct descent. This is exactly what the typological diagram of the family tree furthers: those fossils that are of the same time range cannot be placed on the same branch if they differ in stage; the more primitive form must be put on a diverging branch. However, Mayr reasoned that with the understanding of species as polytypic, it was conceivable that one or more 'advanced races' of a given species reach a higher grade while 'more conservative races' of the same species are absorbed in the process, remain stagnant in isolation, or die out (Mayr 1963, 337–39; see also Simpson's diagrammatic experimenting on these issues in the same volume, 1963a, 13).

As we have seen, different readings of the same author were not uncommon. Thus, in the same text in which Mayr embraced Coon's model, he also claimed that it was an improvement on Weidenreich's, because Weidenreich did not consider distribution in space and time but only morphology (Mayr 1963, 337). This last observation is contradicted by the fact that already in an article of 1940, Weidenreich had actually identified exactly the problem of the contemporaneity of 'more and less advanced' specimens and resolved it in a similar way Mayr did more than twenty years later: the term "ancestor" was not to be understood in the sense of individuals giving rise to each other in a genealogical tree, or in the sense of species descending from each other in a typological tree.

It did not necessarily mean "direct consanguinity" between two fossils, but rather that some specimens of a species gave rise to specimens of the subsequent species (Weidenreich 1940, 380).

Dobzhansky's synthesist allies, Mayr and Simpson, not only were in friendly exchange with Coon but also reviewed *The Origin of Races* favorably.[1] Simpson (1963b) interpreted Coon's tenets sympathetically and he defended the book against the critique of racism. Both Simpson (1963b) and Mayr (1963) in their reviews continued the widespread derision of the so-called 'egalitarians' as committing the folly of denying that races even exist. In his review of Coon's *The Origin of Races*, Dobzhansky showed himself in agreement with Coon so far as he considered the latter's views extensions on Weidenreich's interpretations. He criticized Coon for the (implicit) assumption that *Homo erectus* and *Homo sapiens* had overlapped, and that these two different (and thus by inference genetically isolated) species gave rise to the present single species of *Homo sapiens*. Where Dobzhansky understood Coon to radically diverge from Weidenreich, even though Coon dedicated his book to him and positioned himself in line with the great anatomist, was when Coon claimed that *Homo sapiens* evolved from *Homo erectus* not once but in five local transformations at different times (Dobzhansky in Dobzhansky, Montagu, and Coon 1963, 360 and 364–66).

Coon seems not to have been aware of the significant differences of his views either to those of Weidenreich or to those of Dobzhansky. After reading Dobzhansky's *Mankind Evolving* (1962), Coon had written to the author that he was in the process of publishing very similar views in *The Origin of Races* of the same year.[2] But Dobzhansky also expressed these differences diagrammatically. In terms of a diagrammatics of relatedness, rather than in Coon's table of parallel columns, for Dobzhansky human evolution and kinship had to be conceptualized as "a cable consisting of many strands; the strands – populations, tribes and races – may in the course of time subdivide, branch or fuse; some of them may fade away and others become more vigorous and multiply. It is, however, the

---

1 For an in-depth treatment that arrives at the conclusion that this seeming paradox of disagreement between the synthesists is rather a symptom of larger differences, see Jackson and Depew 2017, 181–85.

2 Coon to Dobzhansky, 26 May 1962, American Philosophical Society Library, Dobzhansky Papers Mss.B.D65, Series I: Correspondence, Coon, Carlton S.

whole species that is eventually transformed into a new species." And the political effect of these (diagrammatic) differences was that Coon's contrary interpretation in *The Origin of Races* was used by organizations resisting the desegregation decision of the Supreme Court by claiming that Black people lagged behind White people some 200,000 years in their development (Dobzhansky in Dobzhansky, Montagu, and Coon 1963, 360 and 364–66, quote on 365; Dobzhansky's review also appeared in the *Scientific American*: Dobzhansky 1963c; see further 1963a, 138, 146–48).

Montagu added that Coon's scenario of five *Homo-erectus* subspecies evolving independently into *Homo sapiens* demanded "the most remarkable example of parallel or convergent evolution in the history of animate nature" (Montagu in Dobzhansky, Montagu, and Coon 1963, 361–63, quote on 361). In similar terms as Dobzhansky, Montagu set a "tangled skein of man's biological history" (ibid.) against Coon's independent "evolutionary scale[s]" (Coon 1962, vii), taking explicit issue with this anachronistic diagrammatic thinking in evolutionary ladders (Montagu in Dobzhansky, Montagu, and Coon 1963, 361–63, 362). The accusation was that Coon's understanding of 'racial' relations was stuck deep in the nineteenth century. Washburn (1964), too, proceeded diagrammatically when critically discussing Coon's alignment with Weidenreich. He reproduced Weidenreich's network of human evolution under genetic exchange (see Figure III.8) to elucidate his comparison of Coon's and Weidenreich's opinions. Washburn emphasized that, although *Gigantopithecus* and *Meganthropus* might no longer be viewed as close to 'early man' as Weidenreich had interpreted them, Weidenreich's unilinear model was very different from Coon's but close to those of Dobzhansky and the American anthropologist and single-species proponent C. Loring Brace (see Brace et al. 1964; on these issues, see also Hawks and Wolpoff 2003).

In concluding, we might state that, like Coon's, Weidenreich's model did not fit the traditional anthropological tree that stood for a common origin at one center, at which ever higher stages of hominids evolved that subsequently spread geographically, replacing the forms that were encountered. He suggested a relating network (Weidenreich 1940, 381–82). At the same time, Weidenreich's humanist frame in *Apes, Giants, and Man* differed from Coon's tone that was seen by many as racist, and he did not propose separate origins for the living human 'races'. Nonetheless, it seems that the difference to Gates' theory of independent 'racial' evolution (up until the more recent historical times), with 'racial' groups as actually having species status, was more marked. Of course, Coon was a much more renowned anthropologist than Gates, and his anthropological treatise was published close to fifteen years later than Gates'. These are some of the reasons why it was his book, especially, that escalated the dispute with Dobzhansky. Some of the issues involved in the relation of these scientific models to particular political stances may be further enlightened by inquiring into Gates' eugenics, which will also reveal another area of treeing.

15. Missing Links to the Eugenic Pedigrees

The fact that some of the scientists treated in this part were active eugenicists points to another source of inspiration for the genealogical or family tree in anthropology. Eugenics peaked from 1900 to the 1930s (as, for example, seen in the number of memberships of the British Eugenics Society), and with it did its core research and propaganda tool, the pedigree to chart the supposedly hereditary transfer of talents, 'defects', diseases, and complex social behaviors, as well as the effects of 'racial crossing'. As Peter J. Aspinall (2018) has shown, it is around 1930 that the use of the terms 'eugenics' and 'genealogical tree' reached its apex. Eugenicists wanted to standardize the technique internationally, and in doing so, they drew on practices from animal breeding.

In the early twentieth century, the American geneticist Charles B. Davenport applied the newly recovered Mendelian rules of inheritance to humans. Davenport was involved in the American Breeders' Association, which contained the Eugenics Committee, the first formal eugenics group in the US (Kimmelman 1983). Now Davenport tried to show the Mendelian transmission of human characters on the basis of pedigrees. In *Heredity in Relation to Eugenics* (1911), he introduced a way of coding information in pedigrees that became standard, at least in the US and Britain (such as squares for males, circles for females, particular shadings for affected persons and heterozygous carriers of the trait of interest). At the same time, he founded the Eugenics Record Office, from where a multitude of mostly young female fieldworkers swarmed out to hospitals, asylums, poorhouses, etc. collecting hundreds of thousands of pedigree charts that should allow insights into the inheritance (the Mendelian transmission) of characters from polydactyly to 'feeblemindedness', criminality, and 'pauperism'. But such pedigrees

 https://doi.org/10.11647/OBP.0396.18

should also demonstrate degeneration, and they were thus not only widely distributed through textbooks but also in eugenic propaganda material (with an emphasis on the pedigrees, see Mazumdar 1991, 58–95; Shotwell 2021; more generally, see Allen 1986).[1]

As we have seen, Darwin had brought genealogical reasoning to an understanding of the human family and the organismic world at large. In the footsteps of Davenport and with the rise of human genetics in general, figures like Gates tried to apply the genealogical approach in the eugenic sense to anthropology. In studies of 'racial crossing', approaches of physical anthropology could merge with the genealogical ones to trace the inheritance of the color of skin, hair, and eyes as well as the shape of heads, hair, eyes, lips, noses, or limbs through generations. In *Heredity and Eugenics* (1923), Gates adapted the family trees of other researchers to chart the heredity of 'abnormalities'. However, still in the 1920s, when head of the Botany Department at King's College London, he began to carry out pedigree studies, thus initiating a long-time project of collecting pedigrees himself, especially of 'racially mixed' families.

In contrast to biometric approaches in anthropology that measured the individual as part of a population but without necessarily putting it in direct relation to others, the genealogical approach used the genetic method of tracing individual pedigrees and thus the inheritance of 'racial' differences through successive generations. My example pedigree, Figure III.16, came out of a study of 1924, when Gates visited Bear Island in Lake Temagami (Northeastern Ontario, Canada) (Gates 1928). This was about the time when his interest in human genetics and anthropology began to take a stronger hold on his research. For the rest of his life, he undertook shorter and longer expeditions in different parts of the globe, collecting anthropometric data with an emphasis on the study of 'racial crossing'. In these projects, he also included genealogical-genetical research on blood groups and blood group frequency studies (Gates 1956; Gates Papers KCL; Fraser Roberts 1964).

1 Mazumdar (1991, 58–95) shows how human pedigrees were used in different ways. While American eugenicists mostly favored a Mendelian approach in pedigree studies, in Britain there was also a strong biometric group. However, many eugenicists simply used pedigrees to demonstrate that a trait was hereditary, without further theoretical ambition. Finally, pedigree charts of a somewhat different kind were also central to the German racial hygiene movement.

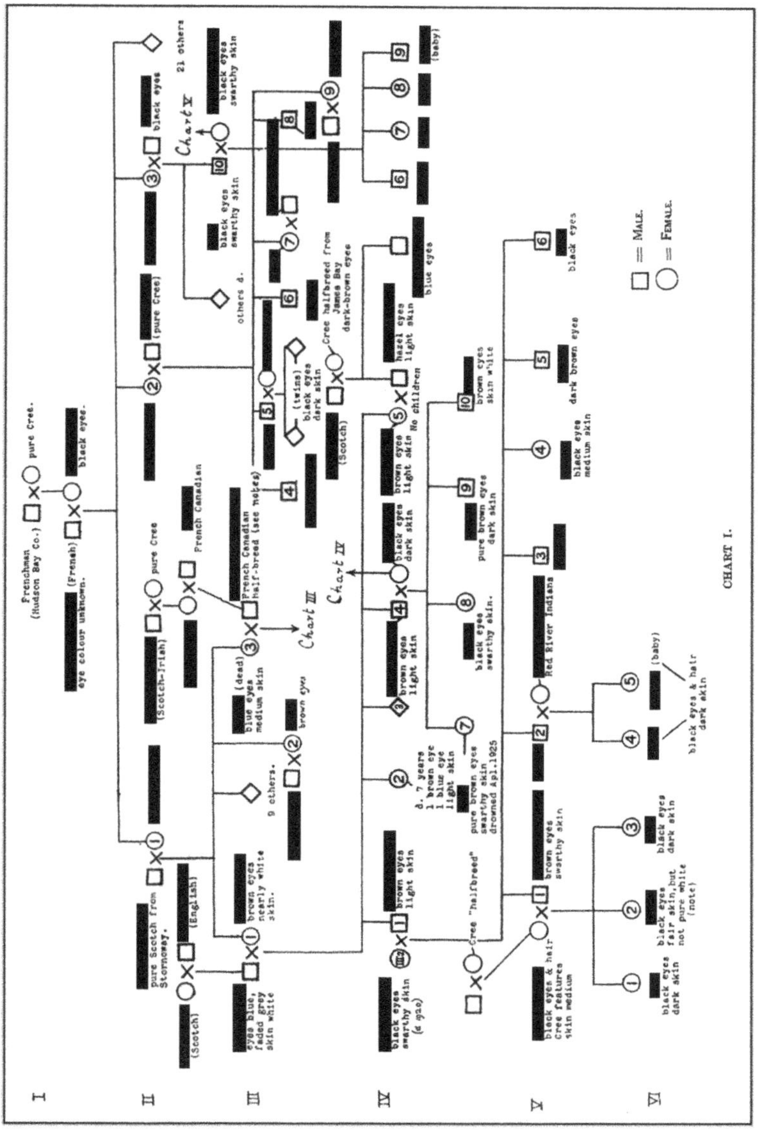

Fig. III.16 Pedigree of eye color, complexion, and hair color in a family of European and First Nations descent. Used with permission of John Wiley and Sons – Books, from Reginald Ruggles Gates, "A Pedigree Study of Amerindian Crosses in Canada" (*The Journal of the Royal Anthropological Institute of Great Britain and Ireland* 58.2 [1928]: 511–32), Chart 1, p. 521. Permission conveyed through Copyright Clearance Center, Inc. © Royal Anthropological Institute of Great Britain and Ireland, all rights reserved.

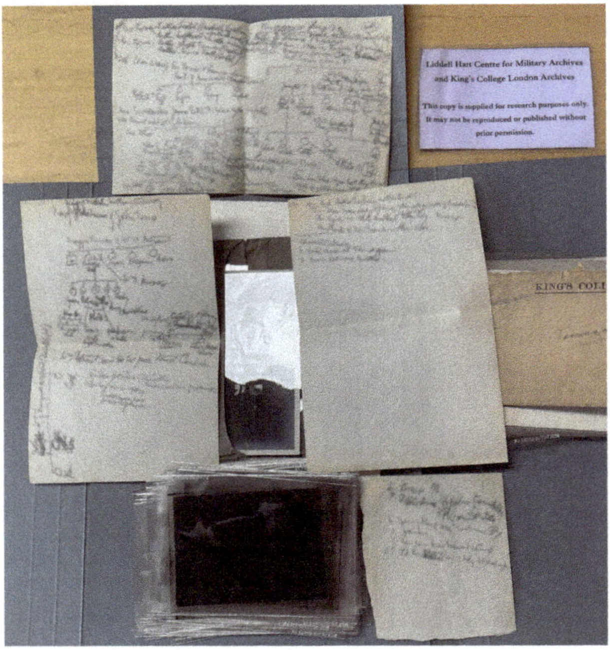

Fig. III.17 Collecting pedigrees, measurements, and photographs in Ontario (King's College London Archives, Gates, Professor Reginald Ruggles [1882–1962], K/PP65, 5/4/2), all rights reserved, with kind permission from King's College London Archives. The sketches of pedigrees trace eye color, complexion, and hair color through a family of European and First Nations origins. The data entered Figure III.16.

When travelling on Bear Island, Gates considered himself in the footsteps of such American anthropometrists as Morton and Aleš Hrdlička, and he included the cephalic index in his measures. Gates used the help of a White Canadian, female intermediary to approach 'mixed-race' families. He took their photographs and recorded their pedigrees, in conjunction with data on features and skin, eye, and hair color over six generations. For reckoning ancestry, he followed the pioneer Galton's system of notation (Galton 1869, 50–53). Figure III.17 shows some diagrammatic fieldnotes and photographs from this research that entered Gate's 1928-publication and specifically the pedigrees, one of which is shown as Figure III.16. The compilation of such pedigrees was intended to allow insights into the number of genetic factors affecting the characters, to determine the dominant and recessive ones, as well as to see if they were correlated (Gates 1928). Towards the end of his endeavors in what he called 'racial genetics', Gates (1963) still thought that 'racial' characteristics like aspects of skulls, noses, skin, hair, etc. were (in contrast to medical characteristics) determined by one to a few genes usually without showing dominance. Blood groups, on the contrary, were determined by a single dominant gene.

If Gates already in the 1920s demanded a concerted global effort to investigate 'racial mixing', it was in 1936 that he began to ask institutions, professionals, and the general public through calls in medical journals and the press for their cooperation in the newly founded Bureau of Human Heredity to collect information and data, particularly in the form of pedigrees. The Bureau was directed by a council that represented medical and scientific bodies in Great Britain and chaired by Gates himself. The British National Human Heredity Committee had been founded in 1932 for the collection of data and the study of human pedigrees (in collaboration with the Galton Laboratory) as a branch of the International Human Heredity Committee, itself founded by the International Federation of Eugenic Organizations (Press Cuttings, Vol. 3, 1936–54, Gates Papers KCL, 9/3; Gates 1936b; 1939).

Gates in general considered 'miscegenation' as disadvantageous. Already in *Heredity and Eugenics* (1923), he established a hierarchy of 'races' that constituted something like a racist time warp between the Paleolithic, Neolithic, and modern times, when he declared many Indigenous peoples to be in the Stone Age and Aboriginal Australians to be remnants of the Paleolithic, mentally on the level of the Neanderthals, and thus "wholly incapable of coping with the white man's civilization" (225). Gates reasoned that the 'main races' had evolved in isolation from each other for such a long time and had psychologically and culturally progressed at such different rates that it would have been "folly to suppose that crosses between a progressive and a primitive race can lead to a desirable result [...]" (ibid.; see also the literature on the negative consequences of 'miscegenation' that Gates kept: Gates Papers KCL, 10/3). However, in the case of the northern Ontarian mixed populations mentioned above, Gates figured that they, through amalgamation of characters and natural selection, were more progressively adapted to their living conditions than each of the 'races' from which they originated.

Overall, the study of 'racial mixing' should throw light on the origin of 'races'. Gates considered that the recent phase of 'racial' evolution, in which 'original races' crossed, was more amenable to research than the earlier phases of human evolution, in which novel variations had appeared to produce 'new races' (Gates 1928). That Gates regarded his research into family pedigrees and hominid phylogeny as closely connected also becomes evident from the fact that he thought the occurrence and inheritance of 'abnormal mutations' threw light on the appearance of 'racial' and specific differences in the course of evolution through repeated/parallel mutation (Gates 1948, Chs. 5 and 11). Thus, the charts showing the effects of 'racial mixing' in a family were not so much about traits, individuals, or families, as about 'races'. While this was also the case for the diagram of human phylogeny in *Human Ancestry* (see Figure III.2), the one in *Human Ancestry* was meant to represent a deeper, less easily accessible time of 'racial' evolution in isolation. To the contrary, these pedigrees of 'racially mixed' families established close relationships between the living populations, even if these relations were rarely condoned and most often seen as creating imbalances in body and mind. These pedigrees were supposed to protocol the breakdown of the natural order of 'racial distinctions' – distinctions that between the larger human groups amounted to species status for Gates: "[I]ntermixture of *unrelated* races is from every point of view undesirable, at least as regards race combinations involving one primitive and one advanced race" (1923, 232, my emphasis). In the "genetical anthropology" (1929, 294) Gates envisioned, eugenic pedigrees and anthropological (or phylogenetic) family trees were interlinked:

> It is, therefore, clear that miscegenation between, for example, the [W]hite races and African races – which for ages have been undergoing separate evolution which must have been at very different rates, assuming that both are descendants from the same original stock – is wholly undesirable from a eugenic or any other reasonable point of view. (Gates 1923, 233)

Heredity and Eugenics (1923) and its 'revision and expansion' in *Heredity in Man* (1929) did not provoke ethical outrages (e.g., C. T. R. 1924; F. S. 1924), but some thought there was not enough biometry treated – a criticism Gates rejected (Gates 1931) – or synthesis and evaluation of the literature discussed (Woodrow 1932). One commentator thought enough so to demolish the 1929 book (ß 1930). Others found the Mendelian explanation of the pedigrees not entirely convincing (G.

M. M. 1930; see also Press Cuttings, Vol. 1, 1915–31, Gates Papers KCL, 9/1). These issues continued after Gates moved to the US. By the time the second volume of *Medical Genetics and Eugenics* (1943) appeared, the Eugenics Record Office had been closed down (1939) after a scientific committee had pronounced the pedigree data of little informational value a few years before (Shotwell 2021, 86, and generally for the flaws in such pedigree research). The volume was made up of lectures by Gates, the American geneticist Laurence H. Snyder, and Hooton. Once again, Gates' presentation of data on 'race crossings' was considered "uncritical" in a scientific rather than ethical sense ("Medical Genetics and Eugenics. Volume 2" 1944; for another review that raised scientific issues with Gates' contribution, see Glass 1945).

The problems with Gates' pedigree method were highlighted also with regard to the two-volume *Human Genetics* of 1946 (something like a second and expanded edition of *Heredity in Man*). A reviewer for the *Lancet*, for example, found many mistakes, including in Gates' reading of pedigrees, and, labelling Gates a botanist, warned that the volumes could be used "purely as a work of reference" (28 June 1947, Press Cuttings, Vol. 3, 1936–54, Gates Papers KCL, 9/3). Once more, an assessment of the vast literature cited as well as a treatment of the statistical methods to analyze human pedigrees were missed (Dodson 1948).[2] While it was often described as encyclopedic, the British geneticist and psychiatrist J. A. Fraser Roberts even called the book dangerous as a guide to the nonexpert.[3] It was nonetheless mostly still welcomed as a service to scientists and scholars. Washburn seems to have been among the few who not only noticed that Gates was twisting and bending genetics to make the pedigrees fit Mendelian rules (because they could be explained by nurture), but who also took issue with Gates' eugenic propaganda and his concomitant attack on Boas (Washburn 1947; on the

2 On the fact that Mendelism, practiced as pedigree studies, became a purely visual method (devoid of statistics) with geneticists such as William Bateson or Davenport, see Mazumdar 1991, 58–95. Davenport and the American geneticists more generally were criticized for their approach by Pearson and others.

3 *Bulletin of Hygiene*, September 1947, 22.9, 603, Press Cuttings, Vol. 3, 1936–54, Gates Papers KCL, 9/3 – containing further examples; for a general response to reviewers by Gates, see "*Human Genetics* and the Reviewers", Gates Papers KCL, 4/74/2; for one to the geneticist Hans Grüneberg, see Gates Papers KCL, 4/81/13/a.

reverse adjustment, of pedigrees to demonstrate Mendelian character distributions, see Teicher 2022).

All in all, the reviews I have encountered expressed hardly any indignation on ethical grounds, even though Gates was an outspoken eugenicist (for some of Gates' eugenic propaganda, see Press Cuttings, Vol. 2, 1931–36, Gates Papers KCL, 9/2). Rather, the commentators had concerns regarding the science. In general, it appears that reviewers of Gates' books on human genetics and eugenics mainly thought of him as a man with the time and patience to write reference works, while finding him deficient to some extent even in this respect. This was also the judgment of Gates' mentor Hooton regarding *Human Ancestry* (Hooton in Gates 1948, xivi). Hooton's stance furthermore illustrates how Gates' views on the deteriorating effect of 'racial mixing' eventually did come to attract harsh criticism, especially where White and Black populations were concerned. Hooton (1935) himself had long since allowed for the fact that studies of 'race hybridization' had shown that it did not lead to infertility, that it did not produce inferior humans, and that simple Mendelian unit character inheritance did not apply. Heredity in humans was far too complex to predict character distribution by the Mendelian laws.

Hooton was not only ambiguous in his (racial) science but also in his (racial) politics. Although he published racist theories and was socially conservative, Elazar Barkan (1992, 310–18) has shown that when Boas was looking for cooperation in the campaign against racism in the US in 1935, he found support in Hooton. At that time, Gregory refused a charter fellowship of the Galton Society because some of its members praised Hitler. Gregory had to "[...] admit that being a scientist I am also a *Homo sapiens*".[4] Hooton, who showed understanding for Gregory's decision, when invited for a conference answered the Executive Secretary of the American Eugenics Society in the negative: "I have felt for many years that this society has been mixing up racial discrimination with eugenics propaganda and I emphatically do not approve of such a policy and do not wish to be associated with it."[5] The reprimand agrees with

4 Gregory to Hooton, 21 May 1935, Hooton Papers PMA, G, Correspondence William Gregory, Box 10, Folder 13.

5 Hooton to George Reid Andrews, 4 May 1936, Hooton Papers PMA, A, Correspondence American Eugenics Society, Box 1 (A), Folder 6. Note that while

Hooton's published reprovals of racism and simultaneous propagation of eugenics, but it also illustrates how Gates' remaining steadfast with regard to issues of race and eugenics, and their interrelation, increasingly isolated him.

In 1947, the Dean of Liberal Arts of Howard University received a petition by eighteen academics to dismiss Gates from his fellowship based on teaching outdated and racist ideas. Two years later, *Pedigrees of [Black] Families* (Gates 1949) appeared. The number of pedigrees included had risen to 218 (mostly collected by his students of genetics at Howard University among their own families and friends). Yet Gates was yet again applauded for digesting a great amount of knowledge by colleagues. Rather than triggering ethical censure, the book was depreciated for its lack of statistical analyses of gene frequencies and for not double-checking the pedigrees' genetic interpretations with twin studies (Spuhler 1950; for further comments, see Press Cuttings, Vol. 3, 1936–54, Gates Papers KCL, 9/3). Although Gates had been forced to resign from Howard, he held a research fellowship in the Biology Department at Harvard between 1950 and 1954, followed by one at Harvard's Peabody Museum. Gates was able to get some funding for his research travels to study 'racial crossings' until the end of his life, also from segregationists. He seems to have been more at ease with the political and scientific climate in Japan, Australia, or India, where he met scientists eager to collaborate, point him to interesting areas for studying 'interbreeding', and inform him which people were amenable to such studies and which were not (Brown 2016, 238–91).

In 1952, Gates attacked the revised UNESCO Statement on Race for its claim that 'racial intermixture' produces no biological disadvantage.[6] Similarly, some ten years later, he was the first signatory of the introduction to Carleton Putnam's *Race and Reason* (1961, vii–viii), in which full support was lent to Putnam's use of 'science' for the cause of 'racial' segregation, while accusing the 'egalitarians' of ideologically motivated harassment, political corruption of science, and distortion of the truth. The signatories emphasized their agreement with Putnam's

Hooton did not want to figure on the advisory list, he remained ordinary member of the society.

6 "Disadvantages of Race Mixture", *Nature*, 22 November 1952, 170.4334, 896, Press Cuttings, Vol. 3, 1936–54, Gates Papers KCL, 9/3.

understanding that there were vast differences between human groups not only in physical appearance, but also in psychological quality, mental ability, and general potential. This they presented as a 'fact' which they considered of preeminent importance for reasonable and beneficial politics and policy. Putman was closely involved with the International Association for the Advancement of Ethnology and Eugenics that in 1959 had been co-founded by Garrett. Gates, too, was part, sometimes even listed as co-founder, of the association that was "dedicated to preventing race mixing, preserving segregation, and promoting the principles of early 20th century [sic] eugenics and 'race hygiene'" (Winston 1998, 179).

In 1961, the American Anthropological Association distanced itself from such abuses of their fields in an unanimously passed resolution, and the following year, the American Association of Physical Anthropologists followed suite, in direct reference to *Race and Reason*, which was used in high-school classrooms. As a consequence, Coon, who to a large extent sympathized with Putnam, resigned from his presidency of the latter association (Jackson 2001). In 1962, Gates, shortly before his death, co-initiated the journal of the International Association for the Advancement of Ethnology and Eugenics – *Mankind Quarterly* – with like-minded scientists to defend 'the aspect of race' in the study of human heredity and culture and, in effect, to defend white supremacism, antisemitism, racism, and segregation. Again, attacks also on this attempt to (re)include racial anthropology and racist politics were not long in the waiting (Comas 1961; 1962; Gates 1962; Ehrenfels, Madan, and Comas 1962; "Our Readers Write" 1962; Gates and Gregor 1963). *Mankind Quarterly* connected an international network of 'miscegenation' researchers and was sponsored by segregationists. In fact, *Mankind Quarterly* is still running, and the association also published Gates' *The Emergence of Racial Genetics* (1963) after his death (Schaffer 2007; Gates Papers KCL, 4/92; for the pro-segregation and pro-apartheid literature in Gates' possession, see Gates Papers KCL, 4/106; for more on the scientific-political backlash to the UNESCO Statement on Race, see Cassata 2008; on Gates, see also Barkan 1992, 168–76).

This was long beyond the point where eugenics and racial anthropology had maneuvered themselves into an intellectual and ethical "blind alley", as Weidenreich (1946a, 89) had called it. Weidenreich had also taken issue with racial classification on the basis of blood group frequencies (79–80), which was increasingly seen as a way out of this dead-end. Indeed, the notion that genetic studies – in contrast to a racist physical anthropology – would be scientifically objective and politically neutral goes back to blood group research (Sommer 2008). As mentioned above, Gates had been an early protagonist in blood group frequency studies, collecting blood from peoples in different parts of the world, and he had been secretary of a committee appointed by the British Association for the Advancement of Science to investigate blood groups among Indigenous peoples in various parts of the world from 1935 to 1939 (Gates Papers KCL, 4/50). Gates also combined blood group analyses with the pedigree method (see Figure III.18). Blood groups enabled the checking of parentage in family pedigrees.

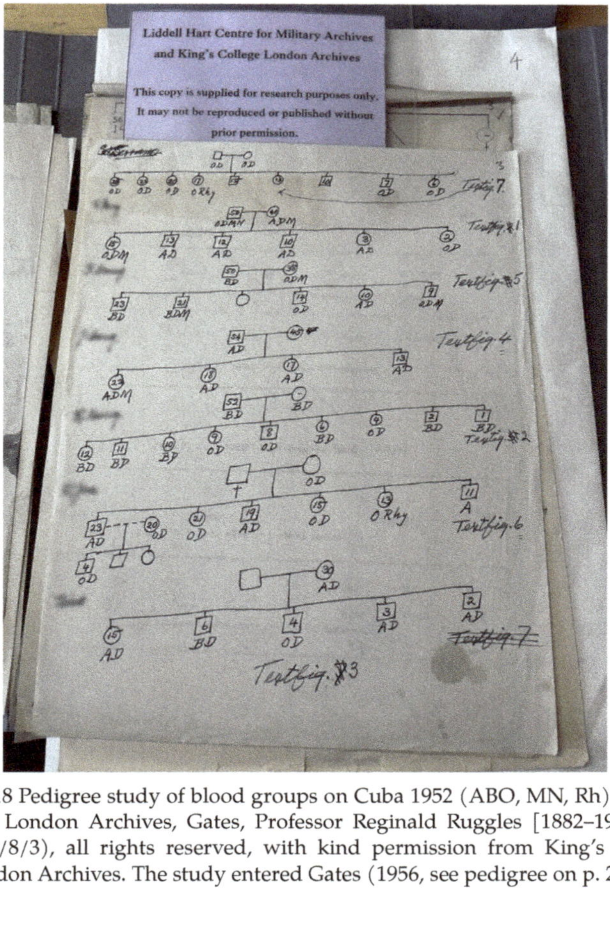

Fig. III.18 Pedigree study of blood groups on Cuba 1952 (ABO, MN, Rh) (King's College London Archives, Gates, Professor Reginald Ruggles [1882–1962], K/PP65, 4/8/3), all rights reserved, with kind permission from King's College London Archives. The study entered Gates (1956, see pedigree on p. 235).

Also Coon made the following observation regarding the usefulness of blood group frequency studies to racial anthropology in his *The Origin of Races* of 1962, which included an appendix of tables giving a broad spectrum of (statistical means and ranges of) cranial, facial, and dental measurements for fossil and living specimens:

> In studying racial differences in living men, physical anthropologists are now relying less and less on anthropometry and more and more on research in blood groups, hemoglobins, and other biochemical features. This is all to the good because the inheritance of these newly discovered characteristics can be accurately determined. In them, racial differences have been found, differences just as great as the better known and much more conspicuous anatomical variations. Being invisible to the naked eye, they are much less controversial than the latter in an increasingly race-conscious world. To me, at least, it is encouraging to know that biochemistry divides us into the same subspecies that we have long recognized on the basis of other criteria. (Coon 1962, 662)

In *The Living Races of Man* of 1965, Coon again discussed the classification of humans based on blood group distributions as carried out by the American immunologist William C. Boyd. Boyd had engaged in the compilation of blood group data and saw in the blood group studies a robust means of classifying 'races' (e.g., Boyd 1939; 1952; 1963; Schneider 1996; Sommer 2016a, 259–63). In *The Living Races of Man*, Coon explained that blood gene frequencies established the Movius Line (a geographical barrier introduced on the basis of archeological evidence), grouping the "Caucasoids" with the "Congoids" and "Capoids", on the one hand, and the "Mongoloids" and "Australoids", on the other. But there was by then "a much more technical, mathematical study made by two professional geneticists with the help of a computer" that supported this basic grouping (Coon 1965, 287). Coon reproduced the family tree of human populations of 1965 by the "two professional geneticists", Luigi Luca Cavalli-Sforza and A. W. F. Edwards, that was based on the comparison of five blood group systems between fifteen populations.

Cavalli-Sforza's and Edwards' populations were turned into "races" in Coon's account, and he stated that these "Racial Relationships Based on Blood Group Frequencies" (Coon 1965, Fig. 7, 288) confirmed the establishment of 'racial' relations on the basis of other genetic factors, as well as by means of physical anthropology as carried out in his *The Origin of Races* (1962). However, Coon thought that what he was studying, and what Cavalli-Sforza and Edwards 'reconstructed', were the 'racial' relations as they had been in place before the major migrations (prior to 1492) that "have greatly complicated the racial geography of the world" (Coon 1965, 288). The tree diagram was the structure assumed to underly 'racial' relatedness prior to these great complications of "the racial geography", when 'races' had migrated from a common origin and diversified in isolation. These approaches therefore still upheld the notion that there had once been 'pure races'. And the 'pure races' could be recovered by the study of the current 'races' that constituted mixtures thereof. There were few scientists, among them Weidenreich, who contested this notion by arguing that there had never been any such thing as 'pure human races' and therefore a tree-shaped human relatedness. Rather, genetic exchange had taken place "ever since man began to evolve" (Weidenreich 1946a, 82).

With these considerations and the return to the 'true' tree diagram in genetics, we are entering the topics of Part IV. Blood group, protein, and later DNA sequence studies were considered politically neutral ways to continue the project of determining human groups and their relations, which had run into trouble with physical anthropology's emphasis on 'racial history and classification' and their meaning for the present. As the perspectives of Foucault and Deleuze on the diagrammatic skeleton of societies as a certain physics of power indicate, however, there are no innocent, or socially neutral, relating diagrams. When population geneticists such as Cavalli-Sforza and Edwards upheld the tree to (re)construct human relations, even though their science and politics differed markedly from the basic assumptions of racial anthropology, they continued an iconography with baggage. One conception in the baggage was that there had been pure geographical groupings that only in relatively recent history had become admixed. The way of relating the major human groups to each other would change, though, with the origin of human evolution being transferred to Africa and African populations as the first branch of the tree.

PART IV. THE TREE, THE MAP, THE MOSAIC, AND THE NETWORK IN GENETIC ANTHROPOLOGY

In Part III we have witnessed controversies about the adequacy of the tree diagram to represent the nature of human evolution and kinship. In the beginning, when paleoanthropologists could expand their view of hominid evolution into the deeper past with the fossil remains of *Pithecanthropus erectus* (*Homo erectus*) at the end of the nineteenth century, this evolution appeared to be a straight line of descent. However, the notion soon gained ground that the relic, just like the remains of Neanderthals, were those of a genus and a species not on the direct line leading to modern humans. Hominid and human evolution was branching. The tendency of pushing modern human anatomy further back in time, thus relegating known and postulated fossil forms to branches of the main human stem, was carried to a point where the tree seems to have deteriorated into other, sometimes bizarre forms expressing parallel evolution between apes and humans and between different hominid types, even between the human 'races'. In effect, however, such bizarre forms only accentuated the tree diagram's typological, divisive, and essentializing tendencies. It was a trend towards downplaying, if not denying kinship.

Part III ended with the uptake of blood group studies by some anthropologists as a 'cleaner' way of doing the old race science. Indeed, human population genetics was increasingly mathematical and computational, associated with the notion of a statistical and automatized approach that, with its focus on the innermost essence of the human being – the level of the gene – did not seem to be amenable to political impregnation. In fact, the gene advanced to the historical document favored by many (Sommer 2008). In Part IV, I am interested in how the phylogeny – the history, kinship, and diversity – of humans

 https://doi.org/10.11647/OBP.0396.19

was visualized in human population genetics and genomics, including ancient DNA (aDNA) studies. As hinted at at the end of Part III, especially with drivers of the field of human population genetics like Luigi Luca Cavalli-Sforza, the populational and genetic approach upheld the tree diagram, and indeed gave the tree of human evolution and kinship new vigor. However, human population genetics developed from the evolutionary synthesis of Darwinian theory and Mendelian genetics and its mathematization. Being interested in genetic variation within and between populations and the evolutionary factors that could explain this variation, the conceptual and methodological outlook was markedly different from that of the preceding physical anthropology and paleoanthropology. Instead of types, there were now 'races' or populations marked by genetic variability and openness. Gone were extravagances like species or genus status for the human 'races' and preordained evolutionary paths through which taxa evolved in parallel. Nonetheless, we will see how the interest in inner-human diversity, or populations, and its evolutionary history made it difficult to shake off all the baggage from racial anthropology. And with the tree of human populations was also still associated the map or narrative of human origins and independent dispersal across the globe.

This persistence of the tree as a relating diagram in anthropological approaches brings to mind Gilles Deleuze's and Félix Guattari's critique of tree thinking as the classical kind of Western reasoning that assumes single origins and proceeds in a dichotomous way. In the introduction to their book *A Thousand Plateaus: Capitalism and Schizophrenia* (1987 [1980]) that was originally published in 1976, they discussed how it dominated the 'Occident', from agriculture and botany to biology, anatomy, psychology, linguistics, structuralism, informatics, epistemology, theology, ontology, and philosophy. As counter-image to the genealogical tree that creates differences instead of multiplicities, Deleuze and Guattari introduced the dynamic, open, multi-dimensional, and heterogeneous rhizome. The rhizome is an anti-genealogy, it connects by other means than reproduction. In contrast to the rhizome, trees genealogically build hierarchical subject, 'racial', or species positions; they are structures of power. "We're tired of trees", Deleuze and Guattari stated, "[w]e should stop believing in trees, roots, and radicles. They've made us suffer too much. All of arborescent culture is founded on them [...]" (1987 [1980], 15).[1]

Deleuze and Guattari made a special case of evolutionary biology. Even while the radical breaks between representation, represented object, and representing subject were rejected, and the rhizome described as devoid of genetic axes and deep structures, Deleuze and Guattari embraced what they saw as its move from the dendritic to the rhizomatic model: "More generally, evolutionary schemas may be forced to abandon the old model of the tree and descent", adopting "instead a rhizome operating immediately in the heterogeneous and jumping from one already differentiated line to another" (1987 [1980], 10). On the basis of viral horizontal gene transfer and the human technique of genetic engineering, they envisioned a future tree of life that has connecting branches between the phyletic lines. Drawing on knowledge from biology, they echoed the belief that reticulate models that connect branches after they have become differentiated would be more accurate in certain cases than the bush or tree schemas used to represent evolution at the time (endnote 5, 25–26).

In this part, I explore the roles of and tensions between tree, reticulation, and rhizome. Indeed, in genetic approaches to human evolution and kinship, the possibility of accessing entire genomes and of analyzing them in novel ways brought alternative relating diagrams to the fore. The twenty-first century ushered in something like an admixture paradigm. Instead of emphasizing the genetic distances and differences between human populations in a tree, images appeared that focused on the interrelatedness of human populations, breaking up the neat groups at the end of independent lines of descent and spreading them out besides each other in colored mosaics. Furthermore, with the advent of aDNA studies, the understanding of human history and diversity seems to have shifted considerably. The advancing field of aDNA research relied on population genetics, from which it adopted terminologies, methodologies, and visualization techniques (e.g.,

1 Michel Serres, on whom Deleuze and Guattari drew, has also argued for ways of reasoning and representing the world beyond dialectics that are network-shaped. In these approaches, the diagram seems to be an operational term that carries what is captured in the analysis to the side of the analysis itself (Serres 1968, 9–23; see Eco 1989; Gehring 1992, on the last point 95).

Morozova et al. 2016). At the same time, bringing in a deep-historical structure, the inclusion of aDNA data into population genetics shifted the focus more strongly towards processes of gene flow: trees became reticulate, with arrows "jumping from one already differentiated line to another" (Deleuze and Guattari 1987 [1980], 10). But was this really an abandonment of the tree, a replacement with "a rhizome operating immediately in the heterogeneous" (ibid.)?

To find out how the shift towards gene flow and aDNA was reflected – or not – in the field's relating diagrams, I focus on prominent models and tools, on the meaning representations seem to carry regarding human diversity, and on how this meaning fits the assumptions of practitioners. I show that behind the (re)presentation of individual and populational genetic kinship and diversity in terms of gene flow, as mosaic and reticulate, still lurks the hierarchically organized tree that suggests independent (unmixed) histories of discrete populations. At the same time, there are certain lines of reasoning and research in place that seem to have the potential to subvert our very understanding of individuality and identity. But before looking at such decentralizing practices, I pick up the thread where I left it in Part III, with the early human population genetics and its tree-structured diagrams and narratives. According to Deleuze and Guattari, Western dualistic (dendritic) reasoning tends to regard scientific practice and knowledge as insulated, while in reality there exists a rhizomatic formation that "ceaselessly establishes connections between semiotic chains, organizations of power, and circumstances relative to the arts, sciences, and social struggles" (1987 [1980], 7). In Chapter 16, we will witness such heterogeneous connections being forged through population-genetic diagrams.

16. The History, Geography, and Politics of Human Genes

Part III has brought us up to the 1960s, when anthropologists had increasingly begun to take on the results of blood group studies or indeed carried them out themselves. Part III ended with Carlton Coon welcoming a new way of drawing phylogenetic trees. He explained to his readers of *The Living Races* (1965), how computer technologies and genetic data allowed the Italian population geneticist Cavalli-Sforza and the British statistician and geneticist A. W. F. Edwards to create what they called the first evolutionary tree of human populations (reproduced in Coon 1965, Fig. 7, 288). This was before it was possible to sequence DNA. What Cavalli-Sforza and Edwards did was analyze twenty alleles from the five main blood group systems of fifteen populations (three per continent). The analysis of the frequencies of variants of blood group alleles in human populations resulted in a phylogenetic tree of a wild mix of population labels from "English" to "Eskimo (Victoria I)" (Cavalli-Sforza and Edwards 1965, Fig. 5, 929).

Data from Indigenous, supposedly isolated populations was preferred in the endeavor to reveal the original human population relations. Some of the labels used in this tree and others for such populations were a legacy of the kind of racial and colonial anthropology we have met with in the preceding parts. However, the young human population genetics was very different from the racial typology of old. Other assumptions underlay this tree than the ones we have met with in Part III, some publishers of which thought of human varieties as separate species or even genera that had evolved in parallel, thus basically decomposing the tree into disparate stalks. In human population genetics, genetic variation was of central interest and the notion of pure races or race in general was often emphatically rejected. At the same time, the tree – the

 https://doi.org/10.11647/OBP.0396.20

dominant icon to visualize and communicate human evolution, history, and kinship at one glance – continued to organize human diversity into clearly demarcated groups.

Another aspect that we have found to be present in the early tree building of physical anthropology survived into the genetic approaches: the fact that phylogenetic trees could also be maps, or narratives of human dispersal across the globe. This was certainly true for 'the first human population-genetic tree' by Cavalli-Sforza and Edwards; it was a diagrammatic rendering of a narrative of common origin and subsequent differentiation through migration without intermixture. Indeed, Edwards and Cavalli-Sforza (1964, Fig. 1, 75) projected the 'first genetic tree of human populations' on a map even before they published it in the form mentioned above. They assumed in their model that populations evolved in isolation from each other as well as at a constant rate of genetic change, with regular population splitting and speed of migration. Mother populations would split into genetically identical daughter populations, from when they would accumulate genetic differences. Thus, this genetic distance (due to genetic drift) was taken to be proportional to the duration of independent evolution, and it was also taken to be proportional to the geographical distance populations had put between themselves in the course of time: space and time overlapped in the tree of human populations projected on a global map (Edwards and Cavalli-Sforza 1964, 72; Cavalli-Sforza and Edwards 1965, 925; 1967).

It is further interesting to note that in Cavalli-Sforza's and Edwards' 'first evolutionary tree of human populations', the main fork divided "Europeans" and "Africans" from "Asiatics" (1965, 929). Through the way in which this tree was projected on the world map, the origin of migration and the root of the tree were placed somewhere in today's Iran, somewhat reminiscent of the understandings of an Ernst Haeckel or Henry Fairfield Osborn who also imaged the cradle of humankind in the east (Lemuria/South Asia, respectively Mongolia). The time of the 'great synthesis' of paleoanthropology, prehistoric archeology, and the new genetic anthropology under the paradigm of 'out-of-Africa' was still in the future. It was only in the research on mitochondrial DNA (mtDNA) in the 1980s, in some of which Cavalli-Sforza, now as professor at Stanford University, was involved, that the "Caucasian" line began to be closer to the "Oriental" and "Am. Indian" ones than to the "Bantu" or "Bushmen" (Johnson et al. 1983, Fig. 7, 267). This meant, even if still ambiguously, that the main fork in the new mtDNA tree could separate the African populations from 'the rest', and that the root of the tree was about to be planted in Africa.

One influential study, in which mtDNA-samples from 148 people, labelled "Africans", "Asians", "Caucasians", "aboriginal Australians", and "aboriginal New Guineans", were sequenced, suggested that all human mtDNA could be referred back to a single female ancestor who had lived in Africa some 200,000 years ago – our 'African or mitochondrial Eve' (Cann, Stoneking, and Wilson 1987, quotes on 32). The mitochondrial tree that accompanied this 1987 publication once again came with a narrative, or a mental map, in the shape of the recent out-of-Africa and replacement scenario (out-of-Africa model). It suggested that the most recent common modern human ancestor had lived in Africa about 200,000 years ago. No more than 140,000 years ago, modern humans had begun to spread and conquer the globe. In this process, modern humans replaced archaic forms of *Homo,* like the Neanderthals in Europe and Asia, without interbreeding. Two of the researchers of this paper, Mark Stoneking and Rebecca Cann, contributed to *The Human Revolution* volume shortly thereafter, which came out of an international conference at Cambridge (GB) organized by the archeologist Paul Mellars and the paleoanthropologist Chris Stringer. It brought together experts from human evolution, archeology, and molecular genetics to discuss the revolutionary new methods developed in the latter field and their application to human evolution. It signified the advent of a large out-of-Africa consensus (Stoneking and Cann 1989; Stringer and Mellars 1989; Sommer 2015a, 116–30; 2016a, 257–73).

The global genetic history was codified with the grand *The History and Geography of Human Genes* (1994) of Cavalli-Sforza and his Italian colleagues Paolo Menozzi and Alberto Piazza. The authors promised nothing less than to reveal the history of migration and differentiation of entire humankind over the span of the species' existence on the basis of the distribution of mostly classical genetic markers in Indigenous or what were considered isolated populations worldwide. The diagrams – the maps, trees, tables, and graphs – to present data, models, and results from statistical analyses were integral to this goal. Figure IV.1 is a map showing human migration paths adapted from *The History and Geography of Human Genes* (Cavalli-Sforza, Menozzi, and Piazza 1994, Fig. 2.15.1, 156), in which the Americas have been moved from the right of Eurasia (original) to its left with the effect of giving the Mercator projection but cutting off the human journey from Asia into America across the Bering Strait. In fact, *The History and Geography of Human Genes* contains so many maps that it may be described as an atlas. It has an appendix with maps mostly giving frequency distributions of alleles. This appendix makes up by far the larger part of the book, also providing tables of allele frequencies for the populations analyzed and a reference list for the alleles studied. In this way, it is reminiscent of the skull atlases of the nineteenth century discussed in Part I.

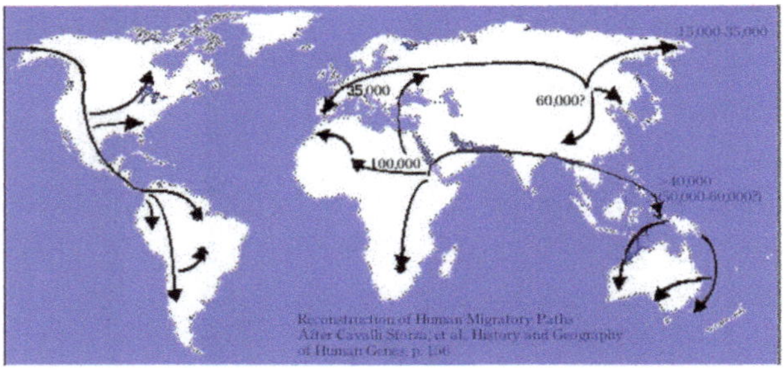

Fig. IV.1 "Reconstruction of Human Migratory Paths After Cavalli-Sforza, et al., History and Geography of Human Genes, p. 156". Drawing by Patrick Edwin Moran (2006). Wikimedia, CC BY-SA 3.0, https://commons.wikimedia.org/wiki/File:Cavalli-Sforza_Human_Migration_Paths.jpg

At the same time, *The History and Geography of Human Genes* (1994) followed in the footsteps of encompassing anthropological treatises like James Cowles Prichard's *Researches into the Physical History of Man* (1813) and subsequent editions in that it begins with a panhuman genetic history succeeded by chapters on Africa, Asia, Europe, America, Australia/New Guinea/Pacific Islands. Also as in Prichard's work, the comparative study of languages constituted a central element in *The History and Geography of Human Genes* (1994). Furthermore, part and parcel of this genetic history was knowledge from archeology, (paleo)anthropology as well as insights about climate, ecology, and human history. Cavalli-Sforza, Menozzi, and Piazza thus also treated results from other approaches to human evolution, such as the multivariate statistics of the renowned anthropologist William Howells, whom we have met in Part III, and they for example used archeological dates to study the constancy of molecular clocks.

Howells, who had followed Earnest Hooton to the Chair of Anthropology at Harvard, pioneered quantitative cranial methodology for the establishment of population relations. His *Skull Shapes and the Map* (1989) presented fifty-seven different measurements on twenty-eight skull series, for example from a village, a 'tribe', a nation, or generally from a region like Tasmania. Firstly, he equated these series with populations, and, secondly, they stood for six major geographic regions of the earth. Howells himself saw this search for specific distinctions between these populations and geographic regions as "analogous to the idea of 'racial' differences of past anthropology, but on an objective and systematic basis, not on one of typology" (1). It was a search for the pattern of human skull variation brought about by processes of differentiation in place before 1492, when intermixture on a global scale would have set in.

Skull Shapes and the Map (1989) together with the preceding *Cranial Variation in Man* (1973a) can be seen as following the old cranial-atlas genre discussed in Part I, with measurements and instruments explained and results tabulated, but Howells did not include images of the skulls. Rather, Howells (1989) produced dendritic diagrams to find out whether the eighteen populations build major geographical clusters. While the skull trees differed between the sexes and with the number of populations included, Howells answered the question in the affirmative. He also used something called principal component analysis – a clustering visualization technique central to Cavalli-Sforza's human population genetics and discussed below. These clustering analyses on the basis of skull measurements, too, were interpreted as confirming the differentiation of major geographic groups. Finally, integrating Neanderthal and other premodern skulls in some analyses, Howells read his findings as supporting the out-of-Africa scenario of human evolution and as in line with those of geneticists like Cavalli-Sforza and colleagues (1988) and Cann and colleagues (1987) (even though Howells' dendrograms did not support an African origin of modern humans).

In *The History and Geography of Human Genes*, Cavalli-Sforza, Menozzi, and Piazza (1994, 66, 72–73, 160) on their part referred to Howells in the context of the question after the right model for human evolution. They granted that Howells' (1973a) method to build trees on anthropometric data had overcome some of the problems in Cavalli-Sforza's and Edwards' (1964) early genetic attempts. However, the analysis of genes seemed to be especially relevant as it was seen to provide the most direct access to human history. Genes were much less than bones affected by environmental factors like climate that were not about naked genealogy but living conditions. This sense of the gene as documenting evolution unperturbed by the common understanding of history brings to light the tensions between the different approaches Cavalli-Sforza and colleagues synthesized. Population genetics was a mathematical and information-technological approach, it reduced history to stochastic change in molecules (Sommer 2015a; 2016a, Ch. 11).

However, despite this severing of phenotype from genotype, the similarity the new genetic approaches showed to Howells' work suggests a lingering association with the phenotype, and in fact racial stereotypes. The association was certainly facilitated by the use of old racial labels (also found in Howells 1989) like "Caucasoid" (Cavalli-Sforza, Menozzi, and Piazza 1994, e.g., 17), "Mongoloid" (e.g., 64), and for Black Africans (e.g., 160). It was also catalyzed by the use of established diagrams like the tree and the tree (or paths of migration and differentiation) on a theoretical or actual map. The combination of conventional diagrams and labels acquired its own life in other disciplines and in diverse public realms. Before beginning to illustrate this with the example of Figure IV.2, let me consider what such labels might mean in the context of human population genetics or genetic history. For the results presented in their magnum opus, Cavalli-Sforza, Menozzi, and Piazza had extracted genetic data on populations from publications (which constituted a data base that was "the result of thousands of more or less haphazard collections and analyses of blood samples" [1994, 157]), using geographic and ethnolinguistic proximity to increase the number of genes per population through population pooling. The 491 populations thus arrived at were subjected to *f*-statistics to estimate the genetic distances between population pairs (coefficient of coancestry). These populations were the substrate for building the detailed trees and maps in the book parts on the different world regions, while more pooling and culling created the forty-two populations which underlay panhuman or global analysis. Finally, in panhuman trees, populations could be further clustered under labels like "Caucasoid" (see, e.g., Figure IV.3).

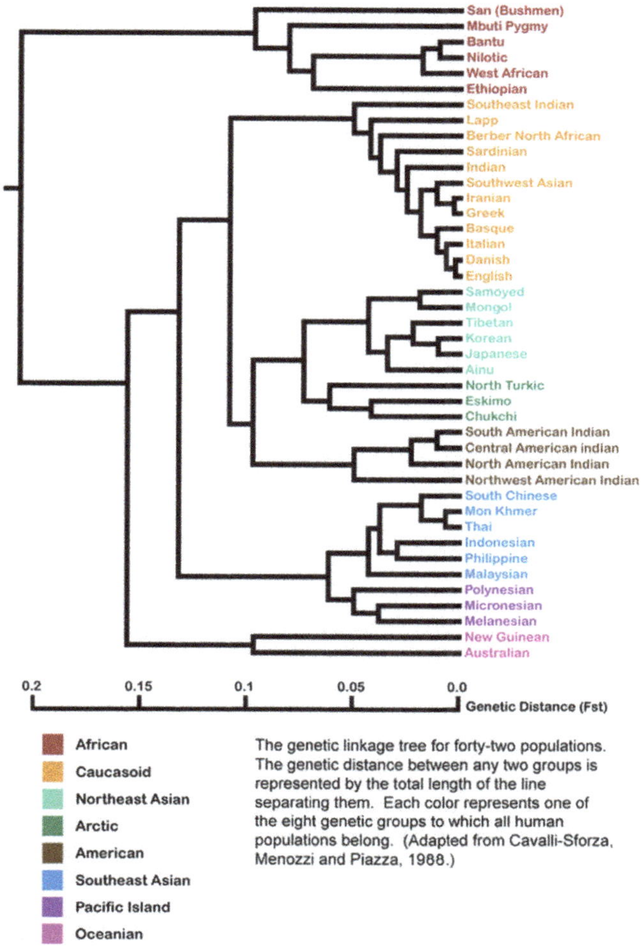

Fig. IV.2 Genetic Tree of Human Populations, "Adapted from Cavalli-Sforza, L.L., Menozzi, P. & Piazza, A,. [sic] *Reconstruction of Human evolution: Bringing together genetic, archaeological, and linguistic data*, 1988". Created by Jonathan Kane (2009 [version between 17 July 2011 and 7 September 2023]). Wikimedia, CC BY-SA 4.0, https://commons.wikimedia.org/wiki/File:Populations.png

Prior to September 2023, my Figure IV.2 was identified on Wikimedia Commons as an adaptation of a population tree by Cavalli-Sforza, Menozzi, Piazza, and Joana Mountain published in the year 1988 (Fig. 1, 6003) reproduced below as Figure IV.3. This tree was again based on classical rather than DNA markers, but, compared to the early study published in 1965, far more alleles sampled across "the world aborigines" (6002) were used. For the original tree of 1988, archeological dates for steps in human expansion across the globe were taken to calibrate genetic differentiation as well as to check for constant rates of genetic evolution. Thus, this tree once again is analogized to a map of human migration across the globe in the shape of bifurcating paths from a common origin.

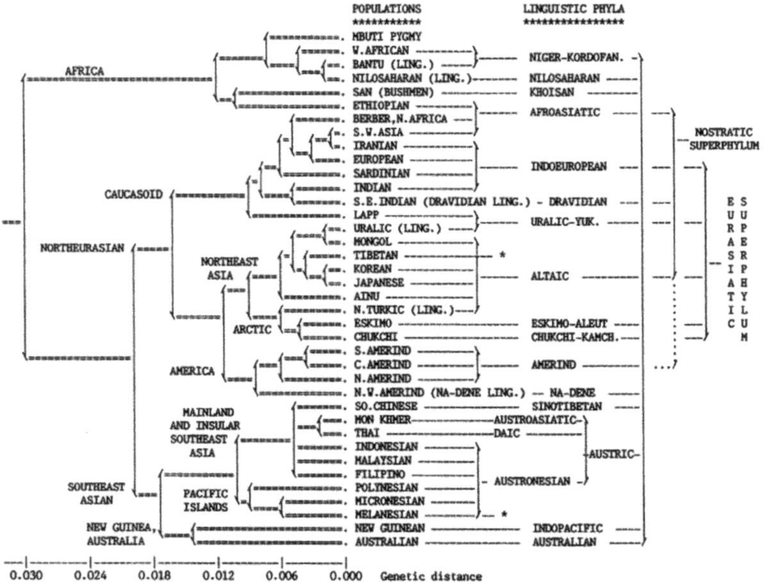

FIG. 1. Comparison of genetic tree and linguistic phyla. See text for details. (Ling.) indicates populations pooled on the basis of linguistic classification. The tree was constructed by average linkage analysis of Nei's genetic distances. Distances were calculated based on 120 allele frequencies from the following systems: *A1A2BO, MNS, RH, P, LU, K, FY, JK, DI, HP, TF, GC, LE, LP, PEPA, PEPB, PEPC, AG, HLAA* (12 alleles), *HLAB* (17 alleles), *PI, CP, ACP, PGD, PGM1, MDH, ADA, PTC, E1, SODA, GPT, PGK, C3, SE, ESD, GLO, KM, BF, LAD, E2, GM*, and *PG*.

Fig. IV.3 "Comparison of genetic tree and linguistic phyla". Luigi Luca Cavalli-Sforza, Paolo Menozzi, Alberto Piazza, et al., "Reconstruction of Human Evolution: Bringing Together Genetic, Archaeological, and Linguistic Data" (*Proceedings of the National Academy of Sciences of the United States of America* 85.16 [1988]: 6002–6006), Fig. 1, p. 6003.

Like Haeckel, Cavalli-Sforza saw in languages a powerful tool to not only identify or classify 'populations' – the abbreviation "ling." in the tree of Figure IV.3 stands for the practice of pooling populations on the basis of language. Cavalli-Sforza also considered the evolution of languages – their common origin and differentiation – as analogous to the evolution of populations (Sommer 2016a, 277–78). The original tree of 1988 that was said to underly Figure IV.2 was thus part of an image that indicated parallels between linguistic and genetic evolution (even if the latter was considered as proceeding more slowly), in that the genetic tree was merged with a linguistic tree to its right (see Figure IV.3). The tree of language evolution as shown in Figure IV.3 supported the story incorporated in the tree of human populations: it suggested that "linguistic phyla" like human populations shared a common origin, but had separated at one point (more or less) far back in time and not mixed again. According to the authors, modern humans had also not interbred with the local archaic humans they encountered in their new homes 'out of Africa'; rather, they came to replace the previous inhabitants (Cavalli-Sforza et al. 1988, 6005).

Thus, possible converging processes in human evolution and history, interactions between languages and peoples, were downplayed by choosing the imagery of the tree. A bifurcating diagram – a tree – cannot truly convey genetic exchange. Possible genetic admixture could be hidden in short branches in trees in which the total length of branches from root to present populations was not forced to be equal by the method of average linkage (or maximum likelihood) that assumes constant mutation rates. With the latter methods, an admixed population would be placed in a tree closely to the parent population with which it is genetically most similar. For the genetic population tree in Figure IV.3, however, it was once again assumed that human populations are discrete, homogenous entities that have had independent evolutionary histories after the last population split (Cavalli-Sforza et al. 1988, 6004). In fact, Cavalli-Sforza and colleagues did only use data from populations that they considered to be "aboriginal, with little or no admixture" (6003). Such trees therefore created a perfect order in what would turn out to be the much messier affair of human genetic history and diversity.

This perfect order was highlighted even more strongly by a Jonathan Kane when he supposedly worked on the originally black and white image published in 1988 (Figure IV.3) to produce Figure IV.2. Kane introduced colors to visually group different populations to eight 'intuitive' larger entities like "American" "to which all human populations belong" (Kane in caption of Figure IV.2). In doing so, he upheld labels, including "Caucasoid", that we have seen established in Part I and that were also used by Cavalli-Sforza and colleagues in Figure IV.3. The very tree shown in Figure IV.2 is actually reproduced on the Wikimedia Black Lives Matter Talk, where such genetic diagrams are criticized as racist for the use of terms like "Mongoloid", "Australoid", "Caucasoid", or similar expressions for Black Africans.[1] While we have seen and will further notice that there are issues associated with such trees other than the labels handed down from early racial anthropology, it is interesting to have a closer look at this issue.

In the original tree of 1988, Cavalli-Sforza and colleagues did use the term "Caucasoid" (Figure IV.3), but the branching within that group, and elsewhere, looks somewhat different than in Figure IV.2. In fact, it seems as though, contrary to the acknowledgement in the caption (until 7 September 2023), the 1988 tree had not been the template for Figure IV.2 at all. Cavalli-Sforza, Menozzi, and Piazza themselves reused their tree of 1988 in their 1994 classic *The History and Geography of Human Genes* (Fig. 2.3.2.A, 78) nearly unchanged, with the small alterations approaching Kane's tree. The names for higher clusters, including "Caucasoid", are still included. Furthermore, in *The History and Geography of Human Genes*, there is a second tree given below (Fig. 2.3.2.B, 78). This image is again in black and white, but it shows the exact same clustering as Figure IV.2, this time without using the term "Caucasoid" or naming any other of the higher clusters. It therefore seems as if Kane created an amalgam of the two trees of 1994, joining the components of both that were most to his liking, rather than having been inspired by the

1 "Talk:Black Lives Matter," *Meta-Wiki*, https://meta.wikimedia.org/wiki/Talk:Black_Lives_Matter, last accessed 18 January 2023. Cavalli-Sforza and colleagues were not alone in these respects. This may be indicated by the work of another influential population geneticist, Masatoshi Nei, who studied human molecular evolution and developed statistical methods from the 1970s. Nei and colleagues showed that "the net gene differences between the three major races of man, Caucasoid, [Black Africans], and Mongoloid, are much smaller than the differences between individuals of the same races" (1985, 41). Nonetheless, the interracial genetic differences were seen to correspond to 'racial divergence times' of up to around 100,000 respectively 50,000 years. Furthermore, while gene flow was acknowledged as an important factor in human evolution, Coon was evoked in support of isolation between the "major races", and on the basis of protein as well as DNA data, phylogenetic trees were built for these as well as for smaller populations.

original of 1988. From Cavalli-Sforza's and colleagues' Figure 2.3.2.A, he took the term "Caucasoid" and in general the naming of higher clusters which he highlighted with colors; from their Figure 2.3.2.B, he took the splitting pattern, including the breaking down of the European group (Cavalli-Sforza, Menozzi, Piazza 1994, Fig. 2.3.2.A and Fig. 2.3.2.B, 78). In fact, before 2011, the caption of Figure IV.2 referred the adaptation not to the original tree in Cavalli-Sforza et al. (1988), but to *The History and Geography of Human Genes* (Cavalli-Sforza, Menozzi, and Piazza 1994).[2]

The appendix of *The History and Geography of Human Genes*, too, contains a colored image, one that superimposes the genetic tree of Figure IV.3 and a mirrored linguistic tree on the world map. However, rather than Kane's distinct colors of Figure IV.2 that emphasize the clear boundedness of continental clusters, Cavalli-Sforza's, Menozzi's, and Piazza's tree-map has colors blend into each other to visualize gradients (color map 8). Like Petrus Camper's and Johann Friedrich Blumenbach's skull series, these colored maps are horizontal and dynamic; they merge human varieties into each other. That genetic trees could be misread, because they suggested human populations to be clearly demarcated entities that evolved in isolation, and because they continued the labelling from early physical anthropology, becomes even clearer when following the story of Figure IV.2 one step further. Looking more closely at the publication history of Figure IV.2 on Wikimedia, one realizes that the citation initially, up to October 2009, did not refer to either Cavalli-Sforza et al. (1988) or Cavalli-Sforza, Menozzi, and Piazza (1994) as the direct source of the tree, but to Berkeley Emeritus-psychologist Arthur Jensen's *The g Factor: The Science of Mental Ability* (1998, Fig. 12.1., 429).[3]

In this book, Jensen brought as much of the available 'evidence' as feasible to bear on the claim that IQ correlates with social achievements such as in education and occupation, and that it also correlates with ethnicity (and gender). It was one in a series of books Jensen was publishing on the topic of intelligence and, like Reginald Ruggles Gates before him, he considered himself in the footsteps of Francis Galton (Jensen 1998, xi). The biggest gap in IQ according to 'this evidence' separated the "[W]hite" from the "[B]lack" communities in America (350). Jensen postulated that this seemingly markable difference in IQ

2 See file history on https://commons.wikimedia.org/wiki/File:Populations.png (30 December 2009), last accessed 16 January 2023.

3 See file history 3 July 2009 on https://commons.wikimedia.org/wiki/File:Populations.png, last accessed 16 January 2023.

had not changed since IQ was being measured and had nothing to do with any cultural bias in the tests. Furthermore, the average differences in IQ that the tests revealed were claimed to be an expression of how strongly they measure *g* (meaning 'general intelligence', or abstract thinking and problem-solving) – the more *g*-loaded a test, the greater would be the difference in "[B]lack and [W]hite IQ" (352). To make these claims look like hard scientific evidence, they were bolstered with measures, formulae, and diagrams, such as a juxtaposition of the normal curves of IQ distribution for "[W]hite and [B]lack populations" (Fig. 11.1., 356; 350–530).

Cavalli-Sforza's and colleagues' population-genetic diagrams came in when Jensen wanted to provide the reasons for the discrepancies in "[B]lack and [W]hite IQ". Introducing *The History and Geography of Human Genes* (Cavalli-Sforza, Menozzi, and Piazza 1994) as "the most comprehensive study of population differences in allele frequencies" (Jensen 1998, 428), or of genetic distances between populations, Jensen reproduced the "average-linkage tree for 42 populations" from *The History and Geography of Human Genes* (Cavalli-Sforza, Menozzi, and Piazza 1994, Fig. 2.3.2.B, 78; Jensen 1998, Fig. 12.1., 429). So this is probably where Kane originally took it from. Between this tree and the tree already published in 1988 for the same set of populations, but using a different distance method (Cavalli-Sforza, Menozzi, and Piazza 1994, Fig. 2.3.2.A, 78; Figure IV.3 above on the left), Cavalli-Sforza, Menozzi, and Piazza observed a remarkable similarity, with the first fission unmistakably separating "Africans from non-Africans" (1994, 77). This is what Jensen so clearly saw, indeed what everybody clearly sees, especially in those tree diagrams in Cavalli-Sforza, Menozzi, and Piazza (1994, 79, and Fig. 2.3.3, 80) that only relate the larger geographical units. Jensen also reproduced one of these as shown in Figure IV.4. In these trees, Cavalli-Sforza and colleagues used the term "Caucasoid", but in the text they disclaimed that "we [...], unlike others [...] [sic] do not give to the clustering obtained in the tree of figures 2.3.2 or 2.3.3 any 'racial' meaning [...]" (1994, 80).

However, also without the use of old racialist or racist labels, trees misrepresent or downplay intra-human kinship – a fact the authors of *The History and Geography of Human Genes* were aware of:

> In conclusion, there has probably been enough intermingling of the clusters that a network representation (i.e., a tree with interconnections between branches) would be highly desirable. But the tree in figure 2.3.3 is probably the best result that can be obtained using present methods, that is, a phylogenetic tree without interconnections. (Cavalli-Sforza, Menozzi, and Piazza 1994, 81)

For Figure 2.3.3, Cavalli-Sforza, Menozzi, and Piazza had clustered the already repeatedly artificially pooled forty-two populations into nine geographic groups. This kind of clustering was unusual, however. The usual procedure was not to join all populations in clusters, but to pick a single, highly localized population to represent each cluster or a vast geographic region. The latter method of sampling and analyzing human variation made it more tree-shaped because the geographically and genetically intermediate populations were not part of the study and thus "links between branches are less likely to be observed" (Cavalli-Sforza, Menozzi, and Piazza 1994, 81). In other words, "[i]t is doubtful whether the sharpness thus acquired is real. Considering that the nine large clusters we have used represent large, geographically contiguous regions [...], it may be almost surprising that the tree we obtained is reasonably reproducible in different bootstrap samples" (ibid.).

It is this "sharpness", however, that was attractive to Jensen. What was important to Jensen in the tree he reproduced from *The History and Geography of Human Genes* (and Kane from him) was that "the greatest genetic distance [...] is between the five African groups [...] and all the other groups" (Jensen 1998, 428), and that he could steer the reader to "[n]ote that these clusters produce much the same picture as the traditional racial classifications that were based on skeletal characteristics and the many visible physical features by which non-specialists distinguish 'races'" (ibid.). In also reproducing one of the diagrams from *The History and Geography of Human Genes* (Cavalli-Sforza, Menozzi, and Piazza 1994, 79) in which only the bigger population clusters – or in Jensen's parlance "the traditional racial classifications" – were linked, or rather separated, in a tree diagram, Jensen rendered both of these claims more fact-like (see Figure IV.4).

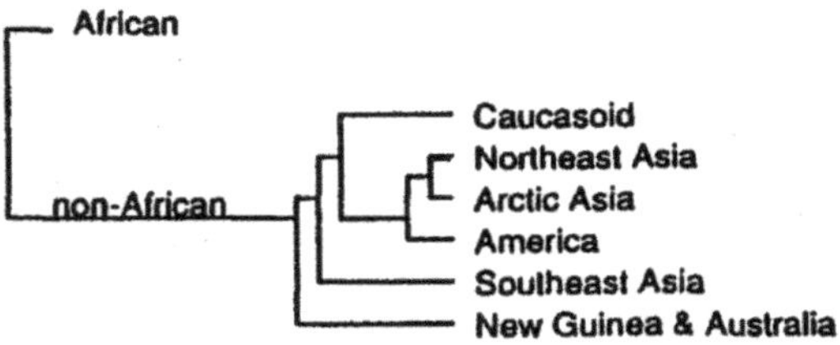

Figure 12.2. A linkage tree based on the average genetic distances between the major clusters among the groups shown in Figure 12.1. (Cavalli-Sforza, L. L., Menozzi, P. & Piazza, A., ***The history and geography of human genes.*** Copyright © 1994 by Princeton University Press. Reprinted by permission of Princeton University Press.)

Fig. IV.4 Diagram reproduced in Arthur Jensen, *The g Factor: The Science of Mental Ability* (Westport, CT: Praeger, 1998), Fig. 12.2., p. 430 (all rights reserved; used with permission of Princeton University Press, from Luigi Luca Cavalli-Sforza, Paolo Menozzi, and Alberto Piazza, *The History and Geography of Human Genes* [Princeton: Princeton University Press 1994], p. 79; permission conveyed through Copyright Clearance Center, Inc.).

To bolster his claims further, Jensen drew on yet another "wholly objective mathematical procedure" (1998, 430), namely principal component analysis. Its introduction into population genetics had been based on a computer program that allowed the representation of genetic variation in a principal component synthetic graphic analysis from a matrix of genetic differences.[4] Principal component analyses are used to detect structure in the relationships between variables, to discover patterns hidden in data. They reduce the dimensionality of data without losing a significant amount of information. To reduce the complexity in the data and the number of factors possibly affecting it, these analyses search for those factors that affect the data most. The first principal component thus accounts for the greatest variance in the data, in our case the largest amount of the genetic difference found, and so forth. In the ideal case, the tree and principal component graphic analysis would be closely related, with the first split in the tree corresponding to the separation of populations by the first principal component (Sommer 2016a, 263–64).

While having this relationship to trees, principal component analyses are maps, most obviously so when synthetic maps are created on their basis in which allele frequencies are transformed into scaled deviations from the sample mean and plotted on the geographical regions from

4 It seems that, mathematically speaking, Karl Pearson (1901) introduced the basic ideas underlying principal component analysis.

where the samples originated. Figure IV.5 represents such a map of the first principal component for the panhuman analysis carried out in *The History and Geography of Human Genes*. It was seen to agree with the first branching of the general genetic tree that splits "Africans" from "non-Africans" (Cavalli-Sforza, Menozzi, and Piazza 1994, 135). (The 'anomaly' that western Europe clustered with Africa was 'corrected' in lower principal component analyses.) In this way, principal component analyses produce grades of gene frequencies across the globe: they are used as a tree, map, and narrative of expansion.

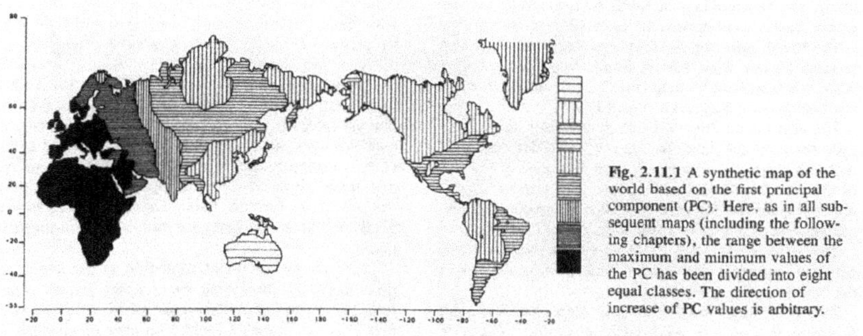
Fig. 2.11.1 A synthetic map of the world based on the first principal component (PC). Here, as in all subsequent maps (including the following chapters), the range between the maximum and minimum values of the PC has been divided into eight equal classes. The direction of increase of PC values is arbitrary.

Fig. IV.5 "A synthetic map of the world based on the first principal component" (all rights reserved; used with permission of Princeton University Press, from Luigi Luca Cavalli-Sforza, Paolo Menozzi, and Alberto Piazza, *The History and Geography of Human Genes* [Princeton: Princeton University Press 1994], Fig. 2.11.1, p. 135; permission conveyed through Copyright Clearance Center, Inc.).

In addition, Cavalli-Sforza, Menozzi, and Piazza (1994, colored maps in appendix) combined the first three principal components to create a color map of the world that was color-coded for "Africans (yellow), Caucasoids (green), Mongoloids, including American Indians (purple), and Australian Aborigenes (red)" (136). While this visualization technique could not inform about expansions (contrary to single components), its coloring suggested "admixtures between Africans and Caucasoids in North Africa and between Caucasoids and Mongoloids in Central Asia" (138).[5] However, Jensen (1998, Fig. 12.3., 431) made use of Cavalli-Sforza's and colleagues' principal component analysis to show that taking the first two components as axes, the populations clustered and were neatly separated from each other in the diagram to form "the 'classic' major racial groups – Caucasians in the upper right,

5 For a critical discussion of reading principal component maps in terms of human expansions, see François et al. 2010.

[Black Africans] in the lower right, Northeast Asians in the upper left, and Southeast Asians (including South Chinese) and Pacific Islanders in the lower left" (Jensen 1998, 430) (see Figure IV.6). Cavalli-Sforza and colleagues therefore referred also to this sort of diagram as a "Principal-component map" (Cavalli-Sforza, Menozzi, and Piazza 1994, Fig. 2.3.5., 82). The conclusion Jensen wanted to draw from the population-genetic trees and maps that he handpicked from *The History and Geography of Human Genes* was that the genetic differences between populations largely explained the phenotypic differences between "races". Natural selection would have worked on gene frequencies leading to differences in physical, behavioral, and mental capacities between the populations (1998, 432–33).

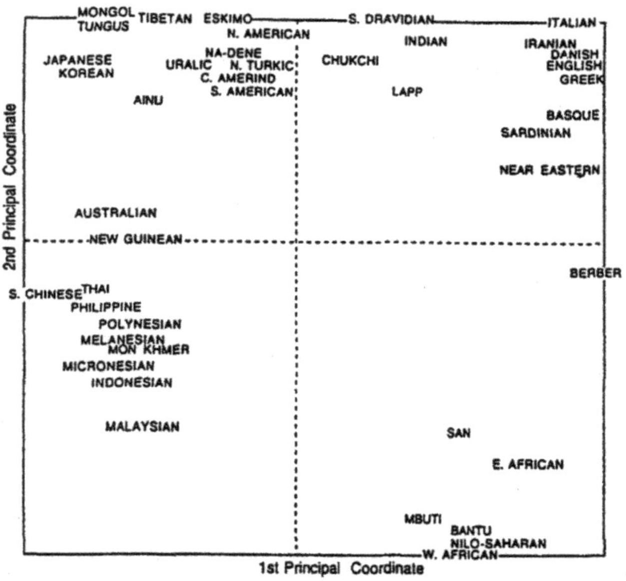

Figure 12.3. A principal components (PC) analysis of the forty-two populations in the Cavalli-Sforza et al. study, showing the bivariate location of each with respect to the coordinates of the first two PCs. The orthogonal dashed lines indicate the mean of each PC. (Cavalli-Sforza, L. L., Menozzi, P. & Piazza, A., ***The history and geography of human genes.*** Copyright © 1994 by Princeton University Press. Reprinted by permission of Princeton University Press.)

Fig. IV.6 Principal component map reproduced in Arthur Jensen, *The g Factor: The Science of Mental Ability* (Westport, CT: Praeger, 1998), Fig. 12.3., p. 431 (all rights reserved; used with permission of Princeton University Press, from Luigi Luca Cavalli-Sforza, Paolo Menozzi, and Alberto Piazza, *The History and Geography of Human Genes* [Princeton: Princeton University Press 1994], Fig. 2.3.5, p. 82; permission conveyed through Copyright Clearance Center, Inc.).

This constituted an abuse of Cavalli-Sforza's and colleagues' research, for whom the genetic differences between populations were less phenotypical or due to natural selection. Directly relating to Jensen's more specific assertions, Cavalli-Sforza had been among those who early on opposed the notion that social structure and cultural potential were genetically based. Cavalli-Sforza and his Stanford colleague, the mathematician Marcus Feldman, tried to refute such allegations with a model for characteristics like IQ that took into account cultural influences (e.g., Cavalli-Sforza and Feldman 1973; for a book-length treatment of cultural transmission, see Cavalli-Sforza and Feldman 1981). This was also directed at policy suggestions such as 'racial' segregation in education or Jensen's claim that compensatory education programs were misguided because the answer to the question "How Much Can We Boost IQ and Scholastic Achievement?" (1969) was 'barely'. The 1960s not only witnessed the civil and minority rights movements, but also a renewed racism in Europe and the United States, one pillar of which was the resurfacing idea of 'race'-related differences in IQ (Sommer 2016a, 290–91). Jensenism, the belief that IQ and 'race' are correlated, was not only fought on paper, but publicly debated (on the controversy, see Panofsky 2014, 71–101). Jensen was symbolically and physically attacked and at times protected by bodyguards due to death threats.

This controversy actually never ended. Following the debates and aggressions of the 1970s, there was the uproar provoked by *The Bell Curve* (Herrnstein and Murray 1994), which positively received Jensenism, and in the wake of which Jensen presented his *The g Factor* (1998). The psychologist Richard Herrnstein and the political scientist Charles Murray asserted that differences in social status between classes and ethnic groups were no longer due to socioeconomic privilege, but that the American society had largely become socially stratified according to differences in intelligence that were highly heritable (Sommer 2016a, 377). Adam Miller (1994) and others have shown how the scholarship on differential intelligence has been linked to the Pioneer Fund (founded 1937) that sponsored research on genetically based differences between the 'races'. Its constituents promoted restrictions to immigration and variants of segregation to curtail intermixture, and worse. At the time of Miller's writing, Jensen, who strongly influenced the public debate about 'racial' abilities, seemingly explaining underrepresentation of African Americans and thus justifying their discrimination, had received over a million dollars from the Pioneer Fund. Scientists associated with the racist journal *Mankind Quarterly* that we encountered in Part III in connection with Gates also figured among the recipients. William H. Tucker (2002) could evidentially link the Pioneer Fund to attempts at repatriating African Americans and to sabotage the Civil Rights Act. Books like *The Bell Curve* used as fodder racist research that was sponsored by the Pioneer Fund.

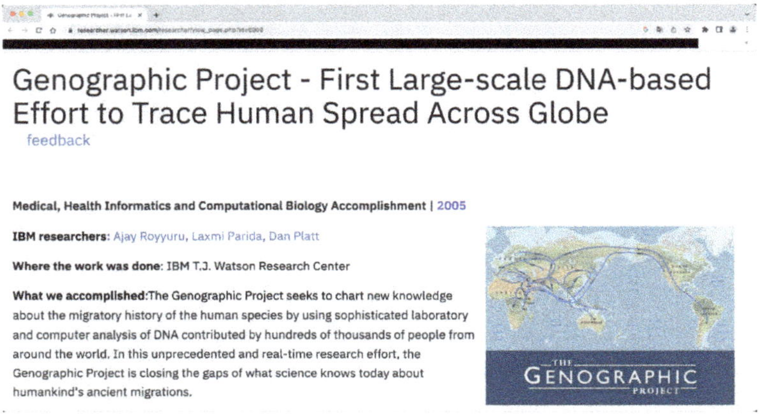

Fig. IV.7 Screenshot taken from a website of the Genographic Project showing a genetic tree-map (https://researcher.watson.ibm.com/researcher/view_page.php?id=6909 [link no longer active], last accessed 17 July 2023).

Cavalli-Sforza was appalled by such scholarship – but Jensen, and to a certain extent Kane, read Cavalli-Sforza's and colleagues' findings, particularly their diagrams, as not simply objectively demonstrating clear-cut differences between human groups in the way a tree shape or a principal component map can, but, in combination with old racial labels, as corroborating racial or racist classifications and stereotypes. The claim for neutrality by human population geneticists like Cavalli-Sforza that seemed to be strengthened by the diagrams is clearly put in jeopardy by the service these trees and maps could render to racist science and politics. Cavalli-Sforza was not only a central driver of human population genetics, he also played an important role in the public perception of this knowledge, not least through trees and maps. He rendered *The History and Geography of Human Genes* (Cavalli-Sforza,

Menozzi, and Piazza 1994), the standard work for specialists, more accessible in *Genes, Peoples, and Languages* (Cavalli-Sforza 2000 [1996]). Throughout his career, Cavalli-Sforza took great efforts to acquaint audiences with the genetic histories his science produced, in popular writings in different languages as well as through exhibition. Last but not least, he co-initiated the Human Genome Diversity Project (HGDP) and was involved in the Genographic Project – large endeavors aimed at finalizing the map of human population migration and the tree of their relatedness (see Figure IV.7) (Sommer 2015a, 123–35; 2016a, Part III).

The call for the HGDP was issued in 1991 and was linked to the canonical *The History and Geography of Human Genes* (Cavalli-Sforza, Menozzi, and Piazza 1994). The concerted population-genetic effort should not only include classical markers and the new autosomal and mtDNA systems, but also advance the Y-chromosomal system with its own tree, map, and narrative. With the Genographic Project, the Y chromosome became a star, and it was especially the Genographic Project and genetic ancestry tracing companies that have made the human population-genetic diagrammatics known to a wide range of people (see Figure IV.7). The Genographic Project was popularized in books and films, it was associated with citizen science, and the (western) people who opted to partake in the project by having their genome analyzed for money were referred to as participants. When the project terminated, there were over one million such participants in more than 140 countries. At the same time, both the HGDP and the Genographic Project were criticized from diverse sides, including the Indigenous Peoples Council on Biocolonialism. The projects were seen as exploitative in the use of Indigenous peoples as 'objects of scientific study' in continuation of nineteenth-century anthropological collecting as treated in Part I. The impression was that researchers would collect bodily material for the realization of their own goals, such as generating histories that might even contradict Indigenous knowledge (e.g., Sommer 2016a, Chs. 13 and 14; on the legacy and ethical issues of the HGDP see in particular Reardon 2005).

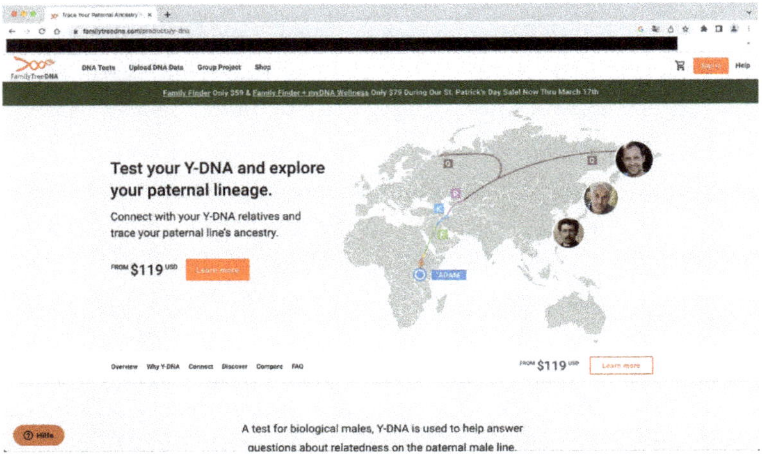

Fig. IV.8 Screenshot taken from a website of the genetic ancestry testing company Family Tree DNA (https://www.familytreedna.com/products/y-dna [image no longer online], last accessed 22 February 2024, with kind permission from FamilyTreeDNA).

The tree and map to render the genealogy and history of human groups thus had a particular revival in human population genetics and its popularization in public projects, books, and films, as well as through its commercialization in ancestry tracing firms. I end this chapter with a screenshot from a genetic ancestry tracing company that shows how a paying costumer might be linked to a branch in the panhuman family tree spread on a map originating from 'Y-chromosomal Adam' in Africa (the counterpart of mitochondrial Eve) (see Figure IV.8). While Figure IV.8 paints a simple picture indeed, Figure IV.7 actually hints at the fact that the tree-on-a-map received more and more branches, increasingly gaining in complexity and losing unidirectionality. Do we still see a tree, or is it a net? It is time to look more closely at the issue of admixture. Let me remark at this point that the sources I analyze throughout Part IV may use terms like 'admixture' differently and do not always clearly differentiate between diverse ways in which 'genes' can move from one population into another. The term 'gene flow' generally refers to the exchange of genetic material between populations, for example through migration. 'Admixture' in a stricter sense implies that two or more populations that have been isolated from each other interbreed to give rise to a new population with a mixed gene pool. In Chapter 17, it is mostly but not exclusively the latter which is at stake.

17. Genetic Trees, Admixture, and Mosaics

We have seen in the last chapter that Cavalli-Sforza's and colleagues' human population genetics was centrally about tree building. From the beginning, the assumptions underlying this approach were also criticized. There was some debate about what constituted the superior kind of data. Howells (1973b), for example, initially held that the genetic tree did not stand for true phylogeny. In his view, serological traits were not the best characteristics for studying population histories, but Howells' critique was not a general one against tree building. To the contrary, as we have seen, he was a tree builder, and also in this paper he included a tree based on cranial measurements (175). Other (physical) anthropologists issued more fundamental criticism, however. Ashley Montagu, C. Loring Brace, and Frank Livingstone denied the very existence of human genetic populations. Livingstone used the concept of the cline (introduced by Julian Huxley [1938b]) to describe the fact that a trait varies continuously not abruptly across space. Furthermore, the frequencies of different alleles did not fall together to form clusters (e.g., Livingstone 1962; see also my discussion of Huxley and Morant in Part III). The tree model was therefore not accurate, and Livingstone (1991) was among those who would demonstrate that the correlation between genetic and geographic distance that underlay tree building could be accounted for by other models than binary fission, such as genetic exchange between relatively stable neighboring populations (similar to the isolation by distance model).[1]

1 Isolation by distance is a special case of gene flow. In this case, genetic exchange mostly takes place between neighboring populations, but genes can also spread to distant populations over many generations using intermediate populations as steppingstones (if there are no absolute barriers between them).

 https://doi.org/10.11647/OBP.0396.21

Another cautioning voice along these lines was the physical anthropologist Gabriel Lasker (1976) who pointed to the particularly difficult situation for human population studies, due to the influences of parallel evolution, culture, and interbreeding. The biochemical methods for studying primate and intra-human phylogenies were essentially the same, but in the latter case the branches of a cladogram could not be read as representing reproductively isolated groups. Such a cladogram could at best be approximate, since the branches in a phylogenetic tree that represented human variants were in reality interconnected. The British-born American statistician, Elizabeth A. Thompson (1975), too, observed that human populations often did not fulfil the criterion of being isolated, non-interbreeding, required by the tree schema, even while her in-depth treatment of the theoretical, evidential, and computational aspects of population-genetic tree building supported the notion that the available genetic data did not warrant more sophisticated models. Thus, also in controversies within the young field of human population genetics itself, the question of whether trees were an adequate representation, or rather gave a false impression of evolutionary history because of degrees of interbreeding, was certainly an issue (see, e.g., also, Kirk 1969; Lalouel 1974; Morton 1974; Cavalli-Sforza 1974).

We have seen that Cavalli-Sforza and colleagues, too, to a certain extent recognized the limits of the tree shape and showed an interest in questions of admixture early on. From the outset, Cavalli-Sforza actually suggested that the tree shape might only work for populations that are geographically far apart, because otherwise "[i]nstead of a 'tree' one may have to estimate a 'network'; such methods do not yet exist" (Cavalli-Sforza 1973, 96; Sommer 2015a, 120–21). With regard to "such methods", the geneticist Ranajit Chakraborty published a review in 1986. Under the premise that "[i]n humans, exchange of genes between populations separated by large geographic distance and wide cultural and/or political barriers have [sic] been in operation since millennia" (1), he discussed the history and state of research on admixture, beginning with Felix Bernstein's studies on the distribution of blood groups published in 1931.

Bernstein, who had worked on the inheritance of blood groups with statistical methods, directed the Institute of Mathematical Statistics at the University of Göttingen (Germany) and lectured on biomathematics.

In the 1931 publication, he presented his attempts at reconstructing the migrations and mixtures of peoples on the basis of current blood group frequencies, such as the dispersal of the B-gene in relatively recent times from central Asia. Bernstein's considerations in general led him to argue against the polyphyletic views of human evolution and kinship that existed at his time and that I have discussed in Part III. He insisted that, during their entire existence, human groups had been part of processes of mixture as well as diversification. Thus, he rejected the image of the tree also for a monophyletic understanding of the origin and kinship of "Menschenrassen" [human races] (17), even while retaining a vegetal metaphor:

> The family tree of humanity does therefore neither resemble the image of a tree, nor the image of several trees grown together, which stem from separated roots, but the intergrowth and intertwining is so manifold, already at the roots, that we must view each putatively pure stem as a mixture [even] with regard to certain very old characteristics. (Bernstein 1931, 19, my translation)[2]

By the time Chakraborty published his review on admixture research in the mid-1980s, there were different methods in use to estimate the relative contributions of ancestral populations to a new hybrid population, some of which were applicable to two ancestral populations, while others allowed for more than two. The models therefore assumed that two or more existing populations gave rise to a new, hybrid population. African Americans were the most studied 'population', followed by the interest in (the Nordic admixture in) Icelanders and (the gentile admixture in) Jews. For over a decade, admixture had also gained attention on the level of the individual (proportions of ancestry for a hybrid individual), again with a special focus on African Americans.[3] Long before commercial

2 "Der Stammbaum des Menschen gleicht deshalb nicht dem Bilde eines Baumes, und auch nicht dem Bilde mehrerer miteinander verwachsener Bäume, die aus getrennten Wurzeln kommen, sondern die Verwachsung und Verflechtung ist eine so vielfältige, bereits von den Wurzeln her, dass wir jeden angeblich reinen Stamm in Bezug auf gewisse sehr alte Eigenschaften als eine Mischung anzusehen haben." Under national socialism, Bernstein lost his position and temporarily emigrated to the US.

3 The medical geneticists Charles J. MacLean and Peter L. Workman positioned their work among other things in the interest in the genetic differences between "races" in gene frequencies with respect to behavioral traits such as IQ (1973a; 1973b, 341).

ancestry tracing companies would pop up, studies even began to suggest the possibility under certain conditions to attribute specific genotypes to 'their populations' (Spielman and Smouse 1976; Smouse, Spielman, and Park 1982).

These strands of research were seen to be in their infancy, and it was hoped that the availability of many DNA sequences would help resolve some of the problems the study of admixtures and times of divergence with classical markers had so far encountered. For the future of admixture research discussed below, it is relevant that it was, on the one hand, assumed that "it may not be far from reality to conclude that admixture of different ethnic groups during the evolutionary history of man has resulted in some degree of homogeneity of genetic variation among populations" (Chakraborty 1986, 35). On the other hand, there also surfaced the notion of originally pure populations. The research demanded precise knowledge of the allele frequencies in all populations in a study. This was seen as a challenge as parent populations may no longer be available "in their original, unaltered form", i.e., "in an unmixed state" (Chakraborty 1986, 21; see also Thompson 1975, 134). Also relevant to the following is Chakraborty's observation that not enough attention was being paid to the historical hypotheses behind the research: "In human populations, admixture generally does not occur with a single sudden influx. The process of admixture in most admixed human groups had been more like the ebb and flow of tidal waves [...]" (1986, 9).

Building on a paper Cavalli-Sforza and Piazza had published in 1975 that mostly defended tree building, in *The History and Geography of Human Genes*, Cavalli-Sforza, Menozzi, and Piazza (1994, 54–9) included a section on admixtures, their estimations and (distorting) effects on tree structures. They mathematically described how to approximate the time that had elapsed between the separation of the ancestral populations and their admixture. They discussed the calculation of the respective percentages of the contributions of ancestral populations to an admixed population (for the case of African Americans). They also introduced an artificially admixed population (a population created from 60%-English and 40%-Ainu ancestry) into the estimation of a population tree to discuss the effects. Finally, the treatment of investigations of differences in autosomal DNA sequences led them to speculate that Europeans resulted from an admixture between Chinese and African populations (with the latter contributing less) – a hypothesis they visualized by drawing on a paper Cavalli-Sforza had co-signed (Bowcock et al. 1991, 168–71) (see Figure IV.9).

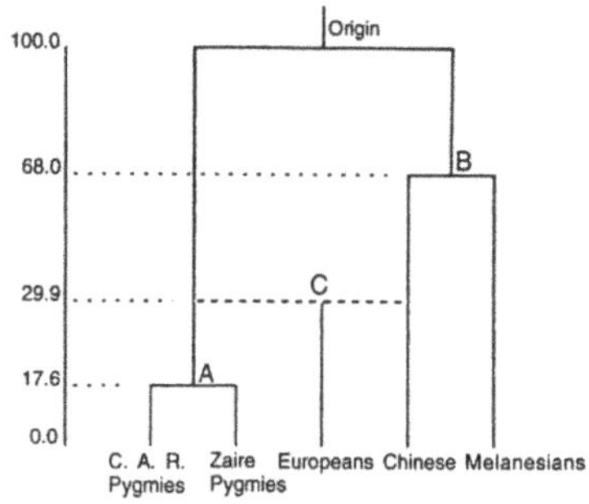

Fig. 2.4.7 A tree calculated by the maximum-likelihood method and showing that admixture between ancestral African and ancestral Chinese was responsible for the genesis of the European population (from Bowcock et al. 1991). C. A. R., Central African Republic.

Fig. IV.9 A tentative breach of the human family tree: Europeans as 'Chinese-African admixture' (all rights reserved; used with permission of Princeton University Press, from Luigi Luca Cavalli-Sforza, Paolo Menozzi, and Alberto Piazza, *The History and Geography of Human Genes* [Princeton: Princeton University Press 1994], Fig. 2.4.7, p. 92; permission conveyed through Copyright Clearance Center, Inc.).

However, Cavalli-Sforza, Menozzi, and Piazza mainly pointed to the problems with regard to admixture studies, especially where the admixture lay deep in the past and the ancestral populations were (genetically) unknown. Thus, they still concluded that although "[i]n theory it is possible to construct a tree with connections between the branches [...]" (1994, 58), in practice, geneticists had so far failed to reconstruct "true networks" (ibid., referring to Lathrop 1982). Generating trees with interconnections required an enormous amount of data. And even such interconnections would be shy of the likely course of history, since "[o]rdinarily population mixtures do not occur in a 'catastrophic' fashion, but are more likely to take place by the continuous slow infusion of individuals [...]" (Cavalli-Sforza, Menozzi, and Piazza 1994, 55). In sum, "[t]he full analysis of reticulate evolution remains an important task for the future" (59). Until then, one might exclude populations suspected of admixture from tree building. In *The History and Geography of Human Genes*, the Cavalli-Sforza and Edwards

(1965) genetic tree of human populations and its projection on a map in Edwards and Cavalli-Sforza (1964) were therefore reproduced with the remark that they assumed independent evolution in the branches of the tree, meaning "no important fusions or exchanges between the branches" (Cavalli-Sforza, Menozzi, and Piazza 1994, 69).

In other words, despite the assumption of admixture (fusions) and gene flow (exchanges), human relatedness was persistently forced into tree shapes; not in a genealogical way, however. In contrast to the genealogical family tree that links individuals on the basis of direct descent, these genetic population trees distance populations on the basis of overall genetic difference. The methods in human population genetics that are more analogous to genealogy were only just on the horizon, as indicated by the mitochondrial trees treated in Chapter 16 that actually (re)constructed the 'descent' of current DNA sequences in the sense of steps of mutations ('maternal lines'). So did studies of polymorphisms in Y-chromosomal DNA ('paternal lines'), the possibilities of which, too, were explored in *The History and Geography of Human Genes.* And in the context of autosomal DNA studies, Cavalli-Sforza, Menozzi, and Piazza expressed the wish that "[o]ne would like to be able to extend this approach including fusions as well as fissions in evolutionary human history, but accurate analysis of a greater number of populations would most probably demand information on many more genes than are available" (1994, 93).

This ability to extend the approach was not so long in the making. By the beginning of the third millennium, new statistical and computational approaches could be brought to bear on the analysis of an unprecedented amount of human genomic data. Expanding on the possibilities of clustering methods such as principal component analysis, statistical software like STRUCTURE (Pritchard, Stephens, and Donnelly 2000), FRAPPE (Tang et al. 2005), and ADMIXTURE (Alexander, Novembre, and Lange 2009) made it possible to group genetic samples into clusters and analyze the degree to which present-day individuals and populations are the result of genetic mixtures. With the introduction of programs for the graphical display of population structures like DISTRUCT (Rosenberg 2004), the visual black box of these seemingly discrete and homogenous entities – human populations – was opened. Individuals and populations came to be represented as colored bar plots indicating their admixed histories. Accordingly, the individual human genome as well as human diversity as such were now widely conceived of as a mosaic. A shift that, as we will see, eventually also registered in popularizations and commercialization.

Software like STRUCTURE allows the allocation of N individuals belonging to n geographically and/or ethnically defined populations to K groups so that these groups have the smallest within-population variation and the highest between-population variance. Starting with K equals 2, the method distributes the N individuals among just two groups, but also graphically visualizes the degree of admixture. This can be repeated with 3 K and so forth. The optimal number of K for the data is estimated in the process and depends on N and n. At the same time, there is a certain tendency to correlate K with conventional geographic regions, with the result that despite its quality of literally bringing to light the intermixed state of individual genomes and the admixed nature of populations, the clustering of individual genomes into populations seems to reify the age-old notion of 'continental races'. This is in fact what happened in a genome-wide and global study with FRAPPE of which Cavalli-Sforza, aged eighty-six, was still a signatory (Li et al. 2008). In this "most comprehensive characterization to date of human genetic variation" (1100), the data of 938 individual genomes from fifty-one populations from the Human Genome Diversity Panel were said to segregate into the five continental groups. In the plotted results for K 7 with the DISTRUCT program, the seven clusters built with FRAPPE on the basis of the individual samples were labeled 'Africa', 'Middle East', 'Europe', 'Central and South Asia', 'East Asia', 'Oceania', and 'America'.

Nonetheless, when experimenting with such programs, it seems that the more fine-grained the analysis becomes, the obscurer the populational structure gets. In other words: the bigger K, the more 'previously pure populations appear as admixed'. This can be indicated by means of an online blogpost by Dienekes Pontikos, on which there is an ADMIXTURE analysis that moves from K 1 up to K 15. Figure IV.10 represents the analysis at K 15. The 15 clusters (K) are not separated by lines in the way usual for such visualizations, but only the 139 smaller populations that were studied and to which the 2,230 individuals whose DNA was analyzed belong ('sample populations'). It is indeed a beautiful mosaic that evokes a cheerful picture of humankind in all colors of the rainbow.

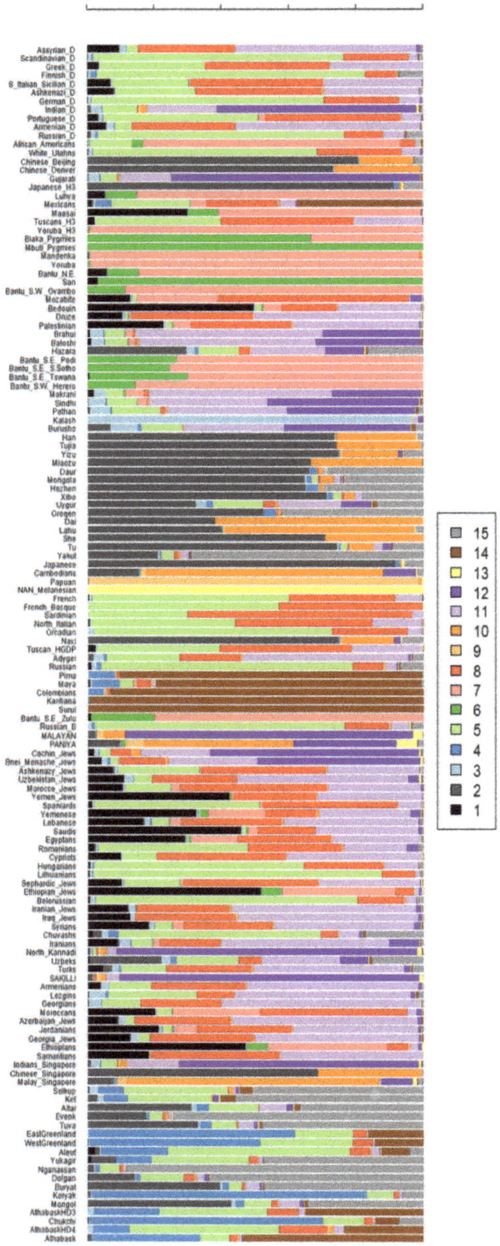

Fig. IV.10 Cluster diagram with K=15 (Dienekes Pontikos, "Human Genetic Variation: The First ? Components," *Dienekes' Anthropology Blog* [15 December 2010], http://dienekes.blogspot.com/2010/12/human-genetic-variation-first.html).

This tendency of 'bursting individuals and populations' seems to stand in stark contrast to the tree structure, which can be shown by Figure IV.11. It is a representation of the same data in the shape of a phylogenetic tree for the fifteen "original/ancestral components or populations" inferred by ADMIXTURE (the 15 K). In this process, the admixture disappears, and we return to a diagram that creates a hierarchical order from "Sub-Saharan" to "Siberian". Instead of a human mosaic, in Figure IV.11 we again see the diaspora, in which populations (in this case fifteen) seem to have differentiated from a common source without converging (see also Sommer 2015a, 134–35; 2016a, 380–83).

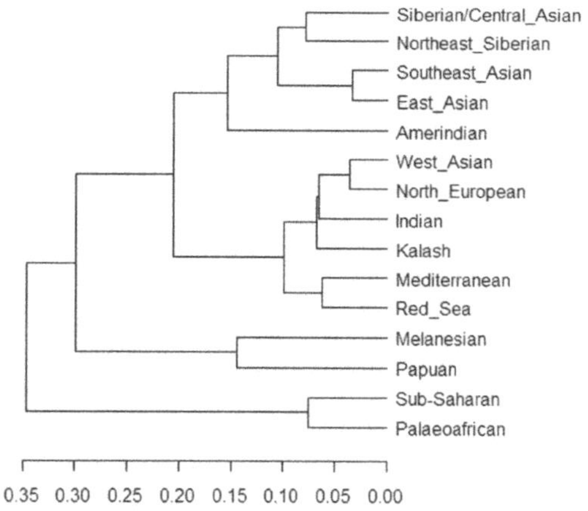

Fig. IV.11 Dendrogram of hierarchical clustering of the 15 ancestral components (Dienekes Pontikos, "Human Genetic Variation: The First ? Components," *Dienekes' Anthropology Blog* [15 December 2010], http://dienekes.blogspot.com/2010/12/human-genetic-variation-first.html).

However, let us take a closer look at the mosaic of Figure IV.10. The 'ancestral populations' (the 15 K) that are so neatly separated in the tree of Figure IV.11 are assumed also in this diagram. Even though the current populations and individuals are shown to form mixtures, they form mixtures of these supposed 'pure ancestral populations' that are marked by the fifteen distinct colors. Thus, the mosaic as well as the tree suggest a genetic order that existed before the major population movements took place. It seems that while admixture has become the center of attention in human population genomics, underneath its colorful diagrams still lurks the conception of originally pure populations hierarchically arranged in a tree – the origination in one population with successive distribution across the globe through fission without fusion. Thus, through altering the number of K, researchers may aim at exposing (tree-like) hierarchical relations between human populations. But assumptions built into STRUCTURE, ADMIXTURE, and similar programs, as well as the number of K assumed, lack rigorous statistical tests, and results may be interpreted subjectively, including as evidencing the existence of traditional 'racial' categories.[4]

Yet, visualizations of ADMIXTURE analyses and similar programs do (at least) show living individuals and current populations as considerably admixed. As a consequence, besides the tree (on a map) visualizations (as shown in Figure IV.8), diagrams that construct humans as genomically of mixed ancestries have also become current in popular and commercial contexts as is indicated by Figure IV.12 (even if with the simultaneous suggestion, through the distinct colors on the map and in the list, that the admixture has been between different, in themselves homogenous, individuals from pure populations).

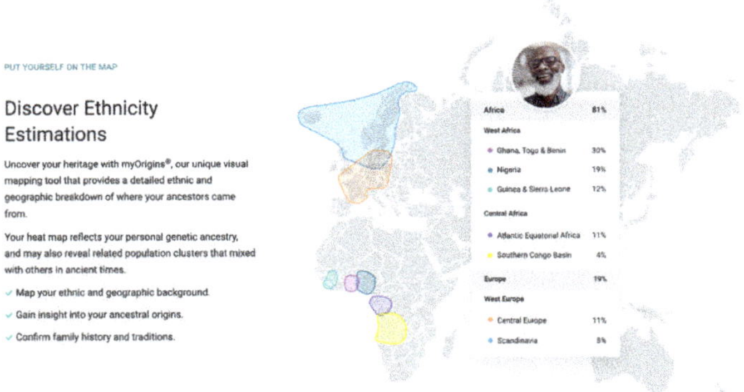

Fig. IV.12 Screenshot taken from a website of the genetic ancestry testing company Family Tree DNA (https://www.familytreedna.com/products/family-finder, last accessed 17 July 2023, with kind permission from FamilyTreeDNA).

4 Programs such as STRUCTURE and ADMIXTURE have been criticized for diverse statistical problems, for the lack of a statistically rigorous justification for the number of K, as well as for the lack of tests for whether the K populations are genetically differentiated to a statistically significantly amount (Alan Templeton, personal communication, 8 January 2024; for a critical discussion of the program, see also Bolnick 2008; on different Bayesian algorithm models that do and do not take into account admixture and geographic information in the determination of population structure, see François and Durand 2010; for an alternative, network approach that does not seem to suggest 'pure' ancestral populations, see Greenbaum et al. 2019).

In stark contrast, trees do not make admixture obvious, even though, besides purportedly giving an image of human relatedness before major intermixtures took place, they at the same time stand for relations between currently living human groups. The owner of the online blog and producer of the diagrams shown as Figures IV.10 and IV.11 is aware of the simplification a visualization as tree encompasses, but, reminiscent of Cavalli-Sforza's approach, he still carries it out.[5] The folding of time, this simultaneity of the non-simultaneous, that is inherent in such genomic trees is further evidenced by the fact that the ancestral population called "Palaeoafrican" in the tree of Figure IV.11 refers to the "Pygmies and San" (!), or rather to genomic data gained from individual human beings belonging to groups who have been given these names by outsiders. And this at a time, as will be of concern in Chapter 18, when aDNA has become part of a new field of enquiry that no longer reconstructs the deeper evolutionary history of modern humans on the basis of current genetic diversity alone (Sommer 2022b, 290–93; Sommer and Amstutz 2024, "Enter Ancient DNA: Mosaic and Trees").

Before moving on to studies that include aDNA in the next two chapters, let us recall the view dominant at that time of the evolution of modern humans and the role archaic humans played therein. In *The History and Geography of Human Genes* (1994), Cavalli-Sforza, Menozzi, and Piazza worked with the tree shape of modern human evolution in support of the out-of-Africa model that assumed no interbreeding with archaic humans outside of Africa. They explicitly rejected the multiregional model of Franz Weidenreich, to the followers of which they, too, mistakenly counted Coon. The misunderstanding seems not to have ended there, because they claimed that the multiregional model assumes parallel evolution of the 'racial' lines in the different parts of the world, whereas, as we have seen in Part III, Weidenreich postulated genetic exchange between the regions and basically one evolutionary line or a network, rather than many parallel lines. Cavalli-Sforza, Menozzi, and Piazza (1994, 62–64) maintained this misrepresentation in word as well as diagram (see Figure IV.13).

5 Dienekes Pontikos, "Human Genetic Variation: The First ? Components," *Dienekes' Anthropology Blog* (15 December 2010), http://dienekes.blogspot.com/2010/12/human-genetic-variation-first.html

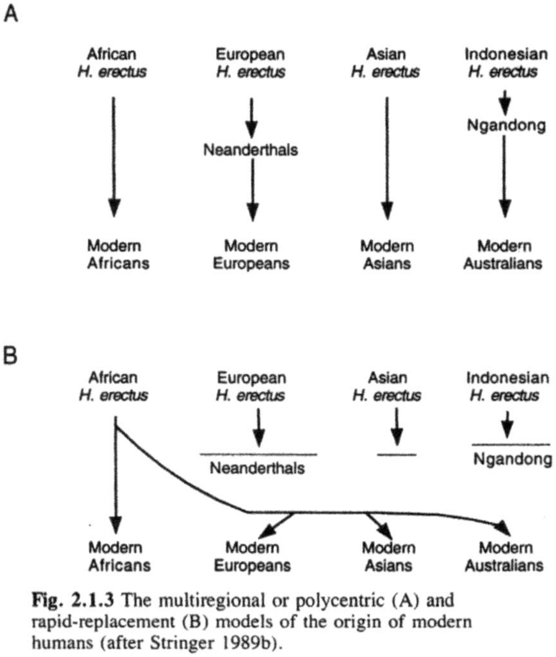

Fig. IV.13 Weidenreich's model distorted to parallel evolutionary lines (A) and juxtaposed to the out-of-Africa replacement model (B) (all rights reserved; used with permission of Princeton University Press, from Luigi Luca Cavalli-Sforza, Paolo Menozzi, and Alberto Piazza, *The History and Geography of Human Genes* [Princeton: Princeton University Press 1994], Fig. 2.1.3, p. 62; permission conveyed through Copyright Clearance Center, Inc.).

The out-of-Africa model, which, when translated into a diagram, renders a tree for modern human evolution like in Figure IV.13B, stood for the notion that modern humans expanded "from Africa to Asia and the rest of the world, rapidly replacing the earlier human types living in these other regions" (Cavalli-Sforza, Menozzi, and Piazza 1994, 63). Although in their treatment of the archeological and paleontological knowledge, Cavalli-Sforza, Menozzi, and Piazza did not completely rule out a little genetic exchange, especially in east Asia, they maintained that "Cro-Magnon seems to emerge essentially unmixed" (65) and stated that "[i]f we look at the two hypotheses shown in figure 2.1.3 [Figure IV.13 above], we conclude with a definitive preference for replacement" (66).

In the next chapter, I engage with the developments taking place with the inclusion of aDNA data. This discussion is set against the backdrop of the preceding chapters, which highlighted the conundrum that while admixture between modern human populations has always been granted to some extent and gene flow between modern and archaic populations has not entirely been ruled out, the prevailing focus has been on building trees. Did the possibilities of including aDNA data in the analyses lead to novel ways of modelling human relatedness? This question again demands reflection on terminology at the outset. In *The History and Geography of Human Genes*, Cavalli-Sforza, Menozzi, and Piazza stated that "interconnected trees are *networks*. In the language of graph theory, trees bifurcate or multifurcate, but their branches do not connect" (1994, 58). However, in the following chapters we will see that there exist different notions of what a tree constitutes, and Chapter 18 will show that trees with a few connecting branches still look very much like trees.

18. Gene Flow and Ancient DNA: Trees with Connecting Branches

Due to technical advancements such as next-generation sequencing and increased accessibility of aDNA in terms of quality, quantity, and time-depth, the potential for aDNA research has significantly expanded from the study of limited individual ancient genomes to the broader scale of population genomics (e.g., Lan and Lindqvist 2019, 21). Most importantly for my context, the once predominant conceptualization of human evolution as a tree on a map, indicating a common origin with subsequent population splits without intermixture, has become increasingly problematic due to advanced technologies and the growing abundance of data, including aDNA data. Indeed, aDNA studies have catalyzed the undermining of the pure tree model for human evolution, and at ever lower segments. Some of the most groundbreaking and surprising findings in aDNA research in fact relate to the genetic contribution of extinct lineages to lines leading to modern human populations as well as evidence of ancient genetic exchange between different archaic lineages (Resendez et al. 2019, 379).

It became clear that Neanderthals had contributed to present 'non-African genomes'. And Denisovans – an archaic hominin established on the basis of DNA from a little finger bone discovered in a cave in the Altai Mountains of southern Siberia – seemed to have contributed to the genomes of modern Papuans, Melanesians, Aboriginal Australians, and other Southeast Asian Islanders, as well as, to a lower degree, to mainland East and South Asians (Green et al. 2010; Reich et al. 2010; for an overview, see Leonardi et al. 2017). Further research suggested possible deep-rooting gene flow from an ancient 'ghost population' and a modern 'ghost population' (genetic traces of unknown ancestors) into

 https://doi.org/10.11647/OBP.0396.22

West African populations as well as large-scale Neanderthal inbreeding in African populations (reviewed in Vicente and Schlebusch 2020, 13).

Despite these developments, however, the diagrams to express hominin and human history and kinship still tended to closely resemble trees. Unlike in the admixture studies discussed in the last chapter, where two or more ancestral groups were conceptualized as having mixed to form a new one, these diagrams suggested that gene flow between groups had been unidirectional and constituted one event of short duration. These events, which were represented by links or arrows connecting tree branches, were often referred to as 'introgression event', 'admixture pulse', or 'episodic migration'. The diagram from a breakthrough-paper of 2014 reproduced as Figure IV.14 serves as an example; it visualizes these short events, pulses, or episodes as darts between the branches of an overall tree structure (Prüfer et al. 2014, Fig. 8, 48).

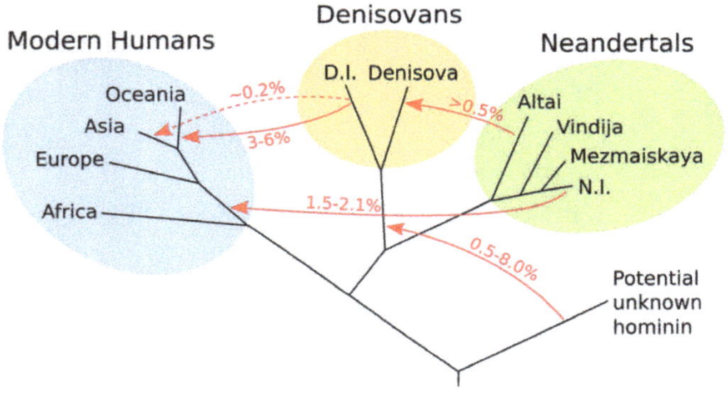

Figure 8. A possible model of gene flow events in the late Pleistocene
The direction and estimated magnitude of inferred gene flow events are shown. Branch lengths and ages gene flows are not drawn to scale. The dashed line indicates that it is uncertain if Denisovan gene flow into modern humans occurred once or more times. D.I. denotes the introgressing Denisovan, N.I. the introgressing Neandertal. Note that the age of the archaic genomes precludes detection of gene-flow from modern humans into the archaic hominins.

Fig. IV.14 "A possible model of gene flow events in the late Pleistocene". Kay Prüfer, Fernando Racimo, Nick Patterson, et al., "The Complete Genome Sequence of a Neanderthal from the Altai Mountains" (*Nature* 505.7481 [2014]: 43–49), Fig. 8, p. 48, https://doi.org/10.1038/nature12886. © Springer Nature Limited, all rights reserved (reproduced with permission from Springer Nature Customer Service Centre GmbH).

At the same time, and as we have found in the preceding chapters of this part, text and diagram were not always completely congruent in this regard, as indicated by the influential 2014 paper from which Fig. IV.14 is taken:

> We present evidence for three to five cases of interbreeding among four distinct hominin populations (Fig. 8). Clearly the real population history is likely to have been even more complex. For example, most cases of gene flow are likely to have occurred intermittently, often in both directions and across a geographic range. Thus, combinations of gene flow among different groups and substructured populations may have yielded the patterns detected rather than the discrete events considered here. (Prüfer et al. 2014, 48)

Furthermore, while in Figure IV.14 the recent human groups are at least embedded in a blue bubble, which we might interpret as genetic exchange among them, in the tree in Figure IV.15 (Kuhlwilm et al. 2016, Fig. 3, 432) that suggests additional gene flow from a population related to modern humans into one of the Neandertal lineages, 'the modern human populations' – constituted by "San", "Yoruba", "French", "Han", and "Papuan" samples – again appear as unmixed among themselves.

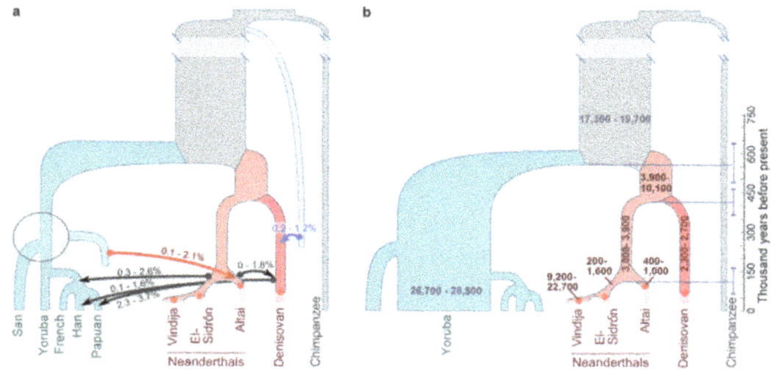

Figure 3. Refined demography of archaic and modern humans
a, Total migration rates of six gene flow events inferred by G-PhoCS. The ranges correspond to 95% Bayesian credible intervals aggregated across runs. Five gene flow events have been previously reported, including gene flow from an unknown archaic group into Denisovans (blue arrow). In addition, we infer gene flow from a population related to modern humans into a population ancestral to the Altai Neanderthal (red arrow). It appears to come from a population that either split from the ancestors of present-day Africans or separated fairly early in the history of African populations (dashed gray box). **b**, Effective population sizes and divergence times inferred by G-PhoCS. The ranges correspond to 95% Bayesian credible intervals aggregated across runs. The horizontal bars (dashed) indicate posterior mean estimates for divergence times. Archaic samples (dots) are located at their estimated ages.

Fig. IV.15 "Refined demography of archaic and modern humans". Martin Kuhlwilm, Ilan Gronau, Melissa J. Hubisz, et al., "Ancient Gene Flow from Early Modern Humans into Eastern Neanderthals" (*Nature* 530.7591 [2016]: 429–33), Fig. 3, p. 432, https://doi.org/10.1038/nature16544.

Finally, some archeologists, geneticists, and paleoanthropologists, including Stringer, who as we have seen had been a key figure in the synthesis of approaches around the out-of-Africa model, rejected many of the proposed mixture events (Stringer 2014; see also Mellars 2006), while granting that it was impossible to pinpoint one geographical or temporal origin of modern human ancestry in Africa (see Bergström et al. 2021, 233). Indeed, it has been observed that

> the revised 'Out-of-Africa' model, or partial replacement model, insists that Africa-related modern humans are the main stream in modern human evolution which has borne the major contribution to the present-day populations, and the dispersed modern humans from Africa assimilated other archaic populations instead of integrating into the indigenous groups of other regions. (Gao et al. 2017, 2162)

This would agree with many of the diagrams representing the new, aDNA-related view of human evolution, with their tree shape that includes connecting arrows. The direction of the darts in these diagrams suggests that the focus is on the modern human populations that came 'out of Africa'; the local archaic humans are merely seen as contributing a bit to that "main stream", as Xing Gao of the Chinese Academy of Sciences and colleagues put it, even if this was corrected for the Y chromosome and mtDNA that were found to have been introduced from the modern human into the Neanderthal lineage (Bergström et al. 2021). And yet, the researchers who added this new arrow in the tree shown as Figure IV.16 conceded that "trees are poor representations of genetic history" (233).

The observations so far are obviously connected to the development of mathematics and technologies to study human and hominin history and diversity on the basis of modern and ancient DNA. Programs like STRUCTURE and ADMIXTURE as well as the older method of principal component analysis that I have treated in the last chapter assess the genetic similarity between individuals and the extent to which populations form distinct clusters. However, the integration of aDNA presents problems, not least due to sample sizes, quality, and chronological and geographic representativity. Significantly, these procedures do not have underlying demographic models or hypothesis testing components, and the recovered genetic substructures could have been brought about by several different population histories: "This results in inference that can be easily steered by subjective interpretation of individual researchers [...]" (Loog 2020, 3). Therefore, even though researchers may assume that living people and populations are a product of admixture between a certain set of distinct ancestral groups that once existed in the past, the observed genetic patterns could be the result of other demographic histories. For example, one cannot differentiate between admixture and other kinds of gene flow, or between one or several events (which may render ADMIXTURE a misnomer).

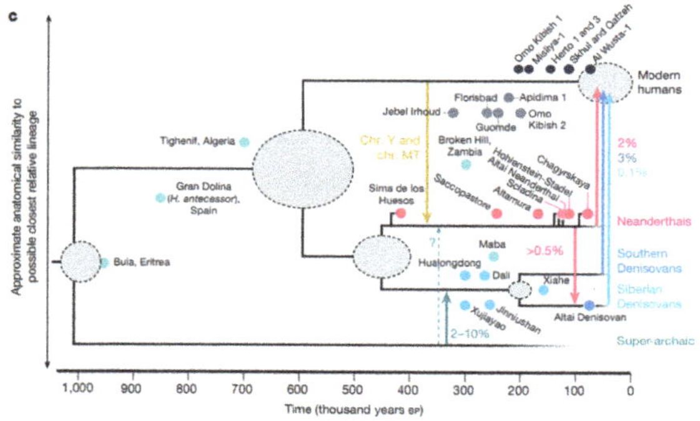

Fig. 3 | Separation of modern human and archaic ancestries in the past one million years (phase 1). a, Locations of key *H. sapiens*, Neanderthal, Denisovan and other archaic human fossils from the past 500 thousand years. Pale colours indicate uncertain but possible lineage assignments. **b**, Chronology of archaic human populations that are unlikely to have contributed to modern human ancestry. These include *Homo naledi*, *Homo floresiensis* and *Homo luzonensis*[143]. The timeline is the same as in **c**. **c**, Chronology and probable ancestry history of the separation between modern human and archaic human ancestries. Selected fossils older than 80 thousand years and their possible lineage attributions (as in **a**) are indicated. The placement of the fossils along the vertical axis reflects our assessment of how closely related they might be to the genetic ancestries. Chr. MT, mitochondrial chromosome; chr. Y, Y chromosome. Grey circles represent uncertainty around timing or population topology.

Fig. IV.16 "Separation of modern human and archaic ancestries". Anders Bergström, Chris Stringer, Mateja Hajdinjak, et al., "Origins of Modern Human Ancestry" (*Nature* 590.7845 [2021]: 229–37), Fig. 3c, p. 234, https://doi.org/10.1038/s41586-021-03244-5.

These might be some of the reasons why, despite their popularity, programs like STRUCTURE, ADMIXTURE, and fineSTRUCTURE were not sufficient for many researchers especially when working with aDNA. Researchers often referred to the early history of human population genetics, and specifically to Cavalli-Sforza's work as discussed in the preceding chapters, when accounting for the fact that they wanted methods that could do both – model population histories and relations and formally test for gene flow (Pickrell and Pritchard 2012). In other words, partly due to that early history of the field, methods were developed to describe population-tree topologies that could include gene flow events. These methods analyze the allele frequency patterns among populations and compare the amount of genetic drift in populations to establish population histories (*f*- and D-statistics) (on such methods in general, see, e.g., Pathak 2020; also Schaefer, Shapiro, and Green 2016).

In my context, the graph-building techniques are of particular interest. These are supplementary to the results from *f*- and D-statistics and "analyse the genetic diversities of many populations and suggest an elaborate tree-like topology, illustrating their mutual relationships" (Pathak 2020, 13). Such tools build trees of populations (based on drift patterns) that explain their evolutionary histories including episodic migrations (gene flow) or admixtures (TreeMix, MixMapper, qpGraph). It is especially in these contexts that the terms 'gene flow' and 'admixture' might be used interchangeably or 'admixture' is used to refer to single introgression events. Kay Prüfer et al. (2014) relied on *f*- and D-statistics and Figure IV.14, taken from their paper, is a "maximum likelihood drift tree of populations using TreeMix" (supplementary information, 55). The diverse techniques are suitable for different purposes and different data sets, and all have their inherent assumptions, their possibilities, and limitations, as well as pitfalls that may be exacerbated in the case of aDNA (Pathak 2020). But what is most important to my purpose is that graph-based models like TreeMix infer a tree structure (only in subsequent steps 'correcting' for admixture or gene flow events), which becomes evident in Figure IV.17.

The researchers from whom Figure IV.17 is taken assumed that human population history is tree-like to simplify the search for a maximum likelihood graph. While this technique may have been computationally efficient – a standard desktop computer could provide the tree structure in five minutes and test for gene flow in only a few hours – it "modeled migration [gene flow] between populations as occurring at single, instantaneous time points", even though this was seen as "a dramatic simplification of the migration process" and the question of the relevance of continuous versus discrete mixture was said to be an open one. The researchers expressed the expectation that with an improved search algorithm, the assumption of 'treeness' could eventually be relaxed (Pickrell and Pritchard 2012, 9, and, including quotes, 13).

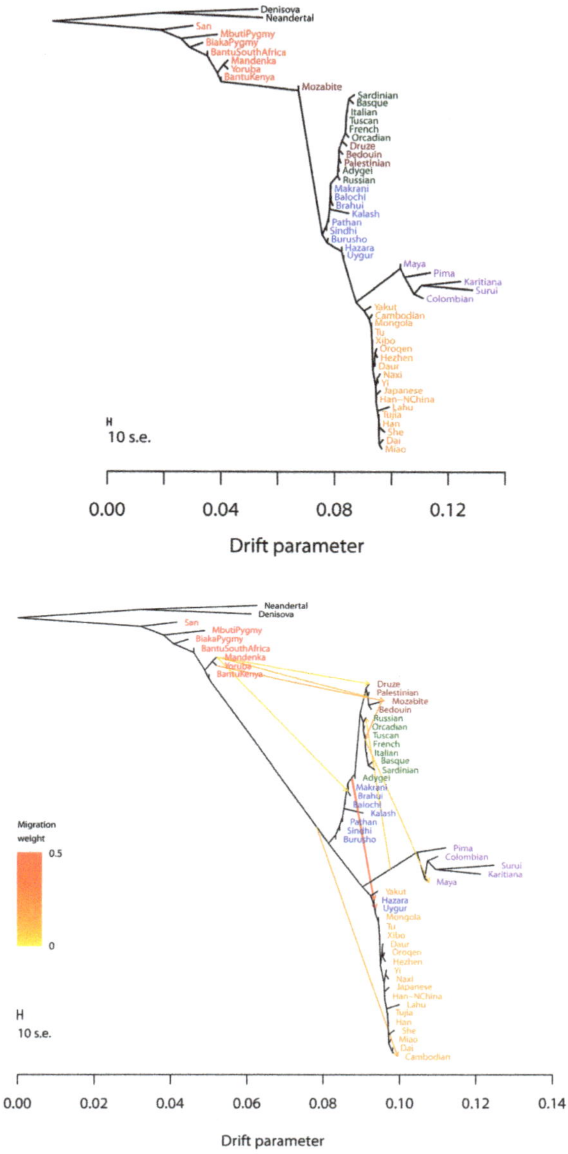

Fig. IV.17 (Above) is the inferred maximum likelihood tree of human phylogeny relating modern and archaic humans without considering gene flow between them, and (Below) is the same tree allowing for ten gene flow events between continental groups of modern humans (TreeMix). Joseph K. Pickrell and Jonathan K. Pritchard, "Inference of Population Splits and Mixtures from Genome-Wide Allele Frequency Data" (*PLOS Genetics* 8.11 [2012]: 1–17), Figs. 3a and 4, p. 8 and p. 10, https://doi.org/10.1371/journal.pgen.1002967. CC BY 4.0.

The appearance of a tree-like structure of human history and relatedness, or rather diversity, may also be enhanced because admixture graphs like qpGraph enable researchers to focus on admixture between populations of interest, hiding the admixed status of populations beyond the scope of a study (Lipson 2020, 1664). qpGraph and qpAdm are part of the ADMIXTOOLS software package that is mainly used for admixture studies and was developed by Nick Patterson of the David Reich Lab (Patterson et al. 2012).[1] In the case of qpGraph, the researchers need to define the number of admixture events as well as which populations are admixed, while in the case of TreeMix, the determination of the phylogeny is automated, but the users decide the list of populations and the number of admixture events. This, for TreeMix together with the fact that the program starts from an unadmixed tree (which is a problem especially if many populations are admixed), is seen as the main drawback of such approaches (e.g., Lipson 2020, 1666.). It has also been observed that tools that require a model for the histories of the populations not in question in an analysis (nontarget populations) might lead to erroneous admixture results if these histories are modelled wrongly – again, especially in aDNA studies.[2]

This knowledge about population histories is not necessary for the statistical tool qpAdm (which applies the common ideas associated with f_4-statistics and) that can identify plausible admixture histories and estimate admixture proportions. It has become a widely used method especially in aDNA studies to test whether the genetics of a certain population can be explained by admixture between two or more source populations. This statistical tool is seen to yield accurate results even when data coverage is low, data is missing to a high degree, or aDNA is damaged. However, it is yet again cautioned that ancient and present-day DNA should not be analyzed together and that qpAdm should not be used for population histories that might include extended periods of gene flow. The tool assumes a single pulse in a short time, even though "real population histories often involve continuous gene flow that occurs over a prolonged period of time" (Harney et al. 2021, 13). In fact,

1 See, further, the Reich Laboratory website: https://github.com/DReichLab/AdmixTools

2 In the paper in which Joseph K. Pickrell and Jonathan K. Pritchard (2012) introduced the tool TreeMix, they interchangeably talked of admixture and gene flow. Mark Lipson (2020) and others only refer to these tools as admixture tools.

also in a case of continuous gene flow, qpAdm might suggest plausible admixture proportion estimates as the result of a single pulse.[3]

Some tools are not only able to approximate rates of gene flow between different branches from sequence data, but also past population sizes and the dates of population splits, one of them being the software package G-PhoCS (Generalized Phylogenetic Coalescence Sampler) that was applied in the construction of Figure IV.15. In most cases, however, tools for dating admixture events (ROLLOFF, ALDER, MALDER) once again assume only one admixture pulse and can therefore not capture continuous mixing of populations. As we have seen, and as also suggested by the trees in Figure IV.17, in which the second tree 'allows for ten admixture events' but not for continuous exchange, this constitutes a more general issue:

> One question is whether changes in populations over time are typically gradual – owing to consistent, low-level gene flow between neighboring populations – or punctate, with migration events rapidly altering the genetic composition of a region. One line of work on modeling human history explicitly assumes the latter [...]. (Pickrell and Reich 2014, 382–83)[4]

This latter approach has been found statistically inconsistent if gene flow does not correspond to single admixture events.[5]

---

3 Nick Patterson explained that the motivation for the development of these software tools was that point-wise gene transfer was easier to model. Thus, the reasons were entirely mathematical, i.e., these models were mathematically tractable, while the graph tools followed "naturally" (personal interview with Nick Patterson, 15 August 2023). The statistics and software are continuously being developed, so that, at the point of writing this, there already exists an ADMIXTOOLS 7.0.2. In fact, on the basis of re-analyses of published population histories with findGraphs (part of ADMIXTOOLS 2), Robert Maier et al. (2023) criticized that there are alternative, and even better fitting, models for population histories than the published ones. With regard to the admixture events, they stated that "even this approach [exploration with findGraphs] can lead to potentially unstable results as relaxing the assumption of parsimony (that fewer admixture events is more likely) can lead to qualitatively quite different equally well-fitting topologies [...]" (22).

4 On the analytical tool DATES for the inference of admixture timing, see Narasimhan et al. 2019; on the methodological developments with aDNA in general, see, for example, Orlando et al. 2021, 11–13 on principal component analysis, ADMIXTURE, and *f*-statistics.

5 As we have seen, programs like TreeMix "cannot distinguish between a single, virtually instantaneous admixture event, versus multiple, recurring admixture events, versus continuous gene flow, or versus gene flow with isolation by

While the supposition of such 'punctate' events and its implementation in analytical tools were among the factors that seem to have favored the persistence of tree-like images of human population histories, it has been more generally observed that most population-genetic models "rely on the assumption that the relationship between populations can be represented as, essentially, a phylogenetic tree, i.e. as abrupt splits between different branches of the tree, followed by independent evolution with potential for subsequent episodes of gene flow between them" (Loog 2020, 8). It has been pointed out that measures such as past population sizes, population splits, divergence times, and specific admixture events only make sense under such tree assumptions and might be artefacts thereof (Templeton 2018b, 223).

At the other end of the spectrum, rather than contemplating that the models might oversimplify population history among other things because they cannot account for continuous gene flow between 'lineages', researchers have instead observed that statistical methods may artificially produce genetic signatures of archaic introgression events when the data could be interpreted on the basis of alternative scenarios such as ancestral population structure. If the 'ancestral African population' was structured due to non-random mating, this could mean that some living human groups share more genetic variants with archaic ones than others, without introgression having taken place. Another possibility is aDNA contamination with modern DNA, which would render the archaic samples 'more modern', mimicking archaic admixture (Gopalan et al. 2021). And yet, even while possibly questioning archaic introgression in favor of the assumption of deep population structure, the approaches via tree building seem to have arrived at more and more reticulate relating diagrams as shown in Figure IV.18, including the possibility of population mergers and continuous gene flow – a topic I will continue in the final chapter (Chapter 20).

---

distance" (Templeton 2023, 13). Inconsistency is thereby a formal property from statistics. While, with increasing amounts of data, a good statistic should converge to the true value, an inconsistent statistic with probability 1 approaches a false inference with increasing data (Alan Templeton, personal communication, 8 January 2024).

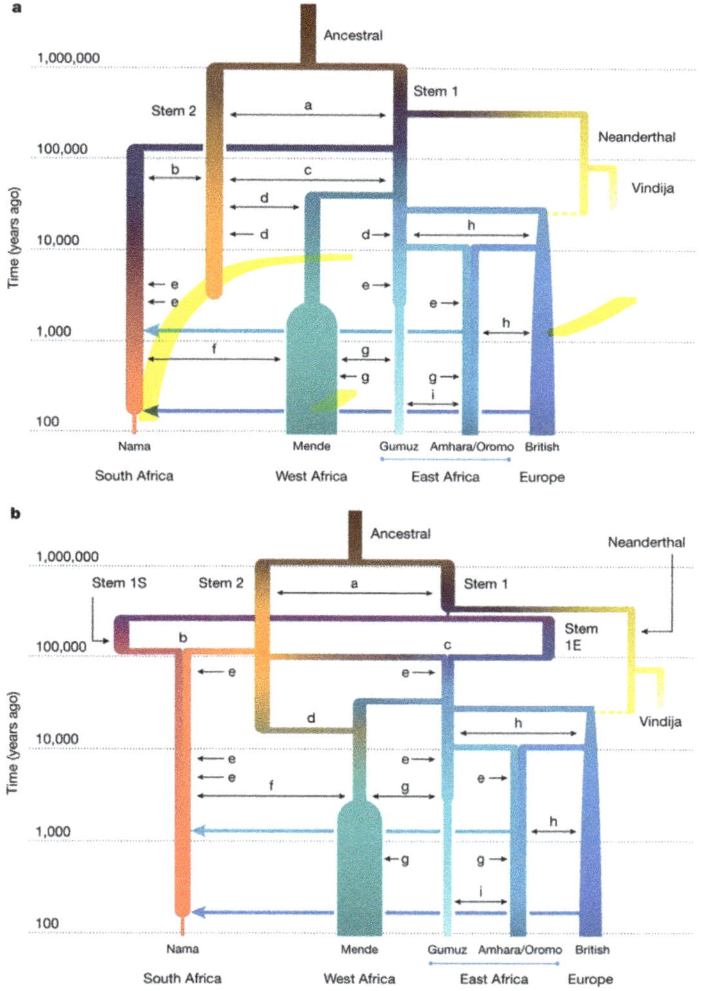

Fig. IV.18 Human phylogeny for 'Africa' including continuous gene flow (small letters) and population mergers. Aaron P. Ragsdale, Timothy D. Weaver, Elizabeth G. Atkinson, et al., "A Weakly Structured Stem for Human Origins in Africa" (*Nature* 617.7962 [2023]: 755–63), Fig. 3, p. 756, https://doi.org/10.1038/s41586-023-06055-y. © The Authors, under exclusive license to Springer Nature Limited, all rights reserved (reproduced with permission from Springer Nature Customer Service Centre GmbH).

Let me first recapitulate. I have begun this part with a look at the visualization of human history, diversity, and kinship in early human population genetic research when the tree (on a map) was fundamental.

Against this background, I have identified something like a visual paradigm shift with the advent of programs like STRUCTURE and ADMIXTURE and the concomitant interest in processes of mixing and in individuals and populations as being intermixed. At the same time, whole-genome analyses in such programs first suggested the age-old Blumenbachian clustering into five groups. Furthermore, while a certain drive beyond the categories of 'the individual' and 'the population' seems to be inherent in such analyses and visualizations, there is also a pull in the opposite direction in the notion of 'originally pure ancestral populations or races'. This pull finds its strongest expression in the shape of trees.

With the advent of population-genomic aDNA research, the focus on admixture and introgression increased and was given a deeper history. However, in modelling and visualizing, the amount of contact and genetic exchange between groups that researchers esteemed likely tended to be minimized, leaving us with trees that include a few arrows between branches. This was probably due to several factors, one of them being ways of thinking and doing that are handed down from one generation of researchers to the next and that may be disproportionately shaped by particularly influential scientists and laboratories (see e.g., Gokcumen 2020, 69). There is also the history of methodological and technological developments in a stricter sense as in the necessity to build on what is already there and the fact that statistical analyses aim at reducing the complexity of data or fit it to parametric models. Although more complex models were appearing on the horizon, human population genomics, also with the inclusion of aDNA data, instantiated tree thinking and tree building that at times rendered human populations distinct, homogenous entities. To find out more about the reasons for these issues, it is helpful to consider the ways in which practitioners themselves account for the history of their field (Sommer and Amstutz 2024, "Enter Ancient DNA: Mosaic and Trees", "Conclusion").

19. The (Diagrammatic) Narratives of Genetic Revolutions

Historians of science Elsbeth Bösl and Elizabeth Jones have written about the development of aDNA research in cycles of proclaimed revolutions. The first cycle commenced with the search for the oldest DNA using polymerase chain reaction technology in the 1990s; this was followed by the second hype cycle in the field, with the advent of next-generation sequencing in this millennium (Jones and Bösl 2021; see also Bösl 2017). Here, I am particularly interested in how the continuities and breaks with classical population genetics were narrated. In a video on YouTube (2018a) as well as in his popular book of the same title, *Who We Are and How We Got Here* (2019), the influential American aDNA researcher David Reich (prominent both within science and in a broader public context) explained that he had been brought up intellectually in the tradition of Cavalli-Sforza:

> This book is inspired by a visionary, Luca Cavalli-Sforza, the founder of genetic studies of our past. I was trained by one of his students, and so it is that I am part of his school, inspired by his vision of the genome as a prism for understanding the history of our species. (Reich 2019, xvii)

As we have seen, Cavalli-Sforza had been among those who brought about 'the first revolution' in human population-genetic studies when reconstructing modern human population history based on allele frequencies and later DNA sequences. A broad consensus was reached that this history could be modelled as a tree with its young root in Africa, from where humans successively populated the globe, splitting into independent lines.

 https://doi.org/10.11647/OBP.0396.23

However, according to Reich, "Cavalli-Sforza's maps" (2019, xix) were wrong. The second, "ancient DNA revolution" (ibid.) showed that the present-day genetic structure of human populations was not sufficient to reconstruct ancient events because, contrary to Cavalli-Sforza's expectations, people had mixed and blurred the genetic patterns of the past, and there had been major migrations to the effect that people occupying a particular geographic region today might not be entirely representative of, or descended from, those who lived there in the past. Cavalli-Sforza seems not to have been right in his assumption that the past was a much simpler place than the present. His reliance on what he thought to be isolated populations that provided a direct link into history was misguided (also Reich 2019, 219, 259).

So even though Reich honored the legacy of the early pioneers as transmitted in *The History and Geography of Human Genes* (Cavalli-Sforza, Menozzi, and Piazza 1994), he moved "[t]oward a new history and geography of human genes informed by ancient DNA" (Pickrell and Reich 2014, title). Reich referred to the founder of the new field as Svante Pääbo, who with his colleagues had developed genome-wide aDNA analyses that eventually gave them access to Neanderthal and Denisovan genomes. Reich was invited to collaborate with Pääbo in 2007, who was at the Max Planck Institute for Evolutionary Anthropology in Leipzig (Germany). This was due to the fact that Reich and the mathematician and computational geneticist, Nick Patterson, Reich's close collaborator since the early 2000s, had made advances in the study of population admixtures. When research results began to point towards interbreeding of Neanderthals and modern humans, they were skeptical. Pääbo had received postdoctoral training in the very genetics laboratory out of which had come the decisive results to initiate a consensus around the out-of-Africa model that excluded interbreeding with archaic humans. Reich himself was biased against the notion that modern humans interbred with Neanderthals due to his having been emersed in 'the Cavalli-Sforza paradigm' that, too, was built on the out-of-Africa model (Reich 2019, 36). Yet, from their aDNA research, a picture emerged in which modern-human–Neanderthal hybrid populations had once occupied Europe and lived across Eurasia, many of which had died out, but some left behind genetic traces in present-day humans.

After seven years of spending time in Pääbo's laboratory, Pääbo helped Reich install his own, the first to focus on the study of whole ancient human genomes in the US. Within a few years, more than half of the published genome-wide aDNA came from Reich's laboratory at Harvard University. Reich was part of the endeavor that led to the overthrow of

> the 'serial founder effect' models [7,8], which proposed that populations have remained in the locations they first colonized after the out-of-Africa expansion, exchanging migrants only at a low rate with their immediate neighbors until the long-range migrations of the past 500 years [9–12]. (Pickrell and Reich 2014, 377)

Reich was among those who showed that "[i]nstead, the past 50'000 years of human history have witnessed major upheavals, such that much of the geographic information about the first human migrations has been overwritten by subsequent population movements" (378). Most significantly, it became clear that "new types of models – with admixture at their center – are necessary for describing key aspects of human history [...]" (ibid.).

In accordance with this move to new models, Reich verbally deconstructed the tree model: "The avalanche of new data that has become available in the wake of the genome revolution has shown just how wrong the tree metaphor is for summarizing the relationship among modern human populations" (2019, 77). Indeed, Reich went on to echo statements made by much earlier opponents of the tree model for human evolution, whom we met in Part III, like Julian Huxley in the 1930s. Instead referring to his contemporary Alan R. Templeton whom I discuss at the end of this chapter, Reich wrote that

> [...] while a tree is a good analogy for the relationships among species – because species rarely interbreed and so like real tree limbs are not expected to grow back together after they branch – it is a dangerous analogy for human populations [...] Instead of a tree, a better metaphor may be a trellis, branching and remixing far back into the past. (Reich 2019, 81)

Indeed, Reich stated that "[t]here was never a single trunk population in the human past. It has been mixtures all the way down" (2019, 82).

At the same time, he referred to the *f*-statistics and D-statistics they used in testing for mixing that "evaluate whether a tree model is an accurate summary of real population relationships" (78). In fact, in a paper the first signatory of which was Patterson, they wrote that "[t]hese methods are inspired by the ideas by Cavalli-Sforza and Edwards (1967) [a paper I discussed in Chapter 16], who fit phylogenetic trees of population relationships to the F_{st} values measuring allele frequency differentiation between pairs of populations" (Patterson et al. 2012, 1065–1066). Patterson, who has co-led the David Reich Lab for some twenty years and has been the driving force behind the mathematical and computational developments (e.g., the software in the package ADMIXTOOLS, Patterson et al. 2012), described Cavalli-Sforza as "a hero for David and me" (personal interview with Nick Patterson, 15 August 2023).

So there is testimony to the handing down of ideas, models, and diagrams of human history and kinship from geneticist to geneticist and laboratory to laboratory and of a few dominant and more or less "vertically integrated" laboratories with the necessary financial, technical, and human resources to carry out successful aDNA research (Pickrell and Reich 2014, 385; personal interview with Nick Patterson, 15 August 2023). This might be part of the reason why despite the rhetoric against the tree and in favor of the trellis, what was built were trees with a few connecting branches or arrows. Rather than models that express that "changes in populations over time are typically gradual – owing to consistent, low-level gene flow between neighboring populations", we find visualizations of admixture and introgression as "punctate, with migration events rapidly altering the genetic composition of a region" (Pickrell and Reich 2014, 382–83).

This contradiction is paralleled by another regarding the nature of these populations. Reich declared that aDNA research had proven wrong the assumption of many people "that humans can be grouped biologically into 'primeval' groups, corresponding to our notion of 'races', whose origins are populations that separated tens of thousands of years ago" (Reich 2019, xxviii). Rather, aDNA research revealed that human diversity had changed radically in the course of evolution, so that today's populations are complex admixtures of populations from the past which themselves were admixed. However, even though Reich wrote of "our interconnected human family" (22), the diagrams remained tree-like. Furthermore, despite the 'admixture-instead-of-races' narrative, he regarded it as "undeniable that there are nontrivial average genetic differences across populations in multiple traits" (253) and that "[t]he average time separation between pairs of human populations since they diverged from common ancestral populations [...] is far from negligible on the time scale of human evolution" (258, also 265). In fact, Reich has been at the center of a controversy about the issue of race in science that has, among other things, led to a critical statement signed by sixty-seven researchers (Opinion, BuzzFeed 2018). The critique has not only been triggered by Reich's *Who We Are and How We Got Here* (2019), but mainly by a provocative opinion Reich penned in *The New York Times*, urging people to take seriously the differences between human populations that scientific research had and would make known (Reich 2018b; particularly far-reaching claims regarding differences between human 'races' on the basis of population genetics have been made by the journalist Nicholas Wade [2014]).

This leads to another aspect of the stories population geneticists tell. It has to do with the controversy between out-of-Africa proponents and multiregionalists that predates the molecular approach to human evolutionary history (see Part III). While, as we have seen, the first scenario is organized around a relatively late radiation of modern humans from Africa across the globe, the rival multiregional model stresses the significance of local continuity in human evolutionary history. In the latter view, local *Homo erectus* populations gave rise to the modern human geographical varieties. Rather than assuming a relatively recent last common ancestor, and thus a human 'racial divergence' as recent as to coincide with *Homo sapiens*, the process is regarded as reaching further back, to when the supposedly first migrations out of Africa were undertaken by *Homo erectus*. In this scenario, *Homo sapiens* evolved locally from archaic populations that stood in genetic exchange with each other. Hence, the multiregional hypothesis is associated with less taxonomic diversity in the hominid record, and with a more linear phylogeny, including local Neanderthal populations as ancestral to modern humans.

According to narratives of some of today's geneticists, it was human population genetics that refuted the multiregional model in the 1980s when it lent support to the out-of-Africa or mitochondrial Eve model, but then came the second, aDNA-driven revolution, and the pure out-of-Africa model was overthrown (e.g., López, Van Dorp, and Hellenthal 2015, 57–59; Reich 2019, 4–5; Gokcumen 2020, 61–62; Gopalan et al. 2021, 200). But what exactly do the findings coming out of the aDNA laboratories mean for the controversy? The answer to this question varies between researchers, and it is not always given in its full complexity. For even without the inclusion of aDNA, there was already a wealth of scenarios that differed in the location of modern human origins in Africa, the number of migrations and dispersals out of Africa, the route(s) taken, and in whether there were migrations back into Africa, as well as in the timing of events and the assumed amount of gene flow (see, e.g., López, Van Dorp, and Hellenthal 2015).

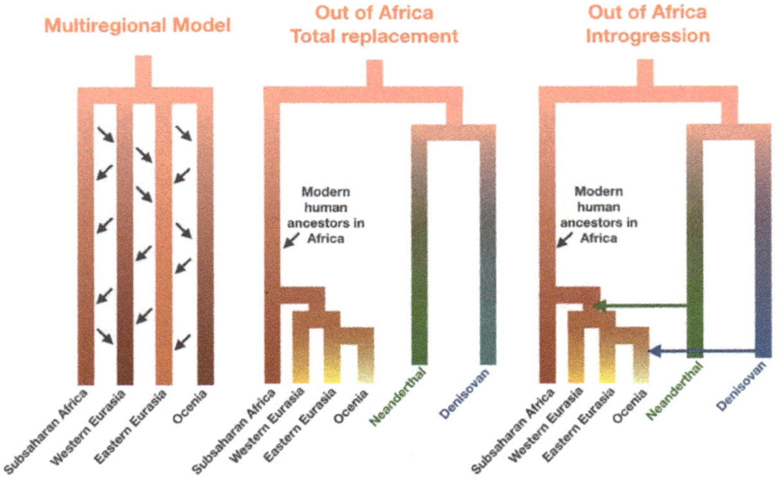

Fig. IV.19 "the three broad models of recent human evolution". Omer Gokcumen, "Archaic Hominin Introgression into Modern Human Genomes" (*Yearbook of Physical Anthropology* 171.S70 [2020]: 60–73), Fig. 1, p. 63. © 2019 American Association of Physical Anthropologists, all rights reserved (reproduced with permission by John Wiley and Sons and Copyright Clearance Center).

Furthermore, a model similar to those that emerged from aDNA studies was also developed from morphological evidence for introgression of archaic humans into modern humans in Eurasia, and it was referred to by its creator, the paleoanthropologist Fred H. Smith, as the assimilation model. Interestingly, Smith and colleagues reproduced the figure from Prüfer et al. (2014, Fig. 8, 48) (see Figure IV.14 above) as an affirmation of their assimilation model, confirming that the tree has 'simply' acquired a few thin connecting arrows (Smith et al. 2017, 132–33; on this model, see also Ackermann et al. 2019). Nonetheless, in continuation of what I have found in Chapter 13 of Part III, a simplified historical succession of dominant models may be recounted in a series of diagrams, as in the case of Figure IV.19: the out-of-Africa model won over the multiregional model in the 1980s with the comparison of mtDNA from living individuals of different human populations, only to be replaced by a more complicated, 'reticulate model' with the aDNA studies that suggested introgression from archaic forms.

Thus, in the telling of the history of human population genetics at the time of aDNA research, diagrammatic means similar to those we have observed in Part III are still used, only that the aDNA model now triumphs at the end: to the left is the multiregional model with a linear diagram standing for anagenesis, in the middle the out-of-Africa model with a tree-shaped phylogeny standing for cladogenesis, and to the right is the reticulate model with a tree that shows connecting darts. Accordingly, the reticulate model is called "Out of Africa Introgression" model in Figure IV.19. It has also been referred to as the leaky replacement model, meaning an out-of-Africa model in which complete replacement of archaic forms by modern humans outside Africa has given way to the assumption of low degrees of introgression from archaic into modern populations (e.g., Nielsen et al. 2017; as we have seen, this has more recently been supplemented with the replacement of the mtDNA and Y chromosome in Neanderthals by modern humans [Liu et al. 2021]). In sharp contrast to a tradition I have documented in Part III, which tended to equate Weidenreich's phylogenetic network with a candelabra model of parallel hominin and 'racial' evolution, Omer Gokcumen (2020) of the Evolutionary and Anthropological Genomics Laboratory at the University at Buffalo does justice to the multiregional model that can be seen as originating in Weidenreich's diagram by including arrows to symbolize gene flow throughout hominin evolution.

Nonetheless, some researchers think the aDNA revolution was more significant. Reich actually wrote of a synthesis between the out-of-Africa and multiregional models, and he conceded that the species status of the Neanderthals, as well as the Denisovans, had become uncertain through the establishment of local interbreeding with modern humans (2019, 49–50, 56). Besides Africa, eastern Eurasia was confirmed as an important region of human evolution, and the picture that emerged of hominin existence some 70,000 years ago increased in complexity, with highly diversified groups like the Neanderthals and Denisovans, and the small Flores forms from today's Indonesia, living at the same time and to some degree in contact with modern humans (62–64). Also 'the beginning of our story in Africa' has come to be presented differently in some papers, to the degree that an 'African multiregionalism' is proposed, with a gradual and mosaic development of 'modern human traits' among differentiated Pleistocene groups that were distributed across the continent and interconnected by gene flow in various degrees. In fact, in this view, and as I will explore further in Chapter 20, the biological and paleoanthropological species concept as well as the notions of 'archaic' and 'modern' need to be reconsidered. Simple tree-like demographic models for Africa, even if they include gene flow between branches, appear untenable to some researchers (Scerri et al. 2018; Galway-Witham, Cole, and Stringer 2019; Vincente and Schlebusch 2020). Instead, reminiscent of Julian Huxley's verbal images encountered in Part III, the diagrammatic metaphor of a braided river has been suggested for modern human origins in Africa (Yong 2018). Thus,

> [c]onsidering the increasing number of ancient individuals identified with recent archaic ancestries, past hominins may have mixed frequently, opening the question of whether archaic and modern human should be regarded as distinct lineages or rather points taken from a continuous spectrum of genetic diversity that was genetically connected throughout the past ~500 kyr similar to that of present-day human populations (20, 22, 23). (Liu et al. 2021, 1479)

At the same time, it seems that the picture aDNA studies have generally painted is one of complex population (pre)histories, with migration, mixture, replacement, and extinction repeatedly changing the genomic structure, including in Africa, rather than being one of local continuity, as in the multiregional model (Klein 2019; for an inclusion of fossil evidence, see also Stringer 2014). That the so-called revolution was not really overturning the treeness of human evolution and kinship may be illustrated by a summary diagram from the review paper that provided the above quote. It includes "[m]ultiple pulses of introgression" as well as the replacement of Neanderthal mtDNA and Y (Liu et al. 2021, Fig. 2, 1482, quote from caption) (see Figure IV.20). It is an orderly picture that, rather than conveying the explosive potential of subverting categories such as human 'races' or even hominin species, suggests neat separations.

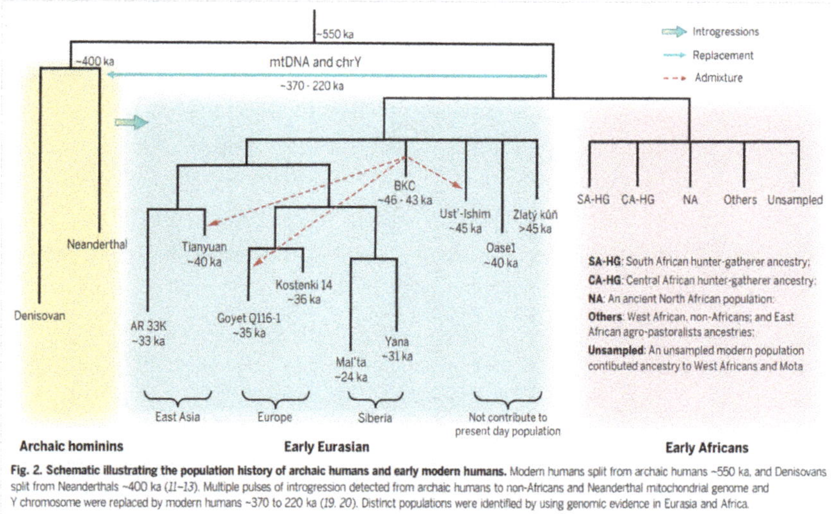

Fig. IV.20 "Schematic illustrating the population history of archaic humans and early modern humans". From Yichen Liu, Xiaowei Mao, Johannes Krause, et al., "Insights into Human History from the First Decade of Ancient Human Genomics" (*Science* 373.6562 [2021]: 1479–84), Fig. 2, p. 1482. Reprinted with permission from AAAS © The American Association for the Advancement of Science, all rights reserved ("Readers may view, browse, and/or download material for temporary copying purposes only, provided these uses are for noncommercial personal purposes. Except as provided by law, this material may not be further reproduced, distributed, transmitted, modified, adapted, performed, displayed, published, or sold in whole or in part, without prior written permission from the publisher").

Both narratives, the one of human genetic history and the one of the history of human population genetics, have been told in different ways by those sympathetic towards the multiregional model. Nonetheless, they may use the same diagrammatic language as found in Figure IV.19 (e.g., Templeton 2018a, Fig. 6.2, 115, modified from Fagundes et al. 2007, Fig. 1, 17615, which is actually a paper in support of the out-of-Africa model). Researchers like the American geneticist and statistician Templeton agree that the pure out-of-Africa model that assumes total replacement of archaic by modern humans in Eurasia has been proven wrong. But in 2013, he considered something like a downsized multiregional model the best fit to existing data. Templeton criticized not only the pure out-of-Africa model with its denial of any interbreeding between modern and archaic humans but also the admixture-models that only allow for minor interbreeding (events). To him, human evolution has been dominated by gene flow and admixture, which has upheld humanity as a single evolutionary lineage. He did not accept the scenario according to which populations developed in relative isolation from one another (and only mixed at a later stage). In his view, the family tree – with or without connecting arrows – is no adequate model of human evolution for any period. One might rather have to think of a trellis (Templeton 2013, 267–70 on the trellis, Fig. 3, 268, for an image; see also Finlayson 2013).

Multiregionalists see genetic as well as archeological and paleoanthropological data as compatible with a model that combines significant migration and distribution events with regional lines of descent and gene flow between regions (mediated by isolation by distance). This is regarded as having maintained human variation within one species, including the archaic human forms like *Homo erectus*, Neanderthals, or Denisovans (e.g., Wolpoff 2020). Although such models are reminiscent of Weidenreich's network of humanity from the 1940s (see Part III), the multiregional models have rather become a compromise between aspects of the tree (on a map) and the uniform (geographic) network. The respective diagrams contain visual elements of both. An early diagram by Templeton (2005, Fig. 9, 50) told of three migrations out of Africa (arrows), beginning with *Homo erectus*. The image also showed regional evolutionary developments (vertical lines) that were interconnected through gene flow (diagonal lines) (see Sommer 2015a, 135, 137). In the newer version of this diagram represented in Figure IV.21, Templeton's trellis of human evolution appears more tree-shaped in the lowest part. The thin diagonal lines indicating gene flow between regions no longer go all the way down to *Homo erectus*, and with regard to the most recent expansion out of Africa, the model is described as mostly out-of-Africa with limited admixture (Templeton 2018b, Ch. 7, containing Fig. 7.4, 207; see also Templeton 2018a, Fig. 6.3, 120; Wadell 2018, in the same volume, arrived at the conclusion that the original out-of-Africa model has been mainly supported by new findings).

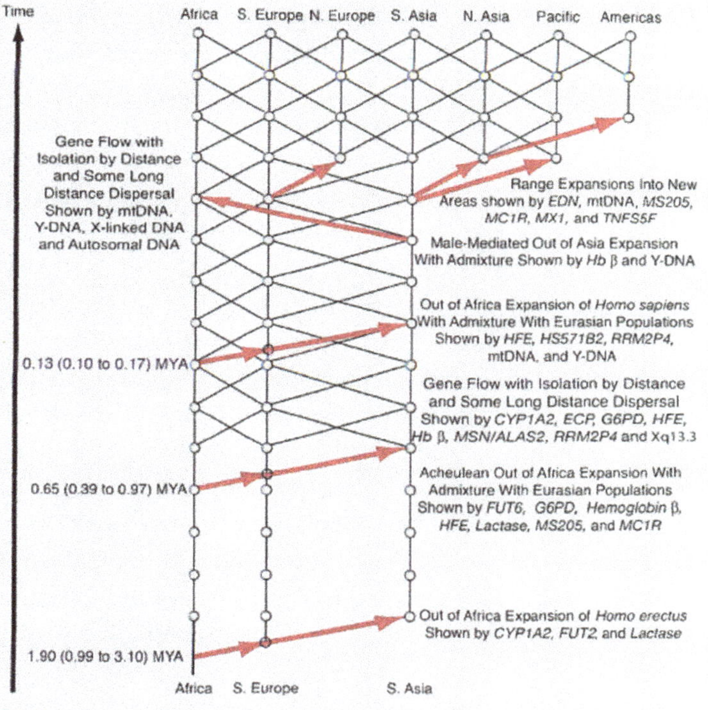

FIGURE 7.4

The model of human evolution over the past two million years that emerges from nested-clade phylogeographic analysis of 25 haplotype trees scattered throughout the human genome, including mtDNA. *Vertical lines* show descent within a broad geographic area, *diagonal lines* show gene flow between areas, and *red arrows* show major population range expansions. When range expansions occurred into regions already occupied by other human populations, the *vertical lines* of descent are not broken to indicate that the expansion was accompanied by admixture. The maximum likelihood estimates of the dates of the three out-of-Africa expansion events are given on the left, along with their 95% confidence intervals in parentheses. The other range expansion events all occurred within the last 50,000 years, but are difficult to estimate from haplotype tree data as there are too few mutations for accurate estimation. The genomic regions that underlie a particular inference are given with the inference.

Fig. IV.21 "model of human evolution".

The diagrammatic changes from 2005 to Figure IV.21 in 2018 actually lead back to an important aspect of statistics that has come up several times before: hypothesis testing. Templeton had developed a method for testing the null hypothesis of no gene flow between two geographic regions from some time in the past up to the present. This test significantly indicated gene flow in the early Pleistocene, but it could not be ruled out that the result was affected by more recent genetic exchange. In 2009, he developed a more refined test to check the null hypothesis of no gene flow in a specific time interval in the past. This more refined test showed highly significant gene flow among human populations from the mid-Pleistocene onwards, but could not reject the null hypothesis of no gene flow for the early Pleistocene. Since Templeton's diagrams were based upon statistically significant rejections of null hypotheses, he removed the trellis structure in the early Pleistocene. Though there was evidence of gene flow in that period, it was insufficient to reject the null hypothesis of no gene flow (personal communication, 8 January 2024).

At the same time, the mixture of modern and archaic humans in Eurasia had gained strong support from aDNA studies. Templeton saw in the results from aDNA studies further refutation of the population-tree model of human evolution. They confirmed network or trellis models that foreground gene flow and admixture since at least the mid-Pleistocene. The trees and their concomitant assumptions were "artifacts of using computer programs that force a treelike structure upon the data even if the data are not treelike" (2018a, 227). Similarly, Templeton regarded the genetic differences between Neanderthals, Denisovans, and modern humans to be insufficient to even regard them as subspecies (226). Diagrams such as given in Figure IV.21 therefore clearly testify to alternative ways of envisioning hominin diversity and kinship, and there is an increasing number of contenders in the race to (diagrammatically) re-define humans and human relatedness. To these revolutionary issues I now turn in my final chapter of this last part of the book.

20. Deconstructing the Tree Diagram to a Mess – or at least a Net

> Even [tough] our brains search for a simple origin story, what we find is a beautiful mess. (Gokcumen 2020, 69)

The Linnean system is hierarchical and assumes clear-bounded entities or taxa. However, there are scientists, among them evolutionary anthropologists Isabelle C. Winder and Nick P. Winder (2014), who have argued that the tree-like Linnean order is still too strongly taken to be the norm, with mechanisms of reticulation, or heterarchical evolution, viewed as the exception. In fact, reticulation appears in many species of plants, insects, and mammals, including the primates, where it most often (but not exclusively) happens at the subspecies and species level. Thus, Winder and Winder (2014) have demanded a rethinking of the models of hominin evolution. Morphological and genetic data supported the notion that the species boundaries between hominins in Pleistocene Eurasia had been open and that genetic exchange across these boundaries had taken place. The mosaic appearance of traits in the Plio-Pleistocene fossil hominins suggested "a reticulating lineage exploring a complex, multi-dimensional space of possible morphologies and repeatedly generating and re-generating new combinations of traits" (306). The intra-specific structure of today's *Homo sapiens* might be similar to the structure of reticulations at higher taxonomic levels in other primates and to the structure that once existed between different hominin species.

These observations point in the direction of a possible paradigm shift, wherein different questions may be asked, such as: in view of gene

 https://doi.org/10.11647/OBP.0396.24

flow between species, is the biological species concept still meaningful? And how much gene flow must there be to finally undermine the hierarchical Linnean model, including the systematic and phylogenetic tree? Different diagrams are associated with these competing models. The first model of reticulate evolution in Figure IV.22 no longer has a tree structure, and the taxonomic system it suggests is not purely hierarchical but cross-cutting like Winder's and Winder's interpretation of the mosaic of characters in the fossil record of the hominin lineage.

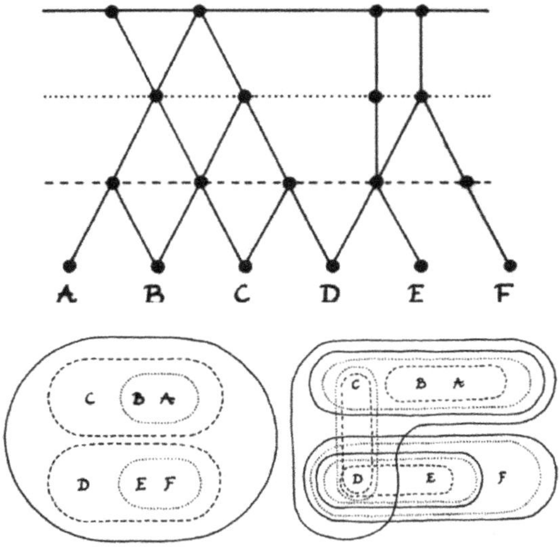

Fig. IV.22 Reticulate evolution and its cross-cutting taxonomy (top and bottom right) as opposed to the hierarchical taxonomy suggested by a tree-like phylogeny (bottom left). Isabelle C. Winder and Nick P. Winder, "Reticulate Evolution and the Human Past: An Anthropological Perspective" (*Annals of Human Biology* 41.4 [2014]: 300–311), Figs. 4 and 5, p. 308. All rights reserved, reprinted by permission of the publisher (© Taylor & Francis Ltd, http://www.tandfonline.com).

Similarly, the molecular phylogeneticist and bioinformatician David A. Morrison has criticized that "if we approach phylogenetics from the tree perspective then our only choice is to consider reticulations as additional (and unusual) occurrences" (2014a, 632). In fact, he found reticulation often to be "'the last resort'" (633), the last possible evolutionary explanation that is taken into consideration. Conversely, Morrison described trees as a subset of networks in the sense that a tree is a network without reticulations. In his perspective, all phylogenies are networks, some of which are more tree-like than others. If a tree is a simplified network – as the genomic methods may suggest – "all trees are networks but not all networks are trees" (Morrison 2016, 457; also, 2014b). Most importantly, in phylogenetics, "[a] 'tree (possibly with reticulations)' is a less useful idea than a 'network (which will be more or less tree-like)'" (Morrison 2014a, 635). Analyses should thus not start from a tree and add some reticulations, but from a network.

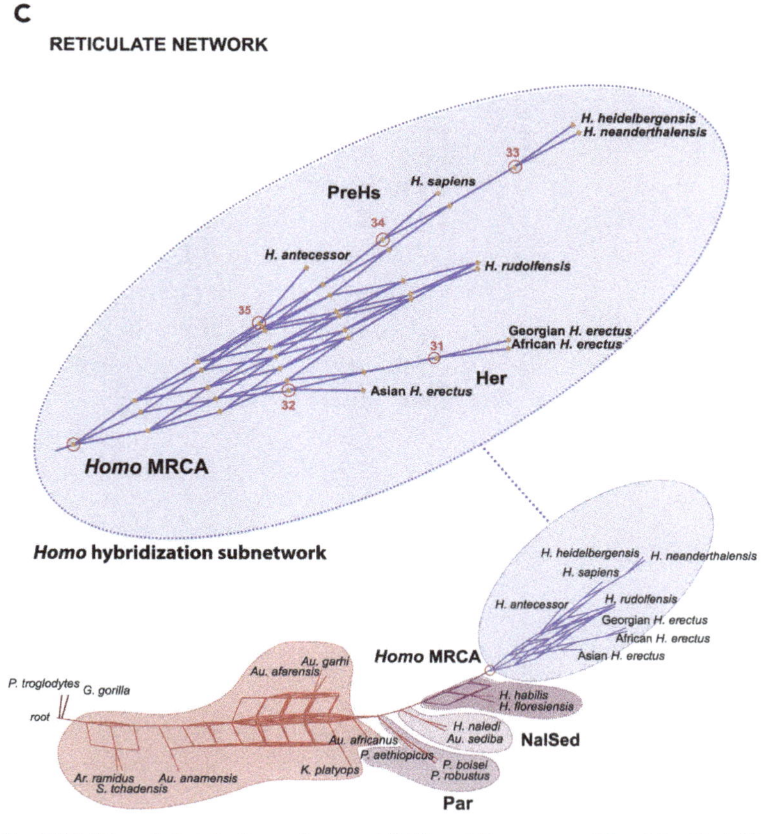

Fig. IV.23 "*Homo* hybridization subnetwork". Miguel Caparros and Sandrine Prat, "A Phylogenetic Networks Perspective on Reticulate Human Evolution" (*iScience* 24.4 [2021]: 1–31), Fig. 4, p. 10, https://doi.org/10.1016/j.isci.2021.102359 © The Authors.

There are two groups of models: evolutionary history networks versus data presentation networks. The first entail hypotheses about evolutionary history, while the second simply describe the data, i.e., what complexities there are, which parts of the data contradict others, etc. With the second method, if the latter is the case, one has to figure out whether the contradictions are due to mistakes or whether different genetic histories are mixed together in the same organisms. Morrison warns that the two approaches may arrive at the same model, but one should not confuse the methods. He anticipates that in the future, biologists will start their investigation of data with the underlying complexity and work out the patterns from there, rather than setting out with assumptions regarding evolutionary history, and particularly not with the one that it is simple (personal interview with David Morrison, 7 November 2023).[1]

Contextualizing their paper in such network perspectives as taken by Isabelle C. Winder, Nick P. Winder, and Morrison (whom they cite), archeologist Miguel Caparros and paleoanthropologist Sandrine Prat (2021) combined a Maximum Parsimony and Phylogenetic Networks method (SplitsTree software) in the analysis of phenotypic craniodental features of twenty-two hominin species. They first arrived at a consensus tree, out of the conflicting trees suggested by different aspects of the data, which means a loss of phylogenetic information. To get access to this lost information, they proceeded to construct a consensus network and reticulate network and concluded that reticulation was a more informative framework to explain the relationships between the species of *Homo*.[2] Figure IV.23 represents their "*Homo* hybridization subnetwork" from the reticulate network (Caparros and Prat 2021, Fig. 4, 10).[3]

Analyses similar to the one conducted by Caparros and Prat, focusing on features pertaining to the cranium or teeth, are carried out on the basis of genetic data. Researchers may produce a series of trees for different genome regions and then try to combine them into one tree

1 It seems that within human population genomics, however, it is the first method which might be gaining ground more easily (see below). Starting from a network and pruning it using rigorous statistical criteria is seen as a consistent inference procedure, and if a tree might correspond more closely to the information in the data, one might just as well arrive at it by this method (Templeton, personal correspondence, 8 January 2024).

2 For another example where the tree (arrived at by TreeMix) did not fit the studied population-genetic history but a network approach (program SpaceMix) led to statistically and historically satisfactory results, see, e.g., Pugach 2016.

3 See, for example, also the work of biological anthropologist Rebecca R. Ackermann, e.g., Ackermann et al. 2019. Questions regarding species concepts, species status, and the role of processes like introgression, hybridization, or continuous gene flow within the hominin line/s have a long history in paleoanthropology; for a discussion among some of the central figures, see, for example, Holliday 2003; for a more general discussion of trees and networks in connection with the program SplitsTree, see Huson and Bryant 2006.

of human populations. This is because different regions of the genome have different evolutionary histories. Indeed, the current understanding of a genome undermines everyday notions of genealogy and identity. In contrast to mtDNA that is handed down 'intact' from mothers to children, or the Y chromosome that is transmitted solely from fathers to sons, the nuclear DNA is freshly amalgamated between mother and father each generation, when both egg and sperm contribute one set of chromosomes. Beyond that, the chromosomes are regularly broken up and put together in new ways, thereby combining two different genealogical lines (that of the mother and father) on one chromosome, which will be passed on in this state to the next generation. In other words, different chromosomal fragments (so-called haplotype blocks) have their own ancestry or genealogy, rendering genomes – like the fossil record – mosaic in nature. Thus, individual chromosomal segments will 'tell' their own histories (e.g., Reich 2019, 10–16).

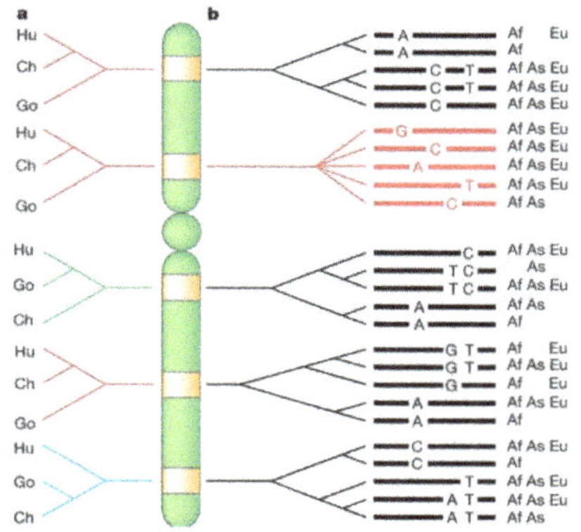

a, The interspecies relationships of five chromosome regions to corresponding DNA sequences in a chimpanzee and a gorilla. Most regions show humans to be most closely related to chimpanzees (red) whereas a few regions show other relationships (green and blue). **b,** The among-human relationships of the same regions are illustrated schematically for five individual chromosomes. Most DNA variants are found in people from all three continents, namely Africa (Af), Asia (As) and Europe (Eu). But a few variants are found on only one continent, most of which are in Africa. Note that each human chromosome is a mosaic of different relationships. For example, a chromosome carried by a person of European descent may be most closely related to a chromosome from Asia in one of its regions, to a chromosome from Africa in another region, and to a chromosome from Europe in a third region. For one region (red), the extent of sequence variation within humans is low relative to what is observed between species. The relationship of this sequence among humans is illustrated as star-shaped owing to a high frequency of nucleotide variations that are unique to single chromosomes. Such regions may contain genes that contribute to traits that set humans apart from the apes.

Fig. IV.24 The human genome "as a mosaic of haplotype blocks". Svante Pääbo, "The Mosaic That Is Our Genome" (*Nature* 421.6921 [2003]: 409–412), Fig. 2, p. 410, https://doi.org/10.1038/nature01400 © Springer Nature Limited, all rights reserved (reproduced with permission by Springer Nature Customer Service Centre GmbH).

As a consequence, Pääbo explained as early as 2003 that "[r]ather than thinking about 'populations', 'ethnicities' or 'races', a more constructive way to think about human genetic variation is to consider the genome of any particular individual as a mosaic of haplotype blocks" (410). For certain haplotype blocks in the genome, an individual from Europe might be more closely related to persons in Africa or Asia than to other Europeans. Even the genetic histories of humans and other apes are "entangled" in this way, with some human genome regions exhibiting closer relations to gorillas than to chimpanzees and bonobos (Pääbo 2003, 409) (see Figure IV.24).

Thus, some researchers have argued that, regarding intra-human phylogeny, also producing a series of trees for different genome regions and then combining them into one tree of human populations is faulty, because there are no discrete entities like populations and there is no hierarchical arrangement of such geographical entities in a tree. If one takes into account all the available data to infer phylogenetic relationships, rather than a few markers considered to be particularly informative regarding ancestry, a lack of both hierarchy and discreteness is the result (and Ancestry Informative Markers were not developed for inference of population-level patterns but for the mapping of genomic regions in individuals). Molecular systematist Rob DeSalle and colleagues instead speak of "rampant polyphyly" (2017, 104), with ancestry being more about parts of the genome in different individuals that can be traced back to the same point in the history of those genomes.

Something like this seems to be at play in what was referred to as "the first ever world-wide family tree" (Currin 2022, title). Stanford statistical geneticist Anthony Wilder Wohns and colleagues (2022), including Patterson and Reich, referred to the unified genealogy of thousands of modern and ancient genomes as a tree and they started with the assumption that there was recombination. From the huge dataset of individual genomes (mainly recent and from the 1000 Genomes Project, the Human Genome Diversity Project, and the Simons Genome Diversity Project) a dated and located tree sequence of multiple correlated trees along the genome was built in an iterative approach. The researchers first merged the modern data, inferred a tree sequence for each autosome, and carried out the respective estimations. Then they integrated the archaic (Neanderthal and Denisovan genomes) and ancient samples with the modern samples and re-inferred the tree sequence. The result was seen as a step in the direction of arriving at "the genealogy of everyone" (6).

Resonating with DeSalle's and colleagues' "rampant polyphyly" constituted by the different parts of human genomes, Wohns et al. (2022) followed specific genome blocks back through generations, tracking how they mutated and moved (recombined, and migrated across the globe in human carriers), reconstructing the ancestral lines of the haplotype fragments found in the dataset (and inferring some twenty-seven million ancestral haplotype blocks on the way).[4] While being called an "inferred tree sequence of chromosome 20" (Anthony Wilder Wohns, personal communication, 6 December 2023), Figure IV.25 suggests this new understanding of human genomic history, kinship, and diversity to be rather rhizomatic.

Have we finally grown tired of trees, as Deleuze and Guattari had? Have we arrived at levels of analytical depth in population genomics that atomize genealogy as we know it into changing rhizomatic dynamics that depend on the kind and number of data we use, and that connect parts of the genome across once closed and hierarchically related entities? Have these technologies put an end to the tree's definitions of fixed and hierarchical subject, 'racial', and species positions? It is interesting that Deleuze and Guattari favored the diagram of the map, which they conceived of as an experiment on reality, as an open, undirected process. Figure IV.25 seems to have turned the tree-on-a-map image into a rhizome on a globe that

4 What Anthony Wilder Wohns and colleagues (2022) carried out was a so-called Ancestral Recombination Graph (ARG) inference that constructs a series of trees for individual genome sites over chromosomes in a given dataset of genomes. Boundaries between trees mark ancestral recombination sites, i.e., sites at which chromosome segments that differ in their genealogies were brought together through ancestral cross-over recombination. Wohns et al. used the algorithm *tsinfer*. Since it assumes that the frequency of an allele is correlated with its age, it has been judged unsuitable for ARG inference involving modern human, Neanderthal, and Denisovan genomes in another study (Schaefer, Shapiro, and Green 2021, 1). This study by Nathan K. Schaefer, Beth Shapiro, and Richard E. Green from the University of California, Santa Cruz used a different algorithm (SARGE) working with shared alleles and shared inferred ancestral recombination events. They used a parsimonious approach (minimal number of necessary recombination events to allow for the data), drawing on Song and Hein (2005). A sequence of trees should be built for the sites found in the data, so that when moving along the genome, a change in tree topology would refer to a recombination. The sequence segments of a particular tree are the haplotype blocks that come with specific evolutionary histories. These trees are combined in the minimal ancestral recombination graph. Schaefer and colleagues found among other things that Neanderthal admixture could not be accounted for by a single ingression pulse into modern humans. Instead, they reached a picture of many small-scale population-specific admixture events that suggested a complex history of admixture throughout Eurasia (2021, 9).

is remaking the world from the Eurocentric Mercator projection to one centered around Africa, losing any sense of unidirectionality.[5]

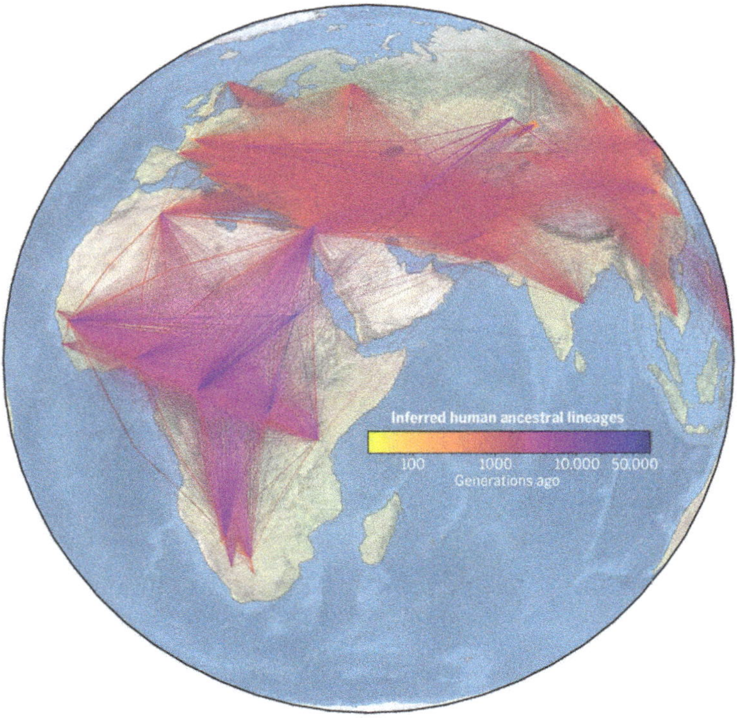

Visualizing inferred human ancestral lineages over time and space. Each line represents an ancestor-descendant relationship in our inferred genealogy of modern and ancient genomes. The width of a line corresponds to how many times the relationship is observed, and lines are colored on the basis of the estimated age of the ancestor.

Fig. IV.25 "Visualizing inferred human ancestral lineages over time and space". From Anthony Wilder Wohns, Yan Wong, Ben Jeffery, et al., "A Unified Genealogy of Modern and Ancient Genomes" (*Science* 375.6583 [2022]: 1–9), p. 1, https://doi.org/10.1126/science.abi8264. Reprinted with permission from AAAS © The American Association for the Advancement of Science, all rights reserved ("Readers may view, browse, and/or download material for temporary copying purposes only, provided these uses are for noncommercial personal purposes. Except as provided by law, this material may not be further reproduced, distributed, transmitted, modified, adapted, performed, displayed, published, or sold in whole or in part, without prior written permission from the publisher").

5 Nonetheless, Wohns stated that "[k]ey findings from our paper are readily apparent [in the figure], including the ancient lineages in Africa, some ancient lineages corresponding to the archaic genomes from Siberia, generally a larger number of lineages within continents, and a few particularly ancient lineages leading to Papua from Africa and Siberia" (personal communication, 6 December 2023).

Such perspectives may indeed seem liberating. To move away from the bounded notion of a species, a population, and even an individual towards understandings of greater interconnectedness may suggest a way out of identitarianism, racism, and speciesism. However, Winder and Winder (2014, 307) have cautioned that notions of a polyphyletic human species and different phylogenies for different ethnic groups might just as well feed into the kinds of racism we have observed in the preceding parts of this book. Furthermore, as we have seen, the notion of different segments of a genome having their separate genealogies can still be associated with the understanding that some segments derive from African ancestors while others derive from European ancestors, etc., which people easily link to the continental racial categories of old (e.g., Reich 2019, 147–50). Nonetheless, thinking along the lines of different parts of individual genomes having separate genealogies, connecting across what have previously been conceived as closed species, 'races', and organisms that have their fixed place within the hierarchical system of trees creates opportunities for new and nonhierarchical kinds of relatedness.

After all, and as mentioned at the outset of this chapter, the deconstruction of the human family tree is a special case of a larger challenge levelled at the tree of life by philosophers as well as biologists with the insight that different areas of the genome did not evolve in congruence. It was the growing knowledge of horizontal gene transfer between branches of the tree of life in nature and genetic engineering in the laboratory that served Deleuze and Guattari as an example of 'making rhizome': "More generally, evolutionary schemas may be forced to abandon the old model of the tree and descent", adopting "instead a rhizome operating immediately in the heterogeneous and jumping from one already differentiated line to another" (1987 [1980], 10). Today, certainly more than ever, the assumption of a tree of life, or of a generally dichotomous phylogenetic system, is in jeopardy. We not only know that procaryotes (the vast majority of life) exhibit lateral gene transfer and that many plant and animal species hybridize. A major issue is also endosymbiosis, such as of chloroplasts, mitochondria, and other organelles of eukaryotic cells.

Therefore, while some concede that the tree retains its epistemic value as a model – and therefore hold it as unproblematic that "[c]onstructing trees is the starting point for nearly every study in evolutionary biology today" (Velasco 2012, 624; e.g., also O'Malley and Koonin 2011) as long as biologists are aware of their model-status – others advocate for a paradigm-shift towards network or web thinking also in the context of the tree of life (e.g., Doolittle 1999; Doolittle and Bapteste 2007; Bapteste and Dupré 2013; for a review of some of the network literature, see Whitfield 2012; on the controversy, see O'Malley, Martin, and Dupré 2010; O'Malley and Koonin 2011). Was "[t]he tree of life [...] always a net", because "[n]ature was always a genetic engineer" (Helmreich 2003, 351)? Such a view might well challenge traditional understandings of the organic world as falling into and being aptly represented by hierarchal relations between more or less discrete categories. Reminiscent of Darwin's tangled bank that we have found in tension with the tree of life in Part II, such a view might rather suggest forms of relatedness that further an ecosystem-oriented thinking along the lines of coalitions and shared environmental risks (Helmreich 2003; 2009; Bapteste, Bouchard, and Burian 2012; more generally, Schmidt-Burkhardt 2009, 178). At the same time, these new kinds of biological relationships – these new kinds of relating diagrams – too, do not carry meaning in and of themselves and can be instrumentalized for different politics of life and of the human.

Postscript

Diagrams have been used to relate humankind in anthropology for centuries. They have been introduced as tools to create human types and establish or deny particular relations between them. These relations have mostly been hierarchical. Diagrams have been developed as ways of sharing, measuring, and comparing human remains by representing the relations of parts on paper and for communicating results. But diagrams were also used to experiment with these relations, as when morphing one skull shape into another. Even treeing could be a largely experimental practice, which we have seen especially for Charles Darwin. At the same time, diagrams like trees and maps seem mostly to have been instruments to promote one's view of human diversity rather than to arrive at such a view. Even in genetic anthropology, where relating diagrams may be produced automatically, the way in which computer programs were and are built largely predetermines the general diagrammatic structure of human history and diversity. Tree- and map-like images transported and transport narratives of human migration and differentiation, with or without communicating interbreeding. Diagrams have thus reduced complex theories and (even more complex histories) to seemingly intuitive icons and provided these theories with (the appearance of) objectivity, possibly as combinations of lines, images, letters, and numbers. The way this has been done has sometimes resulted in a mismatch between diagram and intended meaning.

Throughout this long history of relating diagrams, I have found no linear development, such as from chain to tree to net. There were different kinds in competition at all times and compounds of elements from various types. Trees may still transport the meaning of a progressive and lineal arrangement or evolution, while chains in natural history multiplied to form 'trees' and nets or other three-dimensional structures. Trees and maps were often combined, and

 https://doi.org/10.11647/OBP.0396.25

tree-like structures incorporated network aspects. Anthropological diagrams could be inspired by religious and secular genealogies and maps, breeding pedigrees, even *arbores consanguinitates*, and by forms used in natural history more generally as well as in other sciences like linguistics and embryology.

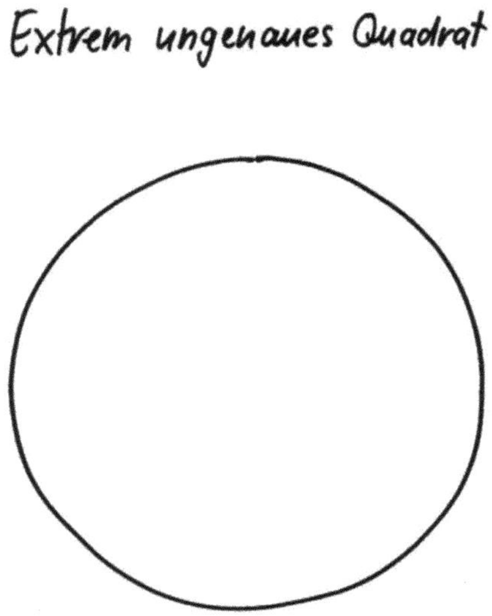

Fig. P.1 'Extremely imprecise square' (by Beni Bischof, reproduced in Bischof 2022, p. 117, all rights reserved, published with kind permission by the artist).

We have seen how the introduction and standardization of a diagrammatics of 'race' in anthropology to categorize and classify, to differentiate and hierarchically arrange humans was a long and arduous process, accompanied by controversies and failures. At the same time, we have witnessed how, once established, a diagrammatic form could survive new ways of conceptualizing human relatedness. Especially the human family tree that encompassed human diversity has been used to convey very different messages. While the tree-like diagram started out as a classificatory icon, the tree bloomed in the evolutionary paradigms, in which it could express approaches as diametrically opposed as evolutionary polygenism and human population genetics, even aDNA admixture research. At times, diagrams were referred to as trees, despite resembling bamboo stalks or a bed of flowers; indeed, 'trees' have come in very variable shapes – from pure line structures to naturalistic images.

This relates to Charles Sander Peirce's differentiation between token and type and the observation that we tend to read diagrams as types rather than tokens. When we perceive a geometrical figure on the blackboard, we abstract from aspects such as the breadth and color of the chalk line and from the fact that it does not run perfectly straight (Stjernfelt 2000, 366). We had to learn to grasp human relatedness as tree-shaped, but once we had learned to do so (which was a very long time ago), it became challenging to unlearn, or not to perceive a family tree even in a phylogeny that only vaguely resembles a tree.

The Swiss artist Beni Bischof has captured this phenomenon in one of his humorous drawings that is shown in Figure P.1. A circle does not have to be perfect for us to see a circle; there is no way it could be a square. Or, read differently, a square needs to be a very imperfect one indeed to become a circle. So how to unlearn? Also in this respect, we may profit from the artist's comment in the interview that accompanied Figure P.1 among other images: "I observe my surroundings closely, question them often also visually, and play with that. Also with a point, which stands at the beginning of a drawing. A point can actually be anything" (Bischof 2022, 107, my translation).[1] One is reminded of the centrality of manipulation for Peirce's icon, with the geometrical figure as a prototype because a theorem is tested in the experimentation with the diagram (Stjernfelt 2000, 359).[2] But what Bischof rather seems to suggest is that we must train ourselves in visual critique, in questioning the seemingly obvious, as Fran Ross (1974) has done with her diagrams in *Oreo* – with the cookie itself standing for a relating diagram. How is that achieved? Bischof proposes that "[o]ne changes the points of view, simply does the opposite for once, or questions everything, be it a point, a square, or a line" (Bischof 2022, 107, my translation).[3] After all, as expressed in Figure P.2, a circle looks very different from the side.

1 "Ich beobachte meine Umgebung genau, hinterfrage sie oft auch visuell und spiele vor allem dann damit. So auch mit einem Punkt, der am Anfang einer Zeichnung steht. Ein Punkt kann ja alles sein [...]."

2 "The truth, however, appears to be that all deductive reasoning, even simple syllogism, involves an element of observation; namely, deduction consists in constructing an icon or diagram the relations of whose parts shall present a complete analogy with those of the parts of the object of reasoning, of experimenting upon this image in the imagination, and of observing the results so as to discover unnoticed and hidden relations among the parts" (Peirce 1885, 182).

3 "Man wechselt die Ansichtsweisen, macht einfach mal das Gegenteil oder hinterfragt alles, sei es ein Punkt, ein Quadrat oder eine Linie."

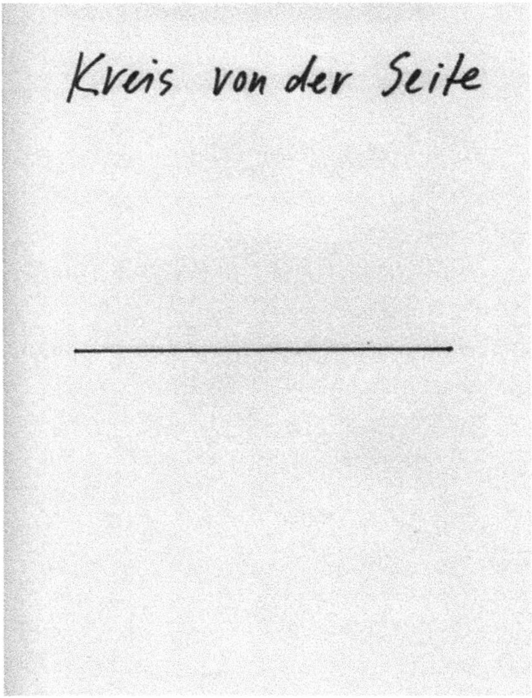

Fig. P.2 'Circle from the side' (by Beni Bischof, all rights reserved, published with kind permission by the artist).

If diagrams as naturalized and deep-rooted in our visual culture as a square or a circle can be questioned, played with, joked about, then so can a tree. This, one practices until it sticks: "Once we become aware of that [possibility], one might be able to train it. Like a muscle in the brain" (Bischof 2022, 107, my translation).[4] We have witnessed critiques of the tree of human 'races' throughout the book and have ended with demands of the demise of the tree of human populations, even the tree of life. The human family tree has increasingly grown connecting arrows and, at least for some researchers, has been replaced by networked structures, as for Gilles Deleuze and Félix Guattari (1987 [1980]) the tree could become rhizomatic or rhizome, and the rhizome may grow branching structures or roots. It is unclear, however, what this would mean for the politics of human relatedness. Are meandering rivers, cables, entangled

4 "Wird man sich dessen bewusst, kann man das vielleicht trainieren. Wie einen Muskel im Gehirn."

skeins, networks, or trellises inherently better relating diagrams in an ethical sense? Some of these diagrams have been brought in position (verbally and/or visually) against those in use in racist and polygenist anthropologies and eugenics. The deconstruction of the notion of more or less contained individuals, 'races', populations, and even species and their hierarchical relations, as they are communicated in trees, by some scientists today, does seem to carry subversive potential. But we should be wary of making any inferences from knowledge in the biological sciences about social relations. They have too often led astray.

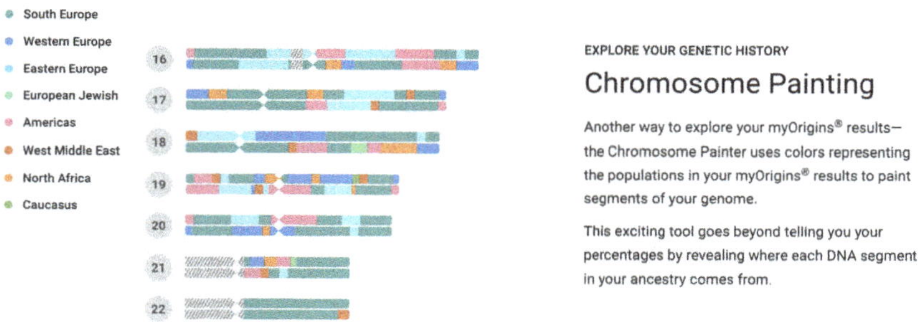

Fig. P.3 "Chromosome Painting" (Family Tree DNA, screenshot of https://www.familytreedna.com/products/family-finder, last accessed 6 July 2024, with kind permission from FamilyTreeDNA).

Chromosome painting, as advertised in Figure P.3 by the genetic ancestry and wellness company Family Tree DNA, sounds like fun. The practice represents a customization of the new insights from genomics, exploiting this deconstruction of the individual as squarely fitting into one ethnicity, as having a straightforward ancestry. No, we are mosaics, like the populations we live in. But wait. We can still be reassured by the fact that the bits of our chromosomes stem from seemingly monochrome ancestral populations that are listed on the left of Figure P.3: from "South Europe" to "Caucasus". As we have seen for scientific practice itself, so too in the popularization and commercialization of science, notions of originally pure populations that at some time in history started to interbreed continue to underly the mosaic. Even when appearing to be pure fun, relating diagrams are political.

Relating diagrams have been part and parcel of racist anthropologies and eugenics. They have been enmeshed in arguments over slavery, in justifications of imperialism, colonialism, war, segregation, and so forth.

Diagrams on paper and in interaction with text have worked to provide inequality, exploitation, and violence with the veneer of inevitability. More than that, they have been built on them. Anthropologists objectified the sampled people and their communities by studying their remains, by distributing and reproducing these remains, and not least through turning them into diagrams – mobile inscriptions that reduced human beings to readable and measurable angles, proportions, and volumes. Most of all, behind the diagrams of human relatedness, whether tree or network, there remain the practices of collecting. The historian Samuel J. Redman (2016) has engaged with the demand for human remains in the United States from about the Civil War, following the pioneer plunderers who supplied Samuel George Morton and his contemporaries. Museums heaped human remains in spaces known as bone rooms, amateurs and scientists assembled them from all over the world, and the latter engaged in the project of producing seemingly natural classifications of humankind from these remains.

The Army Medical Museum was among the first museums that systematically collected human remains from the American West and globally, mainly through medical officers. This exacerbated the conflict with Native Americans, who tried to protect the bones of their ancestors and of their massacred contemporaries from ending up in a museum. At the end of the nineteenth century, the collection of the Army Medical Museum was transferred to the Smithsonian Institution, which became the primary destination for bone collectors, driven by projects of physical and salvage anthropology. This history led to a situation in which US museums were estimated to hold around half a million remains of Native Americans alone (Redman 2016; Sommer 2016b). *The Washington Post* has conducted an investigation into the collecting history of the physical anthropologist Aleš Hrdlička of the Smithsonian Institution's Natural History Museum, which currently houses over 30,000 human remains. This investigation has triggered a project for repatriation (Dungca and Healy 2023).

We have seen the vital part diagrams played in the study of skulls, and that America was far from the only region where bone collections were amassed. Researchers have engaged with histories of collecting practices and collections in other parts of the world (e.g., Legassick and Rassool 2000; Buklijas 2008; Wagner 2010; Dias 2012; Stoecker,

Schnalke, and Winkelmann 2013; Turnbull 2017; Wiedenmayer and Hotz 2002). And these efforts, too, went hand in hand with restitution projects. But what happened to the collection that stood at the center of Part I? In 1966, Morton's skull collection was donated to the University of Pennsylvania Museum of Archaeology and Anthropology. In the aftermath of the implementation of the Native American Graves Protection and Repatriation Act (NAGPRA) in 1990, over a hundred skulls were restituted to Native American nations. In 2020, in the current movement of the decolonization of museums and their collections, Morton's 'Golgotha', until then held in open storage, has definitively been closed to the public. This has further sparked the discussions about ethical legacies, for example in a participant observation series in *History of Anthropology Review* (Mitchell 2021; also, Michael 2021b):

> [...] the descendant community of the Morton Collection can be said to be all those whose ancestors suffered under Western colonialism, 'specimen' collecting practices, and the brutality of life in the industrializing United States and elsewhere. The one thing the people in the collection had in common was their or their community's disempowerment. (Kakaliouras, 2021, n.p.)[5]

This quote underscores the fact that, while diverse communities have been victims of the stealing and unethical acquisition of human remains, in the United States the NAGPRA refers to Native Americans alone. Following the decision of an advisory committee, the University of Pennsylvania Museum have reburied the remains of nineteen Black Philadelphians from the Morton collection in early February 2024. This sparked controversy, however, because the committee did not consult members of the affected Black communities. This foregrounds that more is at stake, and that more people are involved than the Native Americans to whom the over 300 remaining skulls of such an origin in the Morton collection will eventually be repatriated through federal law. The University of Pennsylvania Museum was also criticized for insufficient research into the provenance of the reburied remains. In fact, a professor at Rutgers University demonstrated that one individual had been the son of a Native American mother (e.g., Brewer 2024).

5 See Sommer 2023a, 26.

And what about blood and DNA? Researchers themselves are well aware that the collection of genetic material from living individuals, too, has grown into a political and public issue in the context of the Human Genome Diversity Project (HGDP). This does not come as a surprise in view of the fact that there are rather smooth continuities from the collection of bones and/or the photographing, fingerprinting, measuring, etc. of subjects in the field globally to the collection of blood in colonial and postcolonial contexts (e.g., Friedlaender 2009, xvi and 244; Sommer 2010b; on blood collecting see, e.g., Radin 2017; Bangham 2020). By the time of the take-off of the HGDP at the beginning of the 1990s, with Indigenous rights movements and increasing worldwide organization, research into human diversity and the preservation of bodily material from Indigenous peoples had become more problematic (for the most comprehensive account, see Reardon 2005). Despite controversies involving the collection of blood and genetic research especially surrounding the HGDP, the resulting collection is still the most complete, public, worldwide archive of human DNA. It has served as a central reference in aDNA research due to its anthropological framework, i.e., its focus on human diversity and what were considered isolated populations (Aneli, Birolo, and Matullo 2022, 4, 7). While tens of thousands of human remains have been repatriated and reburied, blood collections seem to have escaped similar large-scale attention. However, as cultural and medical anthropologist Emma Kowal (2023) documents for Australia, things may be about to change; the National Centre for Indigenous Genomics, overseen by an Aboriginal Australian majority board, was established in 2013. The board has developed a model of research governance concerning the management and use of the approximately 7,000 blood samples collected in Indigenous communities between the 1960s and 1990s.

The ethical concerns regarding aDNA studies of human evolution and kinship are possibly even more pronounced, not least because they depend on human remains. Indeed, while harboring a dream of an aDNA atlas of humanity (Reich 2019, 276–80),[6] the access of scientists

6 There is a public data repository on the Reich Laboratory website (https://reich.hms.harvard.edu/allen-ancient-dna-resource-aadr-downloadable-genotypes-present-day-and-ancient-dna-data). Other public repositories include the Sequence Read Archive and the European Nucleotide Archive.

to archaic and ancient human remains is challenged for several reasons. The NAGPRA demands that state-funded institutions offer the return of cultural and biological remains from groups to which Native Americans can demonstrate a connection, and there are governmental restrictions on the export of samples as in the case of China and Japan – restrictions that are the result of historical expeditions from the West (e.g., Sommer 2016a, 75–82). Although scientists express understanding towards Indigenous concerns, at times one also encounters the feeling that "claims of direct ancestral links between ancient skeletons and groups living today" are "unsubstantiated" (Reich 2019, 167). Some scientists defend the access of science to human remains – hand in hand with their freedom to research and write about biological differences between the sexes and between ethnicities (Coyne and Maroja 2023).

Even if the issue of the destructive extracting of aDNA from rare and irreplaceable (sub)fossil human remains is somewhat alleviated by the new methods of gathering aDNA from sediments, ice, and lake cores (e.g., Liu, Bennett, and Fu 2022), other issues persist.[7] There are significant differences in aDNA research possibilities between the Global North and South, with asymmetries in infrastructure, funding, and training opportunities that are reflected in the number of publications per world region. At the same time, researchers from the Global North continue to collect material and data in the Global South, a practice that has led to labels such as 'helicopter science' or 'parachute research'. There is also the accusation of a continuation of biocolonialism (Arcos 2018). Collecting without local collaboration or acknowledgement, and disrespect for the culture and beliefs of local communities, exacerbate the situation (e.g., Orlando et al. 2021, 20; Dalal et al. 2023, 8–9). Ethical guidelines for research conceptualization, sampling strategies, communication and engagement with communities, as well as data management and stewardship have been suggested (e.g., Fossheim 2013; Wagner et al. 2020; Alpaslan-Roodenberg et al. 2021; Harney et al. 2023).

The diagrams I have treated in this book are part of the history of collecting organismic remains, with the verb 'collecting' being a gross

7 The extraction of such so-called environmental DNA (eDNA) has been identified as the only research strand that originated in the field of aDNA studies itself (Orlando et al. 2021, 17).

euphemism for a large part of this history. And similar struggles as those surrounding collections plague the relating diagrams that are built on them. At this moment still, diagrams like those examined in Part I and beyond, and even the seemingly straightforward, harmless diagrams from human population genetics, evidence their political potential when they are leveraged to support racist statements on social media – it in fact has become clear that such diagrams are systematically weaponized by extremists in the US, even by the white supremacist who committed the Buffalo (New York) massacre in 2022, murdering ten African Americans (Carlson et al. 2022; Coghill and Hayes 2024). This has initiated a debate about what I call 'relating diagrams', as well as about 'race' and the history and politics of population labelling, within the genetic anthropology community and in the media, which reflects growing awareness of the issues involved (National Academies of Sciences, Engineering, and Medicine et al. 2023; Kozlov 2024).

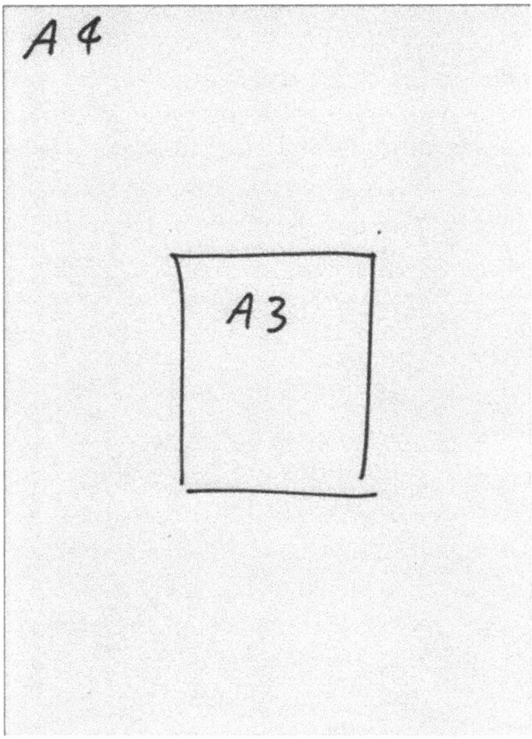

Fig. P.4 A3 on A4 (or tabloid on letter) (by Beni Bischof, all rights reserved, published with kind permission by the artist)

At the same time, some of the relating diagrams I have engaged with stood for the belief in and demands for equality, justice, and democracy, and were positioned against notions of human races or even species and the politics they could entail. I therefore end with another artwork by Bischof that to me is about this experimental and subversive power of diagrams. In a diagram, there are always already alternative ways of relating at play. Diagrams may thus also challenge our engrained perspectives, evoking several viewpoints simultaneously. They also seem to represent their (re)presentational character, like an A3-sized sheet of paper (or American tabloid format) drawn on a physical paper that is defined as A4 (or American letter size): a diagram can reverse relations that are taken for granted – not only in size – and their associated hierarchy of relevance.

References

Archival Sources

Full details of archival sources are given in the main text and accompanying footnotes

American Museum of Natural History Museum Archives (AMNH)

American Philosophical Society Library (APS)

Deutsche Akademie der Naturforscher Leopoldina – Nationale Akademie der Wissenschaften (ed.). *Ernst Haeckel Online Briefedition*, Ernst Haeckel Haus Jena, https://haeckel-briefwechsel-projekt.uni-jena.de/de (EHA Jena)

King's College London Archives (KCL)

Peabody Museum of Archaeology and Ethnology Archives (PMA)

Royal College of Surgeons of England Archives

Wyhe, John van (ed.). 2002. *The Complete Work of Charles Darwin Online*, http://darwin-online.org.uk/ (in Wyhe 2002)

Bibliography

Ackermann, R. R., M. L. Arnold, M. D. Baiz, et al. 2019. "Hybridization in Human Evolution: Insights from Other Organisms." *Evolutionary Anthropology: Issues, News, and Reviews* 28.4: 189–209, https://doi.org/10.1002/evan.21787

Agassiz, L. 1833–43. *Recherches sur les poissons fossiles*. 5 vols. Neuchâtel: Petitpierre.

___. 1833. *Recherches sur les poissons fossiles*. 5 vols., I: *Contenant l'introduction et toutes les questions générales, anatomiques, zoologiques et géologiques*. Neuchâtel: Petitpierre.

Aiyappan, A. 1949. "Review of *Human Ancestry from a Genetical Point of View* by R. Ruggles Gates." *Current Science Association* 18.8: 314.

Alexander, D. H., J. Novembre, and K. Lange. 2009. "Fast Model-Based Estimation of Ancestry in Unrelated Individuals." *Genome Research* 19.9: 1655–56.

Allen, G. 1882. "Obituary: Charles Darwin." *The Academy* 21.521: 306–307.

Allen, G. E. 1986. "The Eugenics Record Office at Cold Spring Harbor, 1910–1940: An Essay in Institutional History." *Osiris* 2.1: 225–64.

Alpaslan-Roodenberg, S., D. Anthony, H. Babiker, et al. 2021. "Ethics of DNA Research on Human Remains: Five Globally Applicable Guidelines." *Nature* 599.7883: 41–46, https://doi.org/10.1038/s41586-021-04008-x

Alter, S. J. 1999. *Darwinism and the Linguistic Image: Language, Race, and Natural Theology in the Nineteenth Century*. Baltimore, MD: Johns Hopkins University Press.

Aneli, S., G. Birolo, and G. Matullo. 2022. "Twenty Years of the Human Genome Diversity Project." *Human Population Genetics and Genomics* 2.4: 1–17, https://doi.org/10.47248/hpgg2202040005

Archibald, J. D. 2009. "Edward Hitchcock's Pre-Darwinian (1840) 'Tree of Life'." *Journal of the History of Biology* 42.3: 561–92, https://doi.org/10.1007/s10739-008-9163-y

___. 2012. "Darwin's Two Competing Phylogenetic Trees: Marsupials as Ancestors or Sister Taxa?" *Archives of Natural History* 39.2: 217–33, https://doi.org/10.3366/anh.2012.0091

___. 2014. *Aristotle's Ladder, Darwin's Tree: The Evolution of Visual Metaphors for Biological Order*. New York: Columbia University Press.

Arcos, M. C. Á. 2018. "Wielding New Genomic Tools Wisely." *Science* 360.6386: 274, https://doi.org/10.1126/science.aat3780

Armstrong-Fumero, F. 2014. "Even the Most Careless Observer: Race and Visual Discernment in Physical Anthropology from Samuel George Morton to Kennewick Man." *American Studies* 53.2: 5–29, https://doi.org/10.1353/ams.2014.0100

Arni, C., M. Sommer, and S. Teuscher (eds.). 2023. *Historische Anthropologie* 31.1. Special Section (Diagrammatik der Abstammung).

Aspinall, P. J. 2018. "How the Use by Eugenicists of Family Trees and Other Genealogical Technologies Informed and Reflected Discourses on Race and Race Crossing During the Era of Moral Condemnation: Mixed-Race in 1920s and 1930s Britain." *Genealogy* 2.3: 1–15, https://doi.org/10.3390/genealogy2030021

Augier, A. 1801. *Essai d'une nouvelle classification des végétaux: conforme à l'ordre que la nature paroît avoir suivi dans le règne végétal; d'ou résulte une méthode qui conduit à la connoissance des plantes & de leurs rapports naturels*. Lyon: Bruyset Ainé.

Augstein, F. A. 1996. "James C. Prichard's Views of Mankind: An Anthropologist Between the Enlightenment and the Victorian Age." PhD thesis, University College London.

Augstein, H. F. 1997. "Linguistics and Politics in the Early 19th Century: James Cowles Prichard's Moral Philosophy." *History of European Ideas* 23.1: 1–18, https://doi.org/10.1016/S0191-6599(97)00004-1

Baer, K. E. v. 1828–37. *Über die Entwicklungsgeschichte der Thiere: Beobachtungen und Reflexion*. 2 vols. Königsberg: Bei den Gebrüder Bornträger.

___. 1859. *Crania selecta ex thesauris anthropologicis Academiae Imperialis Petropolitanae*. Petropoli: Academiae Imperialis Scientiarum.

Bandmann, G. 1966. "Die Galleria Vittorio Emanuele II. zu Mailand." *Zeitschrift für Kunstgeschichte* 29.2: 81–110.

Bangham, J. 2020. *Blood Relations: Transfusion and the Making of Human Genetics*. Chicago: The University of Chicago Press, https://doi.org/10.7208/chicago/9780226740171.001.0001

Bapteste, E., F. Bouchard, and R. M. Burian. 2012. "Philosophy and Evolution: Minding the Gap between Evolutionary Patterns and Tree-Like Patterns." In *Evolutionary Genomics: Statistical and Computational Methods*, ed. M. Anisimova, 2 vols., II, 81–110. New York: Humana Press, https://doi.org/10.1007/978-1-61779-585-5_4

Bapteste, E., and J. Dupré. 2013. "Towards a Processual Microbial Ontology." *Biology & Philosophy* 28.2: 379–404, https://doi.org/10.1007/s10539-012-9350-2

Barkan, E. 1992. *The Retreat of Scientific Racism: Changing Concepts of Race in Britain and the United States Between the World Wars*. Cambridge, UK: Cambridge University Press.

Barsanti, G. 1988. "Le immagini della natura: Scale, mappe, alberi 1700–1800." *Nuncius* 3.1: 55–125.

___. 1992. *La scala, la mappa, l'albero: Immagini e classificazioni della natura fra sei e ottocento*. Firenze: Sansoni.

Bauer, M., and C. Ernst. 2010. *Diagrammatik: Einführung in ein kultur- und medienwissenschaftliches Forschungsfeld*. Bielefeld: Transcript, https://doi.org/10.14361/9783839412978

Beatty, J. 1994. "Dobzhansky and the Biology of Democracy: The Moral and Political Significance of Genetic Variation." In *The Evolution of Theodosius Dobzhansky: Essays on His Life and Thought in Russia and America*, ed. M. B. Adams, 195–218. Princeton, NJ: Princeton University Press.

Bender, J., and M. Marrinan. 2010. *The Culture of Diagram.* Stanford, CA: Stanford University Press.

Bergström, A., C. Stringer, M. Hajdinjak, et al. 2021. "Origins of Modern Human Ancestry." *Nature* 590.7845: 229–37, https://doi.org/10.1038/s41586-021-03244-5

Bernstein, F. 1931. "Die geographische Verteilung der Blutgruppen und ihre anthropologische Bedeutung." In *Comitato Italiano per lo studio dei problemi della popolazione.* Roma: Istituto Poligrafico dello Stato, 227–43.

Bigg, C. 2016. "Diagrams." In *A Companion to the History of Science,* ed. B. Lightman, 557–71. Chichester: Wiley Blackwell, https://doi.org/10.1002/9781118620762.ch39

Bigoni, F., and G. Barsanti. 2011. "Evolutionary Trees and the Rise of Modern Primatology: The Forgotten Contribution of St. George Mivart." *Journal of Anthropological Sciences* 89.1: 93–107.

Bischof, B. 2022. "So ein Punkt kann ja alles sein." Interview M. Köckritz. *Rampstyle* 27.1: 105–121.

Bizzocchi, R. 2010. *Généalogies fabuleuses: Inventer et faire croire dans l'Europe moderne.* Paris: Ed. Rue d'Ulm.

Blair, A. 2010. *Too Much to Know: Managing Scholarly Information before the Modern Age.* New Haven, CT: Yale University Press.

Blanckaert, C. 1987. "'Les vicissitudes de l'angle facial' et les débuts de la craniométrie (1765–1875)." *Revue de Synthèse* 108.3: 417–53.

___. 1989. "L'indice céphalique et l'ethnogénie européenne: A. Retzius, P. Broca, F. Pruner-Bey (1840–1870)." *Bulletins et Mémoires de La Société d'Anthropologie de Paris,* Nouvelle Serie 1.3–4: 165–202.

Blumenbach, J. F. 1775. *De generis humani varietate nativa.* Gottingae: Rosenbuschius.

___. 1790, 1793, 1795, 1800, 1808, 1820. *Decas (altera/tertia/quarta/quinta /sexta) collectionis suae carniorum diversarum gentium illustrata.* Gottingae: Ioann. Christ. Dieterich/Heinrich Dietrich.

___. 1795. *De generis humani varietate nativa.* 3rd ed. Gottingae: Vandenhoek et Ruprecht.

___. 1798. *Über die natürlichen Verschiedenheiten im Menschengeschlechte,* ed. and trans. J. G. Gruber. 3rd ed. Leipzig: Breitkopf und Härtel.

___. 1799. "Observations on the Bodily Conformation and Mental Capacities of [Black Africans]." *Philosophical Magazine* 3.10: 141–47, trans. anonymous.

___. 1804. *De l'unité du genre humain, et de ses variétés,* trans. F. Chardel. 3rd ed. Paris: Allut.

___. 1865. "De generis humani variete nativa." 3rd ed. In *The Anthropological Treatises of Blumenbach and Hunter*, trans. and ed. T. Bendyshe, 145–276. London: Longman, Green, Longman, Roberts, and Green.

Bogen, S., and F. Thürlemann. 2003. "Jenseits der Opposition von Text und Bild: Überlegungen zu einer Theorie des Diagrammatischen." In *Die Bildwelt der Diagramme Joachims von Fiore: Zur Medialität religiös-politischer Programme im Mittelalter*, ed. A. Patschovsky, 1–22. Stuttgart: Thorbecke.

Bolnick, D. A. 2008. "Individual Ancestry Inference and the Reification of Race as a Biological Phenomenon." In *Revisiting Race in a Genomic Age*, ed. B. A. Koenig, S. S.-J. Lee, and S. S. Richardson, 70–85. New Brunswick, NJ: Rutgers University Press.

Bonhoff, U. M. 1993. "Das Diagramm: Kunsthistorische Betrachtung über seine vielfältige Anwendung von der Antike bis zur Neuzeit." PhD thesis, University of Münster.

Bonnet, C. 1745. *Traité d'insectologie: Ou observations sur les pucerons; première partie*. Paris: Durant.

___. 1764. *Contemplation de la nature*. 2 vols. Amsterdam: Marc-Michel Rey.

___. 1773. *Herrn Karl Bonnets Abhandlungen aus der Insektologie*, trans. J. A. E. Goeze, 2 vols. Halle: Bey J. J. Gebauers Wittwe und Joh. Jac. Gebauer.

Bory de Saint-Vincent, J.-B. G. G. M. 1827. *L'Homme (Homo): Essai zoologique sur le genre humain*. 2nd ed. 2 vols. Paris: Rey et Gravier.

Bösl, E. 2017. *Doing Ancient DNA: Zur Wissenschaftsgeschichte der aDNA-Forschung*. Bielefeld: Transcript.

Boule, M. 1908. "L'Homme fossile de La Chapelle-aux-Saints (Corrèze)." *L'Anthropologie* 19: 519–25.

___. 1921. *Les hommes fossiles: Éléments de paléontologie humaine*. Paris: Masson.

Bouquet, M. 1996. "Family Trees and Their Affinities: The Visual Imperative of the Genealogical Diagram." *Journal of the Royal Anthropological Institute* 2.1: 43–66.

Bowcock, A. M., J. M. Herbert, J. L. Mountain, et al. 1991. "Study of an Additional 58 DNA Markers in Five Human Populations from Four Continents." *Gene Geography: A Computerized Bulletin on Human Gene Frequencies* 5.3: 151–73.

[Bowen, F.]. 1860. [Review of] "*On the Origin of Species by Means of Natural Selection, or the Preservation of Favored Races in the Struggle for Life*, by C. Darwin." *The North American Review* 90.187: 474–506.

Bowler, P. J. 1986. *Theories of Human Evolution: A Century of Debate, 1844–1944*. Baltimore, MD: Johns Hopkins University Press.

___. 2021. *Progress Unchained: Ideas of Evolution, Human History and the Future*. Cambridge, UK: Cambridge University Press, https://doi.org/10.1017/9781108909877

Boyd, W. C. 1939. "Blood Groups." *Tabulae Biologicae*, 17.2: 113–240.

___. 1952. *Genetics and the Races of Man*. New York: Little, Brown and Company.

___. 1963. "Genetics and the Human Race." *Science*, New Series, 140.3571: 1057–1064.

Brace, C. L., G. A. Agogino, D. R. Brothwell, et al. 1964. "The Fate of the 'Classic' Neanderthals: A Consideration of Hominid Catastrophism [and Comments and Reply]." *Current Anthropology* 5.1: 3–43.

Braude, B. 1997. "The Sons of Noah and the Construction of Ethnic and Geographical Identities in the Medieval and Early Modern Periods." *The William and Mary Quarterly* 54.1: 103–142.

Bredekamp, H. 2019. *Darwin's Corals: A New Model of Evolution and the Tradition of Natural History*, trans. E. Cleg. Berlin: De Gruyter, https://doi.org/10.1515/9783110680317

Brehm, A. E. 1864–69. *Illustriertes Thierleben: Eine allgemeine Kunde des Thierreichs*. 6 vols. Hildburghausen: Bibliographisches Institut.

Brewer, G. L. 2024. "Penn Museum Buries the Bones of 19 Black Philadelphians, Causing Dispute with Community." *Los Angeles Times*, 3 February 2024, https://www.latimes.com/world-nation/story/2024-02-03/penn-museum-buries-the-bones-of-19-black-philadelphians-causing-dispute-with-community

Brink-Roby, H. 2009. "Natural Representation: Diagram and Text in Darwin's *On the Origin of Species*." *Victorian Studies* 51.2: 247–73.

Broc, P. P. 1837. *Essai sur les races humaines considérées sous les rapports anatomique et philosophique*. Brussels: Établissement Encyclographique.

Broca, P. 1868. "Sur les crânes et ossements des Eyzies." *Bulletins de la Société d'Anthropologie de Paris* 54.T. III/2e: 350–92.

___. 1875 [1865–75]. "On the Human Skulls and Bones Found in the Cave of Cro-Magnon, near Les Eyzies." In *Reliquiae Aquitanicae; Being Contributions to the Archaeology and Palaeontology of Périgord and the Adjoining Provinces of Southern France*, ed. É. Lartet, H. Christy, and T. R. Jones, 97–122. London: Williams and Norgate.

___. 1875. "Instructions craniologiques et craniométriques." *Mémoires de la Société d'Anthropologie de Paris* 2.2: 1–203.

Bronn, H. G. 1837. *XLVII Tafeln mit Abbildungen zur Lethäa geognostica*. Stuttgart: E. Schweizerbart.

___. 1858. *Untersuchungen über die Entwicklungs-Gesetze der organischen Welt während der Bildungs-Zeit unserer Erd-Oberfläche*. Stuttgart: E. Schweizerbart.

Brown, R. W. 2016. "Anglo-Australian Racial Science, Trans-Hemispheric Transactions, and the 'Yellow Peril' in the Anglosphere, 1850–1960." PhD thesis, University of Birmingham, https://etheses.bham.ac.uk/id/eprint/7285/1/Brown17PhD.pdf

Büchner, L. 1868. *Sechs Vorlesungen über die Darwin'sche Theorie von der Verwandlung der Arten und die erste Entstehung der Organismenwelt, sowie über die Anwendung der Umwandlungstheorie auf den Menschen, das Verhältniß dieser Theorie zur Lehre vom Fortschritt und den Zusammenhang derselben mit der materialistischen Philosophie der Vergangenheit und Gegenwart. In allgemein verständlicher Darstellung*. Leipzig: T. Thomas.

Buffon, G.-L. L. 1755. *Histoire naturelle, générale et particulière, avec la description du Cabinet du Roy*. 36 vols., V. Paris: l'Imprimerie royale.

Buklijas, T. 2008. "Cultures of Death and Politics of Corpse Supply: Anatomy in Vienna." *Bulletin of the History of Medicine* 82.3: 570–607, https://doi.org/10.1353/bhm.0.0086

Busk, G. 1861. "Observations on a Systematic Mode of Craniometry." *Transactions of the Ethnological Society of London* 1.1: 341–48.

C. T. R. 1924. "Review on *Heredity and Eugenics*, by R. Ruggles Gates." *Science Progress in the Twentieth Century (1919–1933)* 19.74: 344.

Caldwell, C. 1830. *Thoughts on the Original Unity of the Human Race*. New York: E. Bliss.

Camper, P. 1792. *Über den natürlichen Unterschied der Gesichtszüge in Menschen: verschiedener Gegenden und verschiedenen Alters; über das Schöne antiker Bildsäulen und geschnittener Steine; nebst Darstellung einer neuen Art, allerlei Menschenköpfe mit Sicherheit zu zeichnen*, ed. and trans. S. Th. von Soemmerring and A. G. Camper. Berlin: Voss.

Cann, R. L., M. Stoneking, and A. C. Wilson. 1987. "Mitochondrial DNA and Human Evolution." *Nature* 325.6099: 31–36.

Caparros, M., and S. Prat. 2021. "A Phylogenetic Networks Perspective on Reticulate Human Evolution." *iScience* 24.4: 1–31, https://doi.org/10.1016/j.isci.2021.102359

Carlson, J., B. M. Henn, D. R. Al-Hindi, et al. 2022. "Counter the Weaponization of Genetics Research by Extremists." *Nature* 610.7932: 444–47, https://doi.org/10.1038/d41586-022-03252-z

Carus, C. G. 1843. *Atlas der Cranioscopie, oder, Abbildungen der Schaedel- und Antlitzformen beruehmter oder sonst merkwuerdiger Personen*. Leipzig: August Weichardt.

Cassata, F. 2008. "Against UNESCO: Gedda, Gini and American Scientific Racism." *Medicina nei secoli arte e scienza, Jounal of History of Medicine* 20.3: 907–935.

Castañeda, C. 2002. "Der Stammbaum: Zeit, Raum und Alltagstechnologie in den Vererbungswissenschaften." In *Genealogie und Genetik: Schnittstellen zwischen Biologie und Kulturgeschichte*, ed. S. Weigel, 57–69. Berlin: Akademie Verlag.

Cavalli-Sforza, L. L. 1973. "Analytic Review: Some Current Problems of Human Population Genetics." *American Journal of Human Genetics* 25.1: 82–104.

___. 1974. "Letter: Controversial Issues in Human Population Genetics." *American Journal of Human Genetics* 26.2: 266–71.

___. 2000 [1996]. *Genes, Peoples and Languages*. Harmondsworth: Allen Lane.

Cavalli-Sforza, L. L., and A. W. F. Edwards. 1965. "Analysis of Human Evolution." In *Genetics Today. Proceedings of the XI. International Congress of Genetics, the Hague, the Netherlands, September 1963*, ed. S. J. Geerts, 3 vols., III, 923–33. Oxford: Pergamon.

___. 1967. "Phylogenetic Analysis: Models and Estimation Procedures." *American Journal of Human Genetics* 19.3: 233–57.

Cavalli-Sforza, L. L., and M. W. Feldman. 1973. "Cultural versus Biological Inheritance: Phenotypic Transmission from Parents to Children (A Theory of the Effect of Parental Phenotypes on Children's Phenotypes)." *American Journal of Human Genetics* 25.6: 618–37.

___. 1981. *Cultural Transmission and Evolution: A Quantitative Approach*. Princeton, NJ: Princeton University Press.

Cavalli-Sforza, L. L., P. Menozzi, and A. Piazza. 1994. *The History and Geography of Human Genes*. Princeton, NJ: Princeton University Press.

Cavalli-Sforza, L. L., P. Menozzi, A. Piazza, et al. 1988. "Reconstruction of Human Evolution: Bringing Together Genetic, Archaeological, and Linguistic Data." *Proceedings of the National Academy of Sciences of the United States of America* 85.16: 6002–6006.

Cavalli-Sforza, L. L., and A. Piazza. 1975. "Analysis of Evolution: Evolutionary Rates, Independence and Treeness." *Theoretical Population Biology* 8.2: 127–65.

Chakraborty, R. 1986. "Gene Admixture in Human Populations: Models and Predictions." *American Journal of Physical Anthropology* 29.S7: 1–43, https://doi.org/10.1002/ajpa.1330290502

Chambers, R. 1844. *Vestiges of the Natural History of Creation*. London: John Churchill.

___. 1845. *Explanations: A Sequel to "Vestiges of the Natural History of Creation." By the Author of that Work*. London: John Churchill.

Clark, W. E. Le Gros. 1934. *Early Forerunners of Man: A Morphological Study of the Evolutionary Origin of the Primates*. Baltimore, MD: William Wood.

Clever, I. 2023. "Biometry against Fascism: Geoffrey Morant, Race, and Anti-Racism in Twentieth-Century Physical Anthropology." *Isis* 114.1: 25–49, https://doi.org/10.1086/723686

Coates, B. H. 1834. *Annual Discourse, Delivered before the Historical Society of Pennsylvania, on the 28th Day of April, 1834, on the Origin of the Indian Population of America*. Philadelphia, PN: M'Carty and Davis.

Coghill, A., and G. Hayes. 2024. "Elon Musk Keeps Spreading a Very Specific Kind of Racism." *Mother Jones*, 13 March 2024, https://www.motherjones.com/politics/2024/03/elon-musk-racist-tweets-science-video/

Comas, J. 1961. "'Scientific' Racism Again?" *Current Anthropology* 2.4: 303–340.

____. 1962. "More on 'Scientific' Racism." *Current Anthropology* 3.3: 284–302.

Combe, G. 1822. *Essays on Phrenology, or An Inquiry into the Principles and Utility of the System of Drs. Gall and Spurzheim, and into the Objections Made Against It*. Philadelphia, PN: H. C. Carey and I. Lea.

____. 1826. *Elements of Phrenology*. Philadelphia, PN: E. Littell.

____. 1830. *A System of Phrenology*. 3rd ed. Edinburgh: John Anderson.

Conklin, E. G. 1921. *The Direction of Human Evolution*. New York: Charles Scribner's Sons.

Cook, R. 1988. *The Tree of Life: Image for the Cosmos*. London: Thames and Hudson.

Cooke, K. 2002. "Duty or Dream? Edwin G. Conklin's Critique of Eugenics and Support for American Individualism." *Journal of the History of Biology* 35.2: 365–84.

Coon, C. S. 1962. *The Origin of Races*. New York: Alfred A. Knopf.

____. 1965. *The Living Races of Man*. New York: Alfred A. Knopf.

Cooper Union Museum for the Arts of Decoration. 1961. *The Four Continents*, https://library.si.edu/digital-library/book/fourcontinentsfr00coop

Corbeiller, C. Le 1961. "Miss America and Her Sisters: Personifications of the Four Parts of the World." *The Metropolitan Museum of Art Bulletin* 19.8: 209–223.

Coyne, J. A., and L. S. Maroja. 2023. "The Ideological Subversion of Biology." *Skeptical Inquirer* 47.4, https://skepticalinquirer.org/2023/06/the-ideological-subversion-of-biology/

Cravens, H. 1978. *The Triumph of Evolution: American Scientists and the Heredity-Environment Controversy, 1900–1941*. Philadelphia, PN: University of Pennsylvania Press.

Crull, W. H. 1810. *Dissertatio anthropologico-medica inauguralis, de cranio, eiusque ad faciem ratione*. Groningae: Veenkamp.

Currin, G. 2022. "Scientists Have Created the Frist Ever World-Wide Family Tree." *Interesting Engineering*, 23 February 2022, https://interestingengineering.com/global-family-tree

Cuvier, G. 1800. *Leçons d'anatomie comparée*. 5 vols., II. Paris: Baudouin.

___. 1817. *Le règne animal distribué d'après son organisation, pour servir de base à l'histoire naturelle des animaux et d'introduction à l'anatomie comparée*. 4 vols., I. Paris: Deterville.

___. 1827. *The Animal Kingdom Arranged in Conformity With its Organization. With Additional Descriptions of all the Species Hitherto Named, and of Many not Before Noticed, by Edward Griffith and Others*, trans. anonymous, 16 vols., I. London: Geo. B. Whittaker.

Dalal, V., N. Pasupuleti, G. Chaubey, et al. 2023. "Advancements and Challenges in Ancient DNA Research: Bridging the Global North–South Divide." *Genes* 14.2: 1–17, https://doi.org/10.3390/genes14020479

Darwin, C. R. 1838–51. "'Books to be read' and 'Books Read' Notebook." CUL-DAR119. In Wyhe 2002.

___. 1852–60. "'Books Read' and 'Books to be Read' Notebook." CUL-DAR128. In Wyhe 2002.

___. 1859. *On the Origin of Species by Means of Natural Selection, or the Preservation of Favoured Races in the Struggle for Life*. A Facsimile of the 1st ed. Cambridge, MA: Harvard University Press.

___. 1859 [1964]. "1838.02–1838.07. *Notebook C*: [Transmutation of species]." CUL-DAR122. In Wyhe 2002.

___. 1869 [1859]. *On the Origin of Species by Means of Natural Selection, or the Preservation of Favoured Races in the Struggle for Life*. 5th ed. London: John Murray.

___. 1871a. *The Descent of Man, and Selection in Relation to Sex*. 1st ed. 2 vols., I. London: John Murray.

___. 1871b. *The Descent of Man, and Selection in Relation to Sex*. 1st ed. 2 vols., II. London: John Murray.

Darwin, F. (ed.). 1887. *The Life and Letters of Charles Darwin, Including an Autobiographical Chapter*. 3 vols. London: John Murray.

Daubenton, L. J. M. 1764. "Mémoire sur les différences de la situation du grand trou occipal dans l'homme et dans les animaux." *Histoire de l'Académie Royale des Sciences avec les Mémoires de Mathématique et de Physique*: 568–79.

Davenport, C. B. 1911. *Heredity in Relation to Eugenics*. New York: H. Holt.

Davis, J. B. 1861. "On the Method of Measurements, as a Diagnostic Means of Distinguishing Human Races, Adopted by Drs. Scherzer and Schwarz in the Austrian Circumnavigatory Expedition of the 'Novara'." *Transactions of the Ethnological Society of London* 1.1: 123–28.

___. 1867. *Thesaurus craniorum: Catalogue of the Skulls of the Various Races of Man, in the Collection of Joseph Barnard Davis*. London: Printed for the Subscribers.

___. 1875. *Supplement to Thesaurus craniorum: Catalogue of the Skulls of the Various Races of Man, in the Collection of Joseph Barnard Davis*. London: Printed for the Subscribers.

Davis, J. B., and J. Thurnam. 1865. *Crania britannica: Delineations and Descriptions of the Skulls of the Aboriginal and Early Inhabitants of the British Islands, Together With Notices of Their Other Remains*. London: Taylor.

Dayrat, B. 2003. "The Roots of Phylogeny: How Did Haeckel Build His Trees?" *Systematic Biology* 52.4: 515–27.

Deleuze, G. 1988 [1986]. *Foucault*, trans. and ed. S. Hand. London: Athlone.

Deleuze, G., and F. Guattari. 1987 [1980]. *A Thousand Plateaus: Capitalism and Schizophrenia*, trans. B. Massumi. Minneapolis, MN: University of Minnesota Press.

Demandt, A. 2005. *Über allen Wipfeln: Der Baum in der Kulturgeschichte*. Düsseldorf: Albatros.

___. 2014. *Der Baum: Eine Kulturgeschichte*. 2nd ed. Köln: Böhlau.

DeSalle, R., A. Narechania, M. Zilversmit, et al. 2017. "To Tree or Not to Tree *Homo sapiens*." In *Rethinking Human Evolution*, ed. J. H. Schwartz, 93–108. Cambridge, MA: The MIT Press.

Deschamps, M.-H. 1857. *Étude des races humaines. IIIè mémoire: Méthode naturelle d'ethnologie*. Paris: Leiber et Comelin.

Desmond, A. J., and J. Moore. 2009. *Darwin's Sacred Cause: How a Hatred of Slavery Shaped Darwin's Views on Human Evolution*. Boston, MA: Houghton Mifflin Harcourt.

Desmoulins, A. 1826. *Histoire naturelle des races humaines du nord-est de l'Europe, de l'Asie boréale et orientale, et de l'Afrique australe*. Paris: Méquignon-Marvis.

Dias, N. 2012. "Nineteenth-Century French Collections of Skulls and the Cult of Bone." *Nuncius* 27.2: 330–47, https://doi.org/10.1163/18253911-02702006

Diekmann, A. 1992. *Klassifikation, System, 'scala naturae': Das Ordnen der Objekte in Naturwissenschaft und Pharmazie zwischen 1700 und 1850*. Stuttgart: Wissenschaftliche Verlagsgesellschaft.

Dienekes, P. 2010. "Dienekes' Anthropology Blog: Human Genetic Variation: The First ? Components." *Dienekes' Anthropology Blog*, 15 December 2010, http://dienekes.blogspot.com/2010/12/human-genetic-variation-first.html

Dobzhansky, T. 1942. "Biological Adaptation." *The Scientific Monthly* 55.5: 391–402.

___. 1944. "On Species and Races of Living and Fossil Man." *American Journal of Physical Anthropology* 2.3: 251–65.

___. 1950. "Heredity, Environment, and Evolution." *Science*, New Series, 111.2877: 161–66.

___. 1962. *Mankind Evolving: The Evolution of the Human Species*. New Haven, CT: Yale University Press.

___. 1963a. "Anthropology and the Natural Sciences – The Problem of Human Evolution." *Current Anthropology* 4.2: 138–48.

___. 1963b. "Genetic Entities in Hominid Evolution." In *Classification and Human Evolution*, ed. S. L. Washburn, 347–62. Chicago, IL: Aldine.

___. 1963c. "Review of *The Origin of Races*, by Carleton S. Coon." *Scientific American* 208.2: 169–72.

Dobzhansky, T., A. Montagu, and C. S. Coon. 1963. "Two Views of Coon's Origin of Races with Comments by Coon and Replies." *Current Anthropology* 4.4: 360–67.

Dodson, E. O. 1948. "*Human Heredity*. By Reginald Ruggles Gates." *The American Midland Naturalist* 40.3: 775–76.

___. 1949. "Review on *Human Ancestry from a Genetical Point of View*, by R. Ruggles Gates." *The American Midland Naturalist* 42.3: 765.

Donald, D., and J. Munro. 2009 (eds.). *Endless Forms: Charles Darwin, Natural Science and the Visual Arts*. New Haven, CT: Yale University Press.

Doolittle, W. F. 1999. "Phylogenetic Classification and the Universal Tree." *Science* 284.5423: 2124–28.

Doolittle, W. F., and E. Bapteste. 2007. "Pattern Pluralism and the Tree of Life Hypothesis." *Proceedings of the National Academy of Sciences* 104.7: 2043–2049, https://doi.org/10.1073/pnas.0610699104

Doron, C.-O. 2012. "Race and Genealogy: Buffon and the Formation of the Concept of 'Race'." *HUMANA.MENTE Journal of Philosophical Studies* 5.22: 75–109.

___. 2016. *L'homme altéré: Races et dégénérescence (XVIIe–XIXe siècles)*. Ceyzérieu: Champ Vallon.

Douglas, B. 2008. "Climate to Crania: Science and the Racialization of Human Differences." In *Foreign Bodies – Oceania and the Science of Race 1750–1940*, ed. B. Douglas and C. Ballard, 33–96. Canberra: ANU.

Douglass, F. 1999 [1854]. "The Claims of [Black People] Ethnologically Considered." In *Frederick Douglass: Selected Speeches and Writings*, ed. P. S. Foner and Y. Taylor, 282–97. Chicago, IL: Lawrence Hill.

Duchèsne, A. N. 1766. *Histoire naturelle des fraisiers*. Paris: Didot; C. J. Panckoucke.

Dungca, N., and C. Healy. 2023. "Revealing the Smithsonian's 'Racial Brain Collection'." *The Washington Post*, 14 August 2023, https://www.washingtonpost.com/history/interactive/2023/smithsonian-brains-collection-racial-history-repatriation/

Duperrey, L. I. 1826. *Voyage autour du monde: Exécuté par ordre du Roi, sur la corvette de Sa Majesté, la Coquille, pendant les années 1822, 1823, 1824 et 1825. Histoire naturelle, Zoologie, Atlas*. Paris: Arthus Bertrand.

Dürer, A. 1528. *Hierinn sind begriffen vier Bücher von menschlicher Proportion durch Albrechten Dürer von Nürerberg erfunden und beschuben zu nutz allen denen so zu diser kunst lieb tragen*. Nuremberg: Hieronymus Andreae Formschneider.

Ecker, A. 1865. *Crania germaniae meridionalis occidentalis: Beschreibung und Abbildung von Schädeln früherer und heutiger Bewohner des südwestlichen Deutschlands und insbesondere des Grossherzogthums Baden: Ein Beitrag zur Kenntniss der physischen Beschaffenheit und Geschichte der deutschen Volksstämme*. Freiburg i. B.: Fr. Wagner.

Eco, U. 1989. *Im Labyrinth der Vernunft: Texte über Kunst und Zeichen*. Leipzig: Reclam.

Edwards, A. W. F., and L. L. Cavalli-Sforza. 1964. "Reconstruction of Evolutionary Trees." In *Phenetic and Phylogenetic Classification: A Symposium [Held in the Hartley Laboratories of the University of Liverpool on the 8th and 9th April 1964]*, ed. V. H. Heywood, 11 vols., VI, 67–76. London: Systematics Association.

Ehrenfels, U. R., T. N. Madan, and J. Comas. 1962. "Mankind Quarterly Under Heavy Criticism: 3 Comments on Editorial Practices." *Current Anthropology* 3.2: 154–58.

Eichwald, K. E. v. 1829. *Zoologia specialis quam expositus animalibus tum vivis: Tum fossilibus potissimum rossiae in universum et poloniae in species*. 3 vols. I. Vilnae: J. Zawadzki.

Ellet, E. F. 1867. *The Queens of American Society*. New York: Charles Scribner.

Erickson, P. A. 1986. "The Anthropology of Josiah Clark Nott." *Kroeber Anthropological Society Papers* 65–66.13: 103–120.

Ernst, C. 2014. "Diagramm/Diagrammatik." In *Handbuch Medienwissenschaft*, ed. J. Schröter, 222–27. Stuttgart: J. B. Metzler.

F. S. 1924. "Review on *Heredity and Eugenics*, by R. Ruggles Gates." *Man* 24.3: 45.

Fabian, A. 2003. "The Curious Cabinet of Dr. Morton." In *Acts of Possession: Collecting in America*, ed. L. Dilworth, 112–37. New Brunswick, NJ: Rutgers University Press.

___. 2010. *The Skull Collectors: Race, Science, and America's Unburied Dead*. Chicago, IL: The University of Chicago Press.

Fagundes, N. J., N. Ray, M. Beaumont, et al. 2007. "Statistical Evaluation of Alternative Models of Human Evolution." *Proceedings of the National Academy of Sciences* 104.45: 17614–19.

Finlayson, C. 2013. "Viewpoint: Human Evolution, From Tree to Braid." *BBC News*, 31 December 2013, https://www.bbc.com/news/science-environment-25559172

Fossheim, H. (ed.). 2013. *More Than Just Bones: Ethics and Research on Human Remains.* Oslo: The Norwegian National Research Ethics Committees, https://www.forskningsetikk.no/globalassets/dokumenter/4-publikasjoner-som-pdf/more-than-just-bones_web.pdf

Foucault, M. 1977 (1975). *Discipline and Punish: The Birth of the Prison*, trans. A. Sheridon. New York: Random House.

François, O., M. Currat, N. Ray, et al. 2010. "Principal Component Analysis Under Population Genetic Models of Range Expansion and Admixture." *Molecular Biology and Evolution* 27.6: 1257–68, https://doi.org/10.1093/molbev/msq010

François, O., and E. Durand. 2010. "Spatially Explicit Bayesian Clustering Models in Population Genetics." *Molecular Ecology Resources* 10.5: 773–84, https://doi.org/10.1111/j.1755-0998.2010.02868.x

Franklin, J. 2000. "Diagrammatic Reasoning and Modelling in the Imagination: The Secret Weapons of the Scientific Revolution." In *1543 and All That*, ed. G. Freeland and A. Corones, 53–115. Dodrecht: Kluwer.

Fraser Roberts, J. A. 1964. "Reginald Ruggles Gates. 1882–1962." *Biographical Memoirs of Fellows of the Royal Society* 10.1: 83–106.

Friedlaender, J. S., as told to J. Radin. 2009. *From Anthropometry to Genomics: Reflections of a Pacific Fieldworker*. New York: iUniverse.

G. M. M. 1930. "Review: Heredity in Man. by R. Ruggles Gates." *Man* 30.6: 111.

Galton, F. 1869. *Hereditary Genius: An Inquiry into Its Laws and Consequences*. London: Macmillan.

Galway-Witham, J., J. Cole, and C. Stringer. 2019. "Aspects of Human Physical and Behavioural Evolution During the Last 1 Million Years." *Journal of Quaternary Science* 34.6: 355–78, https://doi.org/10.1002/jqs.3137

Gao, X., F. Peng, Q. M. Fu, et al. 2017. "New Progress in Understanding the Origins of Modern Humans in China." *Science China Earth Sciences* 60.11: 2160–70, https://doi.org/10.1007/s11430-017-9144-1

Garnot, P. 1828. "Mémoire sur les races humaines." In *Voyage autour du monde: Exécuté par ordre du Roi, sur la corvette de Sa Majesté, la Coquille, pendant les années 1822, 1823, 1824 et 1825*, ed. L. I. Duperrey, 7 vols., I, Part 2: *Zoologie*, by R. P. Lesson and P. Garnot, 507–522. Paris: Arthus Bertrand.

—. 1836. "HOMME, *Homo* (Man)." In *Dictionnaire pittoresque d'histoire naturelle et des phénomènes de la nature*, ed. F. É. Guérin, 12 vols., IV, 6–16. Paris: Bureau de Souscription.

Garrett, H. E., and W. M. Krogman. 1950. "On Gates' Human Ancestry." *American Association for the Advancement of Science* 111.2872: 43.

Gates, Ruggles R. 1923. *Heredity and Eugenics*. London: Constable.

___. 1928. "A Pedigree Study of Amerindian Crosses in Canada." *The Journal of the Royal Anthropological Institute of Great Britain and Ireland* 58.2: 511–32.

___. 1929. *Heredity in Man*. London: Constable.

___. 1931. "Heredity in Man." *Science Progress in the Twentieth Century (1919–1933)* 25.100: 690–91.

___. 1936a. "Review of *We Europeans: A Survey of Racial Problems*, by Julian S. Huxley and A. C. Haddon." *Man* 36.9: 161–62.

___. 1936b. "Bureau of Human Heredity." *British Medical Journal* 1.3932: 1018.

___. 1937. "Genetics and Race." *Man* 37.2: 28–32.

___. 1939. "Notes: Bureau of Human Heredity." *Human Biology* 11.2: 287–88.

___. 1946. *Human Genetics*. 2 vols. New York: Macmillan.

___. 1947. "Specific and Racial Characters in Human Evolution." *American Journal of Physical Anthropology* 5.2: 221–24.

___. 1948. *Human Ancestry from a Genetical Point of View*. Cambridge, MA: Harvard University Press.

___. 1949. *Pedigrees of [Black] Families*. Philadelphia, PN: Blackston.

___. 1952. "Studies of Interracial Crossing: I. Spectrophotometric Measurements of Skin Color." *Human Biology* 24.1: 25–34.

___. 1956. "Studies in Race Crossing: IV. Crosses of Chinese, Amerindians and [Black People], and Their Bearing on Racial Relationships." *Zeitschrift für Morphologie und Anthropologie* 47.3: 233–315.

___. 1962. "7. A Propos the Mankind Quarterly." *Man* 62.1: 13.

___. 1963. "Racial Genetics: A New Branch of Anthropology." *Current Anthropology* 4.2: 208–209.

Gates, R. R., and A. J. Gregor. 1963. "Mankind Quarterly: Gates and Gregor Reply to Critics." *Current Anthropology* 4.1: 119–21.

Gates, R. R., L. H. Snyder, and E. A. Hooton. 1943. *Medical Genetics and Eugenics*. 2 vols., II. Philadelphia, PN: Women's Medical College of Pennsylvania.

Gehring, P. 1992. "Paradigma einer Methode: Der Begriff des Diagramms im Strukturdenken von M. Foucault und M. Serres." In *Diagrammatik und*

Philosophie, ed. P. Gehring, T. Keutner, J. F. Maas, et al., 89–105. Amsterdam: Rodopi.

Gessner, S. 2014. "The Use of Printed Images for Instrument-Making at the Arsenius Workshop." In *Observing the World Through Images: Diagrams and Figures in the Early-Modern Arts and Sciences*, ed. N. Jardine and I. Fay, 124–52. Leiden: Brill, https://doi.org/10.1163/9789004263857_006

Gierl, M. 2012. *Geschichte als präzisierte Wissenschaft: Johann Christoph Gatterer und die Historiographie des 18. Jahrhunderts im ganzen Umfang*. Stuttgart: frommann-holzboog.

Giessmann, S. 2007. "Netze als Weltbilder: Ordnungen der Natur von Donati bis Cuvier." In *Verwandte Bilder: Die Fragen der Bildwissenschaft*, ed. I. Reichle, S. Siegel, and A. Spelten, 243–62. Berlin: Kadmos.

Glass, B. 1945. "Review of *Medical Genetics and Eugenics. Volume 2*, by R. Ruggles Gates, L. H. Snyder, and E. A. Hooton." *The Quarterly Review of Biology* 20.1: 85.

Gokcumen, O. 2020. "Archaic Hominin Introgression into Modern Human Genomes." *Yearbook of Physical Anthropology* 171.S70: 60–73.

Gontier, N. 2011. "Depicting the Tree of Life: The Philosophical and Historical Roots of Evolutionary Tree Diagrams." *Evolution: Education & Outreach* 4.3: 515–38, https://doi.org/10.1007/s12052-011-0355-0

Gopalan, S., E. G. Atkinson, L. T. Buck, et al. 2021. "Inferring Archaic Introgression from Hominin Genetic Data." *Evolutionary Anthropology: Issues, News, and Reviews* 30.3: 199–220, https://doi.org/10.1002/evan.21895

Gould, S. J. 1977. *Ontogeny and Phylogeny*. Cambridge, MA: The Belknap Press of Harvard University Press.

___. 1995. "Ladders and Cones: Constraining Evolution by Canonical Icons." In *Hidden Histories of Science*, ed. R. B. Silvers, 38–67. New York: New York Review Book.

___.1996 [1981]. *The Mismeasure of Man*. 2nd ed. New York: W. W. Norton.

___.1997. "Redrafting the Tree of Life." *Proceedings of the American Philosophical Society* 141.1: 30–54.

Green, R. E., J. Krause, A. W. Briggs, et al. 2010. "A Draft Sequence of the Neandertal Genome." *Science* 328.5979: 710–22.

Greenbaum G., A. Rubin, A. R. Templeton, et al. 2019. "Network-Based Hierarchical Population Structure Analysis for Large Genomic Data Sets. *Genome Research* 29.12: 2020–2033, https://doi.org/10.1101/gr.250092.119

Gregory, W. K. 1927. "Did Man Originate in Central Asia? (Mongolia the New World, Part V)." *Scientific Monthly* 24.5: 385–401.

___. 1930. "A Critique of Professor Osborn's Theory of Human Origins." *American Journal of Physical Anthropology* 14.2: 133–63.

___. 1934. *Man's Place Among the Anthropoids: Three Lectures on the Evolution of Man from the Lower Vertebrates*. Oxford: Clarendon.

Gruber, H. E. 2005. "Darwin's 'Tree of Nature' and Other Images of Wide Scope." In *Creativity, Psychology and the History of Science*, ed. H. E. Gruber and K. Bödeker, 241–57. Dordrecht: Springer.

Gundling, T. 2005. *First in Line: Tracing Our Ape Ancestry*. New Haven, CT: Yale University Press.

Gysel, C. 1983. "Les relations du jeune Blumenbach avec Camper vieillissant." *Histoire des Sciences Médicales* 17.2: 135–39.

Haeckel, E. 1866. *Generelle Morphologie der Organismen*. 2 vols. Berlin: Walter de Gruyter.

___. 1868. *Natürliche Schöpfungs-Geschichte: Gemeinverständliche wissenschaftliche Vorträge über die Entwickelungs-Lehre im Allgemeinen und diejenige von Darwin, Goethe und Lamarck im Besonderen, über die Anwendung derselben auf den Ursprung des Menschen und andere damit zusammenhängende Grundfragen der Naturwissenschaft*. Berlin: Georg Reimer.

___. 1870. *Natürliche Schöpfungs-Geschichte: Gemeinverständliche wissenschaftliche Vorträge über die Entwickelungs-Lehre im Allgemeinen und diejenige von Darwin, Goethe und Lamarck im Besonderen* [...]. 2nd ed. Berlin: Georg Reimer.

___. 1874. *Anthropogenie oder Entwickelungsgeschichte des Menschen: Gemeinverständliche wissenschaftliche Vorträge über die Grundzüge der menschlichen Keimes- und Stammes-Geschichte*. Leipzig: Engelmann.

___. 1889. *Natürliche Schöpfungs-Geschichte: Gemeinverständliche wissenschaftliche Vorträge über die Entwickelungs-Lehre im Allgemeinen und diejenige von Darwin, Goethe und Lamarck im Besonderen* [...]. 8th ed. Berlin: Georg Reimer.

___. 1898. *Natürliche Schöpfungs-Geschichte: Gemeinverständliche wissenschaftliche Vorträge über die Entwickelungs-Lehre im Allgemeinen und diejenige von Darwin, Goethe und Lamarck im Besonderen* [...]. 9th ed. Berlin: Georg Reimer.

Hanke, C. 2007. *Zwischen Auflösung und Fixierung: Zur Konstitution von 'Rasse' und 'Geschlecht' in der physischen Anthropologie um 1900*. Bielefeld: Transcript.

Harlan, D. 2018. "Thomas Bateman, *Crania Britannica*, and Archaeological Chronology." *European Journal of Archaeology* 21.1: 57–77, https://doi.org/10.1017/eaa.2017.39

Harney, É., N. Patterson, D. Reich, et al. 2021. "Assessing the Performance of qpAdm: A Statistical Tool for Studying Population Admixture." *Genetics* 217.4: 1–17, https://doi.org/10.1093/genetics/iyaa045

Harney É., K. Sirak, J. Sedig, et al. 2023. "Ethical Considerations When Co-Analyzing Ancient DNA and Data from Private Genetic Databases." *The American Journal of Human Genetics* 110.9: 1447–53, https://doi.org/10.1016/j.ajhg.2023.06.011

Hartkopf, H. 2012. *Franz Weidenreich, ein pfälzischer Weltbürger: Arzt, Politiker, Menschenforscher.* Ubstadt-Weiher: Verlag Regionalkultur.

Hawks, J., and M. H. Wolpoff. 2003. "Sixty Years of Modern Human Origins in the American Anthropological Association." *American Anthropologist* 105.1: 89–100, https://doi.org/10.1525/aa.2003.105.1.89

Heck, K. 2000. "Ahnentafel und Stammbaum: Zwei genealogische Modelle und ihre mnemotechnische Aufrüstung bei frühneuzeitlichen Dynastien." In *Seelenmaschinen: Gattungstraditionen, Funktionen und Leistungsgrenzen der Mnemotechniken vom späten Mittelalter bis zum Beginn der Moderne*, ed. J. J. Berns and W. Neuber, 563–84. Vienna: Böhlau.

___. 2002. "Das Fundament der Machtbehauptung: Die Ahnentafel als genealogische Grundstruktur der Neuzeit." In *Genealogie und Genetik: Schnittstellen zwischen Biologie und Kulturgeschichte*, ed. S. Weigel, 45–56. Berlin: Akademie Verlag.

Hellström, N. P. 2012. "Darwin and the Tree of Life: The Roots of the Evolutionary Tree." *Archives of Natural History* 39.2: 234–52, https://doi.org/10.3366/anh.2012.0092

___. 2019. *Trees of Knowledge: Science and the Shape of Genealogy*. PhD thesis, Uppsala: Uppsala Universitet.

Hellström, N. P., G. André, and M. Philippe. 2017. "Augustin Augier's Botanical Tree: Transcripts and Translations of Two Unknown Sources." *Huntia* 16.1: 17–38.

Helmreich, S. 2003. "Trees and Seas of Information: Alien Kinship and the Biopolitics of Gene Transfer in Marine Biology and Biotechnology." *American Ethnologist* 30.3: 340–58, https://doi.org/10.1525/ae.2003.30.3.340

___. 2009. *Alien Ocean: Anthropological Voyages in Microbial Seas*. Berkeley, CA: University of California Press, https://doi.org/10.1525/9780520942608

Herder, J. G. 1785. *Ideen zur Philosophie der Geschichte der Menschheit*. 4 vols., I. Riga: Hartknoch.

Herrnstein, R. J., and C. Murray. 1994. *The Bell Curve: Intelligence and Class Structure in American Life*. New York: Free Press.

Hieke, T. 2003. *Die Genealogien der Genesis*. Freiburg i. B.: Herder.

Higton, H. 2014. "Instruments and Illustration: The Use of Images in Edmund Gunter's *De Sectore et Radio*." In *Observing the World through Images: Diagrams and Figures in the Early-Modern Arts and Sciences*, ed. N. Jardine and I. Fay, 180–200. Leiden: Brill.

Hird, D. 1903. *An Easy Outline of Evolution*. London: Watts.

His, W., and L. Rütimeyer. 1864. *Crania helvetica: Sammlung Schweizerischer Schädelformen*. Basel: H. Georg.

Hitchcock, E. 1840. *Elementary Geology*. Amherst: J. S. and C. Adams.

Hoeven, J. v. d. 1860. *Catalogus craniorum diversarum gentium*. Lugduni Batavorum: E. J. Brill.

Holliday, T. W. 2003. "Species Concepts, Reticulation, and Human Evolution." *Current Anthropology* 44.5: 653–73, https://doi.org/10.1086/377663

Hooton, E. A. 1931. *Up from the Ape*. New York: Macmillan.

___. 1935. "Homo Sapiens – Whence and Whither." *Science*, New Series, 82.2115: 19–31.

___. 1946 [1931]. *Up from the Ape*. Rev. 2nd ed. New York: Macmillan.

Horst, M. 1913. *Die 'natürlichen' Grundstämme der Menschheit*. Hildburghausen: N.p.

Hoßfeld, U. 2005. *Geschichte der biologischen Anthropologie in Deutschland: Von den Anfängen bis zur Nachkriegszeit*. Stuttgart: Steiner.

Howells, W. W. 1947. "Review of *Apes, Giants and Man*, by F. Weidenreich." *American Antiquity* 12.4: 277.

___. 1959. *Mankind in the Making: The Story of Human Evolution*. New York: Doubleday.

___. 1973a. *Cranial Variation in Man: A Study by Multivariate Analysis of Patterns of Difference Among Recent Human Populations*. Cambridge, MA: Harvard University Press.

___. 1973b. "Measures of Population Distances." In *Methods and Theories of Anthropological Genetics*, ed. M. H. Crawford and P. L. Workman, 159–76. Albuquerque, NM: University of New Mexico Press.

___. 1989. *Skull Shapes and the Map: Craniometric Analyses in the Dispersion of Modern Homo*. Cambridge, MA: Harvard University Press.

Hoyme, L. E. 1953. "Physical Anthropology and Its Instruments: An Historical Study." *Southwestern Journal of Anthropology* 9.4: 408–430.

Hrdlička, A. 1927. "The Neanderthal Phase of Man." *Journal of the Royal Anthropological Institute of Great Britain and Ireland* 57.2: 249–74.

Humboldt, A. v. 1814. *Researches, Concerning the Institutions & Monuments of the Ancient Inhabitants of America, With Descriptions and Views of Some of the Most Striking Scenes in the Cordilleras!*, trans. H. M. Williams. 2 vols. London: Longman, Hurst, Rees, Orme and Brown, J. Murray and H. Colburn.

Huson, D. H., and D. Bryant. 2006. "Application of Phylogenetic Networks in Evolutionary Studies." *Molecular Biology and Evolution* 23.2: 254–67.

Huxley, J. S. 1938a. "Species Formation and Geographical Isolation." *Proceedings of the Linnean Society of London* 150.4: 253–64.

___. 1938b. "Clines: An Auxiliary Taxonomic Principle." *Nature* 142.3587: 219–20.

___ (ed.). 1940. *The New Systematics*. Oxford: Clarendon Press.

Huxley, J. S., and A. C. Haddon. 1935. *We Europeans: A Survey of 'Racial' Problems*. London: Jonathan Cape.

Huxley, T. H. 1863. *Evidence as to Man's Place in Nature*. London: Williams and Norgate.

___. 1865. "On the Methods and Results of Ethnology." *Fortnightly Review* 1.1: 257–77.

___. 1869. *An Introduction to the Classification of Animals*. London: Churchill.

Huxley, L. (ed.). 1918. *Life and Letters of Sir Joseph Dalton Hooker.* 2 vols. London: John Murray.

Illies, J. 1983. "Im Wunderwald der Stammbäume: Dendrologie einer Illusion." In *Evolution – kritisch gesehen*, ed. A. Locker, 97–124. Salzburg: A. Pustet.

Jackson, J. P. 2001. "'In Ways Unacademical': The Reception of Carleton S. Coon's 'The Origin of Races'." *Journal of the History of Biology* 34.2: 247–85.

Jackson, J. P., and D. J. Depew. 2017. *Darwinism, Democracy, and Race: American Anthropology and Evolutionary Biology in the Twentieth Century*. Milton Park: Routledge, https://doi.org/10.4324/9781315210803

James, E. O. 1966. *The Tree of Life: An Archaeological Study*. Leiden: E. J. Brill.

Jardine, N., and I. Fay (eds.). 2014. *Observing the World through Images: Diagrams and Figures in the Early-Modern Arts and Sciences*. Leiden: Brill, https://doi.org/10.1163/9789004263857

Jensen, A. 1969. "How Much Can We Boost IQ and Scholastic Achievement?" *Harvard Educational Review* 39.1: 1–123.

___. 1998. *The g Factor: The Science of Mental Ability*. Westport, CT: Praeger.

Johanson, D., and M. Edey. 1981. *Lucy: The Beginnings of Humankind. The Dramatic Discovery of Our Oldest Human Ancestor – and the Controversial Change It Makes in Our View of Human Origins.* New York: Simon and Schuster.

Johnson, M. J., D. C. Wallace, S. D. Ferris, et al. 1983. "Radiation of Human Mitochondria DNA Types Analyzed by Restriction Endonuclease Cleavage Patterns." *Journal of Molecular Evolution* 19.3–4: 255–71.

Jones, E. D., and E. Bösl. 2021. "Ancient Human DNA: A History of Hype (Then and Now)." *Journal of Social Archaeology* 21.2: 236–55.

Jones, F. W. 1919. "The Origin of Man." In *Animal Life and Human Progress*, ed. A. Dendy, 99–132. London: Constable.

___. 1929. *Man's Place Among the Mammals*. London: E. Arnold.

Jones, W. 1999 [1807] [1792]. "A Discourse on the Origin and Families of Nations." In *The Works of Sir William Jones: With a Life of the Author, by Lord*

Teignmouth, ed. J. Shore, 13 vols., III, 185–204. London: John Stockdale and John Walker.

Junker, Th. 2019. "Blumenbach's Theory of Human Races and the Natural Unity of Mankind." In *Johann Friedrich Blumenbach: Race and Natural History, 1750–1850*, ed. N. Rupke and G. Lauer, 96–112. London: Routledge.

Kaiser, D. 2005. *Drawing Theories Apart: The Dispersion of Feynman Diagrams in Postwar Physics*. Chicago, IL: University of Chicago Press.

Kakaliouras, A. 2021. "Ignoble Trophies: The Samuel G. Morton Collection, Repatriation, and Redress for the 21st Century." *History of Anthropology Review* 45, https://histanthro.org/news/observations/ignoble-trophies/

Karliczek, A., and M. Jank. 2010. "Quantifizieren, Typisieren, Hierarchisieren? Peter Camper und der Winkel der Natur." In *Natur im Kasten: Lichtbild, Schattenriss, Umzeichnung und Naturselbstdruck um 1800*, ed. O. Breidbach, K. Klinger, and A. Karliczek, 59–78. Jena: Ernst Haeckel Haus.

Keel, T. D. 2013. "Religion, Polygenism and the Early Science of Human Origins." *History of the Human Sciences* 26.2: 3–32.

Keith, A. 1925 [1915]. *The Antiquity of Man*. 2nd ed. 2 vols. London: Williams and Norgate.

___. 1934. *The Construction of Man's Family Tree*. London: Watts.

___. 1937. "History from Caves: A New Theory of the Origin of the Modern Races of Mankind." *British Speleological Association, Caves and Caving*, 1.1: 1–6.

___. 1947. "Review of *Apes, Giants and Man*, by Franz Weidenreich." *Man* 47.7: 103–104.

___. 1948. *A New Theory of Human Evolution*. London: Watts.

___. 1950. *An Autobiography*. London: Watts.

Kellner, B. 2004. *Ursprung und Kontinuität: Studien zum genealogischen Wissen im Mittelalter*. Munich: W. Fink.

Kevles, D. J. 1995 [1985]. *In the Name of Eugenics: Genetics and the Uses of Human Heredity*. Cambridge, MA: Harvard University Press.

Kimmelman, B. A. 1983. "The American Breeders' Association: Genetics and Eugenics in an Agricultural Context, 1903–13." *Social Studies of Science* 13.2: 163–204.

Kirk, R. L. 1969. "Biochemical Polymorphism and the Evolution of the Human Races." In *Proceedings VIIIth International Congress of Anthropological and Ethnological Sciences, 1968, Tokyo and Kyoto*, 159–76. Tokyo: Science Council of Japan.

Klaatsch, H. 1920. *Der Werdegang der Menschheit und die Entstehung der Kultur*, ed. A. Heilborn. Berlin: Bong.

Klapisch-Zuber, C. 2004. *Stammbäume: Eine illustrierte Geschichte der Ahnenkunde.* Munich: Knesebeck.

Klein, R. G. 2019. "Population Structure and the Evolution of *Homo sapiens* in Africa." *Evolutionary Anthropology: Issues, News, and Reviews* 28.4: 179–88, https://doi.org/10.1002/evan.21788

Klein, U. 2003. *Experiments, Models, Paper Tools: Cultures of Organic Chemistry in the Nineteenth Century*. Stanford, CA: Stanford University Press.

Kowal, E. 2023. *Haunting Biology: Science and Indigeneity in Australia*. Durham, NC: Duke University Press, https://doi.org/10.1353/book.115390

Kozlov M. 2024. "'All of Us' Genetics Chart Stirs Unease Over Controversial Depiction of Race." *Nature*, 23 February 2024, https://doi.org/10.1038/d41586-024-00568-w

Krogman, W. M. 1947. "Review of *Apes, Giants and Man*, by Franz Weidenreich." *American Anthropologist* 49.1: 115–18.

___. 1949. "Review of *Human Ancestry from a Genetical Point of View*, by R. Ruggles Gates." *American Association for the Advancement of Science* 110.2844: 20–21.

Kuhlwilm M., I. Gronau, M. J. Hubisz, et al. 2016. "Ancient Gene Flow from Early Modern Humans into Eastern Neanderthals." *Nature* 530.7591: 429–33, https://doi.org/10.1038/nature16544

Kull, K. 2003. "Ladder, Tree, Web: The Ages of Biological Understanding." *Sign System Studies* 31.2: 589–603, https://doi.org/10.12697/sss.2003.31.2.15

Lalouel, J.-M. 1974. "Letter: Controversial Issues in Human Population Genetics." *American Journal of Human Genetics* 26.2: 262–65.

Lamarck, J.-B. 1809. *Philosophie Zoologique* [...]. 2 vols., I. Paris: Duminil-Lesueur.

___. 1815. *Histoire naturelle des animaux sans vertèbres* [...]. 7 vols., I. Paris: Verdière.

Lan, T., and C. Lindqvist. 2019. "Technical Advances and Challenges in Genome-Scale Analysis of Ancient DNA." In *Paleogenomics: Genome-Scale Analysis of Ancient DNA*, ed. C. Lindqvist and O. P. Rajora, 3–29. Cham: Springer International Publishing.

Larson, J. L. 1994. *Interpreting Nature: The Science of Living Form from Linnaeus to Kant*. Baltimore: The Johns Hopkins University Press.

Lartet, É., and H. Christy. 1875 [1865–75]. *Reliquiae aquitanicae: Being Contributions to the Archaeology and Palaeontology of Périgord and the Adjoining Provinces of Southern France*, ed. T. R. Jones. London: Williams and Norgate.

Lasker, G. W. 1976. "What Is Molecular Anthropology?" In *Molecular Anthropology: Genes and Proteins in the Evolutionary Ascent of the Primates*, ed. M. Goodman, R. E. Tashian, and J. H. Tashian. New York: Plenum.

Lathrop, G. M. 1982. "Evolutionary Trees and Admixture: Phylogenetic Inference When Some Populations Are Hybridized." *Annals of Human Genetics* 46.3: 245–55.

Latour, B. 1987. *Science in Action: How to Follow Scientists and Engineers Through Society*. Cambridge, MA: Harvard University Press.

Lawrence, W. 1822. *Lectures on Physiology, Zoology, and the Natural History of Man*. London: J. Smith.

Leakey, L. 1934. *Adam's Ancestors: An Up-to-date Outline of What Is Known about the Origin of Man*. London: Methuen.

Lefèvre, W. 2001. "Natural or Artificial Systems? The Eighteenth-Century Controversy on Classification of Animals and Plants and Its Philosophical Contexts." In *Between Leibniz, Newton, and Kant: Philosophy and Science in the Eighteenth Century*, ed. W. Lefèvre, 191–209. Dordrecht: Springer Netherlands.

Legassick, M., and C. Rassool. 2000. *Skeletons in the Cupboard: South African Museums and the Trade in Human Remains, 1907–1917*. Kapstadt: South African Museum.

Leonardi, M., P. Librado, C. D. Sarkissian, et al. 2017. "Evolutionary Patterns and Processes: Lessons from Ancient DNA." *Systematic Biology*, 66.1: e1–e29, https://doi.org/10.1093/sysbio/syw059

Lepenies, W. 1976. *Das Ende der Naturgeschichte: Wandel kultureller Selbstverständlichkeiten in den Wissenschaften des 18. und 19. Jahrhunderts*. München: Hanser.

Lesson, R. P., and P. Garnot (eds.). 1826. *Voyage autour du monde: Exécuté par Ordre du Roi, Sur la Corvette de Sa Majesté, la Coquille, pendant les années 1822, 1823, 1824 et 1825*. 7 vols., I, Part 1: *Zoologie*. Paris: Arthus Bertrand.

Li, J. Z., D. M. Absher, H. Tang, et al. 2008. "Worldwide Human Relationships Inferred from Genome-Wide Patterns of Variation." *Science* 319.5866: 1100–104, https://doi.org/10.1126/science.1153717

Lima, M. 2014. *The Book of Trees: Visualizing Branches of Knowledge*. New York: Princeton Architectural Press.

Lipson, M. 2020. "Applying F4-Statistics and Admixture Graphs: Theory and Examples." *Molecular Ecology Resources* 20.6: 1658–67, https://doi.org/10.1111/1755-0998.13230

Liu, Y., E. A. Bennett, and Q. Fu. 2022. "Evolving Ancient DNA Techniques and the Future of Human History." *Cell* 185.15: 2632–35, https://doi.org/10.1016/j.cell.2022.06.009

Liu, Y., X. Mao, J. Krause, et al. 2021. "Insights into Human History from the First Decade of Ancient Human Genomics." *Science* 373.6562: 1479–84, https://doi.org/10.1126/science.abi8202

Livingstone, D. N. 2008. *Adam's Ancestors: Race, Religion, and the Politics of Human Origins*. Baltimore, MD: Johns Hopkins University Press.

___. 2010. "Cultural Politics and the Racial Cartographies of Human Origins." *Transactions of the Institute of British Geographers* 35.2: 204–221, https://doi.org/10.1111/j.1475-5661.2009.00377.x

Livingstone, F. B. 1962. "On the Non-Existence of Human Races." *Current Anthropology* 3.3: 279–81, https://doi.org/10.1086/200290

___. 1991. "Phylogenies and the Forces of Evolution." *American Journal of Human Biology* 3.2: 83–89, https://doi.org/10.1002/ajhb.1310030202

Loog, L. 2020. "Sometimes Hidden but Always There: The Assumptions Underlying Genetic Inference of Demographic Histories." *Philosophical Transactions of the Royal Society B: Biological Sciences* 376.1816: 1–10, https://doi.org/10.1098/rstb.2019.0719

López, S., L. van Dorp, and G. Hellenthal. 2015. "Human Dispersal Out of Africa: A Lasting Debate." *Evolutionary Bioinformatics* 11.S2: 57–68, https://doi.org/10.4137/ebo.s33489

Lovejoy, A. O. 1964. *The Great Chain of Being: A Study of the History of an Idea*. Cambridge, MA: Harvard University Press.

Lubbock, J. 1865. *Pre-Historic Times: As Illustrated by Ancient Remains, and the Manners and Customs of Modern Savages*. London: Williams and Norgate.

Lubran, M. 1951. "Review of *Human Ancestry from a Genetical Point of View*, by R. Ruggles Gates." *Man* 51.6: 81–82.

Lucae, J. C. G. 1861. *Zur Morphologie der Rassen-Schädel: Einleitende Bemerkungen und Beiträge, ein Sendschreiben an* [...] *Carl Ernst v. Baer*. Frankfurt a. M.: H. L. Brönner.

Lüthy, C., and A. Smets. 2009. "Words, Lines, Diagrams, Images: Towards a History of Scientific Imagery." *Early Science and Medicine* 14.1–3: 398–439, https://doi.org/10.1163/157338209x425632

Lyell, C. 1832. *Principles of Geology, Being an Attempt to Explain the Former Changes of the Earth's Surface, by Reference to Causes now in Operation*. 3 vols., II. London: John Murray.

___. 1863. *The Geological Evidences of the Antiquity of Man With Remarks on the Origin of Species by Variation*. London: John Murray.

Mackenzie, G. S. 1820. *Illustrations of Phrenology: With Engravings*. Edinburgh: Archibald Constable.

Mackintosh, J., and S. G. Morton. 1836. *Principles of Pathology and Practice of Physic*. 2 vols. Philadelphia, PN: Key and Biddle.

MacLean, C. J., and P. L. Workman. 1973a. "Genetic Studies on Hybrid Populations. I. Individual Estimates of Ancestry and Their Relation to Quantitative Traits." *Annals of Human Genetics* 36.3: 341–51.

___. 1973b. "Genetic Studies on Hybrid Populations. II. Estimation of the Distribution of Ancestry." *Annals of Human Genetics* 36.4: 459–65.

Maier, R., P. Flegontov, O. Flegontova, et al. 2023. "On the Limits of Fitting Complex Models of Population History to F-Statistics." *eLife* 12.4: 1–62, https://doi.org/10.7554/eLife.85492

Marinus, J. R. 1846. "Éloge de A. van den Spieghel, lu dans la séance publique annuelle de l'Académie Royale de Médecine de Belgique, le 29 novembre 1846." *Bulletin de l'Académie Royale de Médecine de Belgique* 5.10: 1–17.

Marks, J. 2010. "The Two 20th-Century Crises of Racial Anthropology." In *Histories of American Physical Anthropology in the Twentieth Century*, ed. M. A. Little and K. A. R. Kennedy, 187–206. Lanham, MD: Lexington Books.

Mayr, E. 1942. *Systematics and the Origin of Species*. New York: Columbia University Press.

___. 1950. "Taxonomic Categories in Fossil Hominids." *Cold Spring Harbor Symposia on Quantitative Biology* 15.1: 109–118.

___. 1962. "Review of *The Origin of Races*, by C. S. Coon." *Science* 138, no. 3538: 420–22.

___. 1963. "The Taxonomic Evaluation of Fossil Hominids." In *Classification and Human Evolution*, ed. S. L. Washburn, 332–46. Chicago, IL: Aldine.

Mazumdar, P. 1991. *Eugenics, Human Genetics and Human Failings: The Eugenic Society, Its Sources and Its Critics in Britain*. London, Routledge.

"Medical Genetics and Eugenics. Volume 2." [n.a.] 1944. *Journal of the American Medical Association* 124.12: 812.

Meigs, J. A. 1861. "On the Mensuration of the Human Skull." *The North American Medico-Chirurgical Review* 5.5: 837–61.

Meijer, M. C. 1999. *Race and Aesthetics in the Anthropology of Petrus Camper (1722–89)*. Amsterdam: Rodopi, Brill.

Mellars, P. 2006. "Going East: New Genetic and Archaeological Perspectives on the Modern Human Colonization of Eurasia." *Science* 313.5788: 796–800.

Michael, J. S. 2017. "Nuance Lost in Translation: Interpretations of J. F. Blumenbach's Anthropology in the English-Speaking World." *N.T.M.* 25.3: 281–309, https://doi.org/10.1007/s00048-017-0173-8

___. 2020a. "Porträts von interessanten Personen: A New Look at J. F. Blumenbach's Typological Labels and the Exemplars He Discussed in His Anthropological Research." *Annals of the History and Philosophy of Biology* 25: 65–101.

___. 2020b. "An 'American Humboldt'? Memorializing Philadelphia Physician and Race Supremacist Samuel George Morton." *Pennsylvania History: A Journal of Mid-Atlantic Studies* 87.2: 279–312.

___. 2021a. "How Blumenbach's Illustrations of Human Racial Variations Were Manipulated" (Poster), https://www.academia.edu/60096372/How_Blumenbachs_Illustrations_of_Human_Racial_Variation_were_Manipulated

___. 2021b. "Black Philadelphians in the Samuel George Morton Cranial Collection." *Program on Race, Science & Society*, 15 February 2021, https://prss.sas.upenn.edu/projects/penn-medicines-role/black-philadelphians-samuel-george-morton-cranial-collection

___. 2023. "'Vedado, donde no se entierran más que negros bozals': The Burial Grounds of 55 Enslaved Africans Whose Skulls Were Acquired by S. G. Morton." *Pennandslaveryproject.org*, https://www.academia.edu/97910431/_Vedado_donde_no_se_entierran_m%C3%A1s_que_negros_bozals_The_burial_grounds_of_55_enslaved_Africans_whose_skulls_were_acquired_by_S_G_Morton

Milam, E. L. 2010. *Looking for a Few Good Males: Female Choice in Evolutionary Biology*. Baltimore, MD: Johns Hopkins University Press.

Milam, E. L., and S. Seth (eds.). 2021. *British Journal for the History of Science Themes* 6. Special Issue (Descent of Darwin: Race, Sex, and Human Nature), https://www.cambridge.org/core/journals/bjhs-themes/volume/9D960225004D54E16FAAA9F1CBEB64FA

Mitchell, P. W. (ed.). 2021. *History of Anthropology Review* 45. Special Issue (The Morton Cranial Collection and the Legacies of Scientific Racism in Museums), https://histanthro.org/news/observations/morton/

Mitchell, P. W., and J. S. Michael. 2019. "Bias, Brains, and Skulls: Tracing the Legacy of Scientific Racism in the Nineteenth-Century Works of Samuel George Morton and Friedrich Tiedemann." In *Embodied Difference: Divergent Bodies in Public Discourse*, ed. J. A. Thomas and Ch. Jackson, 77–98. Lanham: Lexington Books.

Morant, G. M. 1934. "A Biometrician's View of Race in Man." *Man* 34.7: 99–105.

___. 1939. *The Races of Central Europe. A Footnote to History*. London: George Allen and Unwin.

Morgan, L. H. 1871. *Systems of Consanguinity and Affinity of the Human Family.* Washington, DC: Smithsonian Institution.

Morozova, I., P. Flegontov, A. S. Mikheyev, et al. 2016. "Toward High-Resolution Population Genomics Using Archaeological Samples." *DNA Research* 23.4: 295–310.

Morrison, D. 2014a. "Is the Tree of Life the Best Metaphor, Model, or Heuristic for Phylogenetics?" *Systematic Biology* 63.4: 628–38, https://doi.org/10.1093/sysbio/syu026

___. 2014b. "Phylogenetic Networks: A Review of Methods to Display Evolutionary History." *Annual Research & Review in Biology* 4.10: 1518–43, https://doi.org/10.9734/arrb/2014/8230

___. 2016. "Genealogies: Pedigrees and Phylogenies Are Reticulating Networks Not Just Divergent Trees." *Evolutionary Biology* 43.4: 456–73, https://doi.org/10.1007/s11692-016-9376-5

Morton, N. 1974. "Letter: Controversial Issues in Human Population Genetics." *American Journal of Human Genetics* 26.2: 259–62.

Morton, S. G. 1834. *Synopsis of the Organic Remains of the Cretaceous Group of the United States. Illustrated by Nineteen Plates. To Which Is Added an Appendix, Containing a Tabular View of the Tertiary Fossils Hitherto Discovered in North America*. Philadelphia, PN: Key and Biddle.

___. 1839. *Crania americana; or, A Comparative View of the Skulls of Various Aboriginal Nations of North and South America. To Which Is Prefixed an Essay on the Varieties of the Human Species*. Philadelphia, PN: J. Dobson.

___. 1844. *Crania aegyptiaca; or, Observations on Egyptian Ethnography, Derived from Anatomy, History and the Monuments*. Philadelphia, PN: John Penington.

___. 1849a. *Catalogue of Skulls of Man, and the Inferior Animals, in the Collection of Samuel George Morton, M.D., Penn. and Edinb*. 3rd ed. Philadelphia, PN: Merrihew and Thompson.

___. 1849b. "Observations on the Size of the Brain in Various Races and Families of Man." *Proceedings of the Academy of Natural Sciences* 4: 221–24.

Mudford, P. G. 1968. "William Lawrence and The Natural History of Man." *Journal of the History of Ideas* 29.3: 430–36.

Müller-Wille, S. 2014. "Race and History: Comments from an Epistemological Point of View." *Science, Technology, & Human Values* 39.4: 597–606, https://doi.org/10.1177/0162243913517759

___. 2021. "Corners, Tables, Lines: Towards a Diagrammatics of Race." *Nuncius* 36.3: 517–31, https://doi.org/10.1163/18253911-03603001

Narasimhan, V. M., N. Patterson, P. Moorjani, et al. 2019. "The Formation of Human Populations in South and Central Asia." *Science* 365.6457: eaat7487, https://doi.org/10.1126/science.aat7487

National Academies of Sciences, Engineering, and Medicine; Division of Behavioral and Social Sciences and Education; Health and Medicine Division; Committee on Population; Board on Health Sciences Policy; Committee on the Use of Race, Ethnicity, and Ancestry as Population Descriptors in Genomics Research. 2023. *Using Population Descriptors in Genetics and Genomics Research: A New Framework for an Evolving Field*. Washington, DC: National Academies Press, https://www.ncbi.nlm.nih.gov/books/NBK592836/

Nei, M. 1985. "Human Evolution at the Molecular Level." In *Population Genetics and Molecular Evolution: Papers Marking the Sixtieth Birthday of Motoo Kimura*, ed. T. Ohta and K. Aoki, 41–64. Tokyo: Japan Science Society Press.

Nicolucci, G. 1864. *La stirpe ligure in Italia ne' tempi antichi e ne' moderni*. Napoli: Stamperia del Fibreno.

Nielsen, R., J. M. Akey, M. Jakobsson, et al. 2017. "Tracing the Peopling of the World Through Genomics." *Nature* 541.7637: 302–310.

Nott, J. C., and G. R. Gliddon. 1854. *Types of Mankind: or Ethnological Researches, Based Upon the Ancient Monuments, Paintings, Sculptures, and Crania of Races, and Upon Their Natural, Geographical, Philological and Biblical History, Illustrated by Selections from the Inedited Papers of Samuel George Morton and by Additional Contributions from L. Agassiz, W. Usher, and H. S. Patterson.* Philadelphia, PN: J. B. Lippincott, Grambo and Co.

Nott, J. C., and G. R. Gliddon. 1857. *Indigenous Races of the Earth: Or New Chapters of Ethological Inquiry* [...] *Contributed by Alfred Maury, Francis Pulszky, and J. Aitken Meigs*. Philadelphia, PN: J. B. Lippincott.

O'Hara, R. J. 1991. "Representations of the Natural System in the Nineteenth Century." *Biology and Philosophy* 6.2: 255–74.

Oken, L. 1805. *Abriss des Systems der Biologie*. Göttingen: Vandenhoek and Ruprecht.

___. 1813. *Okens Lehrbuch der Naturgeschichte*. 3 vols., I. Jena: August Schmid.

O'Malley, M. A., and E. V. Koonin. 2011. "How Stands the Tree of Life a Century and a Half after *The Origin*?" *Biology Direct* 6.1: 32, https://doi.org/10.1186/1745-6150-6-32

O'Malley, M. A., W. Martin, and J. Dupré. 2010. "The Tree of Life: Introduction to an Evolutionary Debate." *Biology & Philosophy* 25.4: 441–53.

Opinion, BuzzFeed. 2018. "Opinion: How Not to Talk About Race and Genetics." *BuzzFeed News*, 30 March 2018, https://www.buzzfeednews.com/article/bfopinion/race-genetics-david-reich

Orlando, L., R. Allaby, P. Skoglund, et al. 2021. "Ancient DNA Analysis." *Nature Reviews Methods Primers* 1.1: 1–26, https://doi.org/10.1038/s43586-020-00011-0

Osborn, H. F. 1915. *Men of the Old Stone Age: Their Environment, Life and Art.* New York: Scribner.

___. 1927. *Man Rises to Parnassus: Critical Epochs in the Prehistory of Man.* Princeton, NJ: Princeton University Press.

___. 1930. "The Discovery of Tertiary Man." *Science* 71.1827: 1–7.

Osborn, H. F., and E. G. Conklin. 1922. "Proposed Legislation Against the Teaching of Evolution." *Bulletin of the American Association of University Professors (1915–1955)* 8.4: 11–7.

Ospovat, D. 1976. "The Influence of Karl Ernst von Baer's Embryology, 1828–1859: A Reappraisal in Light of Richard Owen's and William B. Carpenter's 'Palaeontological Application of 'Von Baer's Law'." *Journal of the History of Biology* 9.1: 1–28.

"Our Readers Write." [n.a.] 1962. *Current Anthropology* 3.5: 449–50.

Pääbo, S. 2003. "The Mosaic That Is Our Genome." *Nature* 421.6921: 409–412, https://doi.org/10.1038/nature01400

Pallas, P. S. 1766. *Elenchus zoophytorum sistens generum adumbrationes generaliores et specierum cognitarum succintas descriptiones, cum selectis auctorum synonymis.* Frankfurt a.M.: Franciscum Varrentrapp.

Panofsky, A. 2014. *Misbehaving Science: Controversy and the Development of Behavior Genetics.* Chicago, IL: University of Chicago Press.

Pathak, A. K. 2020. "Identifying Admixture and Genetic Ancestry in Human Populations via Genetic Drift Pattern." *Polymorphism* 4.1: 5–20.

Patterson, N., P. Moorjani, Y. Luo, et al. 2012. "Ancient Admixture in Human History." *Genetics* 192.3: 1065–1093, https://doi.org/10.1534/genetics.112.145037

Paul, D. B. 2006. "Darwin, Social Darwinism and Eugenics." In *The Cambridge Companion to Darwin. Part II – Historical Contexts*, ed. G. Radick, 214–39. Cambridge, UK: Cambridge University Press.

Pearson, K. 1901. "LIII. On Lines and Planes of Closest Fit to Systems of Points in Space." *The London, Edinburgh, and Dublin Philosophical Magazine and Journal of Science* 2.11: 559–72.

Peirce, C. S. 1885. "On the Algebra of Logic: A Contribution to the Philosophy of Notation [Continued in Vol. 7, No. 3]." *American Journal of Mathematics* 7.2: 180–96.

___. 1906. "Prolegomena to an Apology for Pragmaticism." *The Monist* 16.4: 492–546.

___. 1998 [1903]. "A Syllabus of Certain Topics of Logic." In *The Essential Peirce: Selected Philosophical Writings*, ed. the Peirce Edition Project, 2 vols., II, 267–88. Bloomington, IN: Indiana University Press.

Philpot, J. H. 1897. *The Sacred Tree.* London: Macmillan.

Pickrell, J. K., and J. K. Pritchard. 2012. "Inference of Population Splits and Mixtures from Genome-Wide Allele Frequency Data." *PLOS Genetics* 8.11: 1–17, https://doi.org/10.1371/journal.pgen.1002967

Pickrell, J. K., and D. Reich. 2014. "Toward a New History and Geography of Human Genes Informed by Ancient DNA." *Trends in Genetics*: 30.9: 377–89, https://doi.org/10.1016/j.tig.2014.07.007

Pierer, J. F., and L. Choulant. 1816. *Medizinisches Realwörterbuch: Zum Handgebrauch practischer Aerzte und Wundärzte und zu belehrender Nachweisung für gebildete Personen aller Stände*. 8 vols., I. Leipzig: Brockhaus.

Pietsch, T. W. 2012. *Trees of Life: A Visual History of Evolution*. Baltimore, MD: Johns Hopkins University Press.

Pouchet, G. 1858. *De la pluralité des races humaines: Essai anthropologique*. Paris: J. B. Baillière.

Poskett, J. 2015. "National Types: The Transatlantic Publication and Reception of *Crania Americana* (1839)." *History of Science* 53.3: 264–95, https://doi.org/10.1177/0073275315580955

___. 2019. *Materials of the Mind: Phrenology, Race, and the Global History of Science, 1815–1920*. Chicago, IL: The University of Chicago Press.

Prichard, J. C. 1813. *Researches into the Physical History of Man*. London: John and Arthur Arch.

___. 1833. "Abstract of a Comparative Review of Philological and Physical Researches as Applied to the History of the Human Species. By J. C. Prichard, M.D. F.R.S." In *Report of the First and Second Meetings of the British Association for the Advancement of Science; at York in 1831, and at Oxford in 1832*, ed. Members of the Report of the British Association for the Advancement of Science, 529–44. London: John Murray.

___. 1836–47. *Researches into the Physical History of Mankind*. 3rd ed. 5 vols. London: Sherwood, Gilbert, and Piper.

___. 1836. *Researches into the Physical History of Mankind*. 3rd ed., 5 vols., I. London: Sherwood, Gilbert, and Piper.

___. 1841. "Crania Americana [...] By Samuel George Morton [...] Communicated by Dr. Prichard, M. D." *Journal of the Geographical Society* 10.1: 552–61.

___. 1843. *The Natural History of Man*. London: H. Bailliere.

___. 1847. *Researches into the Physical History of Mankind*. 3rd ed., 5 vols., V. London: Sherwood, Gilbert, and Piper.

___. 1851. *Researches into the Physical History of Mankind*. 4th ed., 5 vols., I. London: Houlston and Stoneman.

Priest, G. 2018. "Diagramming Evolution: The Case of Darwin's Trees." *Endeavour* 42.2–3: 157–71.

Priest, G., P. Findlen, and S. De Toffoli (eds.). 2018. "Tools of Scientific Reason: The Practice of Scientific Diagramming from Antiquity to the Present." *Endeavor* 42.2–3: 49–188, https://doi.org/10.1016/j.endeavour.2018.07.001

Pritchard, J. K., M. Stephens, and P. Donnelly. 2000. "Inference of Population Structure Using Multilocus Genotype Data." *Genetics* 155.2: 945–59.

Prüfer, K., F. Racimo, N. Patterson, et al. 2014. "The Complete Genome Sequence of a Neanderthal from the Altai Mountains." *Nature* 505.7481: 43–49, https://doi.org/10.1038/nature12886

Pugach, I., M. Rostislav, V. Spitsyn, et al. 2016. "The Complex Admixture History and Recent Southern Origins of Siberian Populations." *Molecular Biology and Evolution* 33.7: 1777–95, https://doi.org/10.1093/molbev/msw055

Putnam, C. 1961. *Race and Reason: A Yankee View*. Washington, DC: Public Affairs.

Quatrefages, J. L. A. de. 1861a. *Unité de l'espèce humaine*. Paris: L. Hachette.

___. 1861b. "Histoire naturelle de l'homme: Unité de l'espèce humaine. VII. Les théories polygénistes. Objections générales: Croisement des groupes humains." *Revue des deux mondes (1829–1971)* 32.2: 436–64.

Quatrefages, J. L. A. de, and J. É. Th. Hamy. 1882. *Crania ethnica: Les crânes des races humaines décris et figurés après les collections du Muséum d'Histoire Naturelle de Paris, de la Société d'Anthropologie de Paris, et les principales collections de la France et de l'étranger*. 2 vols. Paris: Librairie J. B. Baillière.

Quine, M. S. 2019. "The Destiny of Races 'Not Yet Called to Civilization': Giustiniano Nicolucci's Critique of American Polygenism and Defense of Liberal Racism." In *National Races: Transnational Power Struggles in Science and Politics, 1840s–1940s*, ed. R. McMahon, 69–104. Lincoln, NE: University of Nebraska Press, https://doi.org/10.2307/j.ctvjsf4cz.7

Radin, J. 2017. *Life on Ice: A History of New Uses for Cold Blood*. Chicago, IL: University of Chicago Press, https://doi.org/10.7208/chicago/9780226448244.001.0001

Ragan, M. A. 2009. "Trees and Networks Before and After Darwin." *Biology Direct* 4.43, https://doi.org/10.1186/1745-6150-4-43

Ragsdale, A. P., T. D. Weaver, E. G. Atkinson, et al. 2023. "A Weakly Structured Stem for Human Origins in Africa." *Nature* 617.7962: 755–63, https://doi.org/10.1038/s41586-023-06055-y

Ratcliff, M. J. 2007. "Duchesne's Strawberries: Between Growers' Practices and Academic Knowledge." In *Heredity Produced: At the Crossroads of Biology, Politics, and Culture, 1500–1870*, ed. S. Müller-Wille, 205–228. Cambridge, MA: MIT Press, https://doi.org/10.7551/mitpress/3482.003.0014

Reardon, J. 2005. *Race to the Finish: Identity and Governance in an Age of Genomics*. Princeton, NJ: Princeton University Press.

Redfield, A. M. 1858. *Zoölogical Science, or Nature in Living Forms*. New York: E. B. and E. C. Kellogg.

Redman, S. J. 2016. *Bone Rooms: From Scientific Racism to Human Prehistory in Museums*. Cambridge, MA: Harvard University Press, https://doi.org/10.4159/9780674969711

Regal, B. 2002. *Henry Fairfield Osborn: Race and the Search for the Origins of Man*. London: Routledge.

Reich, D. 2018a. "Who We Are and How We Got Here." *The Summit on Pike, Seattle*, 17 October 2018, Town Hall, Seattle, *YouTube* (21 December 2018), https://www.youtube.com/watch?v=Ef4OlJwzxxE

___. 2018b. "How Genetics Is Changing Our Understanding of Race." *The New York Times*, 23 March 2018, https://www.nytimes.com/2018/03/23/opinion/sunday/genetics-race.html

___. 2019. *Who We Are and How We Got Here: Ancient DNA and the New Science of the Human Past*. Oxford: Oxford University Press.

Reich, D., R. E. Green, M. Kircher, et al. 2010. "Genetic History of an Archaic Hominin Group from Denisova Cave in Siberia." *Nature* 468.7327: 1053–1060, https://doi.org/10.1038/nature09710

Resendez, S. D., J. R. Bradley, D. Xu, et al. 2019. "Structural Variants in Ancient Genomes." In *Paleogenomics: Genome-Scale Analysis of Ancient DNA*, ed. C. Lindqvist and O. P. Rajora, 375–91. Cham: Springer International, https://doi.org/10.1007/13836_2018_34

Retzius, A. A. 1859 [1860]. "Present State of Ethnology in Relation to the Form of the Human Skull." In *Annual Report of the Board of Regents of the Smithsonian Institution: Showing the Operations, Expenditures, and Condition of the Institution for the Year 1859*, ed. Board of Regents, 251–70. Washington, DC: Thomas H. Ford.

Reumann, M. G., and A. Fausto-Sterling. 2001. "Notions of Heredity in the Correspondence of Edwin Grant Conklin." *Perspectives in Biology and Medicine* 44.3: 414–25, https://doi.org/10.1353/pbm.2001.0058

"Review of '*Human Ancestry' from a Genetical Point of View*, by R. Ruggles Gates." [n.a.] 1948. *Bios* 19.3: 208.

Rheinberger, H.-J. 1986. "Aspekte des Bedeutungswandels im Begriff organismischer Ähnlichkeit vom 18. zum 19. Jahrhundert." *History and Philosophy of the Life Sciences* 8.2: 237–50.

___. 1990. "Buffon: Zeit, Veränderung und Geschichte." *History and Philosophy of the Life Sciences* 12.2: 203–223.

Rheinberger, H.-J., M. Hagner, and B. Wahrig-Schmidt (eds.). 1996. *Räume des Wissens: Repräsentation, Codierung, Spur*. Berlin: De Gruyter.

Richards, R. J. 2002a. "The Linguistic Creation of Man: Charles Darwin, August Schleicher, Ernst Haeckel, and the Missing Link in Nineteenth-Century Evolutionary Theory." In *Experimenting in Tongues: Studies in Science and Language*, ed. M. Dörries, 21–48. Stanford, CA: Stanford University Press.

___. 2002b. *The Romantic Conception of Life: Science and Philosophy in the Age of Goethe*. Chicago, IL: The University of Chicago Press.

___. 2002c. *Was Hitler a Darwinian? Disputed Questions in the History of Evolutionary Theory*. Chicago, IL: The University of Chicago Press.

___. 2018. "The Beautiful Skulls of Schiller and the Georgian Girl: Quantitative and Aesthetic Scaling of the Races, 1770–1850." In *Johann Friedrich Blumenbach: Race and Natural History, 1750–1850*, ed. N. Rupke and G. Lauer, 142–76. London: Routledge, https://doi.org/10.4324/9781315184777-9

Rieppel, O. 2010. "The Series, the Network, and the Tree: Changing Metaphors of Order in Nature." *Biology & Philosophy* 25.4: 475–96, https://doi.org/10.1007/s10539-010-9216-4

Roggenbuck, S. 2005a. "Die Genealogische Idee in der vergleichenden Sprachwissenschaft des 19. Jahrhunderts: Stufen, Stammbäume, Wellen." In *Generation: Zur Genealogie des Konzepts – Konzepte von Genealogie*, ed. S. Weigel, O. Parnes, U. Vedder, et al., 289–314. Paderborn: W. Fink.

___. 2005b. *Die Wiederkehr der Bilder: Arboreszenz und Raster in der Interdisziplinären Geschichte der Sprachwissenschaft*. Tübingen: Narr Francke Attempo.

Rolle, F. 1866. *Der Mensch, seine Abstammung und Gesittung im Lichte der Darwin'schen Lehre*. Frankfurt a. M.: J. C. Hermann.

Roque, R. 2010. *Headhunting and Colonialism: Anthropology and the Circulation of Human Skulls in the Portuguese Empire, 1870–1930*. London: Palgrave Macmillan.

Rosenberg, N. A. 2004. "Distruct: A Program for the Graphical Display of Population Structure." *Molecular Ecology Notes* 4.1: 137–38, https://doi.org/10.1046/j.1471-8286.2003.00566.x

Ross, F. 1974. *Oreo*. New York: New Directions.

Ruschenberger, W. S. W. 1838. *A Voyage Round the World; Including an Embassy to Muscat and Siam, in 1835, 1836, and 1837*. Philadelphia, PN: Carey, Lea, and Blanchard.

Ruse, M. 1996. *Monad to Man: The Concept of Progress in Evolutionary Biology*. Cambridge, MA: Harvard University Press, https://doi.org/10.4159/9780674042995

Russell, S. E. 1916. *Form and Function: A Contribution to the History of Animal Morphology*. Chicago, IL: University of Chicago Press.

Rutherford, H. W. 1908. *Catalogue of the Library of Charles Darwin now in the Botany School, Cambridge. Compiled by H. W. Rutherford, of the University Library; With an Introduction by Francis Darwin*. Cambridge, UK: Cambridge University Press.

Salonius, P. 2020. "The Tree of Life in Medieval Iconography." In *The Tree of Life*, ed. D. Estes, 280–343. Leiden: Brill, https://doi.org/10.1163/9789004423756_014

Saucerotte, C. 1834. *Elémens d'histoire naturelle: Présentant dans une suite de tableaux synoptiques, accompagnés de figures, un précis complet de cette science.* Paris: Aug. Delalain, Germain-Ballière.

Scerri, E. M. L., M. G. Thomas, A. Manica, et al. 2018. "Did Our Species Evolve in Subdivided Populations Across Africa, and Why Does It Matter?" *Trends in Ecology & Evolution* 33.8: 582–94, https://doi.org/10.1016/j.tree.2018.05.005

Schaefer, N. K., B. Shapiro, and R. E. Green. 2016. "Detecting Hybridization Using Ancient DNA." *Molecular Ecology* 25.11: 2398–412, https://doi.org/10.1111/mec.13556

___. 2021. "An Ancestral Recombination Graph of Human, Neanderthal, and Denisovan Genomes." *Science Advances* 7.29: 1–16, https://doi.org/10.1126/sciadv.abc0776

Schaffer, G. 2007. "'Scientific' Racism Again? Reginald Gates, the *Mankind Quarterly* and the Question of 'Race' in Science After the Second World War." *Journal of American Studies* 41.2: 253–78, https://doi.org/10.1017/s0021875807003477

Scharf, S. T. 2009. "Identification Keys, the 'Natural Method', and the Development of Plant Identification Manuals." *Journal of the History of Biology* 42.1: 73–117.

Scherzer, K., and E. Schwarz. 1858. *On Measurements as a Diagnostic Means for Distinguishing the Human Races: A Systematic Plan Established and Investigated by the Undersigned, for the Purpose of Taking Measurements on Individuals of Different Races During the Voyage of H.I.R.M.'s Frigate "Novara" Round the World*. Sydney: Printed for private circulation only.

Schleicher, A. 1861. *Compendium der vergleichenden Grammatik der indogermanischen Sprachen*. Weimar: Böhlau.

Schmidt-Burkhardt, A. 2009. "Wissen als Bild: Zur diagrammatischen Kunstgeschichte." In *Logik des Bildlichen: Zur Kritik der ikonischen Vernunft*, ed. M. Heßler and D. Mersch, 163–87. Bielefeld: Transcript.

Schneider, B., C. Ernst, and J. Wöpking (eds.). 2016. *Diagrammatik-Reader: Grundlegende Texte aus Theorie und Geschichte*. Berlin: De Gruyter.

Schneider, W. H. 1996. "The History of Research on Blood Group Genetics: Initial Discovery and Diffusion." *History and Philosophy of the Life Sciences* 18.3: 277–303.

Schultz, A. H. 1948. "Review of *Human Ancestry from a Genetical Point of View*, by R. Ruggles Gates." *The Quarterly Review of Biology* 23.2: 146–47.

Schwalbe, G. 1899a. "Ziele und Wege einer vergleichenden physischen Anthropologie." *Zeitschrift für Morphologie und Anthropologie* 1.1: 1–15.

___. 1899b. "Studien über Pithecanthropus erectus Dubois." *Zeitschrift für Morphologie und Anthropologie* 1.1: 16–240.

___. 1904. *Die Vorgeschichte des Menschen*. Braunschweig: F. Vieweg und Sohn.

___. 1906. *Studien zur Vorgeschichte des Menschen*. Stuttgart: E. Schweizerbartsche.

___. 1914. "Kritische Besprechung von Boule's Werk: 'L'homme fossile de La Chapelle-Aux-Saints' mit eigenen Untersuchungen." *Zeitschrift für Morphologie und Anthropologie* 16.3: 527–610.

Sera, G. L. 1917. "La testimonianza dei fossili di antropomorfi per la questione dell'origine dell'uomo." *Atti della Società Italiana di Scienze Naturali e del Museo Civico di Storia Naturale di Milano* 56: 25–156.

Sergi, G. 1908. *Europa: L'origine dei popoli Europei e loro relazioni coi popoli d'Africa, d'Asia e d'Oceania*. Milano: Bocca.

___. 1909. "L'apologia del mio poligenismo." *Atti della Società romana di antropologia* 15: 187–95.

Serres, M. 1968. *Hermès I: La communication*. Paris: Les Éditions de Minuit.

Seth, S. 2016. "Darwin and the Ethnologists: Liberal Racialism and the Geological Analogy." *Historical Studies in the Natural Sciences* 46.4: 490–527, https://doi.org/10.1525/hsns.2016.46.4.490

Shapiro, H. L. 1959. "The History and Development of Physical Anthropology." *American Anthropologist* 61.3: 371–79.

Shotwell, M. 2021. "The Misuse of Pedigree Analysis in the Eugenics Movement." *The American Biology Teacher* 83.2: 80–88, https://doi.org/10.1525/abt.2021.83.2.80

Siegel, S. 2009. *Tabula: Figuren der Ordnung um 1600*. Berlin: Akademie Verlag.

Simpson, G. G. 1941. "The Role of the Individual in Evolution." *Journal of the Washington Academy of Sciences* 31.1: 1–20.

___. 1949. *The Meaning of Evolution: A Study of the History of Life and Its Significance for Man*. New Haven, CT: Yale University Press.

___. 1963a. "The Meaning of Taxonomic Statements." In *Classification and Human Evolution*, ed. S. L. Washburn, 1–31. Chicago, IL: Aldine.

___. 1963b. "Review of *The Origin of Races*, by Carleton S. Coon." *Perspectives in Biology and Medicine* 6.2: 268–72.

Sloan, P. R. 1972. "John Locke, John Ray, and the Problem of the Natural System." *Journal of the History of Biology* 5.1: 1–53.

___. 1995. "The Gaze of Nature." In *Inventing Human Science: Eighteenth-Century Domains*, ed. C. Fox, R. Porter, and R. Wokler, 112–51. Berkeley, CA: University of California Press.

___. 2006. "Kant on the History of Nature: The Ambiguous Heritage of the Critical Philosophy for Natural History." *Studies in History and Philosophy of Biological and Biomedical Sciences* 37.4: 627–48.

Smith, F. H., J. C. M. Ahern, I. Janković, et al. 2017. "The Assimilation Model of Modern Human Origins in Light of Current Genetic and Genomic Knowledge." *Quaternary International* 450.1: 126–36, https://doi.org/10.1016/j.quaint.2016.06.008

Smith, G. E. 1924. *Essays on the Evolution of Man*. London: Oxford University Press.

___. 1929. *Human History*. New York: W. W. Norton.

Smith, J. 2009. *Charles Darwin and Victorian Visual Culture*. Cambridge, UK: Cambridge University Press.

Smouse, P. E., R. S. Spielman, and M. H. Park. 1982. "Multiple-Locus Allocation of Individuals to Groups as a Function of the Genetic Variation Within and Differences Among Human Populations." *The American Naturalist* 119.4: 445–63.

Soemmerring, S. Th. v. 1785. *Ueber die körperliche Verschiedenheit des [Afrikaners] vom Europäer*. Frankfurt a. M.: Varentrapp Sohn und Wenner.

Sommer, M. 2005a. "How Cultural Is Heritage? Humanity's Black Sheep from Charles Darwin to Jack London." In *A Cultural History of Heredity III: 19th and Early 20th Centuries*, ed. S. Müller-Wille and H.-J. Rheinberger, 233–53. Berlin: Max Planck Institute for the History of Science.

___. 2005b. "Ancient Hunters and Their Modern Representatives: William Sollas's (1849–1936) Anthropology from Disappointed Bridge to Trunkless Tree and the Instrumentalisation of Racial Conflict." *Journal of the History of Biology* 38.2: 327–65.

___. 2006. "Mirror, Mirror on the Wall: Neanderthal as Mirror and 'Distortion' in Early 20th-Century French Science and Press." *Social Studies of Science* 2.36: 207–240.

___. 2007. *Bones and Ochre: The Curious Afterlife of the Red Lady of Paviland*. Cambridge, MA: Harvard University Press.

___. 2008. "History in the Gene: Negotiations Between Molecular and Organismal Anthropology." *Journal for the History of Biology* 41.3: 473–528, https://doi.org/10.1007/s10739-008-9150-3

___. 2010a. "From Descent to Ascent: The Human Exception in the Evolutionary Synthesis." *Nuncius* 25.1: 41–67.

___. 2010b. Book Review: "*From Anthropometry to Genomics: Reflections of a Pacific Fieldworker*. By Jonathan Friedlaender as told to Joanna Radin. Bloomington: iUniverse, 2009." *American Journal of Human Biology* 22.4: 567–68.

___. 2014. "Biology as a Technology of Social Justice in Interwar Britain: Arguments from Evolutionary History, Heredity, and Human Diversity." *Science, Technology & Human Values* 39.4: 560–85, https://doi.org/10.1177/0162243913520330

___. 2015a. "Population-Genetic Trees, Maps and Narratives of the Great Human Diasporas." *History of the Human Sciences* 28.5: 108–145, https://doi.org/10.1177/0952695115573032

___. 2015b. *Evolutionäre Anthropologie: Zur Einführung*. Hamburg: Junius.

___. 2016a. *History Within: The Science, Culture, and Politics of Bones, Organisms, and Molecules*. Chicago, IL: University of Chicago Press.

___. 2016b. Book Review: "Samuel Redman. *Bone Rooms: From Scientific Racism to Human Prehistory Museums*. Harvard University Press, 2016." *Journal of the Gilded Age and Progressive Era* 15.4: 472–74.

___. 2021. "The Meaning of Absence: The Primate Tree That Did Not Make It into Darwin's *The Descent of Man*." *British Journal for the History of Science Themes* 6.1: 45–61, https://doi.org/10.1017/bjt.2020.14

___. 2022a. "Visualizations in the Sciences of Human Origins and Evolution." In *The Palgrave Handbook of the History of Human Sciences*, ed. D. McCallum, 291–320. Singapore: Palgrave Macmillan, https://doi.org/10.1007/978-981-16-7255-2_26

___.2022b. "Die Familie und der Stammbaum des Menschen in der Anthropologie." In *Genealogie in der Moderne: Akteure – Praktiken – Perspektiven*, ed. M. Hecht and E. Timm, 271–99. Oldenbourg: De Gruyter, https://doi.org/10.1515/9783110718034-017

___. 2023a. "A Diagrammatics of Race: Samuel George Morton's 'American Golgotha' and the Contest for the Definition of the Young Field of Anthropology." *History of the Human Sciences*, January: 1–30, https://doi.org/10.1177/09526951221136771

___. 2023b. "The Human Family Tree." In *cache 3: In the Shadow of the Tree. The Diagrammatics of Relatedness as Scientific, Scholarly, and Popular Practice*, ed. E. Hounsehll and R. Amstutz. Zürich: intercom Verlag, https://cache.ch/shadowofthetree/recurrence/thehumanfamilytree/humanphylogeny

Sommer, M., and R. Amstutz. 2024. "Diagrams of Human Genetic Kinship and Diversity: From the Tree to the Mosaic and the Network?" In *Critical Perspectives on Ancient DNA*, ed. D. Strand, A. Källen, and C. Mulcare. Cambridge, MA: MIT Press.

Sommer, M., C. Arni, and S. Müller-Wille (eds.). 2023. *History of the Human Sciences*. Special Section (The Diagrammatics of Relatedness), https://journals.sagepub.com/toc/HHS/0/0?startPage=1&ContentItemType=research-article&pageSize=10

Sommer, M., C. Arni, S. Müller-Wille, and S. Teuscher. 2024. "In the Shadow of the Tree: The Diagrammatics of Relatedness in Genealogy, Anthropology, and Genetics as Epistemic, Cultural, and Political Practice." *History of the Human Sciences* (forthcoming).

Sommer, M., and V. Lipphardt (eds.). 2015. *History of the Human Sciences* 28.5. Special Issue (Visibility Matters: Diagrammatic Renderings of Human Evolution and Diversity in Physical, Serological and Molecular Anthropology).

Sommer, M., S. Teuscher, S. Müller-Wille, et al. 2018. "In the Shadow of the Tree: The Diagrammatics of Relatedness as Scientific, Scholarly, and Popular Practice." Sinergia-Proposal to the Swiss National Science Foundation, submitted June 1.

Song, Y. S., and J. Hein. 2005. "Constructing Minimal Ancestral Recombination Graphs." *Journal of Computational Biology: A Journal of Computational Molecular Cell Biology* 12.2: 147–69, https://doi.org/10.1089/cmb.2005.12.147

Spiegel, A. v. d. 1632. *De humani corporis fabrica libri decem*. Frankfurt: Impensis & caelo Matthaei Meriani bibliopolae & chalcographi.

Spielman, R. S., and P. E. Smouse. 1976. "Multivariate Classification of Human Populations: 1. Allocation of Yanomama Indians to Villages." *The American Journal of Human Genetics* 28.4: 317–31.

Spuhler, J. N. 1950. "Review of *Pedigrees of [Black] Families*, by R. Ruggles Gates." *Science* 111.2874: 96–97.

Spurzheim, J. G. 1833. *Phrenology, in Connection with the Study of Physiognomy*. Boston, MA: Marsh, Capen and Lyon.

Stanton, W. 1960. *The Leopard's Spots: Scientific Attitudes Toward Race in America 1815–59*. Chicago, IL: The University of Chicago Press.

Stjernfelt, F. 2000. "Diagrams as Centerpiece of Peircean Epistemology." *Transactions of the Charles S. Peirce Society* 36.3: 357–84.

___. 2007. *Diagrammatology: An Investigation on the Borderlines of Phenomenology, Ontology, and Semiotics*. Dordrecht: Springer.

Stocking Jr., G. W. 1968. *Race, Culture, and Evolution: Essays in the History of Anthropology*. New York: FreePress.

___. 1973. "From Chronology to Ethnology: James Cowles Prichard and British Anthropology, 1800–1850." In *Researches into the Physical History of Man*, ed. J. C. Prichard and G. W. Stocking Jr., ix–cx. Chicago, IL: The University of Chicago Press.

Stoecker, H., T. Schnalke, and A. Winkelmann (eds.). 2013. *Sammeln, Erforschen, Zurückgeben? Menschliche Gebeine aus der Kolonialzeit in akademischen und musealen Sammlungen*. Berlin: Ch. Links.

Stoneking, M., and R. L. Cann. 1989. "African Origin of Human Mitochondrial DNA." In *The Human Revolution: Behavioural and Biological Perspectives on the Origins of Modern Humans*, ed. C. Stringer and P. Mellars, 17–30. Edinburgh: Edinburgh University Press.

Stringer, C. 2014. "Why We Are Not All Multiregionalists Now." *Trends in Ecology & Evolution* 29.5: 248–51, https://doi.org/10.1016/j.tree.2014.03.001

Stringer, C., and P. Mellars (eds.). 1989. *The Human Revolution: Behavioural and Biological Perspectives on the Origins of Modern Humans*. Edinburgh: University Press.

ß. 1930. "Review of *Heredity in Man*, by R. Ruggles Gates." *Science Progress in the Twentieth Century (1919–1933)* 25.97: 160–62.

Tang H., J. Peng, P. Wang, et al. 2005. "Estimation of Individual Admixture: Analytical and Study Design Considerations." *Genetic Epidemiology* 28.4: 289–301, https://doi.org/10.1002/gepi.20064

Tassy, P. 1991. *L'arbre à remonter le temps: Les rencontres de la systématique et de l'évolution*. Épistémè essais. Paris: C. Bourgois.

___. 2011. "Trees Before and After Darwin." *Journal of Zoological Systematics and Evolutionary Research* 49.2: 89–101.

Teicher, A. 2022. "How Family Charts Became Mendelian: The Changing Content of Pedigrees and Its Impact on the Consolidation of Genetic Theory." *History of the Human Sciences*, https://doi.org/10.1177/09526951221107558

Templeton, A. R. 2005. "Haplotype Trees and Modern Human Origins." *American Journal of Physical Anthropology* 128.S41: 33–59, https://doi.org/10.1002/ajpa.20351

___. 2013. "Biological Races in Humans." *Studies in History and Philosophy of Biological and Biomedical Sciences* 44.3: 262–71, https://doi.org/10.1016/j.shpsc.2013.04.010

___. 2018a. *Human Population Genetics and Genomics*. San Diego: Elsevier Science & Technology.

___. 2018b. "Hypothesis Compatibility Versus Hypothesis Testing of Models of Human Evolution." In *Rethinking Human Evolution*, ed. J. H. Schwartz, 109–128. Cambridge, MA: The MIT Press, https://doi.org/10.7551/mitpress/11032.003.0008

___. 2023. "The Importance of Gene Flow in Human Evolution." *Human Population Genetics and Genomics* 3.3: 1–22, https://doi.org/10.47248/hpgg2303030005

Thienemann, A. 1910. "Die Stufenfolge der Dinge, der Versuch eines natürlichen Systems der Naturkörper aus dem achtzehnten Jahrhundert." *Zoologische Annalen: Zeitschrift für Geschichte der Zoologie* 3: 185–274.

Thompson, E. A. 1975. *Human Evolutionary Trees*. Cambridge, UK: Cambridge University Press.

Thomson, A. J. 1909. "Darwin's Predecessors." In *Darwin and Modern Science: Essays in Commemoration of the Centenary of the Birth of Charles Darwin and of the Fiftieth Anniversary of the Publication of The Origin of Species*, ed. C. Seward, 3–17. Cambridge, UK: Cambridge University Press.

Toepfer, G. 2011. *Historisches Wörterbuch der Biologie: Geschichte und Theorie der biologischen Grundbegriffe. Band 3: Parasitismus – Zweckmäßigkeit*. Stuttgart: J.B. Metzler.

Trinkaus, E. 1982. "A History of *Homo erectus* and *Homo sapiens* Paleontology in America." In *A History of American Physical Anthropology 1930–1980*, ed. F. Spencer. New York: Academic Press.

Tucker, W. H. 2002. *The Funding of Scientific Racism: Wickliffe Draper and the Pioneer Fund*. Urbana, IL: University of Illinois Press.

Turnbull, P. 2017. *Science, Museums and Collecting the Indigenous Dead in Colonial Australia*. New York: Palgrave, https://doi.org/10.1007/978-3-319-51874-9

Vallois, H. V. 1952. "Monophyletism and Polyphyletism in Man." *South African Journal of Science* 49.3–4: 69–79.

___. 1954. "Neandertals and Praesapiens." *Journal of the Royal Anthropological Institute of Great Britain and Ireland* 84.1–2: 111–30.

Velasco, J. D. 2012. "The Future of Systematics: Tree Thinking Without the Tree." *Philosophy of Science* 79.5: 624–36, https://doi.org/10.1086/667878

Vicente, M., and C. M. Schlebusch. 2020. "African Population History: An Ancient DNA Perspective." *Current Opinion in Genetics & Development* 62.1: 8–15, https://doi.org/10.1016/j.gde.2020.05.008

Vimont, J. 1841. *Traité de phrénologie humaine et comparée, accompagné d'un magnifique atlas in-folio de 120 planches*. Bruxelles: Et. Encyclographique.

Virey, J. J. 1808. *L'art de perfectionner l'homme, ou de la médicine spirituelle et morale*. 2 vols., I. Paris: Deterville.

___. 1824. *Histoire naturelle du genre humain: Nouvelle édition augmentée et entièrement refondue avec figures*. 2 vols., I. Paris: Crochard.

Visser, R. P. W. 1990. "Die Rezeption der Anthropologie Petrus Campers, 1770–1850." In *Die Natur des Menschen: Probleme der physischen Anthropologie und Rassenkunde (1750–1850)*, ed. G. Mann and F. Dumont, 325–35. Stuttgart: Fischer.

Vogt, C. 1863a. *Vorlesungen über den Menschen, seine Stellung in der Schöpfung und in der Geschichte der Erde*. 2 vols., I. Berlin: De Gruyter.

___. 1863b. *Vorlesungen über den Menschen, seine Stellung in der Schöpfung und in der Geschichte der Erde*. 2 vols., II. Giessen: J. Ricker'sche Buchhandlung.

Voss, J. 2010. *Darwin's Pictures: Views of Evolutionary Theory, 1837–1874*. Trans. L. Lantz. New Haven, CT: Yale University Press.

W. H. F. 1887. "Obituary Notice of the Late Professor Busk." *The Journal of the Royal Anthropological Institute of Great Britain and Ireland* 16.4: 403–407.

Wade, N. 2014. *A Troublesome Inheritance: Genes, Race, and Human History*. New York: The Penguin Press.

Wadell, P. J. 2018. "The Phylogenomic Origins and Definition of *Homo Sapiens*." In *Rethinking Human Evolution*, ed. J. H. Schwartz, 139–79. Cambridge, MA: The MIT Press, https://doi.org/10.7551/mitpress/11032.003.0010

Wagner, J. K., C. Colwell, K. G. Claw, et al. 2020. "Fostering Responsible Research on Ancient DNA." *The American Journal of Human Genetics* 107.2: 183–95, https://doi.org/10.1016/j.ajhg.2020.06.017

Wagner, K. A. 2010. "Confessions of a Skull: Phrenology and Colonial Knowledge in Early Nineteenth-Century India." *History Workshop Journal* 69.1: 27–51, https://doi.org/10.1093/hwj/dbp031

Wallace, A. R. 1864. "The Origin of Human Races and the Antiquity of Man Deduced from the Theory of 'Natural Selection'." *Journal of the Anthropological Society of London* 2.1: clviii–clxxxvii.

Ward, F. O. 1858 [1838]. *Outlines of Human Osteology*. 2nd ed. London: Henry Renshaw.

Warren, J. C. 1822. *A Comparative View of the Sensorial and Nervous Systems in Men and Animals*. Boston, MA: J. W. Ingraham.

Washburn, S. L. 1947. "Review of *Human Genetics*, by Reginald Ruggles Gates." *American Anthropologist* 49.3: 488–89.

___. (ed.). 1963. *Classification and Human Evolution*. Chicago, IL: Aldine.

___. 1964. "The Origin of Races: Weidenreich's Opinion." *American Anthropologist* 66.5: 1165–67.

Watson, A. 1934. *The Early Iconography of the Tree of Jesse*. London: Oxford University Press.

Weidenreich, F. 1927. *Rasse und Körperbau*. Berlin: Julius Springer.

___. 1928. "Entwicklungs- und Rassetypen des *Homo primigenius*." *Senckenbergische Naturforschende Gesellschaft: Natur und Museum* 58.1: 1–13, 51–62.

___. 1931. "Das Problem der jüdischen Rasse." *Der Morgen: Monatsschrift der Juden in Deutschland* 7.1: 78–96.

___. 1932. "Die physischen Grundlagen der Rassenlehre." In *Rasse und Geist: Vier Vorträge gehalten in der Senckenbergischen Naturforschenden Gesellschaft in Frankfurt a. M., 1930/31*, ed. F. Weidenreich, W. Peters, E. Kretschmer, et al., 5–27. Leipzig: Johann Ambrosius Barth.

___. 1940. "Some Problems Dealing with Ancient Man." *American Anthropologist* 42.3: 375–83.

___. 1946a. *Apes, Giants, and Man*. Chicago, IL: The University of Chicago Press.

___. 1946b. "Generic, Specific and Subspecific Characters in Human Evolution." *American Journal of Physical Anthropology* 4.4: 413–32.

___. 1947a. "Are Human Races in the Taxonomic Sense 'Races' or 'Species'?" *American Journal of Physical Anthropology* 5.3: 369–72.

___. 1947b. "Facts and Speculations Concerning the Origin of *Homo sapiens*." *American Anthropologist* 49.2: 187–203.

Weinert, H. 1932. *Urspung der Menschheit: Über den engeren Anschluss des Menschengeschlechts an die Menschenaffen*. Stuttgart: Ferdinand Enke.

White, C. 1799. *An Account of the Regular Gradation of Nature in Man, and in Different Animals and Vegetables; and from the Former to the Latter.* London: Printed for C. Dilly, in the Poultry.

Whitfield, J. B. 2012. "Phylogenetic Networks: Concepts, Algorithms and Applications." *Systematic Biology* 61.1: 176–77, https://doi.org/10.1093/sysbio/syr055

Wiedenmayer, F., and G. Hotz. 2002. "History of the Collection of Physical Anthropology in the Natural History Museum Basel, Switzerland." *Bulletin der Schweizerischen Gesellschaft für Anthropologie* 8.1: 41–53.

Wilson, D. J. 1987. "Lovejoy's The Great Chain of Being After Fifty Years." *Journal of the History of Ideas* 48.2: 187–206.

Winder, I. C., and N. P. Winder. 2014. "Reticulate Evolution and the Human Past: An Anthropological Perspective." *Annals of Human Biology* 41.4: 300–311, https://doi.org/10.3109/03014460.2014.922613

Winston, A. S. 1998. "Science in the Service of the Far Right: Henry E. Garrett, the IAAEE, and the Liberty Lobby." *Journal of Social Issues* 54.1: 179–210.

Wohns, W. A., Y. Wong, B. Jeffery, et al. 2022. "A Unified Genealogy of Modern and Ancient Genomes." *Science* 375.6583: 1–9, https://doi.org/10.1126/science.abi8264

Wolpoff, M. H. 2020. "Human Evolution: Multiregional Origins." In *Encyclopedia of Global Archaeology*, ed. C. Smith, 5312–17. Cham: Springer International.

Wolpoff, M. H., and R. Caspari. 1997. *Race and Human Evolution*. New York: Simon and Schuster.

Woodrow, H. 1932. "Review of *Heredity in Man*, by R. Ruggles Gates." *The American Journal of Psychology* 44.2: 400.

Worm, A. 2014. "'*Arbor autem humanum genus significat*': Trees of Genealogy and Sacred History in the Twelfth Century." In *The Tree: Symbol, Allegory, and Mnemonic Device in Medieval Art and Thought*, ed. P. Salonius and A. Worm, 35–67. Turnhout: Brepols.

Wyman, J. 1868. "On the Measurement of Crania." *The Anthropological Review* 6.23: 345–49.

Yong, E. 2018. "The New Story of Humanity's Origins in Africa." *The Atlantic*, 11 July 2018, https://www.theatlantic.com/science/archive/2018/07/the-new-story-of-humanitys-origins/564779/

Yudell, M. 2014. *Race Unmasked: Biology and Race in the Twentieth Century*. New York: Columbia University Press, https://doi.org/10.7312/yude16874

Zuckerman, S. 1949. "Genealogical Guesses: Review of *Human Ancestry from a Genetical Point of View*, by R. Ruggles Gates." *Science Progress (1933–)* 37.148: 740–43.

List of Illustrations

Index

About the Team

Alessandra Tosi was the managing editor for this book.

Adèle Kreager proof-read this manuscript. Anja Pritchard indexed it.

Jeevanjot Kaur Nagpal designed the cover. The cover was produced in InDesign using the Fontin font.

Cameron Craig typeset the book in InDesign and produced the paperback and hardback editions. The text fonts is Tex Gyre Pagella and the heading font is Californian FB.

Cameron also produced the PDF, and HTML editions. The conversion was performed with open-source software and other tools freely available on our GitHub page at https://github.com/OpenBookPublishers.

Jeremy Bowman produced the EPUB edition.

Laura Rodríguez was in charge of marketing.

This book was peer-reviewed by two referees. Experts in their field, these readers give their time freely to help ensure the academic rigour of our books. We are grateful for their generous and invaluable contributions.

This book need not end here...

Share

All our books — including the one you have just read — are free to access online so that students, researchers and members of the public who can't afford a printed edition will have access to the same ideas. This title will be accessed online by hundreds of readers each month across the globe: why not share the link so that someone you know is one of them?

This book and additional content is available at:
https://doi.org/10.11647/OBP.0396

Donate

Open Book Publishers is an award-winning, scholar-led, not-for-profit press making knowledge freely available one book at a time. We don't charge authors to publish with us: instead, our work is supported by our library members and by donations from people who believe that research shouldn't be locked behind paywalls.

Why not join them in freeing knowledge by supporting us:
https://www.openbookpublishers.com/support-us

You may also be interested in:

Photography in the Third Reich
Art, Physiognomy and Propaganda
Christopher Webster (ed.)

https://doi.org/10.11647/obp.0202

Brownshirt Princess
A Study of the 'Nazi Conscience'
Lionel Gossman

https://doi.org/10.11647/obp.0003

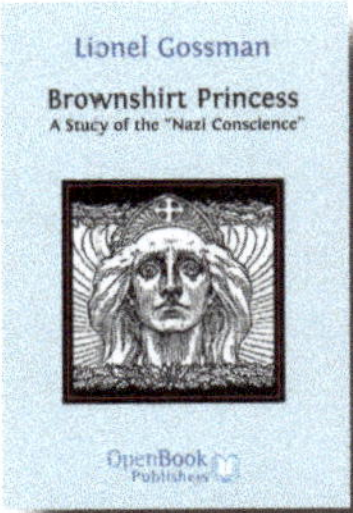

The European Experience
A Multi-Perspective History of Modern Europe, 1500–2000
Jan Hansen; Jochen Hung; Jaroslav Ira; Judit Klement; Sylvain Lesage; Juan Luis Simal; Andrew Tompkins (eds)

https://doi.org/10.11647/obp.0323

www.ingramcontent.com/pod-product-compliance
Lightning Source LLC
Chambersburg PA
CBHW051441270326
41932CB00025B/3395